THE FOUNDATIONS
OF
CHRISTIAN DOCTRINE

by

Kevin J. Conner, B.Th., M.Div., Th.D. (Hon).

The Foundations of Christian Doctrine
© Copyright 1980 by Kevin J. Conner

Joint Publishing through:

Sovereign World International
(Sovereign World Edition 1988)
P.O. Box 777 Tonbridge
Kent TN11 OZS   England
(0) 1732 850598
ISBN# 1-85240-024-2

City Bible Publishing
9200 NE Fremont
Portland, Oregon 97220
1-800-777-6057
www.citybiblepublishing.com
ISBN# 0-914936-38-7

Also available through:

KJC Publications
P.O. Box 300
Vermont
Victoria 3130
Australia

DEDICATION . . .

to my lovely wife, Joyce, who has been a constant source of strength and encouragement to me over many years of Biblical research . . .

and . . .

to my daughter, Sharon, and my son, Mark, who have been a joy and delight and whose lives are evidence of the foundations of Christian Doctrine well laid . . .

and . . .

to my son in law, Frank Damazio, who, along with the Portland Bible College faculty, encouraged me in the production of this text . . .

and . . .

to all those students with whom "The Foundations of Christian Doctrine" have been shared over the past number of years . . .

and . . .

to all those Teachers and Students in the Body of Christ who desire to see that the foundations are not destroyed, but laid properly, upon which Christian doctrine, character and practice may be built.

ACKNOWLEDGEMENT

Due credit and a very special thanks must go to Ken Malmin for his part in the production of this text-book. Many hours were spent in editing, correcting, adjusting and arranging the material, as well as contributing paragraphs and short sections here and there by reason of his communicative skills. It has been a great honor and pleasure to have him serve in this production in a Paul/Timothy relationship.

FOREWORD

Under the original outpouring of the Holy Spirit on the Day of Pentecost about 3000 souls were born into the Kingdom of God and added to the Church.

The Scripture tells us that these new converts "continued stedfastly in the Apostle's doctrine, and in fellowship, and in breaking of bread and prayers" (Acts 2:42).

In a day when all absolutes are under attack and being destroyed in the hearts and mind of this present generation, there is a tremendous need to maintain sound doctrine, that "faith which was once delivered to the saints" (Jude 3). There is great assurance and peace when one can point to and proclaim God's absolutes as written in the inspired, infallible and authoritative Word of God, the Holy Bible.

Again, it should be noted that, not only are the world philosophies attacking the absolutes, many professionals in Christendom are attacking and undermining or laying aside all doctrine, classifying it as "dead", "divisive" or "unnecessary" and thus resorting to a philosophical Gospel devoid of any Biblical theology.

Not only is this so, but we are living in the times of which the Spirit expressly spoke: "that in the latter days some shall depart from THE FAITH, giving heed to seducing spirits, and doctrines of devils" (I Timothy 4:1). Hence the need indeed of "contending for THE FAITH once delivered to the saints" (Jude 3).

The Bible provides various styles of literature such as History, Poetry, Law and Prophecy. There is, however, underlying and flowing through all the Books of the Bible and its various styles of literature, **sound theology.** We know that God did not systematize all these Doctrines; He has left that for us to search out and to explore; but all the Bible writers had solid foundations of theology undergirding all they said and wrote.

In practically every Book of the Bible there may be discovered the basic Doctrines of God, of Christ, of the Holy Spirit, of the Holiness of God, the Sinfulness of Man, and of God's Grace in the Redemptive Plan and the Atonement. There is the Reward for the Righteous and Judgment on the Wicked. The Prophets themselves were founded upon the fundamental facts of God's holiness, righteousness, love and mercy, as well as the revelation of man's sinfulness and need for repentance and redemption.

It is the writer's firm conviction that one is poorly qualified to be a sound interpreter and exegete of the various styles of Bible literature without a solid foundation in theology.

Much interpretation and exposition arises out of the theological principles one holds, hence the need for sound theology. The arguments or excuses used against doctrine are dealt within the first chapter of this text and need not be elaborated upon here.

The contents of this text have been the basis for "Systematic Theology" and "Basic Doctrine" Classes in Portland Bible College in the last number of years where the author has been serving as a teacher.

The text has been written in such a way as to provide "SEED to the sower and BREAD to the eater" (Isaiah 55:9-11). The writer has not tried to say all that could be said but has provided both Outline (Seed) and Content (Bread) so that the Teacher (Sower) and Student (Eater) may together be able to expand by a consideration of the Scripture references given. Therefore, to obtain the best and fullest use of this text it is necessary to read and meditate on the numerous Scripture references listed, and not just on the author's comments.

It is the writer's prayer that all who read, study and use this text will follow Paul's exhortation to Timothy when he said "Take heed to thyself, and unto the doctrine; continue in them: for in doing this thou shalt both save thyself, and them that hear thee" (I Timothy 4:16).

Kevin J. Conner
7600 N.E. Glisan Street
Portland, Oregon 97213
U.S.A.

TABLE OF CONTENTS

Chapter 1

THE CHRISTIAN DOCTRINE

It is necessary that Christians be taught sound Bible doctrine and that all doctrine be tested by the full context of the infallible Word of God. Doctrine received, believed and practiced determines a person's character, behavior and destiny.

CHAPTER OUTLINE

I. THE DEFINITION OF DOCTRINE AND THEOLOGY

A. Doctrine
B. Theology

II. THE DIVISIONS OF THEOLOGY

A. Exegetical Theology
B. Historical Theology
C. Dogmatic Theology
D. Biblical Theology
E. Systematic Theology
F. Pastoral Theology

III. THE PURPOSE OF DOCTRINE

A. The Purpose Defined
B. The Purpose Clarified

IV. THE NECESSITY OF DOCTRINE

V. THE CLASSIFICATION OF DOCTRINE

A. The Doctrine of God
B. The Doctrine of Man
C. The Doctrine of Devils

VI. THE SYMBOLS OF DOCTRINE

A. Leaven
B. Wind
C. Rain

VII. THE NATURE OF DOCTRINE
A. Doctrine must be sound
B. Doctrine must be pure
C. Doctrine must be Scriptural
D. Doctrine must be obeyed
E. Doctrine determines character
F. Doctrine affects fellowship
G. Doctrine determines destiny
H. Doctrine and love

VIII. THE PROGRESS OF DOCTRINE

I. THE DEFINITION OF DOCTRINE AND THEOLOGY

A. "Doctrine" means "something taught, teachings, instruction; the principles of religion that are taught; or more literally, 'to teach the substance.' "

In this text we will use the term "doctrine" to refer to the truths of God's Word that are to be taught. The word "doctrine" is used fifty-six times in the Authorized Version. One of these is in Acts 2:42 where we find that the early church converts continued stedfastly in the apostles' doctrine.

B. "Theology" means "the study of God, of religious doctrines and of matters pertaining to Divinity."

The word is derived from two Greek words:

1. "Theos", meaning "God" and

2. "Logos", meaning "Word, or Discourse" Like other sciences, theology is a systematic and logical arrangement of certified facts. Thus in theology facts relating to God and His Word are presented in an orderly and logical manner. While theology refers primarily to the knowledge of God's truth, religion denotes the practice of it. These two must constantly be integrated and united in the life of the believer and the church. John 13:17 "If ye know these things (theology), happy are ye if ye do them (practice)."

II. THE DIVISIONS OF THEOLOGY

A. Exegetical Theology
"Exegesis" means "to lead out, to guide out, to draw out." In theology it refers to the analysis and interpretation of Scripture. Exegetical theology is concerned with Biblical languages, Biblical archeology, Biblical introduction and Biblical hermeneutics.

B. Historical Theology
Historical theology traces Biblical history, church history, and the history of doctrine.

C. Dogmatic Theology
This branch deals with dogma as set forth and formulated in church creeds. The difference between dogma and doctrine should be recognized.

Dogma is man's statement of a truth set forth, as in a creed.
Doctrine is God's revelation of truth as found in the Scriptures.

D. Biblical Theology
Biblical theology traces the progress of truth through the Books of the Bible, seeing the various manners in which each of the writers presented important doctrines.

For example in presenting the Doctrine of the Atonement, Biblical theology would show how this doctrine is dealt with in the Old Testament, the Gospels, the Acts and the Epistles by Paul, Peter, James and John.

E. Systematic Theology
Systematic theology concerns itself with the orderly arrangement into topics of the doctrines concerning God, Man, Angels, Sin and Salvation. It is a systemization of the major fundamental doctrines of Biblical theology.

F. Pastoral or Practical Theology
Pastoral or practical theology deals with pastoral work, Christian education, church administration, etc. Its goal is the practical application of theology in the regeneration, edification and education of man.

III. THE PURPOSE OF DOCTRINE

A. The Purpose Defined

The beginning of Luke's gospel intimates the purpose of doctrine and theology. Luke 1:1-4 "... to set forth in order a declaration of those things which are most surely believed among us ... That thou mightest know the certainty of the things wherein thou hast been instructed."

1. "To set forth" is to draw up a narrative;

2. "In order" means consecutively;

3. "A declaration" means a full declaration, a leading and following through;

4. "Those things which are most surely believed among us", i.e., the things pertaining to the Gospel of the Lord Jesus Christ;

5. "Instructed" means "orally instructed". It comes from the Greek word "katecheo" which means "to instruct by asking questions and correcting answers". The word catechism is derived from it. The word "instructed" is used also in Luke 1:4; Acts 18:25; and Romans 2:18.

The purpose of doctrinal and theological studies is to set forth in a systematic order the things which are most surely believed among the true believers. It is to instruct the believer that he may know the certainty of these truths. It is to encourage the believer to contend for "the faith once delivered to the saints" Jude 3.

B. The Purpose Clarified

It is important to recognize that no man can confine God to mere "Articles of Faith" or "Doctrinal Statements". It has pleased God to reveal Himself in the 66 Books of the Bible rather than in just a few doctrinal articles. Church history has proven the fact that man limits himself to such articles and therefore becomes unprepared to advance in God when the light of recovered truth begins to shine. It is for this reason that we see multiplied denominations and organizations within Christendom. For, each time God recovered further truth to His people, Creeds, Confessions and Articles of Faith all played their part in hindering God's people from moving on. Thus God had to step over the boundary walls of doctrinal statements and cause those who would respond to more light to move on with Him.

Truth is ever progressive. Of course it is recognized that God will never reveal anything outside of, or contrary to His Word, but He will continually shine light upon the Word He has given, further clarifying its meaning. (Psalm 43:3) Thus in any study on systematic theology it must be clearly understood that God is not limited to such. He is only limited to the revelation of Himself in the complete Word which He inspired and which He must illumine. Man himself does not know what to believe, therefore God has laid this down in His own Written Word. No system of theology can be the final authority, only as it is subjected to, tested by and found to be in harmony with the authority of the infallible Scriptures.

IV. THE NECESSITY OF DOCTRINE

The Apostle Paul prophesied that "the time will come when they will not endure sound doctrine" II Timothy 4:3.

Today there is a great attack on sound doctrine. There is a turning away from doctrinal matters and a turning to the philosophies of men and doctrines of devils. Many churches have no time for doctrinal preaching or teaching. They have turned to oratory, politics, ethics, book-sermons, or a social gospel saying that doctrine is useless and obsolete. The following are some of the most common objections being cast about. They appear to be sound and spiritual statements, but when followed through to their logical conclusions they become illogical and dangerous.

Objection Number One:
"There is no Biblical record of Jesus or of any of the Apostles formulating or giving any ready-made system of doctrine."

The answer to this should be evident in Acts 2:42. All the writers of the Old and New Testaments had in their writings underlying theological facts concerning the person of God, His nature and being, Man, Sin, and Redemption as well as the other great doctrines of the Bible. They may not be arranged in a systematic order but they are the very foundations of all the books of the Bible.

Objection Number Two:
"The Church does not need doctrine for doctrine has always been divisive, and this is why there are so many denominations."

The answer to this is seen in the emphasis in Scripture on doctrine. Doctrine existed before the church existed. The church does not originate doctrine, God does. It is the person who rejects the doctrines of God who causes the division. One is either for or against it. Of course, there will be those who carnally use the doctrines of the Bible to divide but this is not the fault of the doctrine. It is the one who uses or abuses the doctrine that is wrong. This is certainly no excuse to neglect the right use of doctrine.

Objection Number Three:
"It does not matter what you believe; it only matters who you believe."

The answer to this is that it is impossible to really separate Christ from His doctrine. He and His Word are one. One cannot accept Christ and reject what He teaches. It is possible to accept fragments of His teachings and reject Him. But in a true Bible sense, to accept Christ fully is to accept His doctrine fully. He Himself said, "My doctrine is not Mine, but His that sent Me" John 7:16-17.

Objection Number Four:
"You can be right in your doctrine and wrong in your spirit and that is not acceptable with God, or you could be wrong in your doctrine and right in your spirit and this is more acceptable with God."

This proposes that right attitudes are more important to God than right doctrines. The answer to this is that the statement is part truth and part error. God's ideal is to be right in both attitude and doctrine; not one at the expense of the other.

Objection Number Five:
"Doctrine is dry, dull and dead and is useless for us today; we need practical teaching". Or "experience is more important than doctrine". Again this statement is only partially true. It is to be admitted that oftentimes the presentation of doctrine may be dull and boring. However, the fault is not always with the doctrine, but with the teacher of it. The life of the teaching is the life of the teacher. The answer is not to dispense with doctrine but to know how the teacher must be quickened by the Spirit of God, the one who inspired the Scriptures. As to the latter part of the statement, the end of systematic theology is practical theology. Paul said to Timothy, "But thou has fully known my doctrine, manner of life ..."II Timothy 3:10. Doctrine should lead to life, theory to practice, interpretation to application, teaching to walking. This is God's ideal.

Not only is this so, but experience must always be measured in the light of the Word of God. Experiential theology must be governed by Scriptural theology; the subjective must be governed by the objective; the fallible by the infallible. Otherwise unguarded experience can lead to error.

The Need for Doctrine
In an age of relativism, in which there appears to be no absolutes, it is vital to know that God has absolutes. God, His Word, His truth and His laws stand out as eternal absolutes, unchanged and unchanging, forever reliable. Atheism, agnosticism, relativism, situation ethics, existentialism and other philosophies of men have saturated this generation thus causing a real need for sound doctrine.

This is a day in which all believers need to know:

1) WHO they believe
2) WHAT they believe, and
3) WHY they believe it.

All religions, true or false, all cults, "isms" and idealogies are founded on various doctrines and these teachings received, believed, obeyed and continually practiced determine:

1) Character—what we are
2) Behavior—what we do
3) Destiny—where we go

Strong character is determined by strong beliefs, and clearly defined doctrine makes for clear cut convictions. What a person believes is either molded by the vain philosophies of men or the inspired Word of God. Hence it is absolutely necessary to be founded on the doctrine of Christ.

In the realm of the sciences:
Stars existed before astronomy; man in his ignorance conceives astrology. Flowers existed before botany; man in his ignorance resorts to pantheism. Life existed before biology; man in his ignorance falls to evolution. God existed before theology; man in his ignorance falls into idolatry.

Just as the sciences of astronomy, botany, biology, etc., banish basic errors relative to such, so does the science of theology banish false views of God and creation.

Truth combats error and light dispels darkness. The need is not to fight error or darkness as such, but rather to declare the truth, turn on the light, and thus dispel the error and darkness. False teaching can only be corrected by the Word of God. Thus, whether it be denial of truth, subtraction or addition, misunderstanding, misrepresentation or substitution, only the sum total of the Word can rectify false doctrines. (II Timothy 3:15,16)

V. THE CLASSIFICATION OF DOCTRINE

The Scripture lists several classes of doctrine. However, it will be seen that all doctrine proceeds from three sources; God, Satan or Man. These are also the three sources of thought, which is illustrated in Matthew 16:13-23.

1. **The thought of God** concerning Christ is seen in verses 16-17. There Peter confessed that Jesus was the Christ, the Son of the living God. This indeed was revelation from God concerning His blessed Son.

2. **The thought of Man** is seen in verses 13-14, where people thought that Jesus might be Elijah, or Jeremiah or one of the prophets. Nothing sinful, but only human thinking is seen here. It is human thinking apart from Divine revelation concerning the Christ of God.

3. **The thought of Satan** is seen clearly in verses 21-23 where Peter, who a moment before had received the mind and thought of God, now confessed a thought which he received from Satan, who was opposed to the cross and the Christ of God.

This illustration clearly shows that the mind of man is open to three sources of thought and communication. Therefore all must be tested in the light of the written Word of God.

A. The Doctrine of God

1. Doctrine of God
Deuteronomy 32:2 — "My doctrine shall drop as the rain..."
Proverbs 4:2 — "I give you good doctrine..."

Isaiah 29:24 — "They also that erred in spirit shall come to understanding, and they that that
          murmured shall learn doctrine."
I Timothy 6:1 — "...that the name of God and His doctrine be not blasphemed."
I Timothy 6:3 — "...the doctrine which is according to godliness."
Titus 2:10 — "...that they may adorn the doctrine of God our Saviour in all things."

2. Doctrine of Christ
Hebrews 6:1 — "...the first principles of the doctrine of Christ."
Matthew 7:28 — "...they were astonished at His doctrine." See also Matthew 22:33; Mark 12:38; Mark
          1:27

Jesus taught many things in parables and doctrine. (Mark 4:2) Believers are to reject any one who
does not bring the doctrine of Christ. (II John 9-10) Jesus said "My doctrine is not mine but His that
sent Me. If any man will do His will he shall know of the doctrine whether it be of God or whether it be
of men" John 7:16-17. Jesus taught His Father's doctrine, the doctrine of God. The Father and the Son
were one in doctrine.

3. Doctrine of the Apostles
The early church converts "continued stedfastly in the Apostles doctrine, and in fellowship and
breaking of bread and prayers" Acts 2:42. (Read also Acts 5:28; 13:12; 17:19.) The religious leaders in
the Book of Acts feared the doctrine which the Apostles preached and thus fought and opposed it. All
true ministries in the Body of Christ will teach the Apostles doctrine; nothing more, nothing less.
They will "contend for the faith once delivered to the saints" Jude 3. The New Testament epistles
were written primarily by Apostles. They laid the foundations of revelation. Other ministries must
teach this. In Hebrews 6:1-2 we have a brief yet comprehensive summary of the Apostles doctrine,
from justification unto perfection. We list them in their progressive order.

    a. The Doctrine of Repentance from Dead Works
    b. The Doctrine of Faith toward God
    c. The Doctrine of Baptisms
    d. The Doctrine of Laying on of Hands
    e. The Doctrine of Resurrection from the Dead
    f. The Doctrine of Eternal Judgement
    g. The Doctrine of Perfection

B. The Doctrine of Men
Matthew 15:9 speaks of those who were "teaching for doctrines the commandments of men." Jesus
said that the doctrines and traditions of men make the Word of God of none effect (Mark 7:7-13). Paul
warns the believers not to be "carried about by every wind of doctrine, by the sleight of men, and
cunning craftiness whereby they lie in wait to deceive" Ephesians 4:14. (Hebrews 13:9) We are not to
be subject to the commandments or doctrines of men, nor their vain philosophies. (Colossians 2:8)

The Bible also clearly shows that there are certain doctrines of which the believer is to beware and
which Christ hates.

1. We are to beware of the Doctrine of the Pharisees and the Sadducees.   (Luke 12:1; Acts 23:8;
    Matthew 16:12)

2. The Lord condemned certain doctrines held by the churches in Revelation.

    The Doctrine of Balaam (Revelation 2:14 with Jude 11 and II Peter 2:15)
    The Doctrine of the Nicolaitans (Revelation 2:6,15)
    The Doctrine of Jezebel (Revelation 2:20-24)

We must hate that which Christ hates because of its corrupting influence in the church. God is very concerned about the doctrines His church follows. False cults, hiding under the cloak of Christianity, are founded on 'perversions of the Word of truth. (Read II Timothy 2:16-18; 4:3-4; I Timothy 1:4-6; 3:9; 4:7; 6:4-5; and Titus 1:9). Paul exhorted Timothy and Titus concerning those who would resist the truth, men of corrupt minds, destitute of the truth who had given themselves over to fables, vain babblings and endless genealogies. The Scriptures warn against false apostles, false prophets, false teachers and other ministries, who would bring in false doctrine. (II Corinthians 11:19-20; Matthew 7:15-23; II Peter 2:1-3)

C. Doctrine of Devils

The Scriptures warn us that in the latter times there would also arise doctrines of devils. Paul told Timothy that "the Spirit speaketh expressly, that in the latter times some shall depart from the faith, giving heed to seducing spirits and doctrines of devils..." I Timothy 4:1-3. (Refer also to I Corinthians 10:20-21.) These doctrines of devils are propagated through deceived men. Paul spoke of those who "corrupt the Word of God", that is, they deal deceitfully with the Word. (II Corinthians 2:17) He also spoke of those who were "walking in craftiness, handling the Word of God deceitfully" II Corinthians 4:2. The serpent stood before the woman, Eve, and perverted the Word of God, thus bringing about the Fall of man. Deception was Satan's first weapon in Eden (Genesis 3:1-6), and it is also Satan's last-day weapon. Note the warnings against deception in Matthew 24:4, 11, 24. In Ephesians 4:14 Paul speaks of winds of doctrine, and the trickery of men, their cunning craftiness, whereby they lay in wait to deceive the simple. This is how heresies originate. They arise out of demonic influence, and flow through deceived men.

The Apostle Peter also speaks of those who are unlearned and unstable wresting the truth of the Scriptures to their own destruction (II Peter 3:14-16). The word "wrest" means "to wrench, or torture on the rack" thus perverting and distorting the Scriptures they profess to be teaching. (Exodus 23:6; Deuteronomy 16:19; Psalm 56:5) Eternal judgement is pronounced on all those who "add" or "take away" from the Word of God. They suffer eternal wrath. (Deuteronomy 4:2; Proverbs 30:6; Revelation 22:18-19) Paul uttered a curse on angels or men who preached "another Gospel." (Galatians 1:6-8) False cults in principle preach "another Jesus", receive "another spirit" and proclaim "another Gospel." (II Corinthians 11:4)

All doctrine ultimately proceeds from one of two main sources: the Spirit of Truth or the Spirit of Error. Men can teach either, according to the Spirit they receive and are motivated and influenced by. The Last Days are upon the church, and Satan is releasing his mind, which is expressed through doctrines of demons, in order to deceive mankind. This shows the absolute need of being founded and established in the sound principles of the doctrine of Christ.

The following diagram shows the progression and end of the two streams of doctrine.

DOCTRINE

GOD	SATAN
Spirit of Truth	Spirit of Error
Light	Darkness
Doctrine of God	Doctrine of Satan
Doctrine of Christ	Doctrine of Devils
Doctrine of the Apostles	Doctrine of Man
Believing	Deceiving
Life and Liberty	Death and Bondage

The only sure and infallible test of all doctrine is the complete body of Scripture, working from the part to the whole, and the whole to the part. The prophet said, "To the law (The Word) and to the testimony (of the Scriptures). If they (the spirits) speak not according to this Word, it is because there is no light in them" Isaiah 8:19-20.

VI. THE SYMBOLS OF DOCTRINE
Doctrine is likened to three main things in Scripture, each of which illustrates its power and influence.

A. Doctrine is like Leaven (Matthew 16:5-12)
This is because leaven (yeast) works silently and secretly in the lump of dough, influencing the whole until all is leavened. Leaven has the subtle power to permeate the whole. Leaven here is a symbol of the evil influence of teaching. False doctrine corrupts the pure teaching or meal of God's Word, as well as the person who feeds upon it.

B. Doctrine is like Wind (Ephesians 4:14)
A believer is likened to a tree planted by the rivers of water, to bring forth fruit in his season. (Psalm 1:3) As a tree has to be well rooted to be able to stand the stormy winds that blow, so must the Christian be rooted and grounded in God to stand the false doctrines that are blowing like contrary winds through the earth. Strong winds can uproot trees and false doctrines can uproot the believer who is not rooted in the Word of the Lord.

C. Doctrine is like Rain (Deuteronomy 32:2; Isaiah 55:10-11; Hebrews 6:1-9)
Rain is used here in a good sense referring to heaven-sent teaching. Rain is symbolic of revival, refreshing and restoration after a time of drought or famine. Isaiah speaks of the cycle of rain as representing the cycle of the Word. As the rain cometh down from heaven, and watereth the earth, making it bud, so is the Word which proceeds out of God's mouth. It comes down from heaven, accomplishes that which God sent it to do and returns to Him.

VII. THE NATURE OF DOCTRINE
As we read the New Testament, especially the Pastoral Epistles of Paul, we find frequent references to doctrine. In I and II Timothy there are about 16 specific references to doctrine. A careful study of these references, along with others from the Gospels, Acts and other epistles, shows us the nature of doctrine. In the Pastoral Epistles, doctrine refers to two basic elements.

1. It refers to the art and act of communicating or teaching the truths of God, and Paul encourages both Timothy and Titus to do this. (I Timothy 5:17; Titus 2:1)
2. It also refers to the subject matter or the substance of what is taught. (I Timothy 4:6; II Timothy 3:15-16)

One cannot, in reality, separate these two. The act of teaching involves the content of teaching. Indoctrination is the continuous act of teaching. Doctrine is also synonymous with "the words of faith" (I Timothy 4:6); "sound words" (II Timothy 1:13), and "the faithful Word" (Titus 1:9).

"The faith once delivered to the saints" in Jude 3 speaks of the sum total of the revelation and doctrine as set forth in the Word of God that is to be taught and practiced.

We list several points concerning the nature of true doctrine.

A. Doctrine Must Be Sound
(I Timothy 1:10; II Timothy 4:2-4; Titus 1:9; 2:1)

In the Last Days some will depart from the faith, turn to doctrines of devils and will not endure sound (wholesome, healthy) doctrine. They will turn to fables, stories and traditions of men. (Matthew 22:29; Galatians 1:6-9) Sound doctrine alone preserves from error, and makes for the spiritual health and development of the believer. (I Timothy 4:6)

B. Doctrine Must Be Pure
Job said, "My doctrine is pure" Job 11:4. Heathen religions, as well as various cults under the name of Christianity, hold, teach and practice impure doctrines. The test of the purity of teaching is the purity of life it produces.

C. Doctrine Must Be Scriptural

(II Timothy 3:14-17)
All scripture is inspired of God, including both the Old and New Testaments. These are profitable for:
1. Doctrine
2. Reproof
3. Instruction
4. Correction

Titus 2:1 "Speak thou the things which become sound doctrine." Everything must be tested by the infallible Word of the Lord. The Scripture must be interpreted by proper principles in order to arrive at proper exposition.

D. Doctrine Must Be Obeyed

The believers at Rome "obeyed from the heart that form of doctrine" which had been delivered to them. (Romans 6:17) To really understand truth, it must be obeyed. All doctrine remains only a lifeless theory until it is practiced. Bible doctrines, no matter how true and scriptural, have no affect on man's life unless obeyed. Jesus said in John 7:16-17 "If any man will DO His will, he shall know of the doctrine..." that is, he will know intellectually and experientially, not just theoretically.

Jesus warned us to beware of the doctrine of the Pharisees, (Matthew 16:12) which is capsulized for us in Matthew 23:1-3 "They SAY and they DO NOT." It was a religion of words without deeds, which constitutes hypocrisy. They preached one thing, and practiced another. The Pharisees were often right in their doctrine, being legally meticulous but they did not obey it. All of their theory became a lifeless form. Jesus told us to do what they say, but not what they do because they say and do not. (Matthew 23:3)

Herein lies one of the chief dangers in handling doctrine; that it may become truth apart from experience, truth that is not lived. If one preaches the doctrines of love, holiness, light, fellowship, unity of the Body of Christ, ministry of the Holy Spirit, the Christian family, etc., then he must also obey that doctrine lest he become a modern-day Pharisee. Christian living must accompany Christian doctrine. Paul could say to Timothy, "But thou hast fully known my doctrine, manner of life..." II Timothy 3:10. Paul's life-style was consistent with his doctrine.

E. Doctrine Determines Character

It is a proven fact that doctrine determines character. What a person believes greatly affects what he is. Believing affects being, and being affects doing. If we follow sound doctrine, it will bring about a development of the Divine nature and the character of Christ within us. If we follow false doctrine, it will bring about a corruption of character. Doctrines such as Ultimate Reconciliation and Antinomianism have a damaging affect upon a believer's attitudes and lifestyle.

Paul exhorted Timothy to "take heed to thyself and the doctrine" I Timothy 4:6,13,16. And again, "Give attendance... to doctrine" I Timothy 4:13. Paul spoke of "the doctrine which is according to godliness" I Timothy 6:1-3. That is, God-likeness; holy character and living. Paul wrote to Titus and exhorted him to be an example in doctrine, and "adorn the doctrine" Titus 2:7-10 with II Peter 1:3.

F. Doctrine Affects Fellowship

Doctrine does affect fellowship in that there can be no fellowship unless both parties are walking in the light. (I John 1:1-7) In fact the measure of common light between believers will partially determine the measure of their fellowship.

In Acts 2:42 we find that the converts of the first Pentecost continued stedfastly first in the Apostles' doctrine and second in fellowship. The significance of this order is supported by some of the New Testament epistles.

John, the Apostle of love, wrote to the believers telling them not to receive any who came to their house if they did not bring the doctrine of the Father and the Son. (II John 9-10) He also said not to bid them God-speed, lest they became partakers of their evil teaching and deeds. John taught that believers should not have fellowship with those who propagate false doctrine. However, we must keep in mind what type of doctrinal issues he is telling us to break fellowship over. He is not giving us license to disfellowship over minor areas of doctrine rather only when the most foundational truths are at stake; such as the person of Christ. A good policy to follow is: "In essentials unity, in non-essentials liberty, in all things charity."

Though some may wrongly sacrifice fellowship for doctrine, neither should we sacrifice doctrine for fellowship. Both must be maintained in purity.

G. Doctrine Determines Destiny

Who and what we believe in affects eternal destiny. It is a vain statement to say that it does not matter what a person believes, as long as they are sincere. This is abundantly exemplified in false cults, inside and outside of Christendom, who are zealous and sincere, but sincerely wrong. (II Peter 3:14-15) It is our relationship to Christ which affects our eternal destiny. "What think ye of Christ, whose Son is He?"; and, "What will you do with Jesus which is called Christ?" Matthew 22:42; 27:22. It is on their answer to these two questions that a person's eternal destiny hangs. In Christ is light and life. Outside of Christ is darkness and death.

H. Doctrine and Love

Though all our doctrine be exactly right, scripturally and theologically, if we do not have love we are nothing. (I Corinthians 13:1-6) Paul never said that tongues, prophecy, faith, knowledge or spiritual gifts were nothing. He said I am nothing without love.

God is Love. (I John 4:16) This is the nature of God and all He does is founded on it. So should it be with the people of God. If God's people, who often uphold their own doctrines, would constantly remember that love is the greatest doctrine in the Bible, then all other doctrines would take their proper place in relation to it.

VIII. THE PROGRESS OF DOCTRINE

The prophet Isaiah in speaking to Israel referred to a principle which God used to progressively reveal doctrine in Scripture. In Isaiah 28:9-13, he sets forth the question, the answer and the method of divine instruction.

The Question: "Whom shall He teach knowledge?"
"Whom shall He make to understand doctrine?"

The Answer: "Them that are weaned from the milk, and drawn from the breast."

The Method: "For the Word of the Lord was unto them... precept upon precept; precept upon precept; line upon line, line upon line; here a little, there a little..."

This may be said to be God's method of teaching doctrine. God did not give the full revelation of Himself at once. From Adam to Moses, a period of approximately 2500 years, there was no written Word, or recorded revelation of God in Scripture form. The promises of redemption were in the hearts and mouths of the patriarchs, while the heavens declared the Gospel story in its signs. (Genesis 1:14-19); Psalm 19:1-6) God inspired Moses to write the Pentateuch, Genesis through to Deuteronomy, covering the period of 2500 years from Adam to Moses. Later, the history of Israel under Joshua, Judges, Samuel, and the Kings of Israel and Judah was recorded in the writings of the historical and prophetical books, from Joshua through to Malachi.

The thirty-nine books of the Old Testament took approximately 1100 years to record. No one patriarch, prophet, priest, king or saint ever received the whole doctrine of God at once; but each received "precept upon precept, line upon line, here a little and there a little" until the whole of the Old Testament revelation was completed. Hebrews 1:1-2 tells us "God, who at sundry times (Old Testament times), and in divers manners (in many portions, many ways, fragmentary manners), spake in time past unto the fathers

by the prophets, hath in these last days spoken unto us by His Son..." God communicated His mind/
Word in Old Testament times by signs, shadows, types, ensamples, figures, allegory, dreams and vis
angelic manifestation and prophetic voice.

In New Testament times the doctrinal revelation came through Jesus Christ, God's Son, and then thr
the apostles. (John 1:1-3, 14-18; Acts 2:42; Ephesians 3:1-6) The finality of God's revelation and doct
instruction is in Christ. He is THE ORACLE (the speaking place) of God. (Hebrews 5:12; Romans 3:2; I
4:11) It is no wonder then that the New Testament Canon of 27 books was completed within the
century, in contrast to the 1100 years it took to complete the Old Testament.

Though a compilation of many books, the Bible is to be viewed as one harmonious whole with truth
progressively revealed throughout. Each book is a part of the whole and cannot be understood apart
its relation to the whole.

The way God progressively revealed truth in Scripture suggests the way in which the Bible student sh
handle the doctrines of Scripture; bringing together all that the Bible has to say on the subject to form
the doctrine of it and arrange the elements of that doctrine into a systematic order. All doctrine must
out of and be founded firmly upon the only absolute authority in man's possession, the inspired
infallible Word of God.

Chapter 2

THE DOCTRINE OF REVELATION

The God of the Bible is one who reveals Himself to His creation. God creating man with mental and spiritual faculties indicates His intention that man know Him. However, since the fall of man, these mental and spiritual faculties have been dulled and he cannot of himself discover God. Thus God, in grace and love, has taken the initiative by giving a progressive revelation of Himself consummating in the Lord Jesus Christ. Man can only personally know God through Christ.

CHAPTER OUTLINE

I. THE DEFINITION OF REVELATION

II. THE NECESSITY OF REVELATION

III. PROGRESSIVE REVELATION

A. General Revelation

1. The Revelation of God in Nature

2. The Revelation of God in Conscience

3. The Revelation of God in Human History

B. Special Revelation

1. The Revelation of God in Miracles

2. The Revelation of God in Prophecy

3. The Revelation of God in Christ

4. The Revelation of God in Scripture

5. The Revelation of God in Personal Experience

I. THE DEFINITION OF REVELATION

The Greek word "Apokalupsis" means "an uncovering, to uncover or unveil". It best represents what is meant by "revelation". Most dictionaries define revelation as a disclosure or unveiling; to make known something hidden or secret. It is used in this sense in Scripture. (Ephesians 1:17; 3:3-5; Revelation 1:1; Galatians 3:23; I Peter 1:5; 2 Corinthians 12:1,7; Galatians 1:12) In theology revelation refers to God unveiling Himself to man, and communicating truth to the mind of man which he could not discover in any other way. It is imparted truth which could not be discovered by natural reasoning alone.

Matthew 11:27 "No man knoweth the Son save the Father; neither knoweth any man the Father, save the Son, and he to whomsoever the Son will reveal Him."

Matthew 16:17 "Blessed art thou Simon Barjona for flesh and blood hath not revealed this unto thee but My Father which is in heaven."

I Corinthians 2:10 "...but God hath revealed them unto us by His Spirit."

(Read also Amos 3:7; I Samuel 3:21; Daniel 2:19-30,47; Deuteronomy 29:29; I Peter 4:13; Luke 2:26)

II. THE NECESSITY OF REVELATION

Man being made in the image and likeness of God, has within himself certain faculties which enable him to receive revelation from God. These faculties set man apart from the irrational creatures made by God. Man is superior to animals, in that he is endowed with a will, intelligence, conscience and a spirit which can know and worship God.

However, when man fell so did these faculties. Though he partook of the tree of knowledge of good and evil he fell into a state of spiritual ignorance and darkness. In the Fall, man became totally depraved in spirit, soul and body. His mind, reason and understanding became darkened. He was alienated from the life of God and became an enemy of God in his mind by wicked works. (Ephesians 4:17-18; Colossians 1:21 with Genesis 3:1-6)

The fact that man is a created but fallen being indicates his need of a revelation of God. Unless God takes the initiative and reveals Himself to man, it is impossible for man to discover or know God. Zophar said to Job, "Canst thou by searching find out the Almighty unto perfection?" (Job 11:7)

Paul declared that the world with all its wisdom could not know God, (I Corinthians 1:21) and that no man could know the things of God without the Spirit of God revealing it to him. (I Corinthians 2:11-16)

II. PROGRESSIVE REVELATION

Divine revelation may be instantaneous or progressive. (Isaiah 28:9-13; Hebrews 1:1-2; Matthew 16:17; Deuteronomy 29:29) When viewed as a whole it becomes evident that God's revelation has been given to man in a progressive manner with each successive portion building on the previous. The Bible provides us with an overview of the progress of God's revelation. This may be viewed in two categories, general and special.

A. General Revelation

General revelation includes that which God has revealed of Himself to all mankind.

1. The Revelation of God in Nature

Creation itself suggests that there is a Creator. The existence of an intelligent design in nature precludes the existence of an intelligent designer. The design, beauty, law and order and numerical structure stamped upon all created things point to an intelligent being, above, beyond and greater than all created things. This being is God.

Genesis 1:1 "In the beginning God created the heaven and the earth."
Psalm 19:1 "The heavens declare the glory of God; and the firmament sheweth his handywork."
(Read Psalm 19:1-6; Genesis 1:1-5; Romans 10:17,18 and John 1:1-5)

Nature is God's book by creation, and it has a language and speech which may be heard in every nation. All mankind is held accountable for their knowledge of the revelation of God in nature. "Because that which may be known of God is manifest in them; for God hath shewed it unto them. For the invisible things of him from the creation of the world are clearly seen, being understood by the things that are made, even his eternal power and Godhead; so that they are without excuse." (Romans 1:19-20)

The revelation of God in creation indicates that there is a God who is the creator, designer, architect and sustainer of all that exists. (Acts 14:15-17; 17:24-29; Genesis 1:1; Isaiah 40:12-14) However, the revelation of God in creation is insufficient on its own in that God cannot be personally known through it. Creation reveals that there is a God but does not bring man into contact with Him. It reveals God's power but does not reveal His person. Being insufficient for a personal knowledge of God, nature was meant to point man toward further revelation of Him. It was designed to arouse in man a desire to seek beyond it for the one who made it. He was to look at creation and then beyond it to the creator. Unfortunately, the majority of mankind has chosen not to do so. Man has selected created things, even the works of his own hands, and exalted them to be gods over him. Paul referred to those "who changed the truth of God into a lie, and worshipped and served the creature more than the Creator," Romans 1:25. They corrupted the truth of a creation pointing to God as its Creator and replaced it with a creation that is god in itself.

2. The Revelation of God in Conscience
Conscience is defined as "a knowing with oneself". It is an awareness of right and wrong, with a compulsion to the right. When God created man in His own image and likeness, He placed within man a conscience. This faculty was somewhat inoperative until the Fall of Man, when the violation of the one commandment given to Adam and Eve (Genesis 2:17) set the conscience into motion. Their guilty conscience drove them to hide from God when He sought them.

That man possesses the faculty of conscience is a universally accepted fact. Man is a moral creature, capable of knowing right from wrong. However, the question is, "where did he get this moral sense?" Some suggest that conscience is socially acquired, that is, received from others by their instruction and example. The element of truth in this belief is that man's conscience can be socially conditioned but the error is in stating that man's moral sense is received only from other men. According to Paul, the Gentiles, though never taught the law, had "the law written in their hearts, their conscience also bearing witness, and their thoughts the mean while accusing or else excusing one another;" Romans 2:14-15. This law inherent within man suggests the existence of a supreme law-giver who not only placed this law within man but also holds him accountable to it. Conscience then is a revelation of God, the ultimate law-giver.

The revelation of God in conscience is insufficient on its own for two reasons. First, though the existence of conscience does indicate the existence of a divine law-giver, it does not give a personal knowledge of Him. Second, though the conscience is meant to be an internal witness to the law of God, that witness is fallible. Through sin, a man's conscience may be corrupted, defiled and even seared. (I Corinthians 8:7-10; I Timothy 4:2; Titus 1:15) Only through the blood of Christ and the Word of God can a man's conscience be restored to its rightful role. (II Corinthians 4:2; I Timothy 3:9; Hebrews 9:14; 10:22)

3. The Revelation of God in History
There is a revelation of God seen in the history of the nations of the world. The mysterious rise and fall of nations indicates that somewhere behind the scenes is a sovereign hand, guiding, governing, controlling, raising up and casting down the rulers of these nations.

Deuteronomy 32:8 "When the Most High divided to the nations their inheritance, when he separated the sons of Adam, he set the bounds of the people according to the number of the children of Israel."

Psalm 75:7 "But God is the judge: he putteth down one, and setteth up another."

Daniel 4:32 "...The Most High ruleth in the kingdom of men, and giveth it to whomsoever He will."

Acts 17:26 "And hath made of one blood all nations of men for to dwell on all the face of the earth, and hath determined the times before appointed, and the bounds of their habitation;"

Romans 13:1 "...For there is no power but of God: The powers that be are ordained of God."

God has always been involved in human history. Following are some illustrations of God's involvement in the nations existing in Bible days.

a. God's dealings are seen in the history of the nation of Egypt. (Exodus 9-12; Romans 9:17; Jeremiah 46:14-26; Ezekiel 29-30)

b. God caused the Assyrian Empire to fall. (Isaiah 10:12-19; Ezekiel 31; Nahum 3:1-7)

c. God judged the Babylonian kingdom according to His prophetic word. The drying up of the river Euphrates and the leaving open of the two leaved gates by which the Medo-Persian soldiers entered the city on the night of her fall, attest to the sovereignty of God. (Daniel 1-5; Jeremiah 50-51; Isaiah 47-48; 45:1-5)

d. The Medo-Persian Empire came under the judgement of God in due time. (Isaiah 44:24-45:1-7; Daniel 2; Daniel 7)

e. The Grecian Empire collapsed in God's ordered time. (Daniel 8:1-25; 11:1-35)

f. God foretold through Daniel the rise of the Roman Empire. It also fell at the appointed time. (Daniel 7:7,23; 9:24-27)

g. The history of Israel is one of the most remarkable revelations of God in history. Taken as a nation from the midst of the nations (Deuteronomy 4:34-40) it was brought into covenantal relationship with the Lord at Mt. Sinai. The revelation of God in the Tabernacle of Moses, the Aaronic and Levitical priesthood, the sacrificial system, the feasts, and above all, the moral and civil laws given to them are all evidence that the unseen God was involved in the history of this nation. (Exodus 19-40; Leviticus 1-9) The preservation of the nation of Israel is also a remarkable testimony to the fact that this unseen hand guides the destinies of the peoples of earth. (Esther 1-10) Israel remains today as an indicator of the presence of that sovereign hand.

Though history shows us that there is a sovereign God at work, it does not reveal His person to us. As the others, the revelation of God in human history is insufficient for a personal knowledge of Him. Further revelation is needed.

B. Special Revelation
General revelation is that which is available to all nations of the earth. All mankind has the general revelation of God in nature, conscience and history. Special revelation refers to those acts of God whereby He reveals Himself and His will to specific persons.

1. The Revelation of God in Miracles
A miracle is a supernatural intervention into the laws of nature. There are genuine miracles wrought by God and there are counterfeit miracles wrought by the power of Satan. Throughout human history God has revealed His power and presence in true miracles.

a. The plagues in Egypt were miracles. (Exodus 4-12)

b. The miracles of the magicians were Satanic counterfeits. (Exodus 7:12,22)

c. The opening of the Red Sea and Jordan were miracles. (Exodus 14-15; Joshua 4-5)

d. The manna from heaven and water from the rock were miracles. (Exodus 16-17; I Corinthians 10:1-6)

e. The Gospels and the Acts record numerous miracles; spiritually, physically, and materially in the ministry of Christ and His apostles. (Matthew 8; Acts 3-4, etc.)

f. The Antichrist will perform miracles to deceive the peoples of earth. (Matthew 24:24; II Thessalonians 2:9; Revelation 13:13; Acts 8:9-11)

The Bible is a book of recorded miracles from Genesis to Revelation and its greatest miracle is the resurrection of Christ. Just as counterfeit miracles reveal the presence and power of Satan, so genuine miracles attest to the presence and power of God. The purpose of counterfeit miracles is to deceive and turn men from God. The purpose of true miracles is to bless and turn men to God. Miracles, both ancient and modern are specific revelations of God's power and motivation in dealing with mankind.

2. The Revelation of God in Prophecy

There are two types of prophecy; preaching and and prediction. Though both are inspired and reveal the Word of God, the prediction of future events is the easiest to illustrate.

a. The falls of nations were foretold by the prophets and came to pass years after their utterance with amazing accuracy.
   (1) The fall of Assyria was prophesied in Ezekiel 31.
   (2) The fall of Babylon was foretold in Jeremiah 50-51 and Isaiah 47-48.
   (3) The fall of Egypt as a nation was predicted in Ezekiel 30-31.
   (4) The fall of the Grecian Empire was prophesied in Daniel 8.

b. The coming of Christ was foretold by the prophets.   There were about three hundred prophecies to be fulfilled within the short life time of Christ and most of these had to find fulfillment in the last few hours of His life. These prophecies had been foretold over a thousand years by different writers. They seemed to be impossible to fulfill. Yet God in Christ fulfilled them in great detail.
   (1) Christ was to be the seed of the woman. (Genesis 3:15; Isaiah 7:14; Matthew 1:20-23)
   (2) Christ was to be the seed of Abraham. (Genesis 12:1-3; Matthew 1:1)
   (3) Christ was to be of Tribe of Judah. (Genesis 49:10; Hebrews 7:14)
   (4) Christ was to be born at Bethlehem. (Micah 5:2; Matthew 2:6)
   (5) Christ was to be anointed by the Spirit. (Isaiah 61:1-2; Luke 4:18-20)
   (6) Christ was to minister life and healing. (Isaiah 35; Matthew 8)
   (7) Christ was to ride into Jerusalem upon an ass. (Zechariah 9:9; Matthew 21:4-5)
   (8) Christ was to be sold for thirty pieces of silver. (Zechariah 11:12-13; Matthew 26:15)
   (9) Christ was to suffer the crucifixion. (Psalm 22; Isaiah 53; Matthew 27)
   (10) Christ was to rise from the dead, ascend to heaven and sit at the Father's right hand in King-Priestly ministry. (Psalm 16; Psalm 110; Matthew 22:43-45)

Just as miracles are a revelation of God's power so the fulfillment of prophecy is a revelation of God's infinite knowledge.

3. The Revelation of God in Christ

The general revelations of God in nature, conscience and history are insufficient in that they do not reveal God's person. The special revelations of God in miracles and prophecy are also insufficient in that they only reveal certain of His attributes but not His entire personhood. With all this, there still existed the need for a more personal revelation of God. This need God has met in Christ. Christ is the sum total of the revelation of God including His will, His nature, His person and character. To look at Christ is to look at God, for Christ is the expressed revelation of God in human form.

John 1:1,14 "In the beginning was the Word, and the Word was with God; and the Word was made flesh and dwelt among us..."

John 1:18 "No man hath seen God at any time; the only begotten Son, which is in the bosom of the .Father, he hath declared him."

Colossians 1:15 "Who is the image of the invisible God."

Hebrews 1:1-3 "God... hath in these last days spoken unto us by His Son... the express image of His person."

(Read also Matthew 11:17; John 14:9; Colossians 2:9; II Corinthians 4:3-6; Romans 16:25-26; Amos 3:7; and II Timothy 3:15-16)

Christ is the ultimate revelation of God because He is God.

4. The Revelation of God in Scripture

The revelation of God in Christ is the revelation of the Living Word — the Word made flesh. The revelation of God in Scripture is that of the written Word — the Word inspired and recorded. Because of the various means of revelation, especially in the realm of miracles, spoken prophecy, and Jesus Christ Himself, there was need of a written revelation as a universal expression, which would be available for all mankind. There was need of some revelation that could be given to all the nations, which would correspond exactly with the Christ of God. This revelation is contained in the Bible. The Scriptures were inspired by the Holy Spirit and thus in them we have an infallible revelation of the nature, being and will of God.

5. The Revelation of God in Personal Experience

The fact that God has given a revelation of Himself indicates that He intended man to receive it. Man, being made in the image and likeness of God, has been given mental and spiritual capacity to receive revelation from His Creator. However, the intellectual and spiritual parts of man's being have to come under the illuminating influence of the Holy Spirit in order to be able to receive the revelation of God. (I Corinthians 2:12) The Lord Jesus opened the understanding of the disciples and also breathed His Spirit into their spirits, thus quickening their mental and spiritual capacity for knowing God. (Luke 24:44-45; John 20:22)

The purpose of all the revelation of God is that man may come to know God in a personal way. It is not enough for men to say they know God in nature, conscience, history, miracles or prophecy. Man must come to know God in an experiential way. From the fall of man unto this day, there have been millions of people who have known God in a personal way. The following are some examples from Scripture.

   a. In the Old Testament
      (1) Enoch walked with God (Genesis 5:21-24)
      (2) Noah walked with God (Genesis 6:9,13)
      (3) God revealed Himself to Abraham (Genesis 12:1-3)
      (4) Isaac knew God (Genesis 26:24)
      (5) Jacob had personal dealings with God (Genesis 28:13; 35:1)
      (6) The beloved son Joseph had revelation of God (Genesis 37:5-11)
      (7) God revealed Himself to Moses in the burning bush (Exodus 3:1-5)
      (8) Joshua met the Lord as the Captain of the Host (Joshua 1:1; 5:13-15)
      (9) Gideon had a visitation from God (Judges 6:25)
      (10) The Lord revealed Himself to Samuel in vision (I Samuel 3:2-4)
      (11) David had a personal experience with the Lord (I Samuel 23:9-12)
      (12) Elijah knew God in a still small voice (I Kings 17:2-4)
      (13) Isaiah had a revelation of the holiness of God (Isaiah 6:8)

   b. In the New Testament
      (1) The 12 apostles received a personal experience of God in Christ (Matthew 10:10)
      (2) Jesus is the revelation of God to man personally (Matthew 11:27; 16:17-18)
      (3) Paul had a personal revelation of Jesus Christ (Acts 9:4-6; 18:9)
      (4) The beloved apostle John knew Jesus experientially (John 13:23-25; I John 4:7-11; Revelation 1:1-12)

Much of the revelation in the Old and New Testaments was drawn from the personal experience of the saints. It arose out of the revelation of God to them, in them and then through them. The transforming power of the Gospel today in the lives of sinners is abundant testimony to the revelation of God in personal experience.

Chapter 3

THE DOCTRINE OF THE SCRIPTURES

The Holy Scriptures are a revelation of God, coming from God, and flowing through and to man. They are the only inspired and infallible divine revelation ever given to man and are the supreme authority in all matters of faith and morals. The Scriptures were plenary-verbally inspired. The Holy Spirit breathed upon the human vessels the very thoughts and words He wanted written. This word flowed through the human channels involving their emotions, personalities and frames of reference, without violating such. Yet the Holy Spirit guarded and preserved each thought, phrase and word from any error, omission or inaccuracy.

CHAPTER OUTLINE

I. THE NAMES AND TITLES OF THE INSPIRED BOOK
A look at the Bible, the inspired book, shows that there are a number of names and titles it is called by.

A. The Bible
The Greek word "Biblios" simply means "Book" and from it is derived our English word "Bible".

Though the word "Bible" is not used in Scripture, the Greek word "Biblios" is used often. There are many books referred to as "Bibles" in the Scripture. Some of these are listed below:

The book of Moses. (Mark 12:26)
The book of Isaiah. (Luke 3:4; 4:17-18)
The book of Psalms. (Luke 20:42; Acts 1:20)
The book of the Prophets. (Acts 7:42)
The book of the Law. (Galatians 3:10)
The volume of the book. (Hebrews 10:7)
The blood-sprinkled book. (Hebrews 9:19)
The book to the 7 Churches. (Revelation 1:11)
The little book. (Revelation 10:5-10)
The seven sealed book. (Revelation 5:1-10)
The prophecy of this book. (Revelation 22:7,9,10,18)

The Bible is the Divine Library, consisting of sixty-six separate yet related books. It is THE book of all books, priceless and incomparable. Its two divisions are the Old Testament, having thirty-nine books and the New Testament containing twenty-seven books. Though a compilation of sixty-six books it is really one unified book. The Bible is the only authoritative written revelation of God.

B. The Word of God
Though written by men, the Scriptures are God's Word to man. Over two-thousand times they are spoken of or alluded to as "the Word of God". They are called:

1. The Word of God. (I Thessalonians 2:13; Hebrews 4:12; Ephesians 6:17; Mark 7:13; Colossians 1:25; John 10: 35; Luke 8:11)

2. The Word of the Lord. (Jeremiah 1:2,11; Ezekiel 1:3; Isaiah 1:10; Hosea 1:1; Acts 8:25; II Thessalonians 3:1; I Peter 1:23-25; Isaiah 40:8; I Thessalonians 1:8; 4:15; Acts 13:48)

3. The Word of Christ. (Colossians 3:16)

4. The Word of Life. (Philippians 2:16)

5. The Word of Truth. (Ephesians 1:13)

6. The Word of Faith. (Romans 10:8)

7. The Word. (James 1:21-23; John 1:1-3; Luke 4:4; I Timothy 4:5; Romans 10:17; Acts 4:31; 6:4)

Jesus Christ is the living Word, the Word made flesh, and the Bible is the Written Word. Both are the "Logos". The Living Word is revealed in the Written Word and the Written Word leads us to the Living Word. They are one.

C. The Scriptures
The Word "Scripture" means "a writing" or "writings". It is in contrast with all of the uninspired writings of men. This word is used about twenty-four times in the Gospels and twenty-eight times in the rest of the New Testament. It is found once in the Old Testament. The Writings are:

1. The Scriptures of Truth. (Daniel 10:21)

2. **The Scripture.** (Mark 12:10; 15:28; Luke 4:21; John 2:22; 7:38; 10:35; Romans 4:3; II Timothy 3:16; Galatians 3:8,22; 4:30; Acts 1:1,6; John 19:24,28,36, 37; 20:9)

3. **The Scriptures.** (Matthew 21:42; 22:29; 26:54,56; Mark 12:24; Luke 24:27; John 5:39; Romans 16:26; Acts 13:27; 17:11; II Timothy 3:15; I Corinthians 15:3; John 7:38,42; Romans 1:2; II Peter 3:16)

4. **The Holy Scriptures.** (II Timothy 3:15; Romans 1:2)

D. The Oracles of God.

The word "oracle" literally means "the speaking place". Christianity arises out of a faith in an infinite personal God who has not been silent, but has spoken. The Bible is indeed the Oracle of God, His speaking place. The Law is referred to as the "lively oracles". (Romans 3: (Romans 3:2) The Holiest of All in the temple is also called "The Holy Oracle". (Psalm 28:2)

The first principles of the doctrine of Christ are also the Oracles of God. (Hebrews 5:10:12; 6:1-2) Believers, when ministering the Word of God, are to speak as the Oracles of God. (I Peter 4:11)

E. The Old and New Testaments

The word "Testament" simply means "Covenant". The Bible is divided into two sections relative to the two major covenants, the Covenant of Law (The Old Testament), and the Covenant of Grace (The New Testament).

Though there are nine Divine Covenants in all, God's dealings with man seem to center around these two. While the Old Testament focuses on God's dealings with Israel under the Law Covenant given through Moses, the New Testament focuses on God's dealings with the world under the Grace Covenant given through Christ. Jeremiah, under the Old Covenant, foretold the coming of the New Covenant. (Jeremiah 31:31-34; Hebrews 8:6-13; 10:15-17) Jesus in establishing the New fulfilled the Old. (Luke 22:20; I Corinthians 11:25; Mark 14:24; Matthew 26:26-28; Hebrews 9:15; 12:24; II Corinthians 3:6,14; Matthew 5:17-18; 11:13; Romans 3:21)

II. THE SYMBOLS OF THE INSPIRED BOOK

God likens His Word to many things and each of the symbols used to convey a unique facet of truth to represent it.

A. The Word is like Fire. (Jeremiah 23:29)
It burns, cleanses and purges all that is contrary to its holy standard.

B. The Word is like a Hammer. (Jeremiah 23:29)
It smashes and demolishes evil.

C. The Word is like a Lamp. (Psalm 119:105)
It's an instrument of light and illumination in the darkness.

D. The Word is like a Mirror. (James 1:23)
It reveals to us what we are and what we can be in God.

E. The Word is like Milk. (I Peter 2:2)
It nourishes the young in Christ.

F. The Word is like a Rod. (Revelation 11:1-2)
As a measuring instrument it is the Divine standard in all matters of faith and practice.

G. The Word is like a Seed. (I Peter 1:23; Luke 8:11; James 1:18)
It is a germinating, life producing Word, having the potential of eternal life within it.

H. The Word is like a Sword. (Hebrews 4:12)
It is sharp and two-edged in its operation, separating the things of the flesh and the spirit.

I. The Word is like Water. (Ephesians 5:26; John 15:3; 17:17; Psalm 119:5,9)
It is life giving, refreshing and a cleansing agent.

J. The Word is like Gold. (Psalm 19:7-10; Job 28:1; Proverbs 25:2)
It is of priceless value. The Bible is an inexhaustable gold mine where one can dig out treasures for ever.

K. The Word is like Honey. (Psalm 19:10; Revelation 10:10)
It is sweet to the taste.

L. The Word is like an Ox-goad. (Ecclesiastes 12:11)
It is an instrument which prods the oxen into fulfilling its duties.

M. The Word is like a Nail. (Ecclesiastes 12:11)
It is fastened in a sure place. We can safely hang things on it.

N. The Word is like Bread. (Matthew 4:4; Deuteronomy 8:3; Psalm 119:103; Isaiah 55:10; Exodus 16)
It is the staff of life, ever fresh, and meant for daily consumption.

0. The Word is like a Pearl. (Matthew 7:6)
It is a precious gem. Though formed in darkness, it has the colors of the rainbow when brought to the light.

P. The Word is like an Anchor. (Hebrews 6:18-19)
It holds the believer in safety through every storm.

Q. The Word is like a Star. (II Peter 1:19; Revelation 2:28)
It guides the believer to Christ.

R. The Word is like Meat. (Hebrews 5:14)
It is strength-giving food for the mature.

III. THE DEFINITION OF INSPIRATION
Paul tells us in II Timothy 3:16, "All Scripture is given by inspiration of God, and is profitable for doctrine, for reproof, for correction, for instruction in righteousness: that the man of God may be perfect, thoroughly furnished unto all good works." In this verse the Greek word "Theopneustos", translated "inspiration" simply means "God-breathed". God breathed into Adam the breath of life and he became a living soul. (Genesis 2:7; Acts 17:25) "But there is a spirit in man, and the inspiration of the almighty giveth them understanding." (Job 32:8) The dry bones of Ezekiel's vision needed the breath of life, "but there was no breath in them..." (Ezekiel 37:8,9) Jesus "breathed" upon His disciples on the morning of the resurrection, telling them to receive the breath of the Spirit of life. (John 20:22)

Naturally speaking inspiration is the "act of drawing air into the lungs; inhalation; the act of breathing into". With regard to the Scriptures it speaks of "the influence of the Spirit of God on the mind and soul of man; the Divine influence exerted on the writers of the Scripture, by which they are instructed". (Collins Graphic English Dictionary) Webster's dictionary defines inspiration as "the supernatural influence of the Spirit of God on the human mind, by which the prophets and apostles and sacred writers were qualified to set forth Divine truth without any mixture of error."

IV. THE MODE OF INSPIRATION

A. The Place of Inspiration
The mode or method which God employed in inspiring Scripture must be distinguished from its content and result.

1. Revelation
Revelation is the communication of truth which could not be discovered by natural reason. It is God

unveiling His person and purpose to man. E.H. Bancroft in "Christian Theology" says in his chapter outline that:

a. A Divine Revelation is possible.
b. A Divine Revelation is probable.
c. A Divine Revelation is credible.
d. A Divine Revelation is necessary.

Revelation is possible because of the nature of God. It is probable because of the fact that man is God's creation, and there has to be communication between the Creator and the creature. It is credible because of the character of God, and it is necessary because of the communication gap that exists between God and man through sin.

The Bible is not man's thoughts about God, but primarily God revealing Himself and His purposes to man. Divine knowledge was communicated by the Spirit of God to holy men who recorded it. All that may be known of God in this present life is founded in and upon the Scriptures. In this written revelation of God, God has revealed His nature, character and being. He has revealed the purpose of man's existence and His redemptive plan for mankind. These things could not be found out by the reasonings or intellectual pursuits of men, only by Divine revelation. Some of the things recorded by Moses in the Pentateuch were obviously impossible to discover by natural reasoning. (e.g. Genesis 1-2) Although some other things were recorded by experience and observation, they are no less a revelation from God to man. (Deuteronomy 29:29; Matthew 11:25-27; 16:16-18; I Corinthians 2:9-14; Ephesians 3:2-6)

2. Inspiration
Inspiration describes the process by which the revelation was recorded. While revelation has to do with the impartation of Divine truth, inspiration has to do with the recording of the truth. The Scriptures are an infallible revelation because of inspiration. Inspiration was the power which enabled the men of God to write the Divine revelation without error or defect. (II Peter 1:21) God commanded many men to write things in a Book. (Exodus 17:14; Revelation 1:11; II Peter 1:20-21; Jeremiah 30:2; II Samuel 23:2; II Timothy 3:15-17) Moses, for instance, received the Ten Commandments by revelation, but he recorded them in a book under inspiration.

3. Illumination
Illumination describes the process of the Holy Spirit enlightening man's understanding to be able to receive God's revelation. It is the work of the Spirit to bring revelation, inspiration and illumination. (Luke 24:26-27, 44-45; I Corinthians 2:11-14; John 16:12-15; Acts 17:1-3) Revelation is the reception of truth. Inspiration is the recording of truth. Illumination is the perception of truth, brought about by the influence of the Holy Spirit. (I John 2:20,27)

In the New Testament the word revelation often refers theologically to illumination. (Ephesians 1:17-18 with Psalm 119:18) Believers today are not to receive revelation or inspiration as the Bible writers, but they are to receive illumination. The believer receives illumination on the revelation given by inspiration. Illumination is the supernatural opening of the understanding to receive that which is revealed in God's Word. The Holy Spirit knows what He meant when He inspired the Word. We, therefore, need His illumination.

This is promised to us by the Lord Jesus. (John 15:26; 16:12-13) The Holy Spirit, who is the agent of revelation and inspiration also becomes the agent of illumination.

It should be remembered that there is absolutely nothing to be added to the completed Biblical revelation and anyone who dares to add comes under the curse of God. (Revelation 22:18-19) This excludes all other "inspired books" be they sacred or otherise. The Bible stands alone, as the inspired revelation of God.

E. H. Bancroft, in "Christian Theology" (p.24) says:

"Revelation concerns the discovery of truth. Illumination concerns the understanding of truth. Inspiration concerns the communication of truth."

These may act cooperatively or separately, as the following instances show:

a. Inspiration without revelation. (Luke 1:1-3)
b. Inspiration including revelation. (Revelation 1:1-11)
c. Inspiration without illumination. (I Peter 1:11)
d. Inspiration including illumination (I Corinthians 2:12)
e. Revelation without inspiration. (Exodus 20:1,22)
f. Illumination without inspiration. (I John 2:27)

B. The False Theories of Inspiration

There are various theories of inspiration. A brief consideration shows most of them to be inadequate, incomplete or false.

1. The Natural Theory of Inspiration

This is also spoken of as the Intuition Theory. It holds that the Bible was written by human genius or by men of superior mental insight. Works like "Paradise Lost" by Milton, the poems of Shakespeare and the sacred books of the great world religions are all spoken of as being inspired works, or the product of human genius.

This theory denies the supernatural element in the writing of the Bible. If the Bible is a humanly inspired book, then why is it that the natural man cannot understand it? (I Corinthians 2:12 Amp. N.T.)

2. The Illumination Theory of Inspiration

This theory holds that the Bible was the result of illumination, or a heightening of man's religious perception. It is said that just as believers today receive illumination and are quickened and anointed by the Holy Spirit, so it was with the men who wrote Scripture.

However, as noted in the distinction between revelation, inspiration and illumination, it is possible to have illumination without inspiration, as it is possible to have inspiration without illumination. The Bible writers had revelation, inspiration and at times illumination. (Acts 13:27; Psalm 119:18) The Bible is not just a product of human enlightenment.

3. The Mechanical Theory of Inspiration

This is also spoken of as the Dictation Theory which holds that God dictated the Scriptures to the writers like an executive dictates words to his secretary. It says in effect that the Bible is a verbatim report. This theory makes man a mere machine, like a tape-recorder or typewriter just receiving and recording words. It treats the writers as mere pens used to write the Scriptures, making them similar to Spiritist mediums who write under the control of evil spirits.

While true inspiration does include the fact that words were inspired by the Spirit of God, the mechanical theory destroys the evident personality of the various writers.

4. The Trance Theory of Inspiration

This theory is closely related to the Mechanical theory. It proposes that the writers of the Bible were caught up in a vision or trance-like state and wrote word for word or picture for picture what they saw by the Spirit.

There is no doubt that some visions and words were given this way, but this is an incomplete concept in that it also rules out man's conscious involvement.

5. The Partial Theory of Inspiration

The Partial theory purports that only parts of the Bible are inspired. It teaches that the Bible contains the Word of God, that it is not the Word of God in total.

If this theory is so, then who is the final authority to tell us which part is inspired? It leaves this open to all the opinions of men, and undermines the inspiration and authority of God's Word. The Bible not only contains the Word of God, it is the Word of God.

It is to be recognized that the words or utterances of Satan and evil men certainly were not inspired of God, nor are they God's words, but God did inspire men to record them. (Genesis 3:4-5; Matthew 16:22; Acts 5:38-39)

6. The Thought Theory of Inspiration
This theory is also called the Dynamic Theory of Inspiration. The teaching here is that God simply gave the main thoughts or concepts to the writers, but He allowed them to express them in their own words as they wished. The question to ask in regard to this theory is, "If Divine inspiration extended only to the thoughts given to the writers how can we be assured that they chose the right words to accurately communicate those thoughts? "To be reliable the inspiration of thoughts must extend to the inspiration of the words that convey them."

C. Plenary-Verbal Inspiration
The word "plenary" means "full, complete in every part" and the word "verbal" means "by means of words". Plenary-Verbal inspiration states that the Bible writers were fully inspired even as to their choice of words; that the Bible is completely the Word of God including each and every word.

L. Gausen defines inspiration as "that inexplicable power which the Divine Spirit put forth of old on the authors of the Holy Scriptures in order to guide them even in the employment of the words they used, and to preserve them alike from all error and from all omission". II Peter 1:20,21 "Knowing this first, that no prophecy of the scripture is of any private interpretation. For the prophecy came not in old time by the will of man: but holy men of God spoke as they were moved by the Holy Ghost."

There are two key elements that must be kept in balance to arrive at a Biblical view of inspiration, God's involvement through the Holy Spirit and man's involvement. The Bible has a Divine touch making it infallible and a human touch making it understandable. It is God's Word written by man.

God could have written the Bible Himself as He did the ten commandments (Exodus 32-34) and the words on Belshazzar's wall (Daniel 5), or He could have caused angels to write it as they were somehow involved in the giving of the Mosaic Law. (Exodus 20:19; Psalm 68:17; Acts 7:53; Galatians 3:19) But, He chose to include the goal of the book in its production, that is the uniting of God and man. The reason God is revealing Himself to mankind is to bring them into union with Himself. Thus, He produced this written revelation by uniting Divine and human faculties in a unique way. It is God's Word clothed with humanity.

God wrote the Bible.
For forty different men to write sixty-six books in three languages over a period of sixteen hundred years and have them become one harmonious book is humanly impossible. The unity and progression of thought together with the absence of contradiction indicate the Bible had ultimately one author, God. That the Bible is the Word of God is supported by the fact that phrases such as "God said" are found over three thousand eight hundred times in its pages. And the human writers of Scripture claimed to be channels of God's Word. (Exodus 32:16; Deuteronomy 10:2,4; 9:10; Exodus 24:12; Jeremiah 36:1-4; Exodus 4:10,15; 34:27; Jeremiah 7:27; I Corinthians 2:13; II Peter 1:20-21; Daniel 10:9; Hosea 1:1; Joel 1:1; Haggai 1:1; Zechariah 1:1; Malachi 1:1) God is the author of Scripture. The Bible is His Word.

Men of God wrote the Bible.
Though God is the author of Scripture, He chose to use men to write it. Since the Word was going to man He decided to channel it through man also. It is evident throughout Scripture that God used the writer's frame of reference, cultural background, historical perspective, personality, emotions and experiences. God clothed His revelation with their humanity. Men like Moses, Isaiah, Paul and John have clearly left their mark on Scripture. They, with others, were the writers of the Bible.

Thus, the Bible is a product of both God and man. The miracle of inspiration is that God could channel His revelation through man without detracting from its perfectness; that men using their consciousness could write Divine truth; and that the Holy Spirit could cause men to write the infallible Word of God without violating their personalities. God was able to fully utilize the faculties of fallible men and yet somehow overrule their limitations so as to bring forth an infallible revelation of Himself.

The inspiration of Scripture was :

supernatural, not merely natural
divine, not merely human,
living, not mechanical,
conscious, not trance-like,
plenary not partial,
and verbal, not merely conceptual.

V. The Proofs of Inspiration

A. The Miracles of the Bible
The word "miracle" means "an act of power; a supernatural deed wrought by the power of God". The Bible is not only the product of the miracle of inspiration, it contains accounts of many miracles. Most of the sixty-six books either record or refer to some miracle. The majority of these miracles were confirmed by eyewitnesses.

1. Miracles under Moses
The Books of Exodus and Numbers record mighty miracles under the ministry of Moses, the 10 plagues in Egypt (Exodus 4-12), the opening of the Red Sea (Exodus 14-15), the Manna from heaven for 40 years, the waters out of the rock (Exodus 16-17), and the healing of the people by faith in the lifted serpent of brass (Numbers 21).

2. Miracles under Joshua
Under the ministry of Joshua the Jordan was opened in a similar miracle to the Red Sea (Joshua 3-5), the walls of Jericho collapsed (Joshua 6), and the sun stood still for Israel's victory over their enemies (Joshua 10).

3. Miracles under Samson
The slaying of the lion (Judges 14:6), the water from the jawbone of the ass (Judges 15:15) and the collapse of the Temple in Samson's death were miracles of strength (Judges 16:30).

4. Miracles under Elijah & Elisha
The Books of Kings record miracles under the ministries of these two prophets; the opening of the Jordan (II Kings 2), the healing of the waters (II Kings 2:21-22), the multiplying of the oil (II Kings 4:1-7), the resurrection of the child (II Kings 4:8-37), and many others.

5. Miracles under Christ
Numerous miracles are recorded in the Gospels; in the physical realm, healing of the sick and diseased; in the spiritual realm, exorcism and raising of the dead; in the cosmic realm, walking on the water and stilling the storms. (Matthew 8-9) The greatest of all miracles is that of the resurrection of Jesus Christ.

6. Miracles under the Apostles
The apostles carried on the ministry of Christ performing various miracles of healing and exorcism. (Acts 4:16-22; 6:8; 15:12; 19:11) Just as miracles were a witness to the genuineness of ministry and validity of message in Bible days so miracles today that come by faith based on the Bible are a testimony to its genuineness and validity.

B. Prophecy and Fulfillment
While miracles are an evidence of Divine power, prophecy is an evidence of Divine knowledge. The study of Bible prophecies and their fulfillments provides some of the greatest proofs of the inspiration

of Scripture. That God could cause men to accurately predict events generations before they occurred proves He was involved in their writings.

Predictive prophecy must measure up to four tests to be approved of as valid.

1. The prophecy must be uttered before the events come to pass.

2. The prophecy must be explicit and specific in its predictions, so that there could be no possibility of accidental or coincidental fulfillment.

3. Those who utter the prophecies should have no part in their fulfillment.

4. The events of fulfillment should correspond exactly or accurately with the details of the prophecy in all points.

Bible prophecy meets these qualifications and has been proven to be entirely genuine. It is a miracle of knowledge that has always been correct and impossible to refute. The following are some examples of fulfilled prophecies:

1. The prophecy of judgement on Egypt and its fulfillment. (Genesis 15 with Exodus 4-12; Ezekiel 29-30)

2. Israel's history and dispersion is a remarkable fulfillment of the prophecy of Deuteronomy 28.

3. The prophecy and fulfillment concerning the rise and fall of Assyria also illustrates Divine inspiration. (Isaiah 10 with Ezekiel 31-32)

4. The fall of Babylon under the Medes and Persians was clearly foretold over 100 years before it took place. (Isaiah 44:28-45:1; Isaiah 47-48 with Jeremiah 50-51 and Daniel 1-5)

5. Daniel's prophecies of the rise and fall of Gentile Kingdoms were fulfilled in detail. (Daniel 2, Daniel 7, Daniel 8, Daniel 11) These chapters deal with the rise of Babylon, Medo-Persia, Greece and Rome and ultimately with the Kingdom of Antichrist.

The greatest possible example of prophecy and fulfilment is that which pertains to Messianic prophecy. The only man ever to have explicit details given beforehand of His birth, life, ministry, death, burial and resurrection was the Lord Jesus Christ. This was foretold by thirty different persons, over a period of 4,000 years before Jesus was even born. There were approximately 330 Old Testament prophecies that were fulfilled in the first coming of Christ. Some of these are listed below:

THE PROPHECY / **THE FULFILMENT**

1. Seed of the Woman: Genesis 3:15 — Galatians 4:4
2. Of the line of Shem. Genesis 9:26 — Luke 3:36
3. Seed of Abraham. Genesis 22:18 — Matthew 1:1
4. Seed of Isaac. Genesis 26:2-4 — Luke 3:34
5. Seed of Jacob. Genesis 28:13-14, Number 24:17-19 — Luke 3:34
6. Of the Nation of Israel Deuteronomy 18:18 — Romans 9:4-5
7. Of the Tribe of Judah Genesis 49:10-12 — Hebrews 7:14, Revelation 5:5
8. Of the Family of Jesse. Isaiah 11:1-2 — Matthew 1:6
9. Of the House of David II Samuel 7:12-14 — Matthew 1:1, Romans 1:2-3, Matthew 9:27

10. David's Lord, David's Son
    Psalm 110:1

Revelation 22:16,
Matthew 22:41-46

11. Born of a Virgin, Isaiah 7:14
    Jeremiah 31:22

Matthew 1:18-23

12. Created a New Thing.
    Jeremiah 31:22
13. The Mighty God. Isaiah 9:6-7

Luke 1:34-35
John 1:1-3,14,
I Timothy 3:16
John 3:16, Matthew 3:17
Matthew 1:21

14. The Son Begotten. Psalm 2:7,12
15. The Son's Name. Proverbs 30:4
16. To inherit Throne of David
    Isaiah 9:6-7
17. To be born at Bethlehem. Micah 5:2

Luke 1:31-33
Matthew 2:1-8

18. Slaughter of innocents.
    Jeremiah 31:15
19. The Star of Messiah. Numbers 24:17
20. Out of Egypt. Hosea 11:1

Matthew 2:16-18
Matthew 2:1-2,9-10
Matthew 2:12-15

21. Messiah's Forerunner. Isaiah 40:3
    Malachi 3:1

Matthew 3:1,2-3

22. To be manifested after 483 years.
    Daniel 9:25
23. Messiah's Anointing. Isaiah 61:1-4,
    Psalm 45:7
24. The Fullness of the Spirit.
    Isaiah 11:1-4

Mark 1:15
Luke 4:16-22
Acts 10:38
John 3:34,
Revelation 5:6

25. Ministry for 3 1/2 years.
    Daniel 9:24-27
26. To be 30 years of age.Numbers 4:3
27. Ministry in Galilee.
    Isaiah 9:1-2,8
28. The Prophet like unto Moses.
    Deuteronomy 18:18
29. To be a King and Law-Giver.
    Genesis 49:10
30. The Shepherd-Stone. Genesis 49:24

The 4 Gospels
Luke 3:23
Matthew 4:12-16,
Luke 4:14
Acts 3:19-26
John 6:14
Matthew 5,6,7
(Laws of Kingdom)
John 10:11,
Matthew 21:42-44

31. His zeal for God. Psalm 69:9
32. Must come to the Temple
    Malachi 3:1
33. Ministry of miracles,healings
    Isaiah 35
34. To come in the Name of the Lord.
    Psalm 118:26
35. Gracious in word. Psalm 45:2
36. Speak God's Word by commandment
    Deuteronomy 18:18

John 2:13-17
Matthew 21:12-15,
Luke 2:25-32
Matthew 8,
Matthew 11:4-5

Matthew 21:9-11
John 1:17, Luke 4:22
John 8:28,38
John 12:47-50

37. To speak in Name of God
    Deuteronomy 18:19
38. To speak in parables.
    Psalm 78:1-4

John 5:43

Matthew 13:3-35

39. Half-brothers reject Him.
    Psalm 69:8
40. Rejected by leaders. Psalm 118:22

John 1:11,
John 7:1-5
Acts 4:1-12,
Matthew 21:42-45

41. Not many believe. Isaiah 53:1
42. Spiritual blindness. Isaiah 6:9,
    29:13

John 12:37-38
John 12:39-41
Matthew 13:14

43. Messiah to be 'cut off' after
3 1/2 years. Daniel 9:26
44. To be cut off for our sins
Isaiah 53:8
45. Make reconciliation. Daniel 9:24
46. Sold for 30 pieces of silver
Zechariah 11:13
47. Silver cast down in Lord's House
48. To the Potter. Zechariah 11:13
49. Ride on ass into city.
Zechariah 9:9, Genesis 49:11
50. Betrayed by a friend. Psalm 41:9
51. False witnesses accuse.
Psalm 35:11
52. Dumb as a Lamb before accusers
Isaiah 53:7
53. Smitten and spat upon. Isaiah 50:6

54. Cheek smitten, hair plucked.
Isaiah 50:6, Micah 5:1
55. Stripes of Law.
Deuteronomy 25:1-3, Isaiah 53:5
56. Cursed to hang on a tree.
Deuteronomy 21:23
57. Back as a plowed field.
Psalm 129:3
58. Despised, rejected of men.
Isaiah 53:3
59. Man of Sorrows. Isaiah 53:3
Lamentations 1:12
60. Visage marred, and form.
Isaiah 52:14, Isaiah 53:2

61. Forsaken by disciples.
Zechariah 13:7
62. In prison and judgement.
Isaiah 53:8
63. Hated without a cause. Psalm 69:4
Psalm 109:2-5
64. Forsaken of God. Psalm 22:1
65. A reproach of men. Psalm 22:6, 69:9

66. A broken heart. Psalm 69:20, 22:14
67. Given gall and vinegar in thirst
Psalm 69:21
68. Shake their heads at Him.
Psalm 22:7-8, 109:25
69. Bones out of joint. Psalm 22:14, 17
70. To be stared at. Psalm 22:17

71. Hands and feet pierced
Psalm 22:16, Zechariah 13:6

72. Side to be pierced.
Zechariah 12:10
73. Blood and water cleansings.
Leviticus 14:4-6
74. Parted His garments. Psalm 22:18

Mark 15:25
II Corinthians 5:21

II Corinthians 5:18-21
Matthew 27:3-4
Matthew 26:14-16
Matthew 27:5
Matthew 27:6-10
John 12:12-16,
Matthew 21:1-11
John 13:18-21
Matthew 26:60-61,
Mark 14:55-65
Matthew 26:63,
27:12-14, Acts 8:35
Matthew 26:67-68.
John 18:22

Luke 22:63-64
John 19:1,
I Peter 2:24
Galatians 3:10,13,
I Peter 2:24

Mark 15:15-17
I Peter 2:3-8

Luke 23:27-31
Luke 19:41

John 19:1-5

Matthew 26:30-31

John 18:28

John 15:23-25
Matthew 27:46
Romans 15:1-3,
Hebrews 13:13
John 19:34-37
John 19:29,
Matthew 27:34-48

Matthew 27:39
Crucifixion on the Cross
Matthew 27:36,
Luke 23:35

John 20:27, 19:18,37,
Luke 23:33
John 19:34,
Revelation 1:7

John 19:34-36
John 19:23,
Mark 15:24

75. Cast lots for His vesture Psalm 22:18	John 19:23-24, Matthew 27:35
76. Not a bone to be broken. Exodus 12:46, Psalm 34:20	John 19:33-36
77. Prays for enemies. Psalm 109:4, Isaiah 53:12	Luke 23:34
78. Numbered with transgressors.. Isaiah 53:12	Mark 15:27-28
79. Sun to go down at noon. Amos 8:9-10	Matthew 27:45
80. At even, going down of Sun Deuteronomy 16:6	Mark 15:33-34,42
81. Carried own wood. Genesis 22:9	John 19:17-18, Matthew 27:31-32
82. Commits spirit to God. Psalm 31:5	Luke 23:46
83. Sins of world laid on Him. Isaiah 53:4-12	II Corinthians 5:18-21, I Peter 2:24
84. Burial with the rich. Isaiah 53:9	Matthew 27:57-60
85. Bruised the serpent's head. Genesis 3:15	Hebrews 2:11,14-15, Romans 16:20
86. Bruised by the serpent. Genesis 3:15	Matthew 16:21-24
87. Bruised by the Lord. Isaiah 53:10	Acts 2:23, 3:18
88. Buried for 3 days and nights. Jonah 1:17	Matthew 12:39-40 I Corinthians 15:1-3
89. Body not see corruption Psalm 16:10	Acts 13:33, Acts 2:24-32
90. Ascends on high, gives gifts. Psalm 68:18	Ephesians 4:8-16
91. Sits on right hand of God. Psalm 110:1	Hebrews 1:3,
92. Exalted King-Priest. Isaiah 52:13, Psalm 110:1-4	Mark 16:19 Zechariah 6:12-13

Such an array of prophecies given by so many prophets over such a long time being fulfilled in one person within a few years, and most of them in one day, is an impressive proof that the prophets were inspired when they wrote. The Book of Acts reveals how much the apostles based their preaching of Christ on prophecy and fulfilment concerning Him. They referred back to the writings of the Old Testament prophets and then to their historical fulfilment, Jesus Christ, to prove that He was indeed their promised Messiah.

Acts 3:18 "But those things which God before had showed by the mouth of His prophets, that Christ should suffer, He hath so fulfilled."

Acts 10:43 "To Him give all the prophets witness...."

Acts 13:29 "And when they had fulfilled all that was written of Him..."

Acts 17:2,3 "And Paul, as his manner was, went in unto them, and three sabbath days reasoned with them out of the scriptures, opening and alleging that Christ must needs have suffered, and risen again from the dead; and that this Jesus, whom I preach unto you, is Christ."

Only God can declare the end from the beginning. (Isaiah 40:28; 42:8-9; 43:9-10) Fulfilled prophecy is solid evidence that the Bible was not written by man only. The prophecies written concerning future events could never have been predicted by any man apart from the Spirit of God inspiring him.

C. The Numerical Structure of the Bible
It is impossible to read the Bible without noticing the continuous use of numbers. Practically every

page of the Book has some use of numbers. God Himself is the Divine Numberer, and He has stamped His numerical seal upon the whole of creation. This same seal is also upon the Bible. (Job 14:16; Psalm 90:12; Psalm 147:4; Daniel 5:26; Matthew 10:30)

Numbers are found in Scripture in three ways:

1. Numbers that are specifically mentioned. (Genesis 15:9,13,16; Matthew 19:28; Revelation 12:1 etc.)

2. Numbers that are implied. (Genesis 15:9,10,19-21) The 5 sacrifices, the 8 pieces of the sacrifices and the 10 nations mentioned are here by implication.

3. Numbers that are hidden. There is an ingenious numerical structure hidden in Scripture that is not to be found in any other piece of literature, whether sacred or secular. It is woven into the very fabric of Scripture and was drawn out best by Ivan Panin, a Harvard scholar who put fifty years of research into this subject. He uncovered amazingly complex yet harmonious numerical phenomena throughout much of Scripture. This he found to be true whether he used the place value of words and letters or their numerical value. He also discovered general numerical patterns. For example, the following is only a portion of the numerical phenomena to be found in the genealogy of Christ, in Matthew 1:1-7.

"The number of words in the vocabulary will divide by the number seven.
The number of words beginning with a vowel is divisible by seven.
The number of words beginning with a consonant is divisible by seven.
The number of letters in the vocabulary is divisible by seven.
Of these letters, those which are vowels and those which are consonants will both divide by seven.
The number of words in the vocabulary is divisible by seven.
Of these letters, those which are vowels and those which are consonants will both divide by seven.
The number of words in the vocabulary occurring more than once is divisible by seven. Those occurring only once likewise divide by seven.
The number of words occurring in more than one form is divisible by seven. The number occurring in only one form likewise divides by seven.
The number of nouns is divisible by seven. The number that are not nouns likewise divides by seven.
The number of proper names divides by seven. The male names divide by seven. The female names divide by seven.
The number of words beginning with each of the letters of the alphabet is divisible by seven."

D. The Unity of the Bible

Along with a great diversity the Bible also possesses a marvelous unity. Its diversity is plainly evident in that it is composed of sixty-six different books written over a period of 1600 years. These books were written by approximately 40 different authors living in different cultures and countries, from Egypt to Rome to Babylon. There were kings, statesmen, prophets, peasants, fishermen, herdsmen, priests, tradesmen and prisoners who wrote the Bible in three languages. Their writings include almost every kind of literature including history, law, poetry, prophecy, biography, songs, letters, parables and proverbs. The miracle of this is that they produced an amazingly unified book, each writer contributing certain needed portions that harmonize with but never contradict the whole.

There are three major ways this unity can be illustrated.

1. The Harmony of the Division of the Books

   a. The Old Testament

SEE OPPOSITE PAGE:

THE BOOKS OF THE OLD TESTAMENT

THE LAW	HISTORY 17	PENTATEUCH 5	HISTORICAL PENTATEUCH 5	GENESIS EXODUS LEVITICUS NUMBERS DEUTERONOMY
		HISTORICAL BOOKS 12	PRE-EXILE HISTORY 9	JOSHUA JUDGES RUTH I SAMUEL II SAMUEL I KINGS II KINGS I CHRONICLES II CHRONICLES
			POST-EXILE HISTORY 3	EZRA NEHEMIAH ESTHER
THE PSALMS	POETRY 5	POETICAL BOOKS 5	POETRY (THE HEART) 5	JOB PSALMS PROVERBS ECCLESIASTES SONG OF SOLOMON
THE PROPHETS	PROPHECY 17	MAJOR PROPHETS 5	PROPHETICAL PENTATEUCH 5	ISAIAH JEREMIAH LAMENTATIONS EZEKIEL DANIEL
		MINOR PROPHETS 12	PRE-EXILE PROPHECY 9	HOSEA JOEL AMOS OBADIAH JONAH MICAH NAHUM HABAKKUK ZEPHANIAH
			POST-EXILE PROPHECY 3	HAGGAI ZECHARIAH MALACHI

THE BOOKS OF THE NEW TESTAMENT

NEW TESTAMENT HISTORY 5	HISTORIC FOUNDATIONS 5	MATTHEW MARK LUKE JOHN ACTS
DOCTRINAL EPISTLES 22	CHRISTIAN CHURCH EPISTLES 9	ROMANS I CORINTHIANS II CORINTHIANS GALATIANS EPHESIANS PHILIPPIANS COLOSSIANS I THESSALONIANS II THESSALONIANS
	PASTORAL & PERSONAL EPISTLES 4	I TIMOTHY II TIMOTHY TITUS PHILEMON
	HEBREW CHRISTIAN EPISTLES 9	HEBREWS JAMES I PETER II PETER I JOHN II JOHN III JOHN JUDE REVELATION

This chart, and the one on the preceding page are taken from the books "Old Testament Survey" and "New Testament Survey" Copyright 1976 by Kevin J. Conner and Kenneth P. Malmin.

b. The New Testament

SEE OPPOSITE PAGE:

2. The Harmony of Themes through the Bible

Though the Bible has one primary message it intends to communicate there are scores of themes that are developed consistently through its books. These are like streams of truth that begin in Genesis, flow progressively through the books of the Bible and then empty into Revelation, the sea of fulfilment. The following is a listing of only a few topics that begin in Genesis and end in Revelation.

The Creator	Colossians 1:16
The Beginning	Revelation 1:8
The Seed of the Woman	Matthew 1:23
The Ark of Salvation	Luke 2:30
Isaac, Only Begotten Son	John 3:16
Joseph, Beloved Son	Matthew 3:17

The greatest theme in the Bible centers on the person and work of Christ. The Bible as the written Word of God was meant to reveal He who is the living Word.

3. The Harmony between the Old and New Testaments

The Bible consists of the two major divisions, the Old and New Testaments, both of which have their own unique emphasis. However, each is incomplete without the other and each perfectly compliments the other. There are approximately 6,600 cross references between them which support their interrelatedness. It has been said that:

> The New is in the Old contained
> The Old is in the New explained;
> The New is in the Old enfolded,
> The Old is in the New unfolded;
> The New is in the Old concealed
> The Old is in the New revealed.

E. The Miraculous Preservation of the Bible

The Bible has had a truly remarkable history. Over the last 3,500 years it has not only been the most loved but also the most hated book in existence. No book has ever suffered the persistent opposition that the Bible has, Roman emperors issued edicts ordering its annihilation. Untold thousands of Bibles have been burned and countless Christians have been executed for possessing a copy of it. It has been rejected, corrupted and challenged. Its infallibility and authority have been attacked from every angle. However, through the centuries the Bible has survived all these storms and triumphed over them to remain the most significant book in human history. God's miraculous preservation of His Word is another proof of its inspiration.

F. The Influence of the Bible

The worldwide influence of the Bible is unmatched by any other book. It has touched every nation on the earth and influenced countless cultures. It has been translated into more languages and reproduced in larger quantities than any other book. The Bible has produced the highest results in all walks of life including music, art, law and science. Millions of lives have been changed by its truth and only eternity will reveal its full impact on mankind.

G. The Bible itself claims Inspiration
The Scriptures themselves claim inspiration in three areas.

1. For the Writers
Both Old and New Testament writers state that the words they spoke or wrote were not of themselves, but came from God. (II Peter 1:20-21; I Peter 1:10-12; II Peter 3:2; I Chronicles 28:11,19; II Samuel 23:2; Acts 1:16; Luke 1:70; Deuteronomy 4:2)

2. For the Writings
The writers often claimed that God had spoken to them and told them to write it in a book. (Exodus 17:14; 34:27; 24:4; Deuteronomy 31:22, 26; I Corinthians 2:13; Galatians 1:11-12; Revelation 1:18-20) The writings as a whole also claim inspiration. (II Timothy 3:16; Jeremiah 30:2; Hebrews 2:1-4; Acts 28:25; I Thessalonians 2:13.

3. For the Contents
Scripture claims that its contents are inspired. (II Peter 3:1; Jude 17; I Thessalonians 2:13; Psalm 139:17; Isaiah 55:8-11) "The Word of the Lord" came to the prophets and they spoke or wrote accordingly. The thoughts and the words originated with God in their prophetic utterances. (Isaiah 1:2; 7:3; 43:1; Jeremiah 11:1; Ezekiel 1:3; Hosea 1:1; I Corinthians 14:37; Leviticus 1:1; Deuteronomy 32:48; John 10:35; Matthew 25:42-45; Galatians 3:16; Hebrews 12:26-27)

In summary, these seven proofs together build an irrefutable case that the Bible is above and beyond all other books as the inspired Word of God.

VI. THE RESULTS OF INSPIRATION
The results of inspiration are the genuineness, credibility, canonicity, infallibility and authority of the Scriptures.

A. Genuineness
Genuineness means that something is really what it claims to be, something that is really true. A book is genuine if it is written by the person whose name it bears at the time it claims to have been written.

The Bible is genuine; that is the books were really written by who they say they were. Both Jews and Christians, whose theological views are at variance, agree on the genuineness of the Bible books.

B. Credibility
A book is considered credible if it is entirely truthful on the matter it treats.

1. The Old Testament Books

a. The Lord Jesus Himself confirmed the writings of the Old Testament. He spoke of them as the Law, the Psalms, and the Prophets. (Luke 24:44-45, 25-27) We see His attitude to the Law and the Prophets in Matthew 5:17,18; 11:13; John 10:34-37; Luke 18:31-33; Matthew 23:1-2; 26:54.

Christ endorsed many Old Testament books specifically during His ministry.

Genesis	Mark 13:19; Matthew 19:4-5; Genesis 2:24; John 8:44; Luke 17:26-28; Luke 17:28-30
Exodus	Mark 12:26; Matthew 22:31-32, Matthew 5:21,27; 15:4; 22:32; Luke 24:27; John 6:32; Luke 6:3-4.
Leviticus	Matthew 5:33,43; 19:19; 22:39; Mark 12:31; Luke 10:27.
Deuteronomy	Matthew 22:37; Mark 12:29; Luke 10:27; Matthew 4:1-11

Numbers	Matthew 5:33,43; 19:19; 22:39; Mark 12:31; Luke 10:27; John 3:14.
Psalms	Matthew 22:42-44; 21:16; 27:46; Luke 24:44-45; John 13:18; 10:34; Mark 15:34; Luke 23:46.
Isaiah	Mark 4:12; Luke 4:17-18; Matthew 8:17; Luke 8:10, 22:37
Jeremiah	Mark 11:17; Matthew 21:13; Luke 19:46
Hosea	Matthew 9:13; 12:7
Zechariah	Mark 14:27
Malachi	Luke 7:27; Matthew 11:10
Jonah	Matthew 12:39-40

b. The Apostles also endorsed the Old Testament. (Romans 3:2; II Timothy 3:16; Hebrews 1:1; II Peter 1:21; 3:2; Acts 1:16; 3:18; I Corinthians 2:9-16) As the infallible interpreters of the Old Testament the apostles continually referred to it in their teaching.

c. Historical records provide much proof of the credibility of the Scriptures. Many names mentioned in Scripture are also mentioned in the ancient historical records of other nations.

d. Archeology has confirmed in numerous cases the records of the Scripture.

2. The New Testament
The New Testament writers were absolutely qualified as witnesses to write and bear testimony of the Christ. Samuel Oliver in "Synopsis of Christian Theology" (p.16) says that the facts narrated in the sacred pages contain the truth, the whole truth and nothing but the truth. He further states:

a. The witnesses were in a position to judge accurately concerning the facts which they relate.
b. Their character was such as to preclude the possibility of fraud.
c. They had no interest in making their story good, and, according to the truths they proclaimed, if they were imposters or liars, they state their own doom, "everlasting punishment".
d. Their narratives present every appearance of the most perfect simplicity and candour.
e. Their writings contain several undesigned coincidences, which are a decisive mark of truth.
f. Their testimony is in harmony with contemporary history.

Matthew, Mark, Luke and John were true witnesses of the life of Christ and His miracles. James and Jude and the great apostle Paul were each qualified to write. Each wrote by revelation and inspiration, as well as being eyewitnesses.

Historical records confirm much of the historical data of the New Testament writings. The Scriptures are indeed credible. II Peter 3:15-16; I Corinthians 2:13; 14:31; I Thessalonians 2:13; 4:2; II Peter 3:2; I John 1:1-5; Revelation 1:1)

C. Canonicity
The word "canon" means "measuring rod", and refers to a standard or rule. Canonicity means that the Biblical books have been measured by a standard, have stood the test and have been recognized as being inspired of God.

It has been suggested that it was Ezra the scribe who, after the close of the Babylonian Captivity, gathered the Old Testament books which had been written to that time into the accepted canon. As to the New Testament canon, it was generally accepted with its 27 books by the close of the 4th century.

Henry C. Thiesson in "Lectures in Systematic Theology" (pp. 103-104) states four broad principles by which the New Testament books were tested.

1. As to Apostolicity

Was the book written by an apostle, and if not, was it written by someone in close relation to an apostle to raise it up to apostolic level?

2. As to Contents
Were the contents of such spiritual character to warrant a place in Scripture? This eliminated other spurious writings.

3. As to Universality
Was the book universally accepted by the church in that time? This also helped in eliminating questionable gospels and other writings.

4. As to Inspiration
Was the book inspired? Did it have internal evidence? This became the final test for all New Testament books.

D. Infallibility
By "infallibility" is meant "incapable of error, exemption from any liability to make mistakes". It is the setting forth of divine truth without any mixture or error. H. C. Thiesson in "Lectures in Systematic Theology" (p.78) mentions four possible sources of theology and infallible revelation, that mankind will look to; reason, mystical insight, the church or the Scriptures.

1. Reason
Human reason is inadequate to become the infallible standard for man in matters of faith and morals. Man's reason is limited, fallible and depraved by the fall. To exalt human reason is to dethrone God.

2. Intuition
Intuition, or mystical insight is limited and fallible also. The very nature of fallen man, corrupted by sin, makes all subjective insight potentially corrupted and therefore unreliable as an ultimate.

3. The Church
The Roman Catholic Church claims infallibility which can be viewed in three areas.

a. The Church Infallibility Theory
The Roman Catholic Church asserts that the church is the authoritative and infallible teacher. It claims that God has committed His revelations to it whether written or not. It holds that the church has the constant guidance of the Holy Spirit preserving it from error, which makes it infallible and therefore the supreme authority on all matters of faith and morals. This is based on the belief that since the Bible is an infallible revelation it needs an infallible interpreter, lest its infallibility be rendered useless by the possible error of fallible interpreters.

b. The Papal Infallibility Theory
This is the claim that the Pope, as Supreme Head of the Church of Jesus Christ on earth, is the infallible oracle of the Holy Spirit. Whenever he speaks "ex cathedra" his judgements and words are claimed to be infallible.

c. The Episcopal Infallibility Theory
The claim here is that when the bishops of the church collectively make decisions, that these are infallible and become the final authority for the church.

A brief glance at church history reveals the fallacy of these theories. No church, Pope nor group of Bishops can scripturally claim infallibility. The Scriptures themselves are the only infallible Word of God. The Church did not produce the Word. The Word produced the Church. The Word is not subject to the authority of the fallible church, but the church is subject to the infallible authority of the Word.

E. Authority
Authority arises out of infallibility. If the Scriptures are inspired and infallible, then they must also

become the supreme authority for all Christians concerning their faith and morals. They are the final court of appeals for the life and conscience of all true believers. Reason, conscience and the church must be subjected to the authority of the Word. (Hebrews 1:1; I Corinthians 14:37; I Timothy 6:3-4; Galatians 1:8-9; Nehemiah 8:1,8; Psalm 19:7-11; 119:1,9; Isaiah 8:19-20; Matthew 4:1-11; II Timothy 3:14-16)

II. THE APOCRYPHA

The word "apocrypha" means that which is veiled, secret or closed.

In theology the term apocrypha refers to the 14 books added to the Old Testament by the Roman Catholic Church in 1546 A.D. These books are; I Esdras, II Esdras, Tobit, Judith, Book of Esther, Wisdom of Solomon, Ecclesiasticus, Baruch, Song of the Three Holy Children, History of Susanna, Bel and the Dragon, The Prayer of Manasses, I Macabees and II Macabees.

Most of the rest of Christendom rejects these books from having a place in the canon of Scripture. The following are some of the reasons for this rejection.

1. It is universally acknowledged that they never had a place in the Hebrew canon.

2. They were written in the 400 years between Malachi and John the Baptist when there was no inspired prophetic utterances. This is why the Jews rejected them.

3. They are never quoted in the New Testament by Jesus or the Apostles.

4. They are not found in any catalogue of Canonical Books during the first four centuries of the church.

5. Divine inspiration and authority is claimed by none of the writers and is disclaimed by some of them.

6. None of their writers speak with a message from Jehovah.

7. The books contain many historical, geographical and chronological errors, at times contradicting themselves, the Bible and history.

8. They teach doctrines and uphold practices which are contrary to the canonical Scriptures. (e.g. lying is sanctioned, suicide and assassination are justified, magical incantations and prayers for the dead are taught and approved.)

9. They do not fit into the numerical structure of the canon.

Chapter 4

THE DOCTRINE OF GOD

The Scriptures give us the revelation of the eternal God-head, who has revealed Himself as one God, existing in three Persons, even the Father, the Son and the Holy Spirit; distinguishable but indivisible in essence; co-eternal, co-existent, co-equal in nature, attributes, power and glory. There is but one eternal Godhead, who is one undivided and indivisible essence; and in this one essence there are three eternal distinctions, the Father, the Son and the Holy Spirit.

CHAPTER OUTLINE

I. THE EXISTENCE OF GOD

    A. The Fact of the Existence of God

    B. The Arguments for the Existence of God

II. NON-CHRISTIAN VIEW OF GOD

    A. Theistic Views

    B. Non-Theistic Views

III. THE NATURE OF GOD

    A. God is a Spirit

    B. God is Light

    C. God is Love

    D. God is a Consuming Fire

IV. THE ATTRIBUTES OF GOD

    A. Essential Attributes

    B. Moral Attributes

V. THE ETERNAL GODHEAD

    A. The Godhead

    B. The Oneness of the Godhead

    C. The Threeness of the Godhead

    D. Relationship and Distinction in the Godhead

    E. Heresies Concerning the Godhead

    F. The Athanasian Creed and Doctrinal Statements

    G. The Eternal Characteristics of the Godhead

    H. Illustrations of the Godhead

    I. The Godhead Bodily

VI. THE NAMES OF GOD

    A. Creatorship or Elohistic Names of God

    B. Redemptive or Jehovahistic Names of God

I. THE EXISTENCE OF GOD

A. The Fact of the Existence of God

The Bible does not attempt to prove the existence of God; it simply declares it. The writers of Scripture accepted His existence as a settled fact. The opening line of the Bible simply reads: "In the beginning GOD..." Genesis 1:1.

Belief in the existence of God is absolutely foundational not only to an understanding of the Bible but also to life itself. Hebrews 11:6 tells us that he that comes to God must believe that He is, that He exists and that He is a rewarder of them that diligently seek Him. In other words, belief in the existence of God is a prerequisite to having faith in Him personally. If a person rejects the fact of the existence of God he has no reference point for correctly understanding himself or the world around him.

Nothing can be received or known of God unless one believes in His existence. Faith is the only connecting link between the Creator and the creature, God and man. "Faith is the substance of things hoped for, the evidence of things not seen." Hebrews 11:1. It is the proof of the reality of things not seen. God as a Spirit being is invisible to the human eye, but it is through faith in Him that His existence is substantiated to us.

In that God has given visible proofs of His existence, there is no excuse for not believing in His existence. Paul wrote, "For the invisible things of Him from the creation of the world are clearly seen, being understood by the things that are made, even His eternal power and Godhead; so that they are without excuse". Romans 1:20. David wrote, "The fool hath said in his heart, There is no God." Psalm 53:1.

B. The Arguments for the Existence of God

1. The Cosmological Argument

The Greek word "cosmos" means "world". The Cosmological Argument looks at the world and then argues from the law of cause and effect. The existence of an effect indicates the existence of its cause. The world is here. This raises the question "how did it come to be?" Something or someone must have caused it to come into existence. Man knows of nothing in his world that had no cause behind its existence, thus he must recognize that there is a cause behind the world itself and the universe around it. All things must be traced to a first cause which is God, the Creator. (Genesis 1:1; Psalm 19:1-6; Romans 1:19-20; Hebrews 11:3; 1:1-2)

2. The Teleological Argument

The Teleological Argument is the argument from design and purpose. Not only does the universe of worlds exist, but it has a perfect design. Its elements indicate a purpose for their role and they exist in harmony with each other.

Each blade of grass, each snow flake is seen to have a different yet perfect design. Design proves the existence of a designer. Purpose in creation reveals and argues purposeful creatorship. Could there be: A building without a builder? A watch without a watchmaker? A universe without a controller? An orderly creation without a Creator? An intelligent order without a mind? Laws without a lawmaker? The argument from design and purpose proves the existence of an infinite intelligent being greater than the universe.

3. The Anthropological Argument

The Greek word for man is "anthropos". Man is the "master-piece" of God's creative acts. He was made in the image of God to be the crowning glory of creation. (Genesis 1:1-28; Psalm 94:9) He is far superior to all the animal creation combined. The finest looking ape cannot compare with man in his total being. Intelligent man is one of the greatest arguments for the existence of an intelligent God. The billions of human beings, each distinct and unique, yet all bearing the mark of creatorship upon them, argue the existence of a creator. Evolutionary theories are simply man's attempt to escape from creatorship accountability and responsibility.

4. The Ontological Argument

The Ontological Argument is related to the Anthropological Argument. Not only is man a created intelligent being, he also has an intuitive belief and knowledge of the existence of God. Intuition speaks of understanding or knowledge that man has without the process of reasoning. Man knows intuitively that there is a God. He is born with this knowledge in him. It is sometimes spoken of as the religious instinct within man, which makes him desire to worship something or someone. Man was created to be a worshipper, to worship God. He would not seek to worship God if God had not placed within man this intuitive knowledge of His own existence. This argument is substantiated by the fact that there is a universal belief in a god or gods in every nation on the face of the earth. If man does not accept or find the true God, he makes a deity of his own to worship, thus satisfying this intuitive knowledge. Belief in God is not just the result of cultural conditioning. It is intuitive. (Acts 17:23-24; Romans 1:18-32; John 1:3-7; Psalms 115:1-8)

5. The Moral Argument

Man is a moral being. He possesses an inner sense of right and wrong as well as a sense of responsibility to adhere to what is right and avoid the wrong. The Bible labels this conscience, and views it as being God-given. When a man violates his conscience he is subject to guilt and a fear of punishment. Though the conscience can be conditioned or trained in different directions, it is something common to man inherently. Being universal, it is a witness to the existence of a supreme law-giver and judge who built into mankind this sense of responsibility for the right. (Romans 2:14-15; I Timothy 4:2; Titus 1:15; Hebrews 9:14; John 8:9)

6. The Biological Argument

The Greek word "bios" means "life". It is a scientific fact that life can only come from pre-existent life, not from matter alone. Therefore to trace all life back to its source, we must eventually come back to God Himself. There must be a being who is the ultimate life-source, the originator of all life and the possessor of underived and eternal life Himself. This life-source is God. (Psalm 36:9; John 11:25; 14:6; 10:28; 1:1-5)

7. The Historical Argument

Human history points to an unseen Hand, guiding, governing and controlling the destinies of the nations. For example, Babylon fell on a night when the soldiers forgot to close the gates in the wall through which the great river Euphrates flowed. God's prophets had foretold this over one hundred years before it took place. (Isaiah 45:1-5; Daniel 5) A thorough study of history will uncover many illustrations of the fact that behind it all is the hand of God moving to accomplish His will. (Revelation 17:17) History argues the existence of a God who controls it.

8. The Christological Argument

One of the greatest arguments is the Christological Argument. The Christ of history is a fact and it is impossible to explain the person of Jesus Christ apart from the existence of God. His virgin birth, sinless life, miracles, teaching, death, burial, resurrection and ascension are all unexplainable apart from God. Jesus Christ is the greatest revelation of God's existence. All He was, all He did, and all He said attests to the existence of God. (John 1:1-3, 14-18; 14:6-9; I Timothy 3:16) Christianity and its redeeming work in mankind and the nations of the earth becomes an enigma apart from the existence of God in Christ.

9. The Bibliological Argument

The Bible is a witness to the existence of God. As noted under the Doctrine of Inspiration, the Scriptures surpass all other writings as being divinely inspired . It is impossible for them to have been the product of mere humanity. They evidence the existence of a higher intelligence who sovereignly guided the writers in their work. As an infallible witness of all that the Bible communicates about God, His nature and His purposes must be accepted as accurate.

10. The Argument from Congruity

The word "congruity" simply means "agreement, correspondence, harmony". The nine previous arguments are all in agreement. There is correspondence and harmony between them all. There is not one argument presented which brings a discordant note but all together they form a harmonious whole. This is the argument from Congruity. The fact that the Cosmological, Teleological, Anthropological, Ontological, Moral, Biological, Historical, Christological and Bibliological arguments all blend together in a harmony, constitutes the argument from Congruity. It states concerning the existence of God that if it is not so, then all these related facts are inexplicable. Belief in the existence of a self-existent personal God is in harmony with all the facts of man's mental and moral nature, as well as with the nature of the material universe. Man is left totally without excuse as to the fact of God's existence. It is only wilful ignorance that would reject such conclusive evidence.

II. NON-CHRISTIAN VIEWS OF GOD
A brief consideration of the non-Christian philosophies concerning God show that there are basically two groupings; Theistic and Non-Theistic. The Theistic views hold that there is a god or gods. The Non-Theistic views hold the belief that there is no God at all.

A. Theistic Views

1. The Pantheistic View
Pantheism is made up of two words: "pan" meaning "all" and "theos" meaning "God". It is the belief that God is all and all is God. Pantheism is the theory which regards all finite things as merely aspects or parts of the one eternal self-existent being. It holds that there is no God apart from nature, and that everything in nature is a part or manifestation of God. Trees, birds, flowers, animals, reptiles, etc., are all parts of God. Nature itself is God. Henry Thiesson lists the following types of Pantheism:

a. Materialistic Pantheism
This is the theory of the eternity of matter and the spontaneous generation of life. The universe and nature is the only God that man can worship. Since evolution is the cause for the order of the world, there exists no supreme divine intelligence or being and matter itself is God.

This theory ignores and misreads all the evidence in the material realm that there is a God who exists beyond it. It is easily refuted by the arguments for the existence of God explained earlier in this chapter.

b. Hylozoism or Panpsychism
These are the same theory under different names. It holds that all matter besides having physical properties also has the principle of life in it. To emphasize the physical properties only is a form of materialism. To hold that all physical properties have a principle of life is Hylozoism ("zoe" being a Greek word for "life"). This theory extends beyond materialistic pantheism in a search for a non-material god, but still denies the existence of a supreme personal being and falls short.

c. Neutralism
This theory holds that ultimate reality is neither mind nor matter, but a neutral stuff of which mind and matter are but appearances or aspects. It also is an inadequate extension past mind and matter in a search for God.

d. Idealism
This theory holds that the ultimate reality is of the nature of the mind. It says that the world is the product of the mind, either of the individual mind or of the infinite mind. It is the theory that everything exists only in the mind. It exalts and deifies the person and mind of man, or some universal mind as god.

(1) Impersonalistic Idealism
This says that the ultimate reality is one single mind and/or one unified system. It denies that this mind is personal.

(2) Personal Idealism
Personal Idealism holds that the absolute is a person who includes within himself all finite selves and shares their experiences. It holds that all are part of himself and part of the universal mind, even though this mind thinks his own thoughts besides their thoughts. This theory extends even further, recognizing that nature reveals the existence of a supreme intelligence behind it but falls short by mis-defining that supreme mind.

e. Philosophical Mysticism

Philosophical Mysticism is any philosophy that seeks to discover the nature of reality through the process of thought or spiritual intuition. The idealist distinguishes between himself and the great self. The mystic, however, sees himself as being identified with this great self. In other words, this theory is the deification of self; it is the worship of the latent ego within. It makes man himself God. It claims that the only God to be known is the "God within". This conclusion that man within himself is god, leaves him deceived and far short of an accurate knowledge of God.

These theories do reveal man's intuitive belief in a god but also illustrate man's inability to reject God's revelation of Himself and still come to a true knowledge of Him. In trying to find God in creation they have made creation God and missed the Creator behind it. In attempting to find God in all things they have made all things God.

In Summary:

Pantheism makes nature god and misses the God of nature.

Materialistic Pantheism makes matter eternal and misses the God who made matter.

Hylozoism makes a principle of life god and misses the God who is the source of life.

Neutralism makes some neutral substance god and misses God the creator of all subtance.

Idealism makes the mind god and misses the God who is a real person having a perfect mind.

Philosophical Mysticism makes man himself god and misses the God who made all men.

2. The Polytheistic View

The word "polytheism" is made up of two words; "poly" meaning "many" and "theos" meaning "God". Thus polytheism is the worship of many gods. Most ancient religions were polytheistic, and some still exist today. The Egyptians, Assyrians, Babylonians, Greeks and Romans were polytheistic. They worshipped all sorts of gods. They made gods of all created things, of birds, fish, and beasts. They worshipped the sun, moon and planets. They made gods of virtues and vices. They had semi-gods, demi-gods, and gods who were half-man. The Canaanites and Philistines were polytheistic also. Dagon of the Philistines is supposed to have been a god who was half fish and half man. Thus God continually warned Israel against polytheistic idol worship.

Scripture clearly denounces polytheism, no gods were to take the place of the true God. (Exodus 20:3; Deuteronomy 5:7) No images were to be made of the heathen gods. (Exodus 20:23; 34:17; Leviticus 19:4). No mention was to be made of the other gods. (Exodus 23:13; Joshua 23:7) All idols were to be destroyed, not worshipped or kept as souveniers, lest they become a snare to the Israelites. (Exodus 23:32; Deuteronomy 6:14; 7:4,25) These idols were called "strange gods". (Deuteronomy 10:17) All heathen deities were an abomination. (Deuteronomy 12:31; 20:18; Ezekiel 7:20; Samuel 7:3; Judges 10:16)

To worship other than the one true God is idolatry and such would come under the curse and wrath of God. (Deuteronomy 11:28; 28:14) God alone is the one true God. (Exodus 20:1-3; 18:11; Deuteronomy 10:14-17; I Chronicles 16:25; Psalm 97:9; Jeremiah 2:11; 5:7; 16:20). He is greater than all other gods. (Exodus 15:11; Psalm 95:3)

3. The Dualistic View

Dualism is the theory that there are two distinct principles or gods of eternal and equal power who are at war with each other. In epistemology these two principles are idea and object, or thought and thing. In metaphysics these two things are mind and matter. In ethics they are good and evil, or absolute right and wrong. In religion they are called God and Satan, or good and evil. In nature, they are called light and darkness. The early Gnostics held this view of two Gods in conflict in the universe and that this conflict is generally fought out in and among human beings. This theory is contradictory to God's revelation of Himself in that He is clearly sovereign over all that opposes Him. There is no power equal to His.

4. The Deistic View

Deism is the theory that God is only present in creation by His power, not in His being and nature. It holds that God set the various laws of nature in motion at creation and then left the universe to run itself by these laws. It holds the same concerning man. This view presents an absentee God. A God who wound up the universe like a clock and left it to run on its own, exercising only an indirect oversight over it. Deism teaches that truth about God can be known by reason. It rejects the Bible as a special revelation and says that it is a book on the principles of natural religion. Thus it misses the truths of God's omnipresence and sustaining power as the all-powerful God of creation.

The theistic views are all unsatisfactory. While at their best holding the belief in a God of some sort, they are but man's attempts to discover and define God to human satisfaction.

In Summary:
Pantheism makes all god and misses the God of all.
Polytheism makes many gods and misses the one true God.
Dualism makes good and evil two equal gods in conflict and fails to discover a good God who will judge all evil.
Deism presents an absentee god, a god who has nothing to do with anything he created and misses the omnipresent and omnipotent God.

B. Non-Theistic Views

1. The Atheistic View

a. Practical Atheism
The person who holds to practical atheism is the one who believes there may be a God but lives as if there is none. He has no interest in religion because of hypocrisy among the professors of religion.

b. Dogmatic Atheism
The person holding this view will openly declare his disbelief in the existence of any god.

c. Virtual Atheism
This view generates abstract definitions of God to try and account for the world and life, such as "social consciousness" or "the unknowable" or "the moral order of the universe". In making God so obscure by definition it is virtually atheistic.

d. Critical Atheism
This view denies the existence of God on the grounds that no one can prove or demonstrate the existence of God.

e. Classical Atheism
This view is aimed at denying the god or gods of some particular religion.

f. Rationalistic Atheism
This view enthrones reason and dethrones faith in the existence of God. It claims reason as the only source of knowledge.

Atheism is unreasonable and arrogant in that it ignores all the facts and evidences of the existence of God and then makes a universal conclusion that He does not exist. As David said in Psalm 14:1 "the fool hath said in his heart, there is no God."

2. The Agnostic View
Agnosticism holds that one cannot know whether God exists or not. It neither denies nor affirms the existence of God. A Gnostic is "a knowing one", who says "I know all". An Agnostic is one who says "I cannot know" or "I know nothing". This view holds that we cannot have knowledge as to the existence or nature of God and the universe. It is wilful ignorance. (Acts 17:23)

Three types of Agnosticism are noted here briefly.

a. Positivism

This view holds that there is nothing true beyond observed facts. God cannot be examined as fact, and therefore He does not exist.

b. Pragmatism
This belief holds that there is no special revelation of God, and that human reason is incompetent to discover God if He does exist.

c. Existentialism
This position holds the philosophy that the individual can exercise his free will and do what he likes in a purposeless universe. It is a "no-morality" philosophy because of a "no-God" view.

The atheistic and agnostic views are not tenable. Both are contrary to man's deepest conviction that there is a God to whom man is accountable. They are the attempts of man to escape from a God they know exists.

In Summary
The Atheist says there is no God, and thus sets himself up as God.
The Agnostic says he cannot know whether God exists, and thus makes willful ignorance his God.

III. THE NATURE OF GOD
The Christian believes that unless God takes the initiative and reveals Himself to man, man will stumble on in the darkness of his insufficient reason. (Ephesians 4:17-18; Matthew 11:27) Man's wisdom is foolishness when it comes to knowing God. (I Corinthians 1:19-21) However, the Christian also believes that God has revealed Himself in the Scriptures. Man must accept this self-revelation or else he will not be able to know God. We must rely on the Bible's description of God. The Bible gives us four basic definitions or descriptions of God in His own eternal and essential nature and being.

A. God is Spirit (John 4:24)
God is a Spirit being. He is immaterial and incorporeal. A spirit does not have flesh and bones. (Luke 24:39). This is why God is spoken of as being invisible. (Deuteronomy 4:15-19; Exodus 33:20; John 1:18; Romans 1:20; Colossians 1:15; I Timothy 1:17; I Timothy 6:16) It is also why God forbade Israel to make any visible images or similitudes of Himself. (Deuteronomy 4:14-20; Isaiah 40:25) God is also a personal being. When we speak of God as being a Spirit, this does not mean that He is some impersonal force or entity. He is a person with self-consciousness, selfdetermination, will, intelligence and feeling. (John 4:20-24; Genesis 1:2; II Corinthians 3:17; I Corinthians 2:11). In His personhood He is essentially a spiritual being rather than a physical being.

B. God is Light (I John 1:5)
This refers to the majesty or the glory of God. God is light, and He dwells in unapproachable light whom no man hath seen, nor can see. (I Timothy 6:15-16) God does not just have light; He is light. Light is absolutely pure, impossible to defile. As light, God is eternal, immortal and invisible. (I Timothy 1:17)

C. God is Love (I John 4:17)
Love refers to the very heart of God's nature. God does not just have love, He is love. (John 3:16) Love involves the grace, mercy, kindness, goodness and benevolence of God toward all His creatures.

D. God is a Consuming Fire (Hebrews 12:29)
This refers to the holiness of God's nature. Fire is not God, but God is a consuming fire. This relates to the definition that God is light. The most frequent symbol used of God in the Bible is that of fire. It is always significant of His holiness and absolute righteousness manifested in judgement against sin.

The following are some examples;
The Lamp of Fire. (Genesis 15:17)
The Burning Bush of Fire. (Exodus 3:1-6)
The Altar of Fire. (I Kings 18:24 ,38)
The Coals of Fire. (Isaiah 6:6,7)

The Tongues of Fire. (Acts 2:1-4)
The Lake of Fire. (Revelation 20:15)

IV. THE ATTRIBUTES OF GOD

Attributes are the characteristics or qualities belonging to a person. Thus when we speak of the attributes of God we mean those characteristics or qualities that belong to God as God, that make God who and what He is. The attributes of God fall into two main groupings: essential and moral.

A. Essential Attributes

Essential attributes are those attributes or qualities which essentially belong to God, apart from any relationship to His creatures. They are characteristics of God which make God who He is. These essential attributes can never become attributes of man, because man would then become God. These attributes are also spoken of as being the non-moral or incommunicable attributes of God.

1. God is Eternal

Eternity of being is an attribute of God. Eternal signifies having no beginning or end. God is the Everlasting One. He has always been and will always be. There never was a time when God was not. (Isaiah 43:10) Psalm 90:3 says "From everlasting to everlasting thou art God." God exists from eternity to eternity.

Various Biblical expressions are used of God which declare that He is eternal.

    a. I AM that I AM. (Exodus 3:14; John 8:58)
    b. The Everlasting God. (Genesis 21:33)
    c. In the beginning God. (Genesis 1:1; Hebrews 1:10; John 1:1)
    d. Thy years are throughout all generations. (Psalm 102:24).
    e. The Lord of Hosts, He is the First and the Last. (Isaiah 44:6)
    f. The High and Holy One inhabits eternity. (Isaiah 57:15)
    g. The Eternal God is our refuge. (Deuteronomy 33:27)
    h. God's eternal power and Godhead. (Romans 1:20)
    i. The Alpha and the Omega, the beginning and the ending. (Revelation 1:8)
    j. Him which is (time present), which was (time past), and which is to come (time future)" (Revelation 1:4; 4:8)
    k. The King Eternal. (I Timothy 1:17)

Each of these Scriptures confirm the truth that God is eternal. He is not limited to or by time. He is timeless. Time past, present and future are comprehended in God who is the eternal I AM.

Although the saints receive eternal life and will live forever, as God, such eternal life is given by God. Eternity of being can never be ascribed to man, as it is only an essential attribute of God.

2. God is Self-Existent

God exists in and from Himself. He is the reason for His own existence. As the self-existent one, He does not owe His existence to any other, neither does He depend on any other to sustain it. He is the I AM, the self-sufficient one. God is the source of all life and His life is underived and inexhaustible. Because of this quality of God's being He is absolutely independent of all outside of Himself. This is inapplicable to man, for he is dependent on God for his origin, life and continued existence.

We note several brief statements from Scripture which convey the truth of God's self-existence.
    a. I AM that I AM. (Exodus 3:14; Isaiah 41:4)
    b. I am Jehovah, that is My Name. (Exodus 3:14-15; 6:3)
    c. With Thee is the fountain of life. (Psalm 36:9)
    d. In Him is life. (John 1:4)
    e. The Father God has life in Himself. He has also given the Son to have life in Himself. (John 5:26)
    f. God so loved the world that He gave His only begotten Son that whosoever believes in Him should not perish but have everlasting life. (John 3:16)
    g. God is the King eternal, immortal, invisible. (I Timothy 1:17)

h. The believer who has the Son has life, for God has given eternal life and this life is in the Son. (I John 5:11-13)

i. He is the living God. (Joshua 3:10; Psalm 84:2; I Thessalonians 1:9)

3. God is Immutable

When we speak of God's immutability, we mean that God is unchanged, and unchangeable as to His character and being. The laws of God's being are eternal and unchanging. In His mode of being as Father, Son and Holy Spirit, God is unchanged and unchangeable. In His essential and moral attributes, God is unchangeable. In all of the perfections of His character, God can never change. This is immutability. Several statements based on Scripture attest to the fact that God is immutable.

a. God is the Father of lights and there is no variableness nor shadow of turning with Him. (James 1:17; Psalm 33:11)

b. Jesus Christ is the same yesterday, today and forever. (Hebrews 13:8; 1:12; Psalm 102:27)

c. I am the Lord, I change not. (Malachi 3:6)

d. I AM that I AM. (Exodus 3:14-15)

e. The Strength of Israel will not repent. (I Samuel 15:29; Romans 11:29; Numbers 23:19)

f. Two immutable things are God and His Word. (Hebrews 6:18)

g. God's purposes, plans and power change not. (Romans 4:20-21; Isaiah 46:10; Romans 11:29)

Though God's actions and dealings with man may vary or change, God in His essential and moral attributes never changes. He is eternally the same. Man, however, can and must change to be what God intends him to be.

4. God is Omnipotent

Omnipotence means that God is all-powerful. Nothing is impossible with God. That is, nothing that would be consistent with his Holy nature, character and being. God has the power to do what he wills, yet His power is under the control of his holy and wise will.

Omnipotence also involves the sovereignty of God. God has the absolute right to govern and dispose of His creatures as He pleases. Scriptures which speak of God's omnipotence and sovereignty are noted below:

a. The Lord God omnipotent reigneth. (Revelation 19:6)

b. God is Almighty. (Genesis 17:1; Revelation 15:3)

c. In the beginning God created the heaven and the earth. (Genesis 1:1; John 1:1-3)

d. All things were created by God and for His pleasure. (Revelation 4:11)

e. There is nothing too hard for God. (Jeremiah 32:17,27)

f. God can do all things and no purpose of His can be restrained. (Job 42:2)

g. The universe of worlds are upheld, guided and propelled by God's mighty word of power. (Hebrews 1:1-4, Amplified)

h. With God all things are possible. (Matthew 19:26)

i. No word of God is void of power. (Luke 1:37; Psalm 33:9)

j. Is anything too hard for the Lord? (Genesis 18:14)

k. God does according to His will in the army of heaven and among the inhabitants of the earth. (Daniel 4:35; Matthew 20:15)

l. God can put it in the hearts of men to do His will. (Revelation 17:17)

m. God has mercy on whom He will have mercy and hardens whom He wills. (Romans 9:18)

5. God is Omniscient

Omniscience means that God is all-knowing. He knows all things at all times. He knows all things within Himself, in the universe and in all creatures. Whether things be past, present or future, God knows them all perfectly. There is nothing that He does not know and has not known from eternity. (I Samuel 2:3) God's knowledge is absolute and unacquired. He never has to learn anything. Man can never tell God anything about Himself that God did not already know. This is omniscience.

Omniscience also involves perfect knowledge, perfect understanding and perfect wisdom. Perfect knowledge is the accurate possession of all facts. Perfect understanding is the full perception and interpretation of the facts. Perfect wisdom is the proper application of the facts.

It is because of God's omniscience that He is qualified to be the judge of all men at the Great White Throne of judgement, according to Revelation 20:11-15. Omniscience makes God infallible. He is incapable of error or ommision. It is impossible for God to err in judgement. (I Corinthians 1:24-30; Psalm 104:24; I Timothy 1:17; Ephesians 3:10)

The following are a number of Scriptural statements that attest to God's omniscience.

   a. The eyes of the Lord are in every place, keeping watch upon the evil and the good. (Proverbs 15:3)
   b. No one can hide themselves in secret places from God's eyes. (Jeremiah 23:23-35)
   c. None can hide themselves from the presence of the Lord and God knows our thoughts afar off before they even come into our mind. (Psalm 139:1-10; I Corinthians 3:20)
   d. God's understanding is infinite. (Psalm 147:5; Isaiah 29:15-16)
   e. God knows the hearts of all the sons of men. (Proverbs 15:11; I John 3:20; Genesis 18:18-19)
   f. Known unto God are all His works from the beginning of the world. (Acts 15:18; Romans 11:33)
   g. All things are naked and open to the eyes of the Lord with whom we have to do. (Hebrews 4:12-13; I John 3:20)
   h. God knows Himself in His eternal distinctions as Father, Son and Holy Spirit. (Matthew 11:27; I Corinthians 2:11)
   i. God knows beforehand all that men will do. It was on this basis of foreknowledge that God, by His Spirit, foretold events through the mouth of the prophets concerning the life of the Messiah. (Micah 5:2; Revelation 13:8; Acts 2:23; 3:18; II Timothy 2:19)
   j. God also knows the histories and destinies of all nations and individuals and on the basis of this He foretold the same. (Matthew 10:29; Psalm 33: 13-15; Matthew 6:8,32; 11:21-24; Isaiah 46:9-10; Daniel 2; Daniel 7; Matthew 24; Matthew 25; Acts 15:18; Deuteronomy 31:20-21; Isaiah 44:26 45:7; Proverbs 15:3)

The following words are expressions of God's omniscience also.
Foreknowledge. (Romans 8:29-30; Acts 2:23; I Peter 1:2)
Foreseeing. (Galatians 3:8; Acts 2:31,24)
Foretelling (prophecy). (Acts 3:18-24)
Foreordained. (I Peter 1:19-20; I Corinthians 2:7; I Peter 1:10-12; II Timothy 1:9; Jeremiah 1:4-5)

Only a God who is omniscient could maintain a universe in harmony with itself and meet the needs of all His creatures at one and the same time.

6. God is Omnipresent

Omnipresence means that God is all-present. He is unlimited by space or time. He is everywhere present at all times. He is present universally and simultaneously in all the universe, always. Omnipresence also involves immensity which means that God is present even beyond space. In His omnipresence He fills all things, but in His immensity of being, God is not limited to or by space. God is above and beyond space. Finite space depends upon Him for its existence.
Scriptures which illustrate the fact of God's omnipresence are listed below:

   a. God is not far from everyone of us, for in Him we live and move and have our being. (Acts 17:27-28; Romans 10:6-8; Genesis 28:15-16)
   b. There is nowhere where man can flee from the presence of the Lord. (Psalms 139:7-12; Jeremiah 23:23-24)
   c. Where two or three gather in the name of the Lord, His presence is there. (Matthew 18:20; 28:18-20)
   d. None can hide from God for He fills heaven and earth. (Jeremiah 23:24; Isaiah 66:1)
   e. The whole earth is full of the glory of the Lord. (Isaiah 6:3)
   f. God fills all things. (Ephesians 1:23)
   g. God's presence is with all believers everywhere. (Exodus 3:12; 33:14; Isaiah 43:2)
   h. Heaven and the heaven of heavens cannot contain God. (II Chronicles 6:18; I Kings 8:27; Isaiah 66:1; II Chronicles 2:6)
   i. Wherever man would seek to go from God, be it heaven, earth or Sheol, God's presence will find them. (Psalm 139:7-12; Amos 9:2-4)

B. Moral Attributes

Moral attributes are those characteristics or qualities which belong to God especially in relation to His creatures. These attributes are also those which God intends man to possess and thus they are called communicable attributes.

1. Perfect Holiness

The perfect holiness of God speaks of absolute purity. He cannot sin nor tolerate sin. He is sinless perfection. Holiness is God's inward character and as such it is underived. He is perfectly holy in all He thinks, says, and does. Holiness is the ability to live consistent with the nature of life. Holiness is a major theme in Scripture as the following passages illustrate.

    a. Be ye holy, for I the Lord your God am holy. (Leviticus 19:2 holiness is one of the key words in Leviticus, being used about 45 times)

    b. God commands that Israel be holy as He is holy. (Leviticus 11:44,45; I Peter 1:16)

    c. The Lord is glorious in holiness. (Exodus 15:11)

    d. One who inhabits eternity says His name is holy. (Isaiah 57:15)

    e. God is of purer eyes than to behold evil or iniquity. (Habakkuk 1:13)

    f. The Lord is the thrice holy God. (Isaiah 6:3; Revelation 4:8; Job 6:10 Father, Son and Holy Spirit are holy).

    g. The Lord God Almighty alone is holy. (Revelation 15:3-4)

    h. The redeemed are to worship the Lord in the beauty of holiness. (Psalms 29:2; Exodus 39:30)

    i. Holiness was God's first revelation to Moses, then came deliverance from Egypt's bondage. (Exodus 3:1-15)

    j. Holiness was also the first thing mentioned to Joshua, then came victory over Jericho's walls. (Joshua 5:13-15)

    k. Holiness was the major vision given to the prophet Isaiah, then came his commission to prophesy. (Isaiah 6:1-6)

    l. Holiness was the revelation of God at Mt. Sinai, then came the tabernacle administrations. (Exodus 19:12-25)

    m. Holiness was the emphatic truth in the Tabernacle of Moses in its various places, the Holy Place and the Most Holy (Exodus 26:33; I Kings 6:16)

    n. Offerings must be holy to be presented to the Lord. (Leviticus 1-7; Leviticus 23)

    o. The priesthood must be holy to minister in the sanctuary of the Lord. (Leviticus 8-10)

    p. God's throne is established upon the attribute of holiness. It is the fundamental characteristic of God, even before the revelation of His grace and love. (Psalm 47:8; 89:14; 97:2; Psalm 99:9; Revelation 15:4).

    q. A holy God cannot tolerate sin. (Isaiah 59:1; Habakkuk 1:3)

    r. Jesus Christ is the perfectly Holy One. (Mark 1:24)

    s. The Holy Spirit is sent to the believer to make him holy. (John 14:26; Hebrews 2:11; 12:10; I Peter 1:15-16; Revelation 4:8)

2. Perfect Righteousness

Righteousness and justice are synonymous. Righteousness is holiness in action against sin. The holiness of God demands that sin be judged and the sinner punished. Such punishment is the righteousness and justice of God in action. (Romans 2:8-9; II Thessalonians 1:8) Righteousness is a holy God acting in a just and upright manner towards His creatures. The righteousness of God is His holiness dealing justly with His creatures. This justice is seen in both punishment, (Genesis 2:17; Romans 1:32; 2:8-9) and reward. (Romans 2:7; Hebrews 11:26; Deuteronomy 7:9-13; Psalm 58:11; Matthew 25:21)

The scriptures attest to these statements.

    a. All God's ways are judgement. He is a God of truth and without iniquity, and He is just and right. (Deuteronomy 32:4)

    b. The Judge of all the earth will do that which is right. (Genesis 18:25)

    c. The Lord judges with righteousness. (Isaiah 11:4-5)

    d. Righteousness belongs to the Lord. (Danfel 9:7,14)

    e. The righteousness of God is revealed in the Gospel. (Romans 1:17)

    f. True and righteous are the judgements of the Lord. (Revelation 16:5-7)
    g. The Lord is righteous. (II Chronicles 12:6; Ezra 9:15; Nehemiah 9:33; Isaiah 45:21; John 17:25)
    h. Justice and judgement are the habitation of God's throne. (Psalm 89:14)
    i. Righteousness and true holiness are the characteristics of the new man being conformed to the image of God in Christ. (Ephesians 4:24)

3. Perfect Love

a. The Love of God

Love is the heart of God's nature. God not only has love, God is love. The love of God is the perfection of affection God has which moves Him to give Himself to His creatures continually. This love is not merely an emotion. It is an act of God's will in which He eternally gives Himself.

Love itself is a triunity: there must be the lover, the love and the loved. In the Godhead, love finds its perfect expression in the triunity of the Father (Lover), the Son (Loved), and the Holy Spirit (Love). (Matthew 3:16; John 14:31) In God we have: The Father who so loved that He gave. (John 3:16;17:24) The Son of His love. (Colossians 1:13 margin), and The love of the Spirit. (Romans 15:30; Galatians 5:22) This love in the Godhead is expressed to man, not only in creation, but more perfectly and fully in redemption. The holiness of God judged sin in the atoning work of the Cross, while the love of God made available salvation for the sinner. The following Scriptures give support to this:

    (1) He is the God of Love. (II Corinthians 13:11)
    (2) God is love. (I John 4:8,16)
    (3) God loves His people. (Deuteronomy 7:6-8,13; John 14:23; Psalm 11:7)
    (4) The perfect expression of the love of the Godhead is seen in Calvary. (John 3:16; Galatians 2:20)
    (5) Whoever dwells in love dwells in God. (I John 4:16-19)
    (6) God wants the same kind of love as in the Godhead to be in His own people. (John 17:24-26; 13:34-35)

b. The Goodness of God

The goodness of God is God's providential care for all His creatures. (Psalm 145:9,15,16; Job 38:41; Matthew 6:26; 5:45; Psalm 36:5; 104:21; Acts 14:17; Romans 2:4)

c. The Grace of God

Grace is the undeserved, unearned and unmerited favor of God bestowed upon sinful men. (Ephesians 1:2,6,7; 2:5-8; 3:2; II Timothy 1:2; Titus 1:4; II Thessalonians 3:17-18) Grace includes the longsuffering and forbearance of God towards sinful men. (II Peter 3:9; I Peter 3:20; Romans 2:4; Exodus 34:6; Romans 9:22)

d. The Mercy of God

Mercy is the pity of God upon the miserable condition of the sinner because of sin. (Ephesians 2:4; James 5:11; Psalm 102:13; Romans 11:30-31; Isaiah 55:7; Luke 1:50,72; Exodus 20:6; Titus 1:4; I Timothy 1:2; II Timothy 1:2; Psalm 85:10; Luke 6:36; Matthew 5:45; II Peter 3:9)

e. The Compassion of God

Compassion is sorrow for the sufferings of another with the urge to help. It is pity, sympathy, relating very much to mercy. Jesus was moved with compassion in His ministry. (Matthew 9:36; 14:14; 18:27; 15:32; Luke 15:20; Psalm 78:38; 86:15; 145:8; 130:7; 103:8-18)

f. The Kindness of God

Kindness is the gentle benevolence of God. (Ephesians 2:7; Colossians 3:12; Titus 3:4; Psalm 31:21; Isaiah 54:8,10; Joel 2:13)

Ephesians 2:4-7 "But God, who is rich in **mercy,** for His great **love** wherewith He **loved** us... that in the ages to come He might shew the exceeding riches of His **grace** in His **kindness** towards us through Christ Jesus." Titus 3:4-7 "But after that the **kindness** and **love** of God our Savior toward men appeared, not by works of righteousness which we have done, but according to His **mercy** He saved us... that being justified by His **grace,** we should be made heirs according to the hope of eternal life." Exodus 34:6-7 "The Lord God, **merciful** and **gracious, longsuffering** and abundant in **goodness,** and truth, keeping **mercy** for thousands..."

4. Perfect Faithfulness

The perfect faithfulness of God means that God is absolutely trustworthy, loyal, reliable and true to His Word. His Word is truth and He is absolutely reliable. (Isaiah 25:1; Deuteronomy 7:9; Isaiah 49:7; Deuteronomy 32:4) Faithfulness is applied in Scripture to both God and His Word. God's Word is as sure as Himself. God cannot lie. He is the only true God. (Psalm 89:37; John 17:3; I John 5:20; Psalm 86:15)

   a. God's commandments and testimonies are faithful. (Psalm 119:86, 138)
   b. God is faithful. (I Corinthians 1:9; 10:13)
   c. The faithful God will establish His people. (II Thessalonians 3:3; I Thessalonians 5:24)
   d. Even though men deny themselves, God is faithful and will never deny Himself. (II Timothy 2:13)
   e. Jesus Christ is a merciful and faithful High Priest. (Hebrews 2:17)
   f. God is faithful to His promises. (Hebrews 10:23; 11:11)
   g. He is a faithful Creator. (I Peter 4:19)
   h. God is faithful and just to forgive us when we confess our sins. (I John 1:9)

God desires that this moral attribute be built into the lives of the redeemed also. (Matthew 24:45; 25:21,23; Luke 16:10-12; I Corinthians 4:2; Galatians 3:9; II Timothy 2:2; Revelation 17:14)

Dr. A. H. Strong in "Systematic Theology" (p.248) lists out a schedule of divine attributes as follows:

1. Absolute or Immanent Attributes
   a. Spirituality, involving:
      (1) Life
      (2) Personality
   b. Infinity, involving:
      (1) Self-existence
      (2) Immutability
      (3) Unity
   c. Perfection, involving:
      (1) Truth
      (2) Love
      (3) Holiness
2. Relative or Transitive Attributes:
   a. Related to Time and Space:
      (1) Eternity
      (2) Immensity
   b. Related to Creation:
      (1) Omnipresence
      (2) Omniscience
      (3) Omnipotence
   c. Related to Moral Beings:
      (1) Veracity and Faithfulness or Transitive Truth
      (2) Mercy and Goodness or Transitive Love
      (3) Justice and Righteousness or Transitive Holiness

V. THE ETERNAL GODHEAD

It is well to note at the beginning of this section that no human pen or tongue can define God by mere words, and that the finite mind of man cannot explain the mystery of the Godhead. The Scriptures do not attempt to explain the mystery; they simply declare it. (Colossians 2:2; I Timothy 3:16) Much of the misunderstanding relative to the being of God, especially in the area of the distinctions in the Godhead, has come into the Church because of the terminology and theological phraseology that has been developed through the centuries.

Man cannot know God or what God is like apart from revelation. If God does not reveal Himself to man, it is impossible for him to discover God for himself. Man with all his searching cannot find out God. God Himself must take the initiative. (Job 11:7; Matthew 11:25-27) This God has done in His Word, the Bible. The Word of God is the revelation of God. Without it, we would have no revelation as to His essence, nature and being. Unless man accepts this revelation he will stumble along in the darkness of mere human reason. We must turn to the Scriptures to consider what God has revealed about Himself in His own inner mode of being, realizing that "the secret things belong to the Lord our God; but those things which are revealed belong unto us and to our children for ever, that we may do all the words of this law." (Deuteronomy 29:29)

A. The Godhead

A term used in the New Testament relative to God is "the Godhead". The word refers to that which is Divine, to Deity, involving God's revelation of His own mode of being. Acts 17:29 "...we ought not to think that the Godhead is like unto gold, or silver or stone, graven out by man's device."

Colossians 2:9 "For in Him (Christ) dwelleth all the fulness of the Godhead bodily."

Romans 1:19,20 "For the invisible things of the world are clearly seen, being understood by the things that are made, even His eternal power and Godhead..."

The Bible also reveals that in the Eternal Godhead there are three which are spoken of as the Father, the Son and the Holy Spirit. (Matthew 28:19; 3:16-17; I John 5:7-8; John 14:6-17) The very fact that the Father, Son and Holy Spirit are linked together in the baptismal command (Matthew 28:19) shows that there is co-existence, co-equality in nature, power and attributes, as well as co-eternity of being. Such would not be done with mere creatures, or mere influences. The statement of faith at the beginning of this section declares that "the Eternal Godhead has revealed Himself as one God existing in three Persons, even the Father, the Son and the Holy Spirit; distinguishable, but indivisible in essence, co-eternal; co-equal and co-existent in attributes, power, nature and glory." Said another way, God is one undivided and indivisible Essence, but in the one true God there are three eternal distinctions, the Father, the Son and the Holy Spirit.

Although the Bible never formally speaks of the Person of God, it does reveal the personality of God as Father, Son and Holy Spirit. Thus when we speak of the Persons in the Eternal Godhead, it is not used in the ordinary sense as used of human persons. The Scriptures clearly show that the Father, Son and Holy Spirit each have the characteristics and qualities of personality. The word "trinity" was introduced by Tertullian, one of the early Church Fathers, to define the teaching concerning the Godhead. It simply means "threefold" or "three in one". Though the word "trinity" is not used in the Scriptures, the words "three" and "one" are used and a consideration of these words reveal that the God of the Bible is triune in nature and being.

The God of the Bible is revealed as triune in nature and being. From Genesis to Revelation, whether it be by type or symbol, pattern or created things, shadows or theophanic revelation or manifestation, or whether it be by clear declaration, Scripture shows that GOD is always revealed as One in Three and Three in One, that is, a triunity.

Let us consider the truth that God is one and God is three, as set forth in the Scriptures. In doing so, we find that in the Biblical revelation of God, there are two streams of Scripture concerning His Person, and these are; God is one, and God is three.

It is important to remember, relative to these statements, that if either of these streams are over-emphasized then heresy results. If the stream of Scriptures concerning the fact that God is one is overemphasized, then we lapse into the heresy of Unitarianism, that is, a numerical number one God. On the other hand, if the stream of Scriptures is over-emphasized concerning the fact that God is three, then it results in the heresy of Tritheism, that is, the worship of three separate Gods. It is here that great exegetical balance must be exercised. It is well to remember the phrase previously used in the Statement of Faith, that "we believe in one God, existing in three Persons, distinguishable, but indivisible."

God is One — that is, indivisible
God is Three — that is, distinguishable

The study of the oneness of God must always be in connection with the threeness of God, and the study of the threeness of God must always be in conjunction with the revelation of the oneness of God. Otherwise, either extreme can become heresy. There is a great need for Scriptural balance.

B. The Oneness of the Godhead

The God of the Bible, is revealed as one God. Both the Old Testament and New Testament confirm the fact that there is but one God. Both Testaments declare the unity of God.

1. Old Testament Scriptures:

Deuteronomy 4:35,39 — "The Lord He is God, there is none beside Him."
Exodus 20:3 — "Thou shalt have no other gods before Me."
I Samuel 2:2; II Samuel 7:22 — "There is none beside Thee."
Psalm 86:10; 83:18 — "Thou art God alone."
Isaiah 44:6,8; 43:10; 45:18 — "Beside Me there is no God" Deuteronomy 6:4 — "Hear O Israel, the Lord our God is one Lord."
Each of these verses show clearly that there is but one God, or that God is one, that He is the one and only true God. False religions made many gods but the national tenet of Israel's faith was "Hear O Israel, Jehovah thy God is one Jehovah" Deuteronomy 6:4. The true Hebrew believers were monotheistic not polytheistic; they worshipped the one true God rather than the many gods. (Deuteronomy 4:35; Isaiah 44:6; 45:5)

2. New Testament Scriptures:

Mark 12:29 - "The Lord our God is one God."
I Corinthians 8:4 - "There is none other God but one."
Mark 12:32 - "For there is one God and there is none other but He."
Galatians 3:20 - "God is one."
Ephesians 4:6 - "One God and Father of all."
James 2:19 - "Thou believest there is one God, thou doest well."
I Timothy 2:5; I Timothy 1:17 - "For there is one God."

The New Testament definitely declares the unity of God. Christianity continues the true faith of Israel in the fact that it is monotheistic. It centers around the worship of the one true God.

C. The Threeness of the Godhead

As clearly as the Scriptures teach that God is one, so clearly do the same Scriptures teach that God is three. The Bible teaches the tri-unity of God. The union of three in one. One God manifested in three Persons.

The Scriptures speak of two kinds of unity or oneness; absolute unity and compound unity. This is seen in the use of two Hebrew and two Greek words translated by the word "one" The two Hebrew words are "yachead" and "echad".

YACHEAD speaks of absolute unity, a mathematical or numerical number one. It is used about twelve times in the Old estament, but never to describe the unity of God.

Following are several examples of its use.
  Abraham offered up "his only (yachead) son, Isaac" (Genesis 22:2,12)
"Deliver my darling"(i.e., My only one) (Psalm 22:20)
"They shall mourn for Him, as one mourneth for his only (yachead) son" (Zechariah 12:10)
Refer also to Jeremiah 6:26 and Judges 11:34.

This word is significant of the fact that there is only one way to God, one Son of God, man's one and only Hope of Salvation, and this is through the Lord Jesus Christ. (John 14:1,6)

ECHAD speaks of a compound or collective unity which comprises more than one person, i.e. one crowd, one people, one nation. Following are several examples of this unity.

"These two shall be one (echad) flesh" (Genesis 2:24)
"People gathered together as one" (Ezra 3:1)
"All the rest of Israel were of one heart to make David king" (I Chronicles 12:38).

This Hebrew word "echad" is used hundreds of times in the Old Testament and is usually significant of a compound unity; the unity of more than one. It is this word "echad" which is used concerning the one God.

The two Greek words which carry the same thought as these two Hebrew words are "heis" and "monos". Whenever Scripture speaks of the fact that God is one, it is never referring to a mathematical or number one God, but always to a compound unity; the unity of more than one Person. It speaks of plurality of Divine Persons in the one God. This unity is a compound unity, which is revealed as tri-unity, the union of three in one. Israel's national tenet of faith for centuries has said, "The Lord our God is one (echad) Lord". (Deuteronomy 6:4) This very scripture tells us that God is a compound unity. It states that "Jehovah Elohim" is a united one, uni-plural in nature and being. The word "Elohim" is a uni-plural word implying plurality of divine persons. Yet it was this which preserved Israel from total lapse into heathen polytheistic religions, the worship of many gods. "In that day, there shall be one (Echad) Lord, and His Name one (Echad)." (Zechariah 14:9)

The Hebrew word for a compound unity is again revealed in this text. The unity of God is a compound unity. The oneness of God is not numerical. From Genesis to Revelation, the God of the Bible is never manifested as the singular, solitary numeral, or number one. The oneness of God is a compound unity; one undivided and indivisible essence with three eternal distinctions.

In the Godhead there are three centers of consciousness, spoken of as the Father, the Son and The Holy Spirit. There are not three separate Gods, but three persons in one God, distinguishable but indivisible.

1. Old Testament Scriptures

Genesis 1:1-2 - "In the beginning GOD... and the Spirit of GOD moved on the face of the waters" (John 1:1-3). The word for "God" is "Elohim" plural of the Hebrew word "El". It is a uni-plural word, denoting plurality of divine Persons without stating the number, but which subsequent Scriptures show to be three divine Persons, even the Father, the Son and the Holy Spirit, each active in creation.

Genesis 1:26,27 - God (Elohim, plurality of divine Persons) made man in His (singular possessive) own image, after His likeness.

Genesis 3:22 - "And GOD (Elohim) said: Man is become as one of us, to know good and evil. (Genesis 11:6) Isaiah 6:8 - "The voice of the Lord saying, Who will go for US?" (John 12:41)

All of these verses speak of the plurality of divine Persons in the one God, and generally this Hebrew uni-plural word "Elohim" is used in the Old Testament to speak of the Eternal Godhead. It is the Old Testament equivalent for the New Testament definition of God as Father, Son and Holy Spirit, or, the Godhead.

Isaiah 48:16 - "The Lord God (the Father) and His Spirit (the Holy Spirit) hath sent Me (the Son)".

Isaiah 61:1 - "The Spirit (the Holy Spirit) of the Lord (the Father) is upon Me, because He hath anointed Me" (Luke 4:18)

Psalm 110:1 - "The Lord (the Father) said unto my Lord (the Son), sit Thou at My right hand until I make Thine enemies Thy footstool."

Genesis 19:24 - "Then the Lord (the Son) rained fire and brimstone from the Lord (the Father) out of heaven" Psalm 45:6–7 -"Thy throne O God (the Son cf. Hebrews 1:8–9) is forever... therefore God, Thy God (the Father) hath anointed Thee."

The Old Testament speaks of:
The Father (Isaiah 63:16; Malachi 2:10)
The Son (Psalm 45:6-7; 2:6-7,12; Proverbs 30:4; Isaiah 7:14; 9:6)
The Holy Spirit (Genesis 1:2; Isaiah 11:1-3; 48:16; Genesis 6:3; 61:1; 63:10)

2. New Testament Scriptures

The revelation of God in three Persons is the distinctive ministry of the blessed Son of God. The only way God could be known to man in His inner nature and being of tri-unity was by revelation. God had to reveal Himself. Who could bring or give this revelation? What patriarch, prophet, or saint could reveal God to mankind? No angel nor created being could unveil God in His glory, in the truth of His eternal Godhead as Father, Son and Holy Spirit.

The only Person who could reveal God to man was the very One who dwelt in the bosom of the Father. It had to be one of the Persons in Elohim, one in the Eternal Godhead who alone could reveal God to man. In the counsels of the Eternal Godhead, it was the eternal Son (the Word) who was to come and declare God in His tri-unity of being.

Hebrews 1:1-2 - "God who at sundry times and in divers manners spake unto the fathers by the prophets hath in these last days spoken unto us in the Person of His Son...".

Matthew 11:27 - "No man knoweth the Son, but the Father; neither any man the father, save the Son, and he to whomsoever the Son will reveal Him." John 1:18 - "No man hath seen GOD at any time; the only-begotten Son, who is in the bosom of the Father, He hath declared Him".

The Amplified New Testament says, "No man has ever seen God at any time; the only unique Son, the only begotten God, who is in the bosom (that is, in the intimate presence) of the Father, He has declared Him He has revealed Him, brought Him out where He can be seen: He has interpreted Him, and He has made Him known" (John 1:18)

The clearest revelation of God as triune had to come through one of these divine Persons. Here we have one of the fundamental reasons for the incarnation. The only way God could be revealed to man was by becoming a man. All of this was prophesied and then fulfilled in the Virgin Birth of the Son of God. He was God manifest in the flesh. (Isaiah 7:14; 9:6-9; Genesis 3:15; Matthew 1:21-23; John 1:1-3; 14-18)

It is the New Testament which plainly declares the number of divine Persons to be three, no more and no less. The whole of the New Testament abounds with clear references to three distinct, divine Persons, who are revealed as the eternal Godhead.

The Old Testament veiled the revelation of God. Being the "age of the shadow", when all things pertaining to the inner nature and being of God were veiled in types, shadows and divine names and titles, it remained for the Son of God in the fullness of time to unveil God in His fullness.

Following is a set of Scriptures from the Gospels and Epistles which show the distinction in the Godhead, as Father, Son and Holy Spirit. These verses tell of three distinct Persons, each having distinct ministry and function, yet one in mind and will, one in essence, and one in the purpose, plan and operation of redemption.

Matthew 3:16-17
The **Father's** Voice which spoke from heaven
The **Son** of God in Jordan's waters of baptism
The **Holy Spirit** descending bodily in the shape of a dove

Matthew 28:19
    Baptizing them into the name
      of the **Father,**
      and of the **Son,**
      and of the **Holy Spirit.**

Matthew's Gospel opens and closes with specific revelation of the Godhead, as Father, Son and Holy Spirit.

John 14:16-17
    The **Father** hears the prayer of the Son
    The **Son** prays to the Father
    The **Holy Spirit** as the Comforter will be given

I Corinthians 12:4-6
    Diversities of gifts, but the same **Spirit** (Holy Spirit)
    Differences of ministrations but the same **Lord** (The Son)
    Diversities of operations but the same **God** (The Father)

Ephesians 2:18
    Access unto — The **Father**
    Through Him — The **Son**
    By one Spirit — The **Holy Spirit**

Ephesians 4:4-6
    There is one **Lord** — The Son
    There is one **Spirit** — The Holy Spirit
    There is one **God** — The Father

II Corinthians 13:14
    The grace of our **Lord Jesus Christ** — The Son
    The Love of **God** — The Father
    The Communion of the **Holy Spirit** — The Spirit

I John 5:7-8
    There are three that bear record in heaven:
      The **Father**
      The **Word** (The Son)
      And the **Holy Spirit,**
    and these **three** are **one.** That is, tri-unity, one God, manifested and distinguished in three Persons.

Revelation 4 - 5
    There are three revealed in these chapters of Revelation.
    The one in the throne, the **Father** God
    The Lamb before the throne, the sacrificial **Son**
    The seven lamps of fire before the throne, the **Holy Spirit** in His fulness.

The Lord Jesus, in John's Gospel (chapters 15, 16 and 17) clearly brings to view the divine Persons in the Godhead. The Son prays to the Father to send the Holy Spirit. He prays that the disciples may be "one, as we are one" and that they may be "one in us." (John 17:21-23) The "oneness" here is certainly not a numerical oneness, but a compound unity, the unity of more than one person. Jesus said, "Ye believe in God (the Father), believe also in Me (the Son)" (John 14:1). He continued by saying, "I am the way, the truth and the life; no man cometh unto the Father but by Me" (John 14:6). Paul said, "For there is **one God** (the Father) and **one mediator** between God and men, **the man** (Son of God) Christ Jesus" (I Timothy 2:5).

God has declared that "in the mouth of two or three witnesses shall every Word be established" (Deuteronomy 19:15; Matthew 18:16-20). If God were not three in one (triune), He could never fulfill

His own Word. It would mean that God would have given to man a law which He Himself cannot fulfill. The Father, the Son and the Holy Spirit are three witnesses making a perfect, full and complete witness.

D. Relationship and Distinction in the Godhead

The relationship and distinctions in the eternal Godhead are seen in the following arrangement of the Scriptures pertaining to the Father, Son and Holy Spirit.

1. The Scriptures recognize three as God.
  a. The Father is God. (John 6:27; I Peter 1:2; Romans 1:7)
  b. Christ is God. (John 1:1,18; Titus 2:13; Romans 9:5)
  c. The Holy Spirit is God. (Acts 5:3,4)

2. The Scriptures recognize clear distinctions as Persons.
  The Son recognizes the Father distinct from Himself. (John 5:32,37)
  b. The Father and Son are distinguished as the Begettor and Begotten. (Psalm 2:7; John 1:14-18; 3:16)
  c. The Son recognizes that He was sent by the Father, and that the Holy Spirit will be sent from the Father through the Son. (John 10:36; Galatians 4:4; John 14:16,17; 15:26)

3. The Scriptures recognize three in creation.
  a. The Father in creation. (Exodus 20:11)
  b. The Son in creation. (Colossians 1:16-17; John 1:3; Hebrews 1:2,10)
  c. The Holy Spirit in creation. (Job 33:4; Psalm 104:30; Genesis 1:2; Job 26:13)

4. The Scriptures show the eternity of the Godhead.
  a. The eternity of the Father. (Deuteronomy 33:27; Psalm 90:2)
  b. The eternity of the Son. (Micah 5:2; John 1:1; Philippians 2:6)
  c. The eternity of the Holy Spirit. (Hebrews 9:14)

5. The Scriptures show the omnipresence of the Godhead.
  a. Omnipresence of the Father. (Jeremiah 23:23-24)
  b. Omnipresence of the Son. (Ephesians 1:23; Matthew 18:20)
  c. Omnipresence of the Holy Spirit. (Hebrews 9:14)

6. The Scriptures show the omniscience of the Godhead.
  a. Omniscience of the Father. (Proverbs 15:3; Hebrews 4:12; I John 3:20)
  b. Omniscience of the Son. (John 21:17; Colossians 2:3)
  c. Omniscience of the Holy Spirit. (I Corinthians 2:10)

7. The Scriptures show the omnipotence of the Godhead.
  a. Omnipotence of the Father. (Matthew 19:26)
  b. Omnipotence of the Son. (Philippians 3:21; Revelation 1:8; Matthew 28:18)
  c. Omnipotence of the Holy Spirit. (I Corinthians 12: 8-11)

8. The Scriptures show the immutability of the Godhead.
  a. Immutability of the Father. (Malachi 3:6; James 1:17)
  b. Immutability of the Son. (Hebrews 13:8)
  c. Immutability of the Holy Spirit. (Implied, not stated.)

Though the Father, Son and Holy Spirit maintain these qualities in common, they also remain distinct from each other.

THE FATHER

The Father is God, a distinct person. He is eternal, self-existent, invisible and immortal, dwelling in light which no man can approach unto; whom no man hath seen, nor can see. (I Timothy 6:16; I Timothy 2:5; I Corinthians 8:4; John 6:27; I Peter 1:2; Deuteronomy 32:4; II Samuel 7:14; Psalm 89:26;

Malachi 2:10; Matthew 6:9; Mark 11:25; Luke 12:30; John 4:21-24; II Corinthians 6:18; Philippians 4:19; James 1:17; I John 2:15-16)

THE SON
The Son is God, a distinct Person, co-equal with the Father and the Holy Spirit. He is a distinct personality made visible by the incarnation. The Son was pre-existent. That is, He existed before the world was. He was eternally existent with the Father and with the Holy Spirit. (Micah 5:2; John 8:56-58; John 17:5; I Corinthians 15:47; Philippians 2:6-7; Colossians 1:17; John 1:1-3,14; Revelation 22:13,16)

The Son not only was pre-existent, but pre-eminent above all things except the Father. (Matthew 11:27; Matthew 28:18; Luke 20:41-44; John 3:13,31; Acts 10:36; Ephesians 1:20-22; Hebrews 1:5-6, 4; I Peter 3:22; Revelation 3:14)

The Son is to be worshipped as God. This would be blasphemy and idolatry if the Son were not God, co-equal and co-eternal with the Father and the Holy Spirit. (Matthew 2:11; Matthew 14:33; Luke 24:52; John 5:23; Acts 7:59-60; Galatians 1:5; Hebrews 1:6; II Peter 3:18; Revelation 5:11-14)

The Son is God manifest in the flesh. (I Timothy 3:16; John 1:14-18)

THE HOLY SPIRIT
The Holy Spirit is God, a distinct personality. He is not merely an influence, but a divine Person, co-equal and co-eternal with the Father and the Son. (Genesis 1:2; Genesis 6:3; Isaiah 63:10; Joel 2:28; Matthew 10:20; Luke 12:12; John 14:16-17; John 15:26; Acts 2:4; Acts 5:3-4; Romans 8:14; I Corinthians 3:16; Galatians 4:6; Ephesians 1:13; Hebrews 2:4; Ephesians 4:30; I Corinthians 6:19)

E. Heresies Concerning the Godhead
Early Church heresies concerning the revelation of the Godhead fell into two extremes, Unitarianism and Tritheism.

1. Unitarianism
Unitarianism accepts the existence of one God but either denies, ignores or misconstrues his threeness.

a. Arianism
Arian, an Early Church heretic, taught that the Godhead consisted of one Eternal Person, who, in the beginning, created in His own image, a super-angelic being, the only begotten Son, by whom He made the worlds, and that the Holy Spirit was the first and greatest creature that the Son created. The heresy was that God is a numerically number one God and that the Son and the Holy Spirit are created beings.

b. Sabellianism
Bishop Sabellius, another Early Church heretic, taught that the Father, Son and Holy Spirit were simply three aspects or three manifestations of the absolute number one God. As a person may be a son, then a husband, and then a father, yet the person is the same individual, so it is with God as Father, Son and Holy Spirit.

This also is contrary to the Scriptures which make clear distinctions between Father, Son and Holy Spirit. The Father loves and sends the Son. The Son loves, leaves and then returns to the Father. The Son prays and intercedes with the Father. The Father and the Son send the Spirit. The Spirit intercedes with the Father and takes the place of the Son.

2. Tritheism
Tritheism accepts the threeness of God but rejects His unity. It is an imbalance concerning the revelation of God as Father, Son and Holy Spirit. It denies the unity of the persons in the Godhead and teaches that Father, Son and Holy Spirit are three separated beings, or, in other words, three Gods. The balance is to recognize that Father, Son and Holy Spirit are three distinct personalities in the one God, but not three separate Gods.

F. The Athanasian Creed and Doctrinal Statements

The Athanasian Creed, formulated in the 5th century to combat the heresies concerning the Godhead and to preserve from the two extremes of Unitarianism and Tritheism, undoubtedly is one of the greatest creeds of Early Church history. We quote it fully here.

The Athanasian Creed, A.D. 500

The Eternal Power and Godhead is a trinity. Romans 1:20; Matthew 28:19.

The true Christian faith is this, that we worship one God in trinity and trinity in unity, neither confounding the Persons nor dividing the substance. For there is one Person of the Father, another of the Son, another of the Holy Ghost.

But the Godhead of the Father, of the Son, of the Holy Ghost, is all one, the glory equal, the majesty co-eternal Such as the Father is, such is the Son, such is the Holy Ghost.

The Father uncreated, the Son uncreated, the Holy Ghost uncreated. The Father incomprehensible, the Son incomprehensible, the Holy Ghost incomprehensible.

The Father eternal, the Son eternal, the Holy Ghost eternal, and yet there are not three externals (or infinities) nor three uncreated, nor three incomprehensibles, but one incomprehensible.

So likewise the Father is almighty, the Son almighty, and the Holy Ghost almighty; and yet there are not three almighties, but one almighty or omnipotent.

So the Father is God, the Son is God, the Holy Ghost is God, yet there are not three Gods but one God. For like as we are compelled by the Christian verity to acknowledge every person by himself to be God or Lord; so we are forbidden by the Christian faith to say that there be three Gods or three Lords.

The Father is made of none, neither created not begotten. The Son is of the Father alone, not made, nor created, but begotten.

The Holy Ghost is of the Father and the Son, neither made, nor created, nor begotten, but proceeding.

So there is one Father, not three Fathers, and there is one Son, not three Sons, and there is one Holy Ghost, not three Holy Ghosts.

And in this trinity, none is afore or after the other, none is first and last, none is greater or less than another, but the whole three Persons are co-eternal together, and co-equal, so that in all things, as aforesaid:

"The **UNITY IN TRINITY**, and the **TRINITY IN UNITY** is to be worshipped."

Dr. Dale in the 19th century made the following statements:
"From eternity to eternity GOD is FATHER, SON and HOLY SPIRIT. The Father is God, but not apart from the Son or the Holy Spirit. The Son is God, but not apart from the Father and the Holy Spirit. The Holy Spirit is God, but not apart from the Father and the Son. There is but ONE GOD but in the GODHEAD there are THREE PERSONS. There are not three Gods, but in the life and being of the one God, there are three centers of consciousness, volition and activity, and these are known to us as THE FATHER, THE SON, AND THE HOLY SPIRIT."

The **Father** is all the fulness of the Godhead, invisible, without form, whom no man hath seen or can see.
The **Son** is all the fulness of the Godhead, manifested, made visible.

The **Holy Spirit** is all the fulness of the Godhead, acting immediately upon the creature, and thus making manifest, or revealing, the Father and the Son.
The Father **planned** redemption.
The Son **effected** redemption.

The Holy Spirit **applies** redemption.
The Father is always the Father. The Father is not the Son, nor the Holy Spirit. The Son is always the Son. The Son is not the Father, nor the Holy Spirit. The Holy Spirit is always the Holy Spirit. The Holy Spirit is not the Father nor the Son.

G. The Eternal Characteristics of the Godhead
The Biblical revelation shows us that each person in the Godhead has certain characteristics, manifestations and operations which never change.

The Father is eternally the Father.
The Son is eternally the Son.
The Holy Spirit is eternally the Holy Spirit

The characteristics and attributes of the Godhead are changeless. God is one in operation, but three in revelation and manifestation.

1. Characteristics of the Father
The characteristics of the Father, consistent in every clear statement of Scripture and every God-created type and symbol, are seen in the following:

 a. First Person in mode of operation. The First Cause, the Original, the Source, the Beginning, the Commencement, the Fountain-head of all wisdom. The Absolute. "In the beginning God" (Genesis 1:1)
 b. The Foundation of our redemption. (John 3:16)
 c. The Covenant-Maker and Keeper, the Covenant Promiser.
 d. The Architect, Designer, Controller and Sustainer.
 e. Light, Life and Love.
 f. Glory, Majesty, Unapproachable Light, Holiness and Fire. (I Timothy 6:16; Hebrews 12:29)
 g. Invisible, Spiritual, Eternally the Father.
 h. The Begetter. (John 3:16; 1:10-12)
 i. Omnipotent, Omnipresent, Omniscient, Immutable, Eternal.

2. Characteristics of the Son
The characteristics of the Son, consistent also in all clear statements of Scripture and every God-ordained type and symbol are seen in the following:

 a. Second Person in mode of operation, for the purpose of redemption. Not inferiority, not inequality, but submission and obedience in redemption's plan to the Father's will. The subject one, the obedient Son.

 b. The eternal Word. (John 1:1-3)

 c. The Mediator, Medium, and Umpire between God and man. The Intercessor, the Advocate.

 d. The God-Man. The union of the divine nature and human nature in the one Person. The Word made flesh. (John 1:14-18) God manifest in the flesh.

 e. The Only Begotten Son. The fulness of the Godhead bodily in human form. (Colossians 1:19; 2:9)

 f. Redeemer, Savior, Grace of God personified.

 g. Sacrificial body and blood. The ratification of the covenant by blood.

 h. The central Person of the Godhead. The one in the midst.

 i. The visible revelation and expression of the invisible God in human form. (Romans 1:19-20; Hebrews 1:3)

j. Eternally the Son. Co-equal in power, nature, attributes and glory with the Father and the Holy Spirit.

3. Characteristics of the Holy Spirit

The characteristics of the Holy Spirit are always consistent throughout the Scriptures and the types and symbols of the Spirit are based on the following:

a. The third Person in mode of operation for the purposes of redemption. Not inferiority, nor inequality, but the servant Person in the Godhead, pointing to the Father and the Son.

b. Proceeding from the Father, through the Son. (John 15:26; 16:16)

c. The Inspirer, Revelator, Illuminator of the Word, the written and living Word. The Communicator, the Teacher.

d. The Quickener, the Unction, the Anointing. (I John 2:20,27).

e. The Sanctifying Power, the Indweller in the multitude of believers, the Presence in the Church.

f. Fruitfulness, Fruit of the Spirit, Mother characteristics.

g. Numberlessness, Multiplicity, Exhaustlessness.

h. The Symbolized One, as Rivers, Rain, Fruit, Oil, Fire, Wind, Dove, Seal, Gifts, etc.

i. Eternally the Spirit. Invisible, Co-equal in nature, power, attributes and glory with the Father and the Son.

H. Illustrations of the Godhead

There have been many attempts to illustrate the triunity of God. Undoubtedly the richest types and symbols of the Godhead are those that God has given in His Word. The very fact that God has given so many threes in His Word is sufficient evidence that God was endeavoring to convey some truth concerning His own triune Being. Romans 1:19-20 tells us that "the invisible things of Him are clearly seen, being understood by the things that are made, even His eternal power and Godhead..."

The following are a number of illustrations of triunity from God's Book of natural creation, and then from God's Book of revelation, the Bible.

1. Natural Illustrations of Triunity

a. Light (Genesis 1:1-5)
Light is one - unity
Light is manifested in three major colors golden yellow, scarlet red and heavenly blue.

b. Water
Water is one - unity
Water is manifested in three forms - water, ice and steam.

c. Sun
There is one Sun relative to earth — one major ruling light.
This one Sun manifests threefold power — light, fire, energy.

d. Space
Space is a whole — unity, one
Space has three dimensions — breadth, length, depth.

e. Matter
Matter or substance is one
Matter is also threefold — energy, motion, phenomena.

f. Eternity
Eternity is one — timelessness
Eternity is also threefold — time past, time present, time future.

g. Triangle
A triangle is one complete object — unity
A triangle is also a threesided object.
Take away any one side and the triangle is destroyed.

h. Man
Man is one — a united or whole person.
Man is threefold or a tripartite being — spirit, soul and body; two invisible parts, one visible.
The visible reveals the invisible.

i. Consciousness
Man being a triune being, having spirit, soul and body, has a threefold consciousness.
Conscious means a knowing of oneself.
Spirit is the God-conscious part of man which contacts the spirit realm. Soul is the self-conscious part of man which contacts the inner realm. Body is the sense-conscious part of man which contacts the natural realm. The triunity of man is a mystery, yet a reality. (I Thessalonians 5:23)

2. Biblical Symbols and Types of Triunity
Scripture abounds with glorious symbols and types setting forth the triunity of God. It is the characteristics of these objects, institutions and people that make them illustrations of the Godhead and these should be studied to unfold their meaning. The key to these symbols and types will usually be the central one of the three. This will generally reveal the Son of God as being the Word of God or as the mediator with His sacrificial body and blood.

a. The Sun, Moon and Stars (Genesis 1:14)

The Sun, Moon and Stars are the source of our light and life, and these are the first manifested three in the Bible. These show forth the characteristics of the Godhead.

The Sun — Source of light and life; the Father
The Moon — Becomes as blood; the Son (Revelation 6:12)
The Stars — Multitudinous; the Holy Spirit in the Saints.

b. The Ark of Noah (Genesis 6:14-22)
God commanded Noah to make an Ark according to specifications which He Himself gave. It was made with "lower, second and third stories". This one Ark with three stories is a marvelous type of God. One God who is three Persons: the Father, the Son and the Holy Spirit. It took a triune Ark to bring salvation to Noah and his family from the waters of judgement, and it is the ministry of the triune God to bring salvation to mankind from the coming judgement upon sin and all ungodly flesh (Matthew 24:37-42).

                    First Story ... The Father, Foundation, Beginning
One Ark— Second Story ... The Son, the Door, the Way (John 10:9)
                    Third Story ... The Holy Spirit, the Window, the Illuminator (John 14:26)

c. The Rod, the Rock, the Waters (Exodus 17:1-8)
Another wonderful shadowing forth is that which is found in the history of Israel. Israel thirsted for waters in the wilderness. God heard their cry and instructed Moses to smite the Rock and the water gushed forth.

The Rod — The Father God. He smote the Son on Calvary. It pleased the Father to bruise His Son (Isaiah 53:10). God gave His Son an offering for sin (John 3:16)
The Rock — The Son. Smitten for us. They drank of that Rock which followed them (I

Corinthians 10:4).
The Waters — The Holy Spirit (John 7:37-39). The Holy Spirit flows from the Son as refreshing, life-giving waters. The thirsty may come and drink.

d. The Ark of the Covenant (Exodus 25:10-22; 37:6-9)
The Ark of the Covenant was covered by a Mercy-Seat with two overshadowing Cherubims of Glory. All three were fashioned out of one piece of gold (Exodus 25:17-22; Hebrews 9:5).

One Cherub ... The Father
One piece of gold— Mercy Seat ... The Son, blood-sprinkled
One Cherub ... The Holy Spirit (Romans 3:25)

Between the Cherubim and over the blood-sprinkled Mercy-Seat was the glory of the Lord, the very presence of God. In the midst of that triune typical creation, God communed with His people. (Numbers 7:89)

e. The Rod of Aaron (Numbers 17)
Aaron's rod that budded is another marvelous typical creation of the triunity of God. A God-ordained testimony and miracle. One rod but a manifestation of three.

The Bud ... The Father, Source, Beginning
One Rod— The Flower ... The Son, Crushed, Fragrance
The Almond ... The Holy Spirit, Fruitfulness

f. The Burning Bush (Exodus 3:1-6)
The call of Moses at the burning bush was indeed a revelation of God Himself in triunity.

The Voice ... The Father God (Exodus 3:4-6)
One Bush— The Bush ... The Son, the Root, Branch (Isaiah 11:1-2)
The Fire ... The Holy Spirit (Hebrews 12:29)

g. The God of Abraham, Isaac and Jacob (Exodus 3:14-16)
The three men show forth the characteristics and ministrations of the Godhead, as Father, Son and Holy Spirit.

Abraham ... The Father God, Promise, Covenant.
The God of— Isaac ... The Son, Only Begotten, Sacrifice
Jacob ... The Holy Spirit, Anointer, Fruitfulness

Only three men whom God has been pleased to call Himself the God of: Abraham (as the Father) offered up his only begotten son, Isaac (as Jesus), and Jacob, proceeded from the father Abraham through the son Isaac, and was the third person of that triunity of men, the anointer of the rock Bethel, "the House of God".

h. The Contents of the Ark (Hebrews 9:4)
Beneath the bloodstained Mercy Seat of the Ark were three articles, which again set forth the characteristics of God in type.

The Tables of the Law ... The Father God
The Golden Pot of manna ... The Son (John 6:32-36)
The Rod that budded ... The Holy Spirit, Life, Fruitfulness.

i. The High Priest, Urim and Thummin (Exodus 28)
In the garments of the High Priest we have a glorious prophecy in type of the Godhead bodily. Aaron, as High Priest, had the breastplate of judgement upon him, and within the breastplate the two mysterious stones, called Urim and Thummin, by which he received and communicated the mind of the Lord to the nation of Israel.

Urim, "Lights" ... The Father (James 1:17)
One High Priest— High Priest ... The Son, Mediator, Sacrifice
Thummin, "Perfections" ... The Holy Spirit"

As all Israel was represented before God in the High Priest, so is the whole church of God represented in the Lord Jesus Christ, our Great High Priest, after the Order of Melchisedek, in whom dwells all the fulness of the Godhead bodily.

j. The Three Feasts of the Lord (Leviticus 23)
The Three Feasts of Israel set forth the ministrations of the Godhead also. Passover ... The Son of God, the Lamb (Exodus 12; I Corinthians 5:7) Pentecost ... The Holy Spirit, the Wave Loaves (II Corinthians 3) Tabernacles ... The Father, Fulness, Completeness of Redemption (Hebrews 6:1-2; Matthew 5:48)

k. The Three Coverings of the Tabernacle (Exodus 36:18-19)

Covering of badger's skins ... God the Father over all
Ram's skins dyed red ... The Son, Blood atonement
Goat's hair curtains ... The Holy Spirit, inwrought workings and operations.

It took the three coverings for the one tabernacle, so it is the Godhead who becomes the true coverings for the Church, His tabernacle.

l. The Cherubim and Sword
The Cherubim in plurality, significant of the Father and Holy Spirit. The Flaming Sword, the Word, the Son.(Genesis 3:24; Hebrews 4:12)

m. The Cherubim and Veil (Exodus 26:31-33)
The Cherubim inwrought within the veil, again significant of the operations of the Father and Holy Spirit. The inwrought veil is significant of the veil of Christ's flesh, rent at Calvary in His death. (Hebrews 10:20-21)

n. Three Measures of Meal (Genesis 18:3)
The Meal one type of food, of corn. Three measures of meal, three equal parts of the whole.

o. The Loaves of Bread (Luke 11:5)
One bread, yet three loaves for the friend at midnight.

p. The Angels (Genesis 18-19)
The Lord revealed as three angels. (Genesis 18:16; 19:24)

q. The Leper Cleansing and Anointing (Leviticus 14:12-29)
The leper (as also the Priest) was touched with triunity in cleansing and anointing. One blood, yet a triune application of blood on the right ear, thumb and toe. Then one anointing oil, and again triune application of the oil on the right ear, thumb and toe.

r. The Tabernacle and Temple
One tabernacle, one temple, yet each had three respective places, the Holiest of All, the Holy Place, and the Outer Court.

s. The Earthly Witnesses (I John 5:7-8)
The witness of the water, the witness of the blood, the witness of the Holy Spirit, yet their witness is one, and agrees in one.

The Godhead Bodily
The Scriptures state that the fulness of the Godhead dwells bodily in the Son. (Colossians 1:19; 2:9)

The Lord Jesus Christ is the visible and bodily revelation of the Godhead. He is the visible manifestation of the invisible Persons in God. In the mystery of Godliness, "God manifest in the flesh" (I Timothy 3:16), the Bible shows that the Father and the Holy Spirit indwelt the Son.

The Father indwelt the Son. (John 14:8-11) All that Jesus said and did was by the Father's indwelling. He could say that when we saw Him we saw the Father. However, He never said He was the Father. He was one with the Father in will and purpose. And although in this mystery the Father dwelt in Him, yet He prayed to the Father in heaven. (John 17:1-3) The Holy Spirit indwelt the Son. (John 3:33-34) Jesus received the Holy Spirit without measure. However, Jesus never said He was the Holy Spirit. Thus, in recognizing that the Son is the fulness of the Godhead bodily, it also must be recognized that the Father is not the Son, nor the Son the Father; the Son is not the Holy Spirit, nor the Holy Spirit the Son or the Father. The Father is eternally the Father. The Son is eternally the Son. The Spirit is eternally the Spirit.

The Scriptures declare the dual truth that Jesus is the fulness of the Godhead bodily, and yet the Father, Son and Holy Spirit are three eternal distinctions, distinguishable but indivisible. (Refer to "The Doctrine of Christ")

VI. THE NAMES OF GOD

One of the richest fields of revelation which God has given concerning His own being is that which pertains to the names of God. A name in Scripture is often significant of the nature of a person, whether the name be of angels, men or God. The Hebrews say of God and His name, "Himself is His Name, and His Name is Himself."

The names of God are basically divided into two groups; Creatorship (or Elohistic), and Redemptive (or Jehovahistic) names.

A. Creatorship or Elohistic Names of God

The Elohistic names of God are those names which have to do with the relationship of God with His creation or creatures. The name "El" signifies "to be strong, powerful or mighty." "Elohim" is the plural of "El" and speaks of plurality of divine Persons in the Godhead. El signifies the object of worship rather than a divine name.

When the name "El" is used as a compound name, it is generally associated or used to show some power or attribute of God in relation to His creation or creatures.

Following is the general list of Elohistic names.

1. El - "to be strong, powerful, mighty." It is in the singular. It is used of Father, Son and Holy Spirit.

   The Father is El. (Genesis 14:18-22)
   The Son is El. (Isaiah 7:14) Immanu-El (Isaiah 9:6-9)
   The Holy Spirit is El. (Job 33:4; 37:10)

2. Elohim - Plurality of divine Persons. Used about 2500 times in the Old Testament. (Genesis 1:1) Used of the triune God. (Exodus 3:1-6,15) Used also of the fulness of the Godhead in the Son. (Psalm 45:2,6)

3. El-Elyon - The Most High God. (Genesis 14:18)

4. El-Roi - The God that sees. (Genesis 16:13-14) Omniscience.

5. El-Shaddai - God Almighty, God all-sufficient. (Genesis 17:1)

6. El-Olam - God, the everlasting. (Genesis 21:33) Eternity of Being.

7. El-Beth-El - God of the House of God. (Genesis 31:13; 35:7)

8. El-Elohe-Israel - God, the God of the Prince of God. (Genesis 33:20)

9. Eloah - The one God. (Deuteronomy 32:15; Daniel 2:11)

10. El-Gibbor - The mighty or great God. (Isaiah 9:6; Jeremiah 32:18-19)

11. Elohim-Elyon - God, The Most High. (Psalm 91:1-2; 78:56)

12. Elohim-Saboath - God of Hosts. (Psalm 80:7,14) Omnipotence.

13. Adon or Adonai - Master, Owner or Masters, Owners, Ruler of all. (Psalm 147:5; 86:12)

14. Immanu-El - God with us. (Isaiah 7:14; Matthew 1:21-23). God made flesh. The Incarnate Logos. (John 1:1-3; 14-18)

B. The Redemptive or Jehovahistic Names of God

The redemptive names of God revealed as Jehovah (or Yahweh) are God's own personal and distinct names. The name Jehovah appears in the Authorized Version about 6,823 times and is generally translated as LORD. The Hebrews referred to this name as the unpronouncable or incommunicable name of God. The Hebrew letters for this name are four, the English letters are JHVH or YHWH. These are spoken of as being the four letter tetragrammation.

Jehovah is the I AM THAT I AM. It signifies "to be", or "I will be all that I will be". It tells us that God is the Eternal, the Unchanged and Unchanging One, and He will be all that He is ever needed to be. This is more particularly seen in the compound redemptive names of the Lord. These compound names are always linked with some need of man, and it is here that Jehovah will be all that His people ever need Him to be. He says of Himself "The LORD is My name...this is My memorial unto all generations." (Exodus 3:14,15; 15:3; Isaiah 42:8; Jeremiah 16:21; 33:2; Amos 5:8; 9:6)

1. Jehovah (Yahweh, or Lord) - I AM THAT I AM (Exodus 3:14-15) "I will be what I will be". The Self-Existent One revealing Himself to man in redemptive purpose. (Malachi 3:6)
2. Jehovah-Elohim - The Lord God, the Redeemer-Creator. (Genesis 2:4)
3. Jah - Abbreviated form of Jehovah. (Exodus 15:2; 17:16; Psalm 68:4).
4. Jehovah-Elohim-Saboath - Lord God of Hosts. That is, of the hosts of heaven, creation and creatures. (Psalm 84:8; Jeremiah 15:16)
5. Adonai-Jehovah-Saboath - Master Lord of Hosts. (Psalm 69:6) Adon is singular for Master, and translated Lord in Old Testament. Adonai is plural for the same.
6. Jah-Elohim - Lord God. (Psalm 68:18)
7. Jah-Jehovah - Lord Jehovah (for double emphasis). (Isaiah 12:2; 26:4)
8. Jehovah-Jireh - The Lord will provide. (Genesis 22:14)
9. Jehovah-Rapha - The Lord that heals. (Exodus 15:26)
10. Jehovah-Nissi - The Lord my Banner. (Exodus 17:15)
11. Jehovah-Kanna - The Lord who is jealous. (Exodus 20:5; 34:14; Deuteronomy 5:9)
12. Jehovah-Mekaddeskum - The Lord who sanctifies. (Exodus 31:13; Leviticus 20:8)
13. Jehovah-Shalom - The Lord our Peace. (Judges 6:24)
14. Jehovah-Shaphat - The Lord is Judge. (Judges 11:27)
15. Jehovah-Saboath - The Lord of Hosts. (I Samuel 1:3; Psalm 24:10; 84:1,3)
16. Jehovah-Elyon - The Lord Most High. (Psalm 7:17)
17. Jehovah-Raah (or, Roi) - The Lord my Shepherd. (Psalm 23:1)
18. Jehovah-Hosenu - The Lord our Maker. (Psalm 95:6)
19. Jehovah-Gibbor - The Lord is Mighty. (Isaiah 42:13)
20. Jehovah-Tsidkenu - The Lord our Righteousness. (Jeremiah 23:6)
21. Jehovah-Shammah - The Lord is There, or Everpresent. Ezekiel 48:35)

Each and all of these compound redemptive names show how Jehovah meets every need of man in redemptive power. The ultimate revelation of the redemptive names is to be found in the name of the Lord Jesus Christ.

Jehovah-Jehoshua-Christos - The LORD JESUS CHRIST, or, Jehovah's Savior Anointed. (Matthew 1:21; Acts 2:34-36; Ephesians 1:20-21; Luke 2:11,26,27)

The name of the Lord Jesus Christ is the greatest redemptive name ever to be revealed because it comprehends in a triune name all the compound redemptive names of Jehovah. It is in the name and person of the Lord Jesus Christ that God meets every need of man in redemptive power. The Lord Jesus Christ is God's ordained Redeemer and all Old Testament redemptive names point to and find their consummation in His redemptive name. It is the name of the Godhead bodily. It is a triune name for the triune God. (Colossians 1:19; 2:9; Matthew 28:19-20)

As in the plan of redemption, it has pleased the Father that all fulness dwell in the Son, so it also has pleased the Father that the fulness of the divine or Godhead name, dwell in the Son. All redemptive names are thus comprehended in this triune redemptive name.

Chapter 5

THE DOCTRINE OF THE HOLY SPIRIT

The Holy Spirit is the third divine person of the eternal Godhead, co-equal, co-eternal, and co-existent with the Father and the Son. It is His ministry to convict and convert man as well as to reveal the Son and the Father to the believer. Since the glorification of the Lord Jesus Christ, the Holy Spirit in all His glorious operations is working through all who believe on the Father through the Son. This is why the present era is known as the age of the Holy Spirit.

CHAPTER OUTLINE

I. IMPORTANCE OF DOCTRINE OF THE HOLY SPIRIT

II. THE PERSONALITY OF THE HOLY SPIRIT

A. The Holy Spirit is not an influence
B. The Holy Spirit revealed as a Person

III. THE DEITY OF THE HOLY SPIRIT

A. By Divine Association with the Father and the Son
B. By Divine Distinction between the Father and the Son
C. By Divine Attributes ascribed to Him
D. By Divine Works ascribed to Him

IV. THE WORK OF THE HOLY SPIRIT IN THE OLD TESTAMENT

A. The Work of the Spirit in Creation
B. The Work of the Spirit in Redemption
C. The Work of the Spirit in Inspiration
D. The Work of the Spirit in Israel

V. THE WORK OF THE HOLY SPIRIT IN THE NEW TESTAMENT

A. In the Life and Ministry of the Lord Jesus
B. In the Life of the Individual Believer
C. In the Life and Ministry of the Church
D. In the Unbelieving World

VI. THE SYMBOLS OF THE HOLY SPIRIT

VII. THE TITLES OF THE HOLY SPIRIT

I. IMPORTANCE OF THE DOCTRINE OF THE HOLY SPIRIT

The Doctrine of the Holy Spirit is one of the most important doctrines in the Word of God and is one of the foremost truths of redemption. Therefore the believer should seek to know all he can of the person, ministry and work of the Holy Spirit as revealed in Scripture. From Genesis to Revelation, relative to both creation and redemption, the Holy Spirit is seen in operation. In the midst of the chaotic condition seen in Genesis 1:1-2, we see the Spirit of God moving. "And the Spirit of God moved upon the face of the waters". The final mention of the Holy Spirit is seen in Revelation 22:17 where "... the Spirit and the bride say, come". Between these two verses, the beginning and consumation of the Spirit's work, we have a vast amount of Biblical revelation of the Holy Spirit's ministry. The Holy Spirit is mentioned more than 90 times in the Old Testament with at least 18 different titles also given. In the New Testament the Holy Spirit is mentioned more than 260 times along with 39 different names and titles. Out of the 27 books of the New Testament, only II John and III John have no reference to the Holy Spirit. The Old Testament foretold the coming of "the last days" when the Holy Spirit would be poured out upon all flesh, in contrast to Old Testament times when the Spirit was only available to a select few in Israel. In God's plan, this present age has been given over to the ministry of the Holy Spirit.

These facts emphasize the importance of the believer coming to know, understand, appreciate and experience the person, work and ministry of the Spirit in his life. It is the Spirit who brings to the heart the revelation of the Father and the Son (John 14:15-26). It is fear, formalism and ignorance which rob the Church from studying the doctrine of the Holy Spirit and thus making room for His blessed ministrations.

II. THE PERSONALITY OF THE HOLY SPIRIT

A. The Holy Spirit is not an Influence

The Holy Spirit is not to be looked upon merely as an influence. Many believers are robbed of a personal relationship with the Holy Spirit because they consider the Spirit to be an impersonal influence, power or energy. It is true that the Holy Spirit does influence the life of the believer, and He is revealed as the power of God, but this influence is a personal one. There are several reasons why this misunderstanding has arisen, the chief being the following:

1. The Holy Spirit is spoken of as being "The Spirit of God" and the word "Spirit" (Greek "Pneuma") means "breath" or "wind", which implies the concept of an unseen force (Isaiah 40:7; John 3:5-8).

2. The Holy Spirit is symbolized as being wind, water, fire, oil, a seal, or other impersonal objects. This seems to negate the fact that the Holy Spirit is a divine Person. However, there are many symbols relative to the Son of God also; such as a lamb, a rock, and a lion, yet these things do not negate the Son being a divine Person. Neither do the symbols of the Spirit negate His personality.

3. The Holy Spirit's work seems to be so mystical, secret and invisible. This does not, however, deny personality of the Spirit, for "God is a Spirit" (John 4:24) yet a real divine Person.

4. The Holy Spirit as a divine title seems harder for believers to relate to than the titles "Father" and "Son" (Matthew 28:19). No doubt this is because these titles have a much more human feeling about them than "the Holy Spirit". But this does not deny the personality of the Spirit. Evil spirits are real personalities and their work is evidenced everywhere. Angels are also spirit beings, yet real personalities. Man is a spirit being with soul and body, a real person having corporality (Hebrews 1:7,14; 12:23; Proverbs 20:27; I Timothy 4:1). Thus the Holy Spirit is a real person, though invisible and incorporeal.

There are also several reasons why the believer should not consider the Holy Spirit as a mere influence or impersonal force.

1. It is contrary to the teaching of the Scripture. The Bible shows the Holy Spirit to be a divine Person.

2. It will hinder worship. True worship is a personal activity, a means of personal relationship.

3. It will hinder proper reverence. To speak of the Holy Spirit as an "it" is improper. The Authorized Version (Romans 8:16,26) does speak of the Spirit in this way. However, other translations correct this. In the teaching of Jesus in John's gospel, He uses personal pronouns over ten times concerning the Spirit. Not understanding the personality of the Holy Spirit can cause people to look on the Spirit as something like "this power" and want to purchase it, even as did Simon the Sorcerer (Acts 8:9-24).

4. It will hinder relationship. God desires to have a personal relationship with each one of us. Thus God Himself comes and lives within us through the person of the Holy Spirit. It would be impossible to have any relationship with an impersonal force. We must know the Spirit as our friend, helper, comforter, and indweller. In this way we can honor Him. The believer has more than an "influence" living within him; he has the person of the Holy Spirit.

B. The Holy Spirit Revealed as a Person

The Holy Spirit is revealed in the Scripture to be the third person in the eternal Godhead. This title is often associated with the person of the Father and the person of the Son (Matthew 28:19; II Corinthians 13:14; I John 5:7,8). It would be meaningless to read these Scriptures and see the Father and Son as persons associated with an "influence", i.e. the impersonal Holy Spirit. Personality does not demand corporeality in God as in mankind.

1. The Holy Spirit is referred to with Personal Pronouns

Although the word "Spirit" is in the neuter gender, the Lord Jesus used personal pronouns when He spoke of the Holy Spirit. The pronouns "He", "Him" and "Himself" are used a number of times in John's gospel when speaking of the Spirit. These pronouns are in the masculine gender (John 14:15,16,26; 16:7-14; 15:26-27).

2. The Holy Spirit is spoken of as having personal qualities.

The three main qualities which constitute personality are attributed to the Holy Spirit. The Holy Spirit has:

    a. Mind (Romans 8:27; I Corinthians 2:10-13).
    b. Will (I Corinthians 12:11).
    c. Emotions (Romans 8:26-27; 15:30; Colossians 1:8)

These things are inapplicable to an impersonal influence or power.

3. The Holy Spirit is spoken of under personal titles

Personal titles are given to the Holy Spirit, which again show that He is a divine person. He is called "the Comforter" which also means "the Advocate" (John 14:16,26; 15:26; 16:7). This same title is used of Jesus as a person, meaning "one who stands alongside" (John 14:26). In John 14:16 Jesus speaks of the Holy Spirit as "another Comforter". The Holy Spirit could not take the place of Jesus personally if He was but an impersonal influence. He came to be personally related to the disciples that Jesus was personally related to while on earth. The Spirit came to be personally in them what Jesus was personally to them.

4. The Holy Spirit performs personal acts

    a. The Spirit works (I Corinthians 12:11)
    b. The Spirit searches (I Corinthians 2:10)
    c. The Spirit speaks (Acts 13:2; Revelation 2:7; II Samuel 23:2; Matthew 10:20; I Timothy 4:1)
    d. The Spirit testifies (John 15:26; Nehemiah 9:30)
    e. The Spirit bears witness (I John 5:6)
    f. The Spirit teaches (John 14:26)
    g. The Spirit instructs (Nehemiah 9:20)
    h. The Spirit reproves (John 16:8-11)
    i. The Spirit prays and makes intercession (Romans 8:26)
    j. The Spirit leads (Matthew 4:1)
    k. The Spirit guides the believer into all truth (John 16:13)
    l. The Spirit glorifies the Lord Jesus Christ (John 16:14)
    m. The Spirit brings about regeneration (John 3:5,6)
    n. The Spirit strives with men (Genesis 6:3)

o. The Spirit convicts men (John 16:8)
p. The Spirit sends messengers from God (Isaiah 48:16)
q. The Spirit calls men into ministry (Acts 13:2; 20:28)
r. The Spirit directs men in the service of Christ (Acts 8:29; 10:19; 16:6,7)
s. The Spirit also imparts spiritual gifts to the members of the Body of Christ (I Corinthians 12:7-11)

5. **The Holy Spirit is spoken of as having personal feelings that could not be attributed to an impersonal power.**

a. He can be grieved (Ephesians 4:30)
b. He can be insulted (Hebrews 10:29)
c. He can be lied to (Acts 5:3)
d. He can be blasphemed (Matthew 12:31-32)
e. He can be resisted (Acts 7:51)
f. He can be tempted (Acts 6:9)
g. He can be vexed (Isaiah 63:10)
h. He can be quenched (I Thessalonians 5:19)

The Holy Spirit is a divine Person. He is God indwelling the redeemed and working within the believer to fulfil the will of God. It is the blessed and glorious privilege of all believers to have the conscious joy and knowledge of the Spirit within.

I. THE DEITY OF THE HOLY SPIRIT
The Scriptures also testify to the fact that the Holy Spirit is God, co-equal with the Father and the Son, yet a distinct person in the eternal Godhead.

A. By Divine Association with the Father and the Son
The Father, Son and Holy Spirit are linked together as one in the baptismal command of Jesus (Matthew 28:19). This shows the Holy Spirit to be co-eternal and co-eternal in the Godhead. Each is linked in the triune name (read also II Corinthians 13:14; I John 5:7-8). The teaching of Jesus clearly relates that the Holy Spirit is one with the Father and Himself (John 14:16,26; 15:26; 16:7-13; Acts 2:33). We see the Father, Son and Holy Spirit at Jesus' baptism (Matthew 3:16,17) in the administrations of the Church (I Corinthians 12:4-6), and involved in apostolic benediction (II Corinthians 13:14).

B. By Divine Distinction from the Father and the Son
The Holy Spirit, though one with the Father and the Son is also distinguished from the Father and Son.

1. The Son is sent by the Father and the Holy Spirit (Isaiah 48:12,16).
2. The Spirit descended upon the Son as a dove, as the Father's voice spoke from heaven (John 1:33; Luke 3:21-22).
3. The Holy Spirit is partaker of the triune name, the name of the Godhead to be used in administering baptism (Matthew 28:19).
4. The Son prays to the Father to send the Holy Spirit who is the Comforter (John 14:16,26; 15:26; 16:7-13).
5. The believer has access to the Father, through the Son, by the Spirit (Ephesians 2:18).
6. The Holy Spirit proceeds from the Father through the Son (John 14:26; 15:26).

C. By Divine Attributes being ascribed to Him
The same essential and moral attributes ascribed to the Father and the Son are also ascribed to the Holy Spirit. This could only be so if the Holy Spirit is indeed a Divine Person.

1. Essential Attributes

a. The Holy Spirit is called God (Acts 5:3,4; I Corinthians 3:16; 12:4-6)
b. The Holy Spirit is eternal (Hebrews 9:14)
c. The Holy Spirit is omnipotent (all-powerful) (Luke 1:35)
d. The Holy Spirit is omniscient (all-knowing) (John 14:26; 16:12,13; I Corinthians 2:10; Romans

8:26-27)
e. The Holy Spirit is omnipresent (everywhere-present) (Psalm 139:7-10)
f. The Holy Spirit is the life source (Romans 8:2)

2. Moral Attributes

a. The Holy Spirit is the Spirit of Truth (John 16:13)
b. The Holy Spirit is the Spirit of Love (Romans 15:30)
c. The Holy Spirit is the Spirit of Holiness (Romans 1:4; Ephesians 4:30)

D. By Divine Works being attributed to Him
Divine works are attributed to the Holy Spirit, even as to the Father and the Son. These things attest to His deity.

1. The Holy Spirit was active in the creation of the worlds, as well as in the creation of beasts and man (Genesis 1:1-2; Job 26:13; 33:14; Psalm 104:30).
2. The Holy Spirit was active in the inspiration of the sacred Scriptures (II Peter 1:21; II Timothy 3:16; II Samuel 23:2-3).
3. The Holy Spirit is active in the regeneration of fallen man, in making man a new creation (John 3:3-5).

4. The Holy Spirit is active in the resurrection of the body, which involves a creative act (Romans 8:11).

It should be evident from the preceding paragraphs that the person of the Holy Spirit is seen by Scripture as being God. All that the Scriptures reveal concerning the character and attributes of God can be applied to describe His person. He is the third person of the triune eternal Godhead, and as God the Holy Spirit He is co-eternal, co-existent, and co-equal with God the Father and God the Son. The Bible reveals one God existing in three persons, even the Father, the Son and the Holy Spirit, distinguishable but indivisible.

IV. THE WORK OF THE HOLY SPIRIT IN THE OLD TESTAMENT
Though the Holy Spirit was not available for "all flesh" in Old Testament times, He was seen working especially among the chosen nation of Israel. The Holy Spirit is mentioned over 90 times in the Old Testament books. We note the work of the Spirit in those times in four major areas.

A. The Work of the Spirit in Creation

1. The Spirit of God was active in the creation of the heavens and the earth (Job 26:13; Psalm 33:6; Isaiah 40:12-14).
2. The Spirit of God was active in the restoration of the earth before the creation of man (Genesis 1:1-2).
3. The Spirit of God was the life-giving breath even to the beasts of the earth (Psalm 104:30).
4. The Spirit of God was active also in the creation of man, the masterpiece of God's creative acts (Genesis 2:7; Job 33:4).

B. The Work of the Spirit in Redemption

1. The Spirit of God strove with man in the days of Noah (Genesis 6:3).
2. The Spirit of God quickened Noah to preach the Word as a preacher of righteousness (I Peter 3:18-20).

3. The nation of Israel often resisted the Spirit of God who spoke through the various prophets in their history (Acts 7:51-52).

C. The Work of the Spirit in Inspiration
In the writing of the Scriptures, both Old and New Testament, the Spirit moved upon the prophets giving them revelation, and inspiration, and causing them to write the sacred Scriptures. The Holy Spirit through the prophets foretold the sufferings of Christ and the glory that should follow in the Church by the power of inspiration (II Peter 1:21; II Timothy 3:16; I Peter 1:11,12; Acts 28:25; II Samuel 23:2; Matthew 22:43; Acts 1:16).

D. The Work of the Spirit in Israel

The only nation in which we see distinctive operations of the Spirit was the chosen nation of Israel. Here the Spirit can be seen equipping, inspiring, energizing and clothing men with Himself. The work of the Spirit in the Old Testament saints seemed temporary in contrast to His work in the saints in the New Testament times. The Spirit came only upon a select few in pre-cross days in contrast to the Spirit being available for all in the last days. We note here in outline form the various operations of the Spirit upon the chosen ones in Israel.

1. The Spirit of God enabled Joseph to interpret the dreams of Pharoah (Genesis 41:38).

2. It was the Spirit of God who gave wisdom for the building of the Tabernacle of Moses according to divine pattern (Exodus 28:3; 31:1-6; 35:31).

3. The Holy Spirit quickened the 70 elders to prophesy in the camp of Israel (Numbers 11:16-29).

4. The Judges as deliverers in Israel were equipped by the Holy Spirit for their ministry. Othniel (3:9-10); Gideon (6:34); Jephthah (11:29); and Samson (14:6,19; 15:14).

5. Joshua was equipped with the Spirit of wisdom after Moses had laid his hands on him (Deuteronomy 34:9; Numbers 27:18).

6. The Spirit of the Lord was upon David as king, prophet and psalmist in Israel (I Samuel 16:13; I Chronicles 28:12; II Samuel 23:1-2).

7. King Saul came under the prophetic Spirit after his anointing (I Samuel 10:6,10; 11:6; 19:23).

8. The priests of the Lord had the Spirit upon them (II Chronicles 20:14,17; 24:20; Luke 1:5,67).

9. The prophets were men who had the Holy Spirit upon them in various measures (I Peter 1:10-12; Acts 7:51-52).

    a. Balaam (Numbers 24:2)
    b. Azariah (II Chronicles 15:1-2)
    c. Elijah (I Kings 18:12; II Kings 2:16)
    d. Elisha (II Kings 2:1-18)
    e. Amasai (I Chronicles 12:18)
    f. Zechariah (II Chronicles 24:20)
    g. Micah (Micah 3:8)
    h. Ezekiel (Ezekiel 3:12-14; 8:3; 11:1-5,24)
    i. Daniel (Daniel 4:8-9,18; 5:11,14).
    j. Isaiah (Acts 28:25)
    k. Jeremiah (Jeremiah 1:9; 30:1-2)
    l. Joel (Joel 2:28; Acts 2:16-17)

Thus judges, kings, priests and prophets in Israel experienced the Spirit upon them and were known as the Lord's Anointed. All these men in their offices typified Jesus Christ, The Anointed One, who would have the Spirit upon Him in fulness in New Testament times.

All those who experienced the power and operations of the Holy Spirit upon them could testify that it was indeed "not by might, nor by power, but by My Spirit, saith the Lord of Hosts (Zechariah 4:6)

At the close of the Old Testament period and the ushering in of the New Covenant times there were peculiar and special operations of the Holy Spirit. Undoubtedly this was because of the new era that was about to be brought in with the coming of Messiah and the outpouring of the Spirit upon all flesh. Zacharias and Elizabeth had a unique experience of the Holy Spirit relative to the birth of John the Baptist, Messiah's forerunner (Luke 1:41-42,67). John the Baptist himself, was filled with the Spirit from his mother's womb and ministered in the Spirit and power of Elijah (Luke 1:15-17). Mary, the mother of Jesus was overshadowed by the Holy Spirit in order for the virgin birth of Messiah to take place (Luke 1:46-55). Both Simeon and Anna, a prophetess, came by the Spirit into the Temple at the time of the dedication of the baby Jesus (Luke 2:25-32).

It is worthy to note a number of phrases which describe the Spirit's coming and work in or upon these chosen vessels.

1. The Spirit "came upon" me. (Judges 6:34; I Chronicles 12:18; II Chronicles 24:20). Used also in the sense of the Spirit "clothing" them.
2. The Spirit "came mightily upon" men (Judges 14:6; I Samuel 10:10; 16:13).
3. The Spirit was "in" men, in the sense of indwelling, at times (Genesis 41:38; Numbers 27:18; Daniel 4:8-9; Nehemiah 9:30; I Peter 1:10,11).
4. The Spirit "filled" men, fitting and equipping them for service (Exodus 31:1-7).
5. The Spirit was often "upon" men (Numbers 11:17; 24:2; Judges 3:10; 11:29; II Chronicles 15:1; Isaiah 59:21; 61:1).
6. The Spirit "rested upon" men (Numbers 11:25-26; II Kings 2:15; Isaiah 11:2).
7. The Spirit "moved" upon men (Judges 13:25).
8. The Spirit "entered into" men at times (Ezekiel 2:2; 3:24).

It should be remembered that these expressions happened only to chosen men of God, the select few for whom the Spirit came to equip for divine service. However, as it will be seen, there was a definite difference in these experiences of the Spirit for Old Testament saints as there is in New Testament saints.

V. THE WORK OF THE HOLY SPIRIT IN THE NEW TESTAMENT
Although the Holy Spirit is seen at work in Old Testament times in creation and in Israel, His operations were not available for all mankind. However, the Old Testament prophets clearly foretold a coming day when the Spirit would be poured out upon all flesh, both Israel and Gentile nations together (Joel 2:28-29; Ezekiel 11:19; 36:26,27; Isaiah 44:3; Zechariah 10:1). This could only be fulfilled upon the foundation of the death, burial, resurrection, ascension and glorification of the Lord Jesus Christ. It would be His ministry to receive the fulness of the Spirit as the perfect Man, the Messiah of God, and then pour out that same Spirit upon all flesh and upon those who believe on Him unto eternal life. Upon the acceptance of the finished work of the cross, the believer will find available to him the gift of the Holy Spirit and thus come under His gracious ministrations from regeneration unto glorification (Matthew 3:11; John 1:30-33; Romans 8:25-32).

The Lord Jesus is the pattern Son of God who is the example of the workings of the Spirit in humanity in an unhindered operation. The believer, as a son of God and member of the Church should follow in His steps and come under the same workings of the Holy Spirit (I Peter 2:21; Romans 8:29). We consider in outline the form the operations of the Spirit in Christ the Head, and then in the Church which is His Body.

A. The Holy Spirit in the Life of the Lord Jesus

1. He was born of the Spirit (Luke 1:35; Matthew 1:18-20).
2. He was filled with the fulness of the Spirit (John 3:34).
3. He was led by the Spirit (Matthew 4:1; Luke 4:1).
4. He was empowered by the Spirit (Luke 4:14).
5. He was anointed by the Spirit (Luke 4:18).
6. He spoke and taught by the Spirit (Luke 4:18).
7. He healed the sick by the Spirit (Luke 4:18).
8. He cast out devils by the power of the Spirit (Matthew 12:28).
9. He was justified (vindicated) by the Spirit (I Timothy 3:16).
10. He was offered up on Calvary by the eternal Spirit (Hebrews 9:14).
11. He was resurrected by the Spirit (Romans 8:11; I Peter 3:18).
12. He gave commandments to the disciples by the Spirit (Acts 1:2).
13. He baptized and empowered the Church by the Spirit (Acts 1:5,8).
14. He directs and governs the Church also by the Spirit (Revelation 2:7,11).

Thus the whole life of Jesus as the perfect Man was governed by the Spirit. If Jesus depended upon the Holy Spirit in such a manner, how much more should the believer constantly depend upon the Holy Spirit. All that God has for us and wants to do in us will only be done by the operation of the Holy Spirit in our lives. Hence the need for believers individually and the church corporately to open their hearts to seek the fulness of the Spirit working in them.

B. The Holy Spirit in the Life of the Believer
The life of the believer follows that example of the Lord Jesus.

1. The new birth is brought about by the Spirit (John 3:5,6).
2. The Spirit indwells the believer's spirit (Romans 8:9; I Corinthians 3:16; 6:17; I John 2:27).
3. The Spirit gives assurance of salvation (Romans 8:16).
4. The Spirit fills the believer with Himself (Acts 2:4; Ephesians 5:18).
5. The Spirit, by the baptism in the Spirit, enables the believer to speak in unknown languages (Acts 2:4; 10:44-46; 19:6; Mark 16:17; I Corinthians 14:2,4,18). The expression "baptism in or with the Spirit" is a Scriptural expression and experience (Matthew 3:11; Acts 1:5; I Corinthians 12:13; John 1:33; Luke 3:16).
6. The Spirit speaks to the believer (Acts 8:29; I Timothy 4:1; Revelation 2:7,11,17,29).
7. The Spirit opens the believer's understanding to the things of God (I Corinthians 2:12).
8. The Spirit teaches the believer, and guides him into all truth (John 16:13; I John 2:27).
9. The Spirit imparts life (John 6:63; II Corinthians 3:6).
10. The Spirit brings about renewal (Titus 3:5).
11. The Spirit strengthens the believer's inner being (Ephesians 3:16).
12. The Spirit enables the believer to pray (Jude 20; Romans 8:26-28).
13. The Spirit enables the believer to worship in spirit and in truth (John 4:23-24; Philippians 3:3; I Corinthians 14:15).
14. The Spirit leads the believer (Romans 8:14).
15. The Spirit enables the believer to put fleshly deeds to death (Romans 8:13).
16. The Spirit produces Christ-likeness in character and fruit in the believer's life (Galatians 5:22,23).
17. The Spirit gives a calling to the believer for special service (Acts 13:2-4).
18. The Spirit guides believers into their ministry (Acts 8:29; 16:6,7).
19. The Spirit empowers the believer to witness (Acts 1:8).
20. The Spirit imparts spiritual gifts to the believers as He wills (I Corinthians 12:7-11).
21. The Spirit will bring about the resurrection and immortality to the believers' bodies in the last day (Romans 8:11; I Corinthians 15:47-51; I Thessalonians 4:15-18).

C. The Holy Spirit in the Life of the Church
Not only is the work of the Spirit seen in the individual believer but it is also seen in the Church. The coming of the Holy Spirit to form the Church, the many-membered body of Christ, was foreshadowed in Israel under the Feast of Pentecost, even as the work of Christ was foreshadowed under the Feast of Passover (Exodus 12; Leviticus 23; Acts 2:1-4). The Holy Spirit is the executive agent of the Godhead who came to earth to build the Church that the Lord Jesus said He would build (Matthew 16:16-20). The Holy Spirit could not be given until Jesus Christ was glorified after His death, burial, resurrection and ascension (John 7:38-39).

It is the indwelling work of the Spirit that seems to be the difference between the experience of Old and New Testament saints. It is the distinguishing feature of New Covenant times. This is seen in the baptismal sign which was given to John the Baptist, concerning the Messiah. John 1:33 says "Upon whom thou shalt see the Spirit descending and remaining on Him, the same is He which baptizeth with the Holy Spirit". This qualified Jesus to be the Baptizer in the Holy Spirit.

In the Old Testament the Spirit descended on special ones, equipping and filling them but not remaining or indwelling them continually. Jesus promised His disciples that the Spirit would come and dwell with them and in them and that, as the Comforter, He would abide with them forever (John 14:16-17).

The major features of the Spirit's work in the Church includes the following:

1. The Holy Spirit formed the Church on the Day of Pentecost into a corporate structure, the Body of Christ. He baptized the living members into this spiritual body. Pentecost is called the birthday of the Church (Acts 2:1-4; I Corinthians 12:12-27; Ephesians 1:22-23).

2. The Holy Spirit formed the Church to be the new and living temple of God, setting believers into their places as living stones in the New Covenant temple (I Corinthians 3:16; 6:16; Ephesians 2:20-22).

3. The Holy Spirit brings anointing, illumination and direction to the Church as the New Covenant Priestly Body (II Corinthians 1:21; Psalm 133:1-2; I John 2:20, 27; Ephesians 1:17-18; Acts 10:38; I Corinthians 12:12-13).

4. The Holy Spirit brings gifts and graces to the members of the Church (I Corinthians 12:4-11, 28-31; Romans 12:6-8; Galatians 5:22-23). The gifts of the Spirit are a demonstration in the Church of the Spirit's omnipotence, omniscience and omnipresence. The fruit of the Spirit is the evidence of the nature and character of the Holy Spirit in the members of the Body of Christ.

5. The Holy Spirit is the Agent of direction and government in the Church. The Lord Jesus is the Head of the Church in heaven and He directs His affairs in His Body by means of the Holy Spirit. It is the Spirit who calls, quickens, energizes and equips the various ministries in the Church and every member of the Body of Christ according to their particular place (Acts 13:1-3; 15:28; 20:28; I Corinthians 12:8-11; Ephesians 4:8-12; I Peter 1:12; I Corinthians 2:1-5; Acts 1:8).

Thus as Jesus Christ, the Head of the Body was under total control and domination of the Spirit, and the Spirit was able to flow freely in perfect and unhindered operation, so this is to be manifested in the Church as the visible and mystical Body of Christ in the earth.

D. The Holy Spirit in the World
The work of the Holy Spirit is summarized clearly in John 16:9-11. The Holy Spirit has come with a three-fold ministry in relation to the world; to reprove the world of sin, righteousness and judgement.

1. Of Sin: because they believe not on Christ. The damnable sin is that of unbelief. It is the root sin of all others. This area of reproof or conviction especially deals with the sin of man.

2. Of Righteousness: because Jesus Christ has gone to the Father and at present we do not see Him. This area of conviction involves the righteousness of Christ, as the Savior of men.

3. Of Judgement: because the prince of this world, Satan, was judged at Calvary. This area of conviction involves the judgement of Satan and his hosts and their defeat at Calvary.

The Work of the Holy Spirit in relation to the unconverted is to convince, convict and convert.

An example of this convicting work is seen in Paul's ministry before Felix, when Felix trembled as Paul reasoned with him of "righteousness, temperance and judgement to come"(Acts 24:25) (Acts 1:5-8; 2:37-42; 4:4; 7:51-59; Genesis 6:3).

VI. SYMBOLS OF THE HOLY SPIRIT
Because of the various operations and manifestations of the Holy Spirit's work and ministry, it has pleased the Father that the Spirit be symbolized. These varied symbols set forth the nature, character and function of the Spirit, even as do the symbols of Jesus Christ, the Son of God.

A. Water
(John 7:38,39; 4:4; Psalm 72:6; 87:7; Isaiah 44:3; Exodus 17:6 with I Corinthians 10:4)

The Spirit symbolized as water speaks of the life-giving flow which refreshes and satisfies. It also speaks of washing, cleansing, and fruitfulness.

B. Fire
(Matthew 3:11; Acts 2:3; Isaiah 4:4; Exodus 19:18; Malachi 3:2,3; Hebrews 13:29)

This symbolizes the holiness of God whereby the Holy Spirit is sent forth in judgement to purge, purify, and enliven with zeal.

C. Wind or Breath
(Acts 2:2; John 3:8; Ezekiel 37:9-10; Isaiah 40:7).

These symbolize the life-giving breath of the God in its regenerating power. It underscores the fact that the Holy Spirit is invisible as a person, yet the effect of His work can be seen.

D. Dew
(Psalm 133:1-3; Hosea 14:5)

Dew only comes in the stillness of the night, bringing refreshing to the mown grass. So it is with the refreshing work of the Spirit in the Church.

E. Oil
(Luke 4:18; Acts 10:38; I John 2:20,27; Psalm 23:5)

Oil was distinctly involved in the anointing of the prophets priests and kings to their offices. It speaks of the consecration and supernatural enablement of the Spirit's anointing grace, the illumination of His teaching, the soothing and healing balm of His presence. It is the Spirit who anoints the members of the Church to their priestly functions.

F. The Dove
(Matthew 3:16; Luke 3:22; Genesis 1:2; Matthew 10:16)

The symbol of the dove is used to represent purity, beauty, gentleness and peace, the nature and character of the Holy Spirit.

G. The Seal
(Ephesians 1:13; II Corinthians 1:22; Ephesians 4:30; II Timothy 2:19)

A seal is significant of ownership, genuineness and security. This emphasizes the Spirit's activity confirming to us God's ownership of us, His authority over us and our security in Him.

H. The Still Small Voice
(Genesis 3:8; I Kings 19:11-13)

The Spirit is the voice of God within man bringing a revelation of God's will to him.

I. The Finger of God
(Luke 11:20; Matthew 12:28)

The Spirit is the one who points the accusing finger at the sinner, to bring about conviction with a view to the accused accepting Jesus Christ as his advocate.

J. The First Fruits
(Romans 8:23)

The first fruits were always symbolic of the full harvest to come, so the Spirit's initial work of regeneration points to the full salvation and glorification of the believer before God.

K. The Earnest
(II Corinthians 1:22; 5:5; Ephesians 1:13-14)

The earnest was always a downpayment, a pledge of more to come. So the Spirit's work in salvation is simply the pledge of full and total redemption to come. This symbol is similar to the first fruits.

L. Enduement
(Luke 24:49 with Judges 6:34; Isaiah 61:10)

The symbol of enduement means the clothing of the Spirit upon someone. The baptism of the Holy Spirit is this divine clothing from above. It is the believer's garment for ministry before the Lord.

M. The Number Seven
The number seven is used in relation to the Holy Spirit. It is a number symbolic of fulness, completeness and perfection. It represents the fulness and perfection of the Spirit's operation in the earth.

Three examples show this symbolic truth of the Spirit's work.

> **a. Seven Lamps** (Revelation 1:3-4; 4:5; 5:6) These are symbolic of the Spirit's illumination, revelation and inspiration. Lamps must have oil to have light (Proverbs 20:27).
>
> **b. Seven Horns** (Revelation 5:6) Horns are symbolic of power and defence. Seven horns speak of omnipotence; the Spirit is all-powerful.
>
> **c. Seven Eyes** (Revelation 5:6; Zechariah 3:9; 4:10) Eyes are symbolic of sight, insight, perception, intelligence and discernment. Seven eyes speak of the Spirit's omniscience, fulness and perfection of sight and insight.

VII. TITLES OF THE HOLY SPIRIT
Even as there are numerous names and titles of the Father and the Son in Scripture, so there are of the Holy Spirit. These titles set forth different aspects of the Spirit's character, functions or ministrations. Most of these titles refer to some specific work or operation that the Holy Spirit desires to perform in the hearts and lives of the people of God.

A. Titles of His Deity
This group of titles sets forth the deity of the Holy Spirit and shows His distinction from and association with the Father and Son. A number of them set forth the Spirit as representing either the Father or the Son, but all show His divinity.

1. The Spirit (John 3:6-8)
2. The Holy Spirit (Luke 11:13; Isaiah 63:11)
3. The Spirit of God (I Corinthians 3:16; 2:11)
4. The Spirit of the Lord God (Isaiah 61:1)
5. The Spirit of the Lord (Isaiah 63:14; Luke 4:18)
6. The Spirit of the Living God (II Corinthians 3:3)
7. The Spirit of the Father (Matthew 10:20; Matthew 16:17)
8. The Spirit of Jesus (Acts 16:6-7)
9. The Holy Spirit of God (Ephesians 4:30)
10. The Spirit of Christ (Romans 8:9; I Peter 1:11)
11. The Spirit of Jesus Christ (Philippians 1:19)
12. The Spirit of His Son (Galatians 4:6)
13. The Spirit which is of God (I Corinthians 2:12)

B. Titles of His Attributes and Ministry
This group of titles sets forth more particularly the essential and moral attributes of the Holy Spirit. Each of these attributes are related to some special need of man. It is the Holy Spirit who brings to us the wisdom, faith and power of God Almighty. All that is in God is brought to us by the Holy Spirit. He is to us all that we need.

1. The Spirit of Wisdom (Isaiah 11:2; Ephesians 1:17)
2. The Spirit of Knowledge (Isaiah 11:2)
3. The Spirit of Counsel and Might (Isaiah 11:2)
4. The Spirit of Grace and Supplications (Zechariah 12:10)
5. The Spirit of Judgement (Isaiah 4:4)
6. The Spirit of Burning (Isaiah 4:4)
7. The Breath of the Almighty (Job 32:8; 33:4)
8. The Spirit of Him who raised Jesus from the dead (Romans 8:11; I Peter 3:18)

9. The Power of the Highest (Luke 1:35)
10. The Eternal Spirit (Hebrews 9:14)
11. The Spirit of Holiness (Romans 1:4)
12. The Comforter (John 14:16,26; 15:26; 16:7)
13. The Spirit of love (II Timothy 1:7)
14. The Spirit of Truth (John 14:17; 16:13; 15:26; I John 4:6)
15. The Spirit of Life (Romans 8:2; Revelation 11:11)
16. The Spirit of Adoption (Romans 8:15)
17. The Spirit of Faith (II Corinthians 4:13)
18. The Spirit of Promise (Ephesians 1:13-14)
19. The Spirit of Grace (Zechariah 12:10; Hebrews 10:29)
20. The Spirit of Glory (I Peter 4:14)
21. The Spirit of Power (II Timothy 1:7)
22. The Spirit of Wisdom and Revelation (Ephesians 1:17)
23. The Spirit of Prophecy (Revelation 19:10)
24. The Good Spirit (Nehemiah 9:30; Psalm 143:10)
25. The Free Spirit (Psalm 51:12)
26. The Unction from the Holy One (I John 2:20)
27. The Anointing which teaches us (I John 2:27)
28. The Voice of the Lord (Ezekiel 1:24; Genesis 3:8; Isaiah 6:8)

In conclusion, we see the work of the Spirit in the New Testament is all that it was in the Old Testament, but more so, for now the Spirit is for all people, all believers out of every kindred, tongue, tribe and nation. The Holy Spirit not only "falls upon" (Acts 8:16; 10:44) is "poured out" (Acts 10:45); "comes" (Acts 19:6) but now He indwells, to remain and abide for ever within the heart of the redeemed. This is the promise of the Father to the Son, and the promise of the Son to the believer. The Holy Spirit as the Spirit of Promise brings all the promises of God to fulfilment in the redeemed community.

Chapter 6

THE DOCTRINE OF ANGELS

The Bible clearly teaches the existence of angels as mighty created spirit beings, whose chief duties are to worship and serve God. They are not a race, reproducing themselves, but are a company created to minister to the heirs of salvation. There are two classes of angels, elect and fallen, and man is forbidden to worship either.

CHAPTER OUTLINE

I. INTRODUCTION
II. THE EXISTENCE OF ANGELS
III. THE ORDER OF ANGELS
IV. THE NATURE OF ANGELS
V. THE CHARACTER OF ANGELS
VI. THE TITLES OF ANGELS
VII. THE SERAPHIM
VIII. THE CHERUBIM
IX. THE MINISTRY OF ANGELS
X. THE GODHEAD IN ANGELIC MANIFESTATION
XI. THE ANGEL OF THE LORD
XII. CONCLUSION

I. INTRODUCTION
The doctrine of angelology has been a neglected doctrine for the following reasons:

A. Ignorance concerning what the Scriptures teach on the subject.

B. Unbelief in the supernatural including the existence of angels (which was the doctrine of the Sadducees, Acts 23:8-9).

C. Fear or superstition concerning the unseen realm of spirit beings.

D. Undue adoration, prayer to and worship of angels by some.

The solution to this problem is to be found in a thorough searching of the Word of God. If all that the Bible reveals about angels were known and accepted, the unbelief, fear and undue adoration could be erased. Relying upon the opinions or subjective experiences of man is dangerous. Personal experiences with angels, though often genuine, are an insufficient foundation for building a doctrine upon. The only sure, inspired and infallible revelation upon which we can wholly depend, is the Word of God. All other teachings, subjective experiences or visions of angels, must be tested by it. The Word of God is the "final court of appeal" in all things. Isaiah the prophet put it this way, "To the Law and to the Testimony: if they (spirits from the unseen world) speak not according to this Word, it is because there is no light in them" (Isaiah 8:19-20).

II. THE EXISTENCE OF ANGELS
The Scriptures reveal that God has an everlasting kingdom, and in this kingdom there are created spirit beings called angels. These fall into two categories; good and evil angels. The good angels are concerned with our welfare, the evil are out to cause harm to the human race. There are about three hundred references to angels in the Bible which substantiate their existence. The Hebrew word for angel is "malak" and simply means "an agent, a messenger". It is generally translated "angel" or "messenger". The Greek word for angel is "angelos" which also means "messenger". These words are used of God, of men, and of the angelic beings. Only the surrounding context will clarify which is being referred to, but in most instances it is the angelic beings. In both the Old and New Testaments there are accounts of angels ministering to the people of God. Nearly all of the great men of the Bible exhibited a belief in the existence of angels. The Lord Jesus Christ Himself spoke often of the angels, and was also ministered to by them. (Mark 8:38; 13:32; Matthew 13:41; II Thessalonians 1:7; John 1:51; Hebrews 12:22)

III. THE ORDER OF ANGELS
God is a King who has a universal kingdom. In this kingdom there is divine order (Matthew 6:9-10; II Peter 1:11; Hebrews 12:28). This order seems to involve the Eternal Godhead as Father, Son and Holy Spirit and the various orders of angelic beings. Scripture speaks of archangels, principalities, powers, seraphim, cherubim, the Angel of the Lord and then also the myriads of angels.

A. The Godhead
The eternal Godhead is revealed as Father, Son and Holy Spirit, the Creator and Lord of angels, being worshipped and served by them (Matthew 28:19-20; Colossians 1:16; I Peter 3:22; Revelation 4:11).

B. The Archangels
Hebrew tradition states that there are twelve archangels which is the number of divine government. The whole context of Scripture relative to the number twelve would seem to confirm this tradition. Jesus said that He could have prayed to His Father and immediately be given twelve legions of angels to deliver Him from the multitude (Matthew 26:53). The extra-Biblical books of Enoch and Tobit give the names of seven of these archangels (Enoch 20:1-7; Tobit 12:15). However, the Scriptures specifically name only three that are generally accepted by expositors as archangels.

1. Lucifer
Lucifer means "Day Star", or "Light Bearer", or "Son of the Morning" (Isaiah 14:12-14; Ezekiel 28:11-17; Ephesians 2:2. Lucifer is seen as the archangel who was associated with the throne of God, as the leader of the worship of God among the angelic hosts. Through pride and rebellion he fell from this place. This will be considered under the Doctrine of Satan and Demonology.

2. Michael

Michael is specifically called an archangel. His name means "Who is like God" or "God-like". There are four special accounts of his activities (Daniel 10:21; 12:1-4; Jude 9: Revelation 12:7-9). Michael is the chief prince of the nation of Israel in the Old Testament. His activities are always seen in connection with warfare with Satan and with the resurrection of the body. Many expositors believe he is the archangel that comes with the Lord Jesus in His second advent relative to the resurrection of the saints and the change over from mortality to immortality of the living saints. (I Thessalonians 4:16)

3. Gabriel

Gabriel is generally accepted as an archangel. His name means "Strength of God". There are special occasions where Gabriel is mentioned, and it seems that Gabriel is a prophetic angel, the messenger and interpreter of the prophetic Word concerning the Christ of God. He appeared to Daniel twice and then to Zacharias, John the Baptist's father, and then to Mary, the virgin mother of Jesus. Each of these visitations involve Messianic revelation (Daniel 8:16-19; 9:1-27; 10:8-11; Luke 1:19,26). Gabriel stands in the presence of God and is seen in association with Michael, never with Lucifer

Some writers have suggested that these three archangels each had a third of the angels under them, and that when Lucifer fell, he took his third with him. The other two thirds remained faithful to God and His Word, under their archangels, Michael and Gabriel. It has also been suggested that these three archangels were the archangels of the Godhead, that is, representing the Godhead. Lucifer was the archangel of the Father, Michael the archangel of the Son, and Gabriel the archangel of the Holy Spirit. Their distinctive associations and ministries certainly lend weight to this opinion.

C. The Heavenly Sanhedrin

The Jewish Sanhedrin consisted of seventy elders of Israel, along with the High Priest who was the President. Dr. H. Lockyer quotes in "The Unseen Army" (p.10-11) that Jewish tradition also had seventy angels as princes over the seventy nations into which the human family was divided at the Tower of Babel. These 70 angels constituted the heavenly Sanhedrin. There does seem to be shadows of this on earth in the order of the seventies in Israel's history, and in New Testament revelation as well. Princes or angels of the nations are spoken of (Daniel 10:13, 20-21; Ephesians 3:10; 6:12; Colossians 2:15). Moses set 12 pillars up at Mt. Sinai and had 70 elders with him from the camp of Israel (Exodus 24:1-11). There were 12 wells of water and 70 palm trees at Elim which blessed the nation of Israel also (Exodus 15:27). The Jewish nation had 70 elders which comprised their council. The Lord Jesus chose 12 apostles, and then 70 others for the ministry of healing and preaching the Gospel of the Kingdom (Luke 9:1-2; 10:1-2). If this order was but the earthly shadow and manifestation of the heavenly pattern, then it indeed points to the 12 archangels and the 70 angels of the heavenly council or Sanhedrin.

D. The Multitude of the Angelic Hosts

The Scriptures clearly show that there are legions or myriads of angelic beings. They speak of thousands or multitudes of spirit beings who worship and serve God. (Daniel 7:9-10; Matthew 26:53; Luke 2:13; Hebrews 12:22; Revelation 5:11).

In the vast multitude of angelic hosts, Scripture reveals that there are two groups, elect and fallen angels.

1. **Elect angels** (I Timothy 5:21). These are the angels which did not follow Lucifer in his rebellion.

2. **Fallen angels** (II Peter 2:4; Jude 6,9). These are angels which fell by the sin of self-will. These will be considered under the Doctrine of Satan and Demonology.

Thus the heavenly order and pattern in the Kingdom of God may be understood by the earthly shadow and manifestation in the Kingdom of God on earth.

HEAVENLY ORDER	ISRAEL'S ORDER	N.T. ORDER
Father, Son, Spirit	Abraham, Isaac, Jacob	Father, Son, Spirit
12 Archangels	12 Sons of Israel	12 Apostles
70 Angels	70 Souls	70 Others
Multitude of	Multitude of	Multitude of
Angelic Hosts	Israel's Hosts	Believers in Church

The Scriptures speak of principalities, powers, rulers and wicked spirits in the Kingdom of Satan, which is simply a counterfeit of God's Kingdom. Hence we have some clues as to what the divine order seems to be (Ephesians 1:21; 3:10; 6:12; Colossians 1:16; 2:10,15; I Peter 3:21-22; Romans 8:38).

IV. THE NATURE OF ANGELS

A. **Angels are Created Beings** (Psalm 148:2,5; Colossians 1:16; Revelation 4:11). Angels were created by God, and for God's pleasure. Because angels are created beings, owing their very existence to God, they are finite, limited and dependent beings. They are not eternal, nor self-existent, though they have eternal life given to them by God. Scripture does not tell us exactly when angels were created. It can be assumed, however, that it was early in creation because they sang and shouted for joy at the foundation of the earth (Job 38:4-7).

B. **Angels are Spirit Beings** (Hebrews 1:13-14; 12:22-23; Psalm 104:4; Colossians 1:16). God, who is Spirit, created angelic spirit beings. These angels are ministering spirits, as flames of fire. Because they are spirit beings, they are not limited to the physical or material realm as man is (cf. Luke 24:39) but neither are they omnipresent as God. At times, angels under God could assume human form and perform human deeds (Psalm 78:25; Genesis 18:8; 19:3).

C. **Angels are Immortal** (Luke 20:34-36; I Timothy 6:16). God, the Creator, is immortal and so are the angels. They derive their immortality from God. They are not subject to physical death, as is man, though sometimes permitted to assume human form or appearance.

D. **Angels are a Company** (Luke 20:34-35; Matthew 22:30; Hebrews 2:16). Angels are a company of beings, not a race. That is to say, they are not involved in marriage. Though spoken of in the masculine gender, angels are sexless. They do not reproduce or propagate their kind, as does the human race. They were created as individual spirit beings. The angels which sinned each sinned as individuals, therefore sin is not transmitted as it is in the human race from Adam to his unborn offspring.

E. **Angels are Innumerable** (Daniel 7:9-10; Luke 2:13; Psalm 148: 2-6; Job 25:3; Psalm 68:17; Hebrews 12:22; II Kings 6:17; Revelation 5:11). The angels are an innumerable host, as far as man is concerned. They are as myriad as the stars of light. Only God knows their number. Jesus spoke of "legions of angels" (Matthew 26:53).

F. **Angels are Higher than Man** (Psalm 8:1-4; 103:20; Hebrews 2:7). In the order of created beings, angels are the first before man. The Scriptures show that man was made a little lower than the angels. Man is a triune being consisting of spirit, soul and body, whereas the angels are spirit beings, thus of a higher order. However, angels are not heirs of God as believers are. God is their Creator, but not their Father, as He is of believers. Angels are superior to man, but inferior to Christ who created them. (Hebrews 1:5; 2:6).

G. **Angels are a Freewill Creation** (Isaiah 14:12-14; II Peter 2:4; Jude 6,9) Angels, as men, were created with a free will, having the power of choice. The very fact that some angels sinned shows they all had the power of choice and could either choose to do God's will, or to follow Satanic self-will.

H. **Angels are Personalities** (Matthew 18:10; Psalm 103:20-21; Revelation 4:8) As God is a person, having all the attributes and qualities of personality, so are the angels. They are not mere good or evil influences, but are real personalities, having intelligence and will. Though they have their own character, they are not glorified human beings. Redeemed sinners will never become angels, only like them (Matthew 22:30).

I. Angels are Invisible (Colossians 1:16). As spirit beings, angels are also invisible, though at time they can become visible to human eyes. Once the redeemed are glorified, and the veil of sin is removed, they will be able to see the angelic spirits.

V. THE CHARACTER OF ANGELS

A. Their Worship (Psalm 103:20; Nehemiah 9:6; Hebrews 1:6; Matthew 22:30; Psalm 29:1,2; Luke 2:13; Revelation 4:8; 5:11; Luke 2:13). Elect and holy angels never accept worship of man, though fallen angels seek to be worshipped. Elect angels direct all worship to God and are symbolic of the "church in heaven" (Hebrews 12:22-24). They are worshippers.

B. Their obedience (Matthew 6:10; 26:53; I Peter 3:22; Psalm 103:20-21; Jude 6). The obedience of the elect angels is immediate and unquestioningly perfect. Fallen angels disobeyed God's will and word.

C. Their Wisdom (II Samuel 14:17; 19:27; Ephesians 3:9-10; Matthew 24:36). Angels are wise, but not all-wise, as God is. Their wisdom has increased over the ages of time as they have beheld the dealings of an all-wise God.

D. Their Knowledge (Mark 13:32; I Peter 1:12) Their knowledge, like their wisdom, has increased through the ages also. However, though having wisdom and knowledge, they are not omniscient.

E. Their Meekness (II Peter 2:11; Jude 9) Angels bear in their character the meekness of God. Fallen angels rose up in pride. Elect angels have meekness and humility.

F. Their Strength (Psalm 103:20; II Peter 2:11; II Kings 19:35; Revelation 18:1,21; II Thessalonians 1:7; Acts 5:19; 12:7,23; Matthew 28:2; II Kings 6:17). These Scriptures give examples of the strength and power of angels. One angel slew 185,000 Assyrians in one night when delivering King Hezekiah from danger. Angels, however mighty, are not almighty. They are not omnipotent.

G. Their Holiness (Revelation 14:10; Mark 8:38). Angels possess the attribute of derived holiness. The elect angels, after their probationary period and their victory over Lucifer's appeal to self-will, now have sinless perfection from which it is impossible to fall.

H. Their Patience (Numbers 22:22-35; Matthew 18:10). The angels have the quality of patience, as they wait before God, and do his bidding.

I. Their Modesty (I Corinthians 11:10). Angels are reserved and decent in their behavior before God and those that are heirs of salvation.

J. Their Ability (I Corinthians 13:1). Angels, when sent by God to various persons on earth can speak the languages needed to communicate God's message. They can speak the tongues of men or of angels. Their linguistic ability is seen here.

K. Their Joy (Luke 15:10; I Corinthians 4:9; Job 38:7). Angels rejoiced at the creation of the earth. They also rejoice over God's new creation, repentant sinners.

L. Their Clothing (Revelation 15:1-8). Angels are generally spoken of as being clothed in white raiment, or raiment that is bright as light. No darkness is in them. They are clear and transparent before a holy God.

VI. THE TITLES OF ANGELS

Angels are known by various titles. Just as various titles and names of God are used to bring out various aspects of His nature, being and ministry, so are the designations by which the angels are known.

A. **Watchers** (Daniel 4:13-23; Isaiah 62:6; I Corinthians 4:9). Angels behold this earth as a theatre. They are ever awake. *WATCHMEN*

B. **Gods** (Psalm 8:5; 29:1-2; 97:7). This Hebrew word "Elohim" is used of angels as of God because they are like God as spirit beings. The same word is also used of man. (Psalm 82:6; John 10:33-34).

C. **Hosts of God** (Psalm 33:6; 103:21; Luke 2:13; I Kings 22:19; II Kings 6:17; Daniel 7:10; Nehemiah 9:6; Deuteronomy 17:3). Significant of the armies of God, the heavenly host.

D. **Saints** (Deuteronomy 33:2; Jude 14). Saints means "Holy Ones". It is used both of angels and men (Zechariah 14:5; Matthew 25:31; Daniel 8:13).

E. **Ministering Spirits** (Hebrews 1:13-14; Psalm 103:21). They are the servants of the Creator. Angels, though intermediaries, are not mediators. There is only one Mediator between God and Man, the Man Christ Jesus (I Timothy 2:5; John 14:1,6). Angels are ministering spirits, servants of the Most High God.

F. **Flames of Fire** (Psalm 104:4; Hebrews 12:29). Significant of the holiness of God upon them. Fire is the symbol of divine holiness and burning against sin.

G. **The Elect** (I Timothy 5:21). The angels who refused to follow Satan are now the elect angels. Christ and the saints are also called the elect of God (Luke 18:7; I Corinthians 4:9). The fallen angels are not elect (II Peter 2:4; Jude 6).

H. **Sons of God** (Job 1:6; 2:1; 38:7). It is generally accepted that it is angels that are here referred to as the sons of God. They are created sons of God, not begotten sons of God, as are born again believers.

I. **Morning Stars** (Job 38:7; Isaiah 12:12-14). Angels are as stars of light. Lucifer was the Day-star before his fall. He became a falling star when he sinned against God. God likens both angels and believers to stars (Revelation 1:20).

J. **Sons of the Mighty** (Psalm 89:6; 82:1). The angels are also spoken of as Mighty Ones (Psalm 29:1; Isaiah 13:3)

K. **Angels** (Hebrews 12:22; Psalm 103:20). The word angel simply means agent, or messenger. Angels are God's messengers.

L. **Princes** (Daniel 10:13,20,21; 12:1) Angels are designated as princes over the various nations. Satan is spoken of as being a prince over the world system, and also as having his princes over the nations (John 12:31; 14:30; 16:11; Ephesians 2:2; Colossians 1:16; 2:10,15; Ephesians 1:21; 3:10; 6:12; I Peter 3:22). They are also called principalities.

M. **Thrones** (Colossians 1:16; Romans 8:38). Thrones are symbolic of the rulership of certain angels in God's order.

N. **Dominions** (Colossians 1:16). Dominions speak of lordships or spheres of influence as under the Lord of Angels, Jesus Christ.

O. **Powers** (Colossians 1:16). Powers speak of authorities or administration which God has given to various angels.

NOTE: The word "angel" is used in Scripture of various groupings of persons, and only the immediate context will determine who the "angel-messenger" referred to may be. The references fall into three categories:

1. The Lord Jesus is revealed as the Angel of the Lord (Exodus 3:2-15; 32:34). (Refer to "Angel of the Lord" comments)

2. Ministers of the churches or God's prophets are also spoken of as being "angels" (Revelation 1:1,20; 2:1,8,12; 19:10; 22:16). Israel was God's messenger (Isaiah 42:19). Haggai the prophet was God's messenger (Haggai 1:13). John the Baptist was spoken of as the "Messenger of the Lord" (Malachi 2:7), and Jesus Christ Himself is spoken of as "The Messenger of the Covenant" (Malachi 3:1). The

language used in Revelation concerning "the angels of the seven churches" is inapplicable to angelic spirit beings unless they are fallen angels (II Samuel 19:27; Galatians 4:14).

3. Angelic beings are also God's messengers (Psalm 68:17; 104:4).

Thus only the context will give clues of identification as to which "angel-messenger" is being spoken of.

VII. THE SERAPHIM (Isaiah 6:1-7)
There is only one Scripture reference to the angelic beings called Seraphim. The title interpreted means "The Burning Ones". They are especially seen in relation to the throne and holiness of God. The Seraphim have six wings: two to cover their feet (significant of holy service); two to cover their face (significant of their awe and reverence), and two to fly with (significant of their obedience to God's will). Their constant cry "Holy, Holy, Holy is the Lord of Hosts, the whole earth is full of His glory" magnifies the thrice-holy God. It speaks of the Father, Son and Holy Spirit in absolute holiness of nature and being (Psalm 24:1; 72:19). The Seraphim also ministered the coal of cleansing from the altar to the lips of the prophet Isaiah. Jesus said that the vision Isaiah saw was of the Messiah Himself (John 12:37-41).

VIII. THE CHERUBIM
Though different, the revelation of the Cherubim seems to be linked with that of the Seraphim. The revelation of the Cherubim is much fuller than that of the Seraphim and the Scriptures concerning them seem to fall into three main streams of thought.

A. The Cherubim are Angels
Many expositors hold that the Cherubim are a distinct order of angelic beings, different from the Seraphim, though similar.

B. The Cherubim are the Godhead
H. Lockyer in "The Unseen Army" (p.25), along with other writers, suggests that the Cherubim are representatives or symbolic of the blessed Godhead with the human nature taken into the divine essence.

This seems to be consistent with the full revelation of the Cherubim in Scripture. They generally seem to be symbolic of the Father and the Holy Spirit in association with the Son of God, relative to the plan of redemption.

1. The Cherubim were associated with the Tabernacle in Eden and the Flaming Sword (Genesis 3:24).

2. The Cherubim were inwrought within the veil of the tabernacle of Moses (Exodus 26:1,31; 36:8,35; Hebrews 9:5; 10:19-20).

3. The Cherubim were part of the gold mercy seat on the Ark of the Covenant, in which the Shekinah Glory of God dwelt. (Exodus 25:17-22; I Samuel 4:4; II Samuel 6:1-2 with Romans 3:25).

4. The two great olive Cherubim overshadowed the Ark of the Covenant in Solomon's Temple (I Kings 6:23-35; 7:29,36; 8:6-7; II Chronicles 3:7-14; 5:7-8).

The central one is identified as the Lord Jesus Christ. He is the Flaming Sword, the Inwrought Veil, the Ark of the Convenant, the Blood–Stained Mercy Seat, and the Father and the Spirit are always seen in association with the Son in the work of redemption. The Cherubim are generally seen in association with the eternal Son of God (Numbers 7:89; Psalm 80:1; 99:1; II Kings 19:15; II Samuel 6:2). Though the angels desire to look into the mystery of salvation they are not an integral part of redemption's work (I Peter1:12).

C. The Cherubim are Saints
The third opinion that is held by some expositors is that the Cherubim, especially those seen in vision by Ezekiel and John, are symbolic of the redeemed saints (Ezekiel 1:1-28; 10:1-22; 11:22 with Revelation 4:6-9; 5:9-12). There is no doubt that the Cherubim (or Living Creatures, or Beasts) of Ezekiel and Revelation are connected by many similarities. They are more symbolic of redeemed men in these visions. The details suggest that they are redeemed men representing the redeemed out of every

kindred, tongue, tribe and nation. Man was made a little lower than the angels, yet by redemption's plan, he will be lifted above the angels. The living creatures sing redemption's song, which the angels cannot do.

The Cherubim are also associated with the Throne and Glory of God. Each have the face of a man, a lion, an ox and an eagle, which are symbolic of the saints redeemed from the earth. The Hebrew writers say that the four faces represent the four standards of Israel under which the twelve tribes of Israel gathered (Numbers 2-3). The early Church Fathers likened the four Gospels to the four faces of the Cherubim or Living Creatures.

Gospel of **Matthew**	Face of the **Lion**	King of Wild Beasts
Gospel of **Mark**	Face of the **Ox**	King of Domestic Beasts
Gospel of **Luke**	Face of the **Man**	King of Creation
Gospel of **John**	Face of the **Eagle**	King of Birds

If the Cherubim are symbolic of the image of God, and the Cherubim in Ezekiel and the Living Creatures in Revelation are redeemed men, then it signifies that man by redemption is restored to the image of God, from which he fell, through Jesus Christ. It is probable that this is the truth symbolized in the Cherubim (Genesis 1:26; Romans 8:26-28). Man is to be restored to the image of God through Christ.

IX. THE MINISTRY OF ANGELS

The ministry and function of angels is primarily twofold: worship and service (Revelation 4:11; Hebrews 1:13-14). The elect angels are "ministering spirits sent forth to them who are the heirs of salvation" (Hebrews 1:13-14; Psalm 103:20-21). Jesus said that the angels of God ascend and descend upon the Son of Man, who is the fulfilment of Jacob's ladder. Thus they minister to those who, like Jacob, are the heirs of salvation (John 1:51; Genesis 28:11-12; Matthew 18:10). Angels have access to both heaven and earth. The angels have been given a charge over the saints to keep them in all their ways (Psalm 91:11-12). The angels behold the Father's face as guardian angels (Matthew 18:10). When the saints gather together, it includes the angels as well as the spirits of just men made perfect (Hebrews 12:22-24). If the Lord were to open our eyes we would behold this innumerable company of God's hosts surrounding us for our protection and well-being (II Kings 6:15-17).

Both the Old and New Testaments give abundant evidence of angelic appearances and ministry to the saints.

A. The Old Testament
1. An angel ministered to Hagar and Ishmael (Genesis 16:10; 21:17).
2. Three angels visited Abraham and Sarah (Genesis 18:2).
3. Two angels rescued Lot out of Sodom from the fire and brimstone (Genesis 19:1-24).
4. The Angel of the Lord called to Abraham to spare Isaac his only begotten son, and offer a ram in his stead (Genesis 22:11-15).
5. Jacob experienced the ministry of angels throughout his life (Genesis 28:12; 31:11; 32:1; 48:16).
6. The Angel of the Covenant wrestled with Jacob and changed his name to Israel (Genesis 32:24-32; Hosea 12:4).
7. Moses received the revelation of the Name of God from the Angel of the Lord in the burning bush (Exodus 3:2).
8. Angels were involved in the giving of the Law to Moses at Sinai (Deuteronomy 33:2; Psalm 68:17; Acts 7:35,38,53; Galatians 3:19; Hebrews 2:2).
9. The Angel of His Presence went before Israel to lead and guide them in the cloudy pillar of fire (Exodus 14:19-24; Numbers 20:16; Exodus 23:20; 32:34; 33:2).
10. God sent an angel to warn the prophet Balaam of his disobedience (Numbers 22:30-35).
11. An angel reproved Israel for their compromise and idolatry among the Canaanites (Judges 2:1-4).
12. An angel uttered a curse on those who did not help the Lord in the battle against Israel's enemies (Judges 5:23).
13. The Angel of the Lord encamps around them that fear Him (Psalm 34:7; 35:5-6).
14. An angel destroyed 70,000 Israelites when David sinned in numbering the people without the atonement money (II Samuel 24:16-17; I Chronicles 21:12-30).
15. Elijah was strengthened by an angel who brought food and drink to him. The angel also gave

instruction to him (I Kings 19:5-7; II Kings 1:3,15).

16. God permitted an angel to slay 185,000 Assyrians in one night in judgement (II Kings 19:35; Isaiah 37:36).

17. Daniel was preserved by an angel in the lion's den (Daniel 6:22).

18. The three Hebrew youths were preserved in the fiery furnace by an angel (Daniel 3:20-28).

19. The Angel of the Lord brought interpretative visions and revelation to the young prophet, Zechariah (Zechariah 1:9, 11,19; 2:3; 3:1-6; 4:1-5; 5:5,10; 6:4-5 with Job 33:23).

20. Angels hear the vows that God's people make in the house of the Lord (Ecclesiastes 5:6).

21. The Angel of the Lord appeared to Gideon (Judges 6:11-22) to Manoah (Judges 13:1-21); to Elijah (I Kings 19:5-7), as well as to others. (Refer to "The Angel of the Lord" for further detail)

22. Angel-Princes are over the various nations (Ephesians 2:2; 6:12; Daniel 10:13,20,21; 12:1; John 14:30; II Samuel 24:16-17).

23. Angels were used in judgement and blessing. The same angel that passed over the house of the Israelites that had the sprinkled blood on the door also smote the firstborn of the Egyptians (Exodus 12:18-30).

24. Angels as God's messengers did God's bidding on earth, as well as in the heavens (Psalm 103:20-21).

The Old Testament is indeed replete with angelic ministrations to the heirs of salvation, as well as ministering the judgements of God upon the wilful and rebellious who refused to response to God's dealings.

B. The New Testament

The New Testament also contains many references to angelic ministry. These are seen in the life of the Lord Jesus in the Gospels, then in the Early Church in the Book of Acts and the Epistles, and then it consummates in the Book of Revelation.

1. In the Ministry of the Lord Jesus

As God manifest in the flesh, He was "seen of angels" (I Timothy 3:16; I Peter 1:12). The angels desired to look into the mystery of redemption's plan, and they were ever ready and available to minister to the Lord Jesus. They were created by Him, and for Him, and thus ministered to Him.

a. In His Birth

(1) Angels spoke to Mary (Luke 1:26-38; Matthew 1:21-23).
(2) Angels spoke to Joseph (Matthew 1:20-21; 2:13,19).
(3) Angels spoke to the shepherds (Luke 2:13-15).

b. In His Temptation

Angels ministered to Christ after his temptation (Matthew 4:11; Luke 4:10; Mark 1:13 with Psalm 91:11-12).

c. In His Ministry

Angels ascended and descended upon the Son of Man in ministry (John 1:51).

d. In His Intercession

An angel strengthened Christ inwardly in Gethsemane. Twelve legions of angels were available if He requested help (Luke 22:43; Matthew 26:53).

e. In His Resurrection

Two angels were seen in His empty tomb after the resurrection. An angel rolled the stone away to let the disciples into the tomb (Matthew 28:2-7; Luke 24:23; John 20:12).

f. In His Ascension

Two men in shining garments spoke to the disciples of His ascension and coming again. No doubt there were angels who accompanied Jesus up into heaven (Acts 1:10-11; Luke 24:50-51).

g. In His Advent

Angels will attend Christ in His second coming. They will gather the elect and separate the wicked from them (Matthew 16:27; 25:31; 13:41-43; I Thessalonians 4:16; II Thessalonians 1:7-9; Matthew 24:36).

2. In the Early Church

a. An angel opened the prison doors to release the apostles to witness (Acts 5:19).

b. Philip was sent by an angel to the desert to witness to the Ethiopian (Acts 8:26).

c. An angel instructed Cornelius to send for Peter to hear the words of the Gospel (Acts 10:3,30-32).

d. The angel rescued Peter out of prison the night before he was to be slain (Acts 12:5-11).

e. Herod was smitten dead by an angel for his pride (Acts 12:23).

f. Paul experienced the presence of the angel in the storm on his way to Rome (Acts 27:23).

g. The saints are to judge the angels in due time (I Corinthians 6:3).

h. The saints are forbidden to worship angels (Colossians 2:18; Revelation 22:8-9). All angels were created by Christ to worship him. Only fallen angels seek the worship that rightly belongs to God (Hebrews 1:5; 2:6).

i. Angelic spirits are round about the Church as believers gather to worship Christ (Hebrews 12:22-24; I Corinthians 11:10; 4:9; Ephesians 3:10; I Timothy 5:21).

j. The final ministry of angels is to escort the departed spirit of the saint to Paradise, the immediate presence of God (Luke 16:22; Psalm 91:11-12; Hebrews 1:13-14; Psalm 34:7; Luke 24:50-51). Consider these scriptures in the light of the bodily translation of Enoch, Elijah, and Jesus (II Kings 2:1-11). The Chariots of God are symbolic of divine and angelic transport of the saints.

k. The Scriptures do imply that all have a guardian angel (Matthew 18:10 with Acts 12:5-16).

Thus even though modern day Sadducees may not believe in angels (Acts 23:8), the Bible clearly shows their glorious ministry to the church.

3. The Angels and the Gospel
The angels are never permitted to preach the Gospel to sinners because they can never experience being redeemed from sin. Peter tells us that the angels desire to look into the mystery of our great salvation as foretold by the Old Testament prophets (I Peter 1:9-12). However, God did use the angels to make special announcements relative to the Gospel.

a. The Angel Gabriel announced the birth of Messiah's forerunner to Zacharias (Luke 1:5-25).

b. The Angel Gabriel also announced to the virgin Mary, the birth of the Christ-child, and gave her the name for the baby, Jesus (Luke 1:26-35).

c. Joseph was told by an angel of the incarnation of the Christ-child in his espoused wife, Mary (Matthew 1:18-25).

d. Gabriel had also foretold to Daniel the notable 70 Week Prophecy which involved the coming of the Messiah, and His crucifixion (Daniel 9:24-27).

e. The shepherds in the field heard the angelic announcement of the birth of Jesus and the heavenly host worshipping God. The angel announced the good tidings that the Savior had been born (Luke 2:10-11).

f. The angel could not preach the Gospel to the Ethiopian but did tell Philip where to go in the desert, so he could preach it (Acts 8:26).

g. It was an angel who appeared to Cornelius to send for Peter who would give him "words whereby he could be saved" (Acts 10:1-4,22,44-46; 11:13-14).

h. It was an angel who told Paul that he would testify before Caesar at Rome (Acts 27:23).

Thus the burden of the Gospel is upon those who are redeemed from sin. Angels may give the announcements pertaining to the good tidings, but redeemed sinners must preach it. Then the angels can rejoice greatly when they see sinners respond to the Gospel in true repentance (Luke 15:10).

4. Angels in the Book of Revelation

The Book of Revelation reveals an active involvement of angels prior to the second coming, as well as at the coming of Christ.

a. Innumerable angels worship God and the Lamb (Revelation 5:11).

b. Four angels restrain the winds of judgement blowing upon the earth until the sealing of God's servants (Revelation 7:1).

c. Seven angels sound the seven trumpets of judgement (Revelation 8:2,7,8,10,12; 9:1,13; 11:15).

d. Michael and his angels engage in war with Satan and his angels and cast them out (Revelation 12:7-10).

e. Angelic ministry is evident in the judgements of the earth (Revelation 14:6,8,9,15,17,18,19).

f. An angel announces the fall of Babylon (Revelation 14:8)

g. An angel announces the everlasting Gospel of judgement, warning the earth-dwellers not to take the mark of the beast (Revelation 14:6,9).

h. The wicked are to be tormented in the presence of the Lamb and the holy angels, whose mercy and ministry they have spurned (Revelation 14:10).

i. Angels are used as harvesters in the time of the end, both of the good and the evil (Revelation 14:17-19 with Matthew 13:24-30, 36-43; 13:49-50). These harvests are symbolized under wheat and tares; good and evil fish; and wheat and wine harvests.

j. Angels pour out the seven vials of judgement on unrepentant mankind (Revelation 15-16).

k. An angel reveals the harlot and the bride to John (Revelation 17:1-7; 21:9).

l. John saw an angel standing in the sun calling for the birds and beasts to the supper of the wicked (Revelation 19:17).

m. A mighty and great Angel binds Satan in the bottomless pit for 1000 years (Revelation 20:1-4).

n. The angels will be associated with Christ in the gathering of the redeemed of earth at His second coming (Matthew 16:27; 24:31,36; 25:31; Mark 8:38; 13:27; II Thessalonians 1:7).

There was much angelic activity in New Testament times and Scripture seems to indicate that the Church can expect much more in these last days leading up to the second coming of Christ. Eternity alone will reveal how much ministry angels have rendered to the redeemed of all ages.

X. The Godhead and Angelic Manifestation

It seems evident in the Old Testament that the Godhead was revealed in angelic form occasionally and were called "angels" or "men". God assumed the "form" of angelic manifestation until the incarnation, when the Son would take upon Himself the "form" of man. If God could assume the form of man, who was made a little lower than the angels, then He could certainly assume the form of angels, who were made a little lower than God. Concerning the manifestation of the eternal Son of God in angelic form, there seems to be no doubt among expositors. Here we add the scriptures which imply the appearance of the Godhead in angelic manifestation.

A. The Father (Genesis 18:1-22)

Three men called "Adonai" (plural Hebrew word "Lords") appeared to Abraham in the heat of the day. Abraham stood before one of these angels called "the LORD" (verses 22,33) and made intercession for Sodom and Gommorrah, and especially for his nephew's family. At this time two of these angels went to Sodom to save Lot and his family (Genesis 19:1). Some Hebrew believers see these three angels as a manifestation of the Godhead. In Genesis 19:14,16,24 the three angels are called "Lord". The two angels, also called "men" referred to the fact that "the LORD rained fire and brimstone from the LORD out of heaven" (compare this with Psalm 110:1). Many expositors hold that the angel before which Abraham stood and made intercession was the Father God manifest in angelic form.

B. The Son (Judges 6:11-22; 13:3-21)

Found in Scripture is the frequent manifestation of an angel referred to as the Angel of the Lord, or the Jehovah Angel. This Angel was a manifestation of the eternal Son of God before His incarnation. These manifestations of the Son in angelic form are spoken of as theophanies or Christophanies. The Lord Jesus was "The Messenger (Angel) of the Covenant" (Malachi 3:1). Because this is dealt with much in Scripture, it is considered more fully in the final section of this chapter.

C. The Holy Spirit

A serious consideration of several scriptures in the following passages point to the Holy Spirit appearing in angelic form also. The Holy Spirit was manifested in the Cloudy Pillar, the Shekinah Glory, in the form or shape of a dove, and in some references in the form of an angel. If the three angels revealed to Abraham as the LORD was indeed a manifestation of the Godhead, then one of the angels was the Holy Spirit (Genesis 18:1-4). The Lord spoke to Moses concerning the angel which was to lead Israel to Canaan Land. The name of God was in Him, and He would not pardon Israel's transgressions or sins (Exodus 23:20-25 with Matthew 12:31-32). The language concerning not pardoning transgressions certainly is applicable to the Holy Spirit. The prophet Isaiah speaks of "The Angel of His Presence" which led Israel through the Red Sea and the Cloudy Pillar of Fire (Isaiah 63:9-10). The Holy Spirit can certainly be identified with "the presence of God."

These scriptures point to the manifestation of the Godhead in angelic form. However, the most prominent manifestation is that of the Angel of the Lord, the pre-incarnate Christ of God.

XI. The Angel of the Lord

The final area pertaining to Angelology is that which concerns the mysterious revelation of the Angel of the Lord. It is especially in the Old Testament that we find the appearance of this angel spoken of as the Angel of the Lord, or more correctly, "The Jehovah Angel". Some expositors understand these appearances often to be a theophany or an appearance of the Lord Jesus Christ before His incarnation. A close study of the context and its details will help the student to determine whether this is so or not. Also, the distinction between a theophany and the incarnation of the Lord Jesus Christ will help one's understanding of these appearances.

A. Incarnation

The meaning of the word incarnation is "God clothing Himself with flesh". God clothed Himself in human form in Christ. He was God manifest in the flesh (I Timothy 3:16). When the eternal Son of God was born of the virgin Mary, it was not a mere temporary theophany, it was an incarnation. He is now eternally clothed with a human body. A theophany was a temporary manifestation of God the Son before the cross. The incarnation is the eternal manifestation of God the Son. A theophany was assumed human form, and then dissolved. The incarnation was begotten and born human form, and then, after the resurrection, eternally glorified. Glorified humanity is upon the Christ of God, the eternal Son.

B. Theophany

This word comes from two Greek words: "Theos" meaning "God" and "phaneroo", meaning "appearance". A theophany is simply an appearance of God and more particularly in the Old Testament, a theophany was an appearance of the Son of God before His incarnation. A theophany was a temporary manifestation in human form. Theophanies are also spoken of as being Christophanies, Old Testament appearances of the pre-incarnate Christ.

A theophany was a pre-cross manifestation and revelation of the Lord Jesus Christ before His incarnation. It was anticipatory of His incarnation (John 1:1-3; 14-18).

(a) The Lord Jesus Christ, the uncreated and eternal Son of God, took upon Himself the nature and form of angels, and was revealed as the Angel of the Lord until He took upon Himself the nature and form of man in the virgin birth (Hebrews 2:16; I Timothy 3:16; John 1:1-3, 14-18). Following is a list of the prominent revelations of the Angel of the Lord. Most of them, by their context, point to the pre-incarnate Christ of God.

Jesus Christ (a) form & nature of angel
It is the 'form of man' or human (b) " " " " man
which is raised & now glorified. Glorified humanity became
[illegible] these angels

1. The Lord appeared to Adam (Genesis 2:16; 3:15). He foretold the coming incarnation as the seed of the woman.

2. The Lord translated Enoch to heaven (Genesis 5:24).

3. The Lord spoke to Noah (Genesis 6:9).

4. Abraham received the call of the Lord, or Jehovah Jireh (Genesis 12:1; 22:11-15).

5. The Angel of the Lord ministered to Hagar and Ishmael (Genesis 16:7-11; 21:17).

6. It was the Angel who went before Abraham's servant to prepare the Bride for Isaac (Genesis 24:7,40).

7. Jacob wrestled with the person spoken of as an Angel, a man, and God, and whose name was a wonderful secret (Genesis 31:11; 32:24-32; Hosea 12:3-5). This Angel redeemed Jacob (Genesis 48:16).

8. The Angel in the burning bush who called to Moses was certainly a revelation of the Lord God. He is spoken of as the Angel, whose name is I AM THAT I AM, or the LORD GOD (Jehovah Elohim) (Exodus 3:2,14-15; Numbers 20:16; Acts 7:30,35).

9. There was the revelation of the Angel in the cloudy pillar, leading and guiding Israel to the promised land (Exodus 14:19-24; 32:34; 33:2).

10. The Jehovah Angel gave the Law to Moses, amidst angelic hosts (Acts 7:35,38,53; Galatians 3:19; Hebrews 2:2).

11. Balaam saw the Angel of the Lord with the drawn sword (Numbers 22:22-35; II Peter 2:15).

12. The Captain of the Lord's Hosts who appeared to Joshua was a Christophany (Joshua 5:13-14; with Hebrews 2:10).

13. The Angel warned Israel concerning the disobedience (Judges 2:1-4; 5:23).

14. Gideon was equipped by the Angel of the Lord, whose name was Jehovah our Peace (Judges 6:11-22).

15. Manoah and his wife, the parents of Samson, had a revelation of the Christ of God. This mysterious person is spoken of, in the context, as a man, an angel, and the Lord. His name was Wonderful, or a Wonderful Secret (Judges 13:3-21).

16. God sent an Angel to destroy 70,000 Israelites when David sinned in numbering the people (I Chronicles 21:12-30; II Samuel 24:16-17).

17. An Angel ministered food to Elijah (I Kings 19:5-7; II Kings 1:3,15).

18. The Angel of the Lord slew 185,000 Assyrians in one night, thus saving Judah (II Kings 19:35; Isaiah 37:36).

19. The Lord appeared to Isaiah in vision (Isaiah 6:1-13) with John 12:39-41).

20. The appearance of the fourth man in the fiery furnace is also accepted as a theophany, or Christophany. Nebuchadnezzar spoke of Him as the Son of God (Daniel 3:28).

21. An angel closed the mouths of the lions and preserved Daniel (Daniel 6:22).

22. The Angel who interpreted the visions to Zechariah is spoken of as the Angel of the Lord (Zechariah 1:9,11,19; 2:3; 3:1-6; 4:1-5; 5:5,10).

23. The Angel-Messenger of the Covenant is the Lord Jesus Christ (Malachi 3:1).

The Lord Jesus is not a mere angel or created being. These theophanies were but temporary manifestations where He appeared as an angel, or as a man, before His incarnation.

C. Revelation
The Book of Revelation contains accounts of the risen, glorified Son of God who is seen by John as the Jehovah Angel. A consideration of these references in their contexts will verify this fact.

1. The Angel-Sealer who comes with the seal of the living God points to the Lord Jesus Christ. No ordinary angel can perform such a sealing of the Spirit and name of God (Revelation 7:2).

2. The Angel-Priest with the golden censer, who offers the prayers of the saints on the golden altar before God points to the Lord Jesus Christ. No ordinary angel can take the prayers of the saints and offer them to God. There is one Mediator between God and man, the man Christ Jesus. Prayer and worship to angels is forbidden (Revelation 8:1-3).

3. The Angel-Redeemer, clothed with a cloud, His face as the sun, having the little open book in His hand,whose voice is as the voice of a lion, and who speaks of "My two witnesses" certainly points again to the Lord Jesus Christ not to any servant angelic being (Revelation 10:1-5,8-10; 11:1).

4. The Angel-Avenger who lightens the earth with His glory points to Christ also (Revelation 18:1).

5. The Angel-Binder, who binds Satan and casts him into the bottomless pit for one thousand years also points to Jesus Christ. He is the stronger man who binds the strong man, and then spoils his house. This was judicially accomplished at Calvary (Revelation 20:1-3 with Matthew 12:28-29).

In Scripture, the Son of God is seen as the God-Man, the Messenger of the Covenant (Malachi 3:1-2), the Messenger of Jehovah. He who was the Creator of angels (Colossians 1:16), and is better than angels (Hebrews 1:4-5), and is worshipped by angels (Hebrews 1:6), as the eternal Son of God, was made a little lower than the angels for the redemption of mankind (Hebrews 2:6-9). In the Old Testament, He appeared as an angel, and as a man. In the New Testament, He was born as a man, yet was seen in vision as an angel. He did not become an angel to redeem fallen angels, but He did become man to redeem fallen man. In the Old Testament He was particularly seen as the Jehovah-Angel in theophany. In the New Testament He is seen as the Jehovah-Man in the incarnation.

XII.Conclusion
Eternity alone will reveal the ministry that angels have rendered to the believers, the heirs of salvation (Matthew 18:10; Psalm 91:11-12). The angels will have kept their charge over us. The believer may thank God for the unseen ministry of these ministering spirits (Hebrews 1:13-14; 12:22-24). However, it should be

constantly remembered that man is forbidden to worship angels, as seen in the Colossian heresy, or to go beyond that which is revealed in the Word of God. All worship must go to the Eternal Godhead, Father, Son and Holy Spirit, Creator and Governor of all created beings (Colossians 1:16: 2:18; Revelation 22:9; I Peter 3:22).

Eternity will bring all holy creations together in one great universal worship service, when the redeemed of earth shall gather with the innumerable company of angels in the heavenly Zion, the New Jerusalem, and worship and serve God eternally (Revelation 4-5; Hebrews 12:22-24).

Chapter 7

DOCTRINE OF SATAN AND DEMONOLOGY

The Scriptures teach the existence of Satan who is the originator of sin and the king over a host of fallen angels and spirits who carry out his work. Christ conquered Satan and the kingdom of darkness at Calvary and has commissioned the Church to deliver men from it and bring them into the kingdom of light. The ultimate judgement of Satan and his forces will be when they are cast into the Lake of Fire for eternity.

CHAPTER OUTLINE

I. THE KINGDOM OF DARKNESS
A. Its Reality
B. Its Domain

II. SATAN — THE KING
A. His Origin
B. His Fall
C. His Nature
D. His Activity
E. His Counterfeit
F. His Judgement

III. EVIL SPIRITS — SATAN'S SERVANTS
A. Fallen Angels
B. Demon Spirits
C. Their Nature
D. Their Activity
E. Their Judgement

IV. THE OCCULT
A. Practices of the Occult
B. Warnings Against the Occult

V. CHRIST'S VICTORY
A. In His Perfect Life
B. In His Substitutionary Death
C. In His Resurrection and Ascension

VI. THE MINISTRY OF THE CHURCH

VII. THE BELIEVER AND THE KINGDOM OF DARKNESS

A. The Believer's Position — Legally
B. The Believer's Responsibility — Experientially
C. The Believer's Battleground — Personally
D. The Believer's Spiritual Armoury-Practically

I. THE KINGDOM OF DARKNESS

A. Its Reality
The Scriptures clearly indicate that in the universe and more particularly surrounding this planet earth, there is the kingdom of darkness. It is the very antithesis of the kingdom of God, which is a kingdom of light. Satan is in control of this kingdom and under his authority there are numerous fallen angels and demon spirits. The following illustrates the contrast between Satan's kingdom and God's.

SATAN'S KINGDOM
a) A Kingdom of Darkness
b) A Kingdom of Sin and Unrighteousness
c) A Kingdom of Sickness and Disease
d) A Kingdom of Deception
e) A Kingdom of Sorrow and Death

GOD'S KINGDOM
a) A Kingdom of Light
b) A Kingdom of Holiness and Righteousness
c) A Kingdom of Healing and Health
d) A Kingdom of Truth
e) A Kingdom of Joy and Life

In every nation today there is a tremendous increase of activity in the Satanic realm. The rise of the occult, spiritism and satanism are evidences of this. In I Timothy 4:1-3 Paul warned us that in the last days people would depart from the faith and give heed to seducing spirits and to doctrines of devils (Jude 3).

Believers often either ignore Satan's existence and power or over-emphasize it. A Biblical balance is much needed in these last days. It is only through the Scriptures that a proper understanding of this subject can be gained.

B. Its Domain
The word "domain" refers to "the rule, reign and territory over which a king rules". The domain of the kingdom of darkness is wherever Satan exercises his dominion. The following references describe this domain.

1. It is called Satan's kingdom (Matthew 12:25-26; Luke 11:14-19).

2. It is a kingdom of darkness (Colossians 1:13-14; Revelation 16:10).

3. It influences the kingdoms of this world system (Luke 4:5-6; Revelation 11:15; Matthew 4:8-10).

4. It influences the world kingdoms from the atmospheric heavens or "the heavenly places" (Ephesians 2:2; 3:10; 6:12; Revelation 12:3,7-12).

5. It is diametrically opposed to the kingdom of God in nature, character and purpose.

It is essential to recognize that the extent of Satan's domain is limited by God. He cannot exercise authority where God does not allow.

II. SATAN — THE KING

A. His Origin
It is necessary to see what the Bible teaches about the person of Satan. As all that is in the kingdom of light is patterned after its king, God, so all that is in the kingdom of darkness is patterned after its king, Satan. Each kingdom displays the nature and character of its head. The king represents the kingdom and the kingdom is like the king.

Very little direct information is given in the Scriptures concerning the origin and fall of Satan and his hosts, as evidently took place in the ages past before the creation of man.

Based on the Law of Double Reference (i.e., in speaking of or to one person there is reference to another person beyond or behind them (Genesis 3:14-15; Matthew 16:23). Two main passages of Scripture which describe Satan's origin and fall are Ezekiel 28:1-19 and Isaiah 14:4-23. The language used in these descriptions of the King of Tyre and the King of Babylon certainly goes beyond what could be applied to any earthly rulers, and points to the king behind the kings of this world order. Daniel's prophecy confirms the fact that there are princes of Satan's kingdom behind the princes of the world kingdoms (Daniel 8:20-21; 10:10-13,20-21). Ezekiel 28:1-19; Isaiah 14:4-23 should be read carefully. It is from these passages mainly that the following description of Satan, prior to his fall, is given.

1. Satan is a real personality. He is evil personified and characteristics are ascribed to him. Satan is not an impersonal influence or power. Personal pronouns, intelligence, knowledge, will and action are attributed to him (Job 1:8; 2:1-2; Zechariah 3:1; II Corinthians 2:11; Matthew 4:6; Revelation 12:12; II Timothy 2:26; Matthew 25:41; Isaiah 14:12-13).

2. Satan is a spirit being. Even as angels are spirit beings, even as God is a spirit being, so is Satan.

3. He is a created being, therefore dependent upon God for his very existence (Ezekiel 28:13,15).

4. He was called Lucifer, which means 'day star, son of the morning, or light bearer'. (Isaiah 14:12 with II Corinthians 11:14)

5. He was an anointed cherub in the heavenly sanctuary, just as Old Testament prophets, priests and kings were anointed for office (Ezekiel 28:14,16,18).

6. He was the covering Cherub placed by God to cover the throne. Compare this with the Cherubim on the ark of the covenant in the Tabernacle of Moses, covering the mercyseat (Exodus 37:9 and Ezekiel 28:14-16).

7. He was in Eden, the Garden of God (Ezekiel 28:13).

8. He was in the holy mountain (or kingdom) of God, in the sides of the north (Ezekiel 28:14,16, with Psalm 48:1).

9. He was perfect in the day that he was created (Ezekiel 28:15).

10. He was full of wisdom (Ezekiel 28:12 with James 3:15-16).

11. He was perfect in beauty (Ezekiel 28:12).

12. He was decked with precious stones set in gold (very similar to the stones in the Breastplate of Aaron, Israel's High Priest) (Ezekiel 28:13 with Exodus 28:15-21)

13. He was created with music in his being, apparently being the leader of heaven's worship (Ezekiel 28:13)

14. He was once in the truth (John 8:44).

Such language cannot be fully applied to earthly kings, but goes beyond them to the king behind them. This description indicates that Lucifer was a mighty being, and had been given a high position near the throne of God; an anointed ministry to lead heaven's angelic worship of the triune God.

B. His Fall
These same passages, along with other helpful references, show the cause of Satan's fall and those that fell with him.

1. He was lifted up in pride over his God-given wisdom, anointing and beauty (Ezekiel 28:17; Proverbs 16:18; 18:12; I Timothy 3:6).

2. He exalted himself, and came under condemnation (Isaiah 14:13-14 with I Timothy 3:6).

3. He manifested self-will against God's will (Isaiah 14:13-15). Note the five "I will's" of Lucifer's ambition here.

   a. I will ascend into heaven. Self-will.
   b. I will exalt my throne above the stars of God. Self-exaltation.
   c. I will sit also upon the mount of the congregation in the sides of the north. Self-enthronement.
   d. I will ascend above the heights of the clouds. Self- ascension.
   e. I will be like the Most High. Self-deification.

4. He fell through pride and self-will, the very essence of sin (Isaiah 14:12 with Proverbs 16:18 and Luke 10:18). He wanted to be independent of God. He rebelled against God.

5. He fell as lightning (Luke 10:18 with II Corinthians 11:14).

6. He was also cast down by God in this self-deification (Ezekiel 28:16-17).

7. He was the original sinner, and iniquity (lawlessness) was found in him (Ezekiel 28:15,16,18; I John 3:8).

8. He did not abide in the truth. He was self-deceived (John 8:44).

9. He became a liar and murderer (John 8:44).

10. He is the source of all sin and in him "The Mystery of Iniquity" is personified. He is the original Antichrist (II Thessalonians 2:7 with Genesis 3:1-6). He was the first apostate and caused other angels to sin in heaven.

11. He was permitted to retain his God-given wisdom which became corrupted, and by which he deceives mankind today (Ezekiel 28:17,18; James 3:15).

12. He will eventually be destroyed by fire (Ezekiel 28:18; Matthew 25:41). Many expositors believe that his fall took place before the creation of man, that he was cast out of the immediate presence of God, and that he fell to the earth bringing about the chaotic condition seen in Genesis 1:1-2 (Isaiah 45:18; Jeremiah 4:23-26).

C. His Nature

In Scripture, the name of a person was generally meant to signify the nature, experience or function of that which was named. This is true of the many names of God, of the names of persons, and also of the many names of Satan. The following Scriptural names and titles of Satan reveal the nature, character and work of this fallen archangel. The name with its interpretation is given along with suitable Scriptural references.

1. **Satan** — Adversary, Hater, Opponent, Enemy. Used about 52 times in the Bible (I Chronicles 21:1; Job 1:6-12; 2:1-7; Zechariah 3:1-7; I Kings 11:1, 23-25; II Corinthians 2:11).
2. **Devil** — Accuser, Slanderer, Whisperer. Slanders God to man and man to God. Used about 35 times (Matthew 4:1; 13:39; 25:41; John 8:44; Ephesians 4:27; Hebrews 2:14; Ephesians 6:11; James 4:7; Revelation 12:10).
3. **Serpent** — Enchanter, Beguiler, speaker of subtilty and wisdom perverted to evil ends (Matthew 10:16; II Corinthians 11:3; James 3:15; Genesis 3:1-14; Revelation 12:9,14-15; 20:2; Isaiah 27:1).
4. **Dragon** — Great Enchanting Serpent. Speaks of the vicious beastly nature and rage of Satan (Isaiah 51:9; Ezekiel 29:3; 32:2; Revelation 12:3-17; 13:2,4,11; 16:13; 20:2).
5. **Beelzebub** — Prince of Devils. Derived from Beelzebub or Lord of the Flies, God of the Dunghill. This was a heathen god believed to be ruler of all evil spirits. (II Kings 1:2; Matthew 10:25; 12:24,27;

Mark 3:22; Luke 11:15-19).

6. **God of this Age** — (Luke 4:6; I John 5:19; II Corinthians 4:4; Galatians 1:4; II Thessalonians 2:3-4).
7. **Prince of this World — Prince of the world-system (John 12:31; 14:30; 16:11).**
8. **Prince of the Power of the Air** — (Ephesians 2:2 with 6:12).
9. **Lucifer** — Daystar, Morning Star, Lightbearer, Shining One (Isaiah 14:12).
10. **Belial** — Worthless, Perverse, Lawless (I Samuel 30:22; II Corinthians 6:15; I Samuel 10:27; II Samuel 23:6).
11. **The Enemy** — Hater, hostility (Matthew 13:39).
12. **The Tempter** — Enticer (Matthew 4:3; I Thessalonians 3:5; I Chronicles 21:1; I Corinthians 7:5).
13. **The Wicked One** — (Matthew 13:19, 38-39; I John 5:18-19; 3:12).
14. **Angel of Light** — (Luke 10:18; II Corinthians 11:13-15).
15. **Accuser of the Brethren** — One against, one charging with an offence (Revelation 12:10; with Job 1:6-7; 2:1-2; Zechariah 3:1).
16. **Antichrist** — One over against Christ. Spirit of Antichrist (I John 2:18-22; 4:1-4; II John 7).
17. **Adversary** — The enemy, the opposer (I Peter 5:8).
18. **Murderer** — Killer, destroyer of life (John 8:44).
19. **Liar** (John 8:44).
20. **Sinner** (I John 3:8)
21. **Abaddon or Apollyon** — Destroyer (Revelation 9:11).
22. **Roaring Lion** (I Peter 5:8).
23. **Wolf** (John 10:12).
24. **Thief** — One who steals by subtilty (John 10:10; Luke 8:12).
25. **Wicked One** — Hurtful, evil one (Matthew 13:19).
26. **Fowler** — One out to entrap and ensnare (Psalm 91:3).
27. **King of a Kingdom** (Matthew 12:26-29; Acts 26:18; Colossians 1:13).
28. **Angel of the Bottomless Pit** (Revelation 9:11).
29. **Leviathan** — Great Water Animal (Isaiah 27:1).
30. **Son of Perdition** (II Thessalonians 2:1-12).

D. His Activity

Upon surveying all of the references to Satan's activities in Scripture, it becomes evident that the majority of them refer to his power and work as being centered around deception. It should be understood that Satan's activities are limited by God, especially towards God's children. This is seen clearly in the experience of Job and Satan's attacks against his person, household and possessions (Job 1-2 with Luke 22:31; I Corinthians 5:5; I Timothy 1:20). Though Satan is mighty, he is not all-mighty; though he is wise and knowing, he is not omniscient; though he is powerful, he is not all-powerful. Nor is he omnipresent; he is on God's chain and can only go as far as God permits in affecting mankind.

The activities of Satan may be grouped in seven main areas.

1. Temptation

These Scriptures show Satan's temptations of Christ, believers, and mankind in general. He is the enticer. (Matthew 4:1-11; Mark 1:13; Luke 4:1-13; I Corinthians 7:5; John 14:30; I John 5:18).

2. Sin

He is the originator of rebellion against divine authority (I John 3:8; Ephesians 2:2).

3. Deception

Deception is the greatest power of Satan. Deception was his first weapon in the Garden of Eden, and it is his last day weapon also to deceive the nations of the earth. (Genesis 3:1-4,13; II Corinthians 11:3; I Timothy 2:14; II Corinthians 11:13-15; John 8:44; II Thessalonians 2:9-10; Revelation 13:14; Acts 13:10; Revelation 12:9; 20:2-10; II Corinthians 2:11; Ephesians 6:11; Acts 5:3; I Timothy 5:15; I John 2:22; 4:1-6; II John 7; I Timothy 3:7; II Timothy 2:26; Revelation 2:9,24; 3:9).

4. Accusation

Satan hurls his accusations against the saints continually but the believer can thank God that he has an Advocate, Jesus Christ, interceding on his behalf (Revelation 12:10; Job 1:2; Zechariah 3:1-2).

5. Affliction

He seeks to afflict physically and mentally (I Corinthians 5:5; Luke 13:16; II Corinthians 12:7).

6. Opposition

Satan and his hosts are involved in a great spiritual war against God and His Kingdom (I Chronicles 21:1; Acts 10:38; Revelation 2:10; 12:13,17; 13:7; I Thessalonians 2:18; I Peter 5:8; Revelation 12:4; II Timothy 2:25-26).

7. Death

Death is the greatest power of Satan manifested, but Jesus has conquered death by resurrection (Hebrews 2:14; Jude 9; I John 3:12; John 8:44).

E. His Counterfeit

Man is by nature religious. He was created to worship. If he does not worship the true and living God, by the power of the Holy Spirit, then he often resorts to the counterfeit, accepting another form of religion and worshipping the God of this world, with the help of evil spirits. For this purpose, Satan has a complete counterfeit religion. When Satan said "I will be like God" (Isaiah 14:12-14), he did not mean that he would be like God in character in holiness, but he wanted to be like God in the sense of independence. He wanted to be God and to be worshipped as God. Thus he set up a rival religion, a complete imitation of all that God is and does. Satan's imitation of God is seen in the following list of counterfeits.

1. Satan has a throne (Revelation 2:13).
2. Satan has great depths of doctrines (Revelation 2:24; I Timothy 4:1; I Corinthians 2:10).
3. Satan has a synogogue (Revelation 2:9; 3:9).
4. Satan has a communion table (I Corinthians 10:21).
5. Satan has people sacrifice at his altar (Deuteronomy 32:17; I Corinthians 10:20).
6. Satan has a counterfeit cup (I Corinthians 10:21).
7. Satan gives his doctrines to men to teach (I Timothy 4:1).
8. Satan himself is an angel of light (II Corinthians 11:14).
9. Satan has his messengers, demonic and human (II Corinthians 11:13).
10. Satan has a kingdom (Matthew 12:26).
11. Satan does counterfeit miracles, signs and wonders (Revelation 16:14; Exodus 7:8-12).
12. Satán has false apostles, prophets and teachers (II Corinthians 11:13-14; II Peter 2:1; Mark 13:22; Matthew 13:38).
13. Satan has a city, Mystery Babylon, to oppose the city of God, New Jerusalem (Revelation 17:5).
14. Satan also has a harlot church, to counterfeit the Bride of Christ (Revelation 17:5).
15. Satan and his demons seek to be worshipped (Leviticus 17:7; Deuteronomy 32:17; II Chronicles 11:15; Psalm 106:37; I Corinthians 10:20; Revelation 9:20; Matthew 4:8-10).
16. Satan has his false Christ, the rival of God's Christ (I John 2:18-22).
17. Satan imitates the revelation of the Godhead in his Satanic three in Revelation 13: the Beast (Anti-Father); the Antichrist (Anti-Son) and the False Prophet (Anti-Spirit). (Revelation 16:13-14; John 5:43).
18. Satan's "Mystery of Iniquity" is the counterfeit of God's "Mystery of Godliness" (II Thessalonians 2:7 with I Timothy 3:16).
19. Satan wants to live in human bodies as temples for his demon spirits as God wants to live in human bodies by His Spirit (John 13:27 with I Corinthians 6:19).
20. Satan seals his followers with a name on their forehead, which is the counterfeit of God's name on His people's forehead (Revelation 13:16 with 7:1-3).

F. His Judgement

God could have destroyed Satan and the sinning angels the moment they rebelled. However, in His infinite wisdom He has permitted sin to run its horrible course as a witness to all of its destructive fruit. In God's overall plan, it is evident that He is dealing with Satan in a progressive manner. There are seven steps in the judgement of Satan.

1. The moment he sinned he was cast out of Paradise, the third heaven, which is the immediate presence of God. (Isaiah 14:15; Ezekiel 28:16; Luke 10:18).

2. He was judged in Eden's earthly Paradise, when Satan caused Adam and Eve to sin (Genesis 3:14-15). He is under the irrevocable and eternal curse of God.

3. He was conquered by Christ at Calvary's cross (John 12:31; 16:11; Hebrews 2:14; I John 3:8).

4. He and his hosts are being conquered by the church as they release the captives of the human race who are under his control. (Mark 16:15-20; Acts 26:18; Romans 16:20).

5. He and his angels are to be cast out of heaven to the earth in the time of tribulation at the close of the age. This casting out is the result of an angelic war in the heavens (Ezekiel 28:17; Ephesians 2:2; 6:12; Revelation 12:4-13).

6. He will be cast out of the earth into the bottomless pit for a thousand years at the second coming of Christ (Revelation 20:2-3).

7. He will be loosed out of the bottomless pit for a little season, after which he will be cast into the Lake of Fire and Brimstone for all eternity (Revelation 20:10; Isaiah 14:15; 27:1; Matthew 25:41). The eternal judgement upon Satan will also be the same for all his hosts and all men who choose to serve him in this life.

III. EVIL SPIRITS — SATAN'S SERVANTS

Under Satan's control there is a vast host of evil spirit beings. In Scripture, they are called angels, authorities, principalities, powers, rulers of darkness, wicked spirits, and demons (I Peter 3:22; Ephesians 6:12; 1:21; 3:10; Romans 8:38; Titus 3:1; Colossians 2:5,10; Daniel 10:13,20-21; Luke 22:53; Colossians 1:13). These titles suggest different ranks and levels of authority in Satan's kingdom. Though many scholars see all of the titles as referring to the same beings, there does seem to be a distinction in Scripture between fallen angels and demon spirits.

A. Fallen Angels

There are angels in the kingdom of darkness who function as Satan's messengers (Psalm 78:49; Revelation 12:7-9; Romans 8:38). It is evident that when Satan fell, a vast company of angels fell with him, preferring Satan's will to God's will. These are spoken of in Scripture as fallen angels. It is possible that one third of the angels fell according to the implications in Revelation 12:4.

Peter tells us that God did not spare certain angels which sinned but cast them down to hell (Greek "Tartarus") (II Peter 2:4). Jude tells us also of angels that left their original estate and are now bound in chains of darkness (Jude 6). Some angels are bound in various places of the earth, and other angels are loose (Revelation 9:14-15; II Peter 2:4), able to appear as angels of light (II Corinthians 11:14-15). Satan and his angels are eventually to be cast out of heaven by Michael and his angels (Revelation 12:7-9). The saints will also judge angels (I Corinthians 6:3). Finally, the devil and his angels are to be cast into the Lake of Fire (Matthew 25:41; II Peter 2:4; Jude 6).

NOTE: Expositors are divided over the particular sin of the angels mentioned in Peter and Jude as well as over the time when it took place. The two theories are as follows:

1. That these angels fell with Satan in the eternities past and were not content to remain in their God-appointed positions and responsibilities. Lifted up through pride, they followed with Satan in his rebellion. For this sin they were cast down to Tartarus and now await the Day of Judgement after which they will be cast into the eternal Lake of Fire with their leader (II Peter 2:4; Jude 6; Matthew 25:41).

2. That these angels were "the Sons of God" who co-habited with "the daughters of men", resulting in unnatural offspring or giants (the Hebrew word for giants is "nephilim" which means "fallen ones", Genesis 6:1-4; Numbers 13:1-33). It is suggested that this was "the strange flesh" that is spoken of in II Peter 2:4 and Jude 6, and that the estate and habitation the angels left was heaven, when they came to earth and assumed human bodies for such abominable sins.

The main objections used against the latter theory is that Jesus said that angels neither marry nor are given in marriage (Luke 20:35-36; Matthew 22:30; Mark 12:25).Those who hold the first theory, explain away the latter by saying that "the Sons of God" were the sons of Seth, of the godly line, who intermarried with "the daughters of men" or the ungodly line of Cain. The student is referred to those works which deal more fully with both theories. Sufficient for this text is the fact that certain angels did sin, and however it took place, these angels are bound in Tartarus awaiting the great White Throne Judgement, while other evil angels are still loose doing their work in the earth.

B. Demon Spirits
Concerning the origin of demon spirits, the three primary views are:

1. That they are angels who fell with Satan, some of which are bound while others are still loose (Psalm 78:49).

2. That they are the disembodied spirits of a pre-Adamic race of beings, or some similar creation who fell when Satan and his angels fell.

3. That they are the spirits of the unnatural offspring of angels (the Sons of God) and antediluvian women in the days of Noah (Genesis 6:1-6).

Though the Bible nowhere specifically states their origin, it does reveal them to be real personalities able to think, act and speak, and especially desiring to express themselves through mankind. The difference between demons and fallen angels seem to be that fallen angels do not seek to inhabit a human body, while demon spirits do. It is even possible for them to inhabit animal bodies to express their destructive nature (Mark 5:1-20; Matthew 8:29; John 13:27).

The two words most often used in the New Testament to refer to demons are "devils" and "spirits". The Greek word "daimon" or "daimonion" is translated "devil" or "devils" (Mark 1:34; 16:17; Luke 9:1; 10:17; James 2:19; I Corinthians 10:20-21; Matthew 9:33-34). The Greek word "pneuma" is translated "spirit" and is used of the Holy Spirit, the human spirit or of evil spirits. It should be remembered that there is only one devil, but numerous demon spirits of like nature and character. These wicked spirits are all under Satan's control.

The Scriptures indicate the following things concerning demon spirits:

1. They are Real Personalities
Demon spirits have all the characteristics of real personalities. They possess both will and intelligence and act according to their evil natures (Matthew 8:29-31; Luke 4:35,41; James 2:19).

2. They are Spirit Beings
Even as God is a spirit being, and Satan and angels are spirit beings, so are demons. Thus they are invisible, incorporeal, though often manifesting their nature and character through human beings (Matthew 8:16; Luke 10:17, 20; Matthew 17:18; Luke 9:38-42).

3. They are Satan's Servants
Having chosen to side with Satan in his rebellion, they became his slaves, obligated to do his bidding. Thus the choice they made was really Satan's, and through self- will they became slaves to his will (Matthew 12:22-30).

4. They are Numerous
On one occasion a demon admitted to Jesus that his name was Legion, for "we are many" (Mark 5:9; Luke 8:30; Matthew 12:26-27). As God has legions of good angels at His command, so Satan has legions of demon spirits at his command.

5. They are Symbolized
As God and His Kingdom are known by many symbols, so Satan and his hosts are symbolized by various things. Each symbol brings out some aspect of their nature.

   a. As fowls of the air (Matthew 13:4,19).

     b. As unclean birds in a cage (Revelation 18:1-3).

     c. As unclean frogs (Revelation 16:13-14).

     d. As locusts from the bottomless pit (Revelation 9:1-10).

     e. As an army of horses and horsemen, with lions heads and serpents tails by which they torment mankind (Revelation 9:16-19).

     f. As serpents and vipers (Luke 3:7).

C. Their Nature

There are many kinds of demon spirits under Satanic control, and their names signify their evil work, which is the same as their leader. Demons are totally and morally depraved in character though there seems to be degrees of wickedness in them (Matthew 12:22-30).

    1. Devils — evil spirits, or servants of the Devil (Leviticus 17; Deuteronomy 32:17; Mark 1:34; 16:17).

    2. Evil Spirits (Judges 9:23; I Samuel 16:14,23; Luke 7:21; 8:2; Acts 19:12-13; Matthew 15:22; Acts 5:16; Deuteronomy 32:17).

    3. Unclean Spirits — this title is used about twenty-one times to describe their impure nature (Zechariah 13:2; Matthew 10:1; 12:43; Mark 1:23-27; Acts 8:7; Revelation 16:13).

    4. Dumb Spirits (Luke 11:14; Mark 9:17; Matthew 9:32-34).

    5. Blind and Dumb Spirits (Matthew 12:22).

    6. Deaf and Dumb Spirits (Mark 9:25).

    7. Foul Spirits (Revelation 18:2; Mark 9:25).

    8. Lying Spirits (I Kings 22:22-23; II Thessalonians 2:9-12).

    9. Spirit of Infirmity (Luke 13:11).

  10. Spirit of Divination — Spirit of Python, or Fortunetelling (Acts 16:16) (Acts 8:9).

  11. Seducing Spirits — Religious spirits which bring false doctrines, doctrines of devils (I Timothy 4:1).

  12. Lunatic Spirits — Epileptic and suicidal spirits (Matthew 17:15-18; Mark 9:14-29).

  13. Antichrist Spirits (I John 4:3).

  14. Spirit of Whoredom (Hosea 4:12)

  15. Spirit of the World (I Corinthians 2:12)

  16. Spirit of Error (I John 4:6)

  17. Spirit of Fear (II Timothy 1:7)

  18. Perverse Spirit (Isaiah 19:14)

  19. Familiar Spirit (I Samuel 28:7-8)

D. Their Activity

The activity of demon spirits, as servants of Satan, is best summed up in John 10:10, "The thief comes to steal...to kill and to destroy". These spirits attack mankind spiritually, morally, mentally, physically and emotionally. The following is a list of the things demons do under Satan's control.

    1. They **oppose** God's ministers (Matthew 13:19; II Corinthians 4:4).

    2. They **pervert** the Word of God and seek to hinder the Gospel (I Thessalonians 2:18).

    3. They **hold** their captives (II Timothy 2:26; I Timothy 3:7).

    4. They **blind** the minds of unbelievers (II Corinthians 4:4).

    5. They **sow tares** among wheat (Matthew 13:39).

    6. They **seduce** people. The Greek word "planos", translated "seduce" means that they rove (as tramps) and by implication they are imposters and misleaders. They seek to draw aside from the path; to lead astray, allure, tempt, corrupt, defraud and entice (I Timothy 4:1; Mark 13:22; I John 2:26). A seducing spirit can cause people to be obsessed with a false idea, or doctrinal imbalance.

    7. They **trouble** people (I Samuel 16:14). The Hebrew word for "trouble" means "to make fearful, afraid, to terrify" It speaks of agitation of mind. It speaks of a person being perplexed, uneasy, molested (I Chronicles 10:13-14).

8. They **oppress** people (Acts 10:38). The Greek word "katadunasteuo" means "to exercise dominion against, oppress, and overburden in body or mind".

9. They **vex** people. The Greek word "pascho" involves a person experiencing sensations or impressions (usually painful), feelings, passions and sufferings. The word "vex" also means "to mob, to harass, molest" or "to suffer at the hands of another, to suffer or experience pain" (Matthew 15:22; 17:15; Luke 6:18; Acts 5:16).

10. They **bind** people (Luke 13:16). The Greek word "deo" means "to tie up, confine, fasten (especially by binding cords around)". The woman in Luke 13 was bound with arthritis and had to be loosed in her physical body. (It should be recognized that though physical infirmities may be caused by demons, this is usually not the case).

11. They **deceive** people (Revelation 12:9; Matthew 24:4,5, 11,24).

12. They **possess** people. The Greek word "daimonizomai" means "to be exercised by a demon (to be vexed or possessed with)". Possession denotes both the occupancy and ownership of a person by an evil spirit. It is indwelling control. Possession is to be under the power and control of a demon that has entered the person and can control their faculties at will. Cases of possession caused lunacy, palsy, dumbness, blindness, and enabled fortune-telling. Demons seek to possess human or animal bodies if possible. They hate to be unclothed or disembodied spirits (Matthew 4:24; 8:16,28-34; Mark 5:1-20; Luke 8:26-40; Matthew 9:32,33; 12:22; 15:21-28; Mark 7:24-30; Mark 1:32; 9:14-29; Luke 4:33-35; Acts 8:7; 16:16). No truly born-again believer can be possessed by demons, because the Holy Spirit dwells within the believer's spirit.

13. They **torment** people (Revelation 9:1-11; 16:13-14). Their torment is like the tormenting sting of a locust.

14. They **buffet** people (II Corinthians 12:7). To buffet means "to hit with blow after blow; to punch, to slap and to fight against".

15. They **resist** people (Zechariah 3:1-3). That is, they oppose, stand up against, and act as an adversary against someone.

E. Their Judgement

Scripture reveals that the judgement of evil spirits parallels that of Satan. It is progressive, as is his, and culminates at the same time. Involved in their judgement is their being; conquered and spoiled (Colossians 2:15); made subject to Christ (I Peter 3:22); spared not; cast down to hell; delivered into chains of darkness, reserved unto judgement (II Peter 2:4); reserved in everlasting chains under darkness unto the judgement of the great day (Jude 6); cast out into the earth with Satan (Revelation 12:9); and cast into everlasting fire (Matthew 25:41).

IV. THE OCCULT

A. Practices of the Occult

Though usually oblivious to the fact, man often becomes aware that there is much activity in the spirit realm. Being separated from God by the fall, man throughout the ages has longed to contact this invisible spirit realm. Thus Satan has provided contact with the spirit realm through numerous avenues in the world of spiritism and the occult. All occultic practices are Satan's counterfeit forms of communication. In these last days, as there is an increased activity of the Spirit of God, so it is that Satan increases his activity by demon spirits to counterfeit and resist the workings of the Holy Spirit. The following list of occultic activities has been divided into two sections: those that are specifically mentioned in the Bible, and others which are modern day designations.

1. **Magicians** (Genesis 41:8; Exodus 7:11). Horoscopists (drawing magical lines or circles), Enchanters, Diviners, Astrologers.

2. **Wise Men** (Exodus 7:11). Claimed to have supernatural wisdom from the unseen realm.

3. **Divination** (Deuteronomy 18:10; Acts 16:16). To divine to determine by lot or magical scroll.

4. **Observer of Times** (Deuteronomy 18:10). To cloud over, act covertly, practise magic, to augur from the appearance of clouds.

5. **Passing** through the fire (Deuteronomy 18:10; Leviticus 18:21). Children consecrated to Molech by fire-death.

6. **Enchanter** (Deuteronomy 18:10). A hisser, whisperer, mutterer of enchantments and magic spells.

7. **Witch** (Deuteronomy 18:10). Witchcraft (Galatians 5:20; Exodus 22:18; Leviticus 22:18; Leviticus 20:27; II Chronicles 33:6). To whisper a spell, practise magic.

8. **Charmer** (Deuteronomy 18:10). To fascinate, cast a spell.

9. **Consulter** of familiar spirits. Consulter of demons (Deuteronomy 18:10). Soothsaying (Leviticus 20:27; Deuteronomy 18:11; I Chronicles 10:13; Isaiah 8:19-20; Isaiah 19:3; 29:4). One who has direct fellowship and communication with demons, impersonating spirits who are familiar with a deceased person's life and deceive the living.

10. **Wizard** (Deuteronomy 18:11). A knowing one, a conjurer, a prognosticator. Able to supply information by means of the spirits contacted. (Leviticus 19:31; 20:6,27; I Samuel 28:3,9; II Kings 21:6; 23:24).

11. **Necromancer** (Deuteronomy 18:11). Seeker unto the dead, consults the dead for advice and information.

12. **Astrologers**, Stargazers. Monthly Prognosticators (Isaiah 47:13). Horoscopists, studying the stars to predict events on earth.

13. **Soothsayers** (Isaiah 2:6; Daniel 2:27). Foretelling future events by the appearance of the clouds.

14. **Sorcerers**

   1) Old Testament (Exodus 7:11; Daniel 2:2). Practicer of hidden arts, magician. To whisper a spell, enchant.

   2) New Testament (Greek "pharmakeus" from which we get the word pharmacy) Revelation 9:21; 18:23; 22:15; 21:8. Enchanter with drugs, maker and user of drugs.

Modern Day Occultic List
The word "occult" is a word meaning "to hide, hidden, or concealed things". As Isaiah 2:6 speaks of Israel being replenished from the East with Eastern religious philosophies and occultic practices, so we can see the same happening today.

1. **Astral Projection** — partial or complete separation of soul and soul travel.
2. **Augury** — fortune telling by means of interpreting omens, etc.
3. **Apparition** — appearance of a disembodied spirit or ghost form.
4. **Amulet** — an object said to have magical power.
5. **Astrology** — fortune telling based on a supposed influence of the position of the sun, moon, stars and planets.
6. **Apport** — the appearance and/or disappearance of physical objects.
7. **Automatic Writing** — words written without awareness or conscious effort.
8. **Blood Pact** — a contract signed with Satan in one's own blood.
9. **Black Mass** — celebrated in honor of the Devil.
10. **Charming or Enchanting** — employment of magic, attempts to use spirit power.
   (a) **Clairaudience** — Spiritualistic faculty for hearing voices not normally heard.
   (b) **Clairsentience** — Spiritualistic diagnosis of diseases apart from science.
   (c) **Clairvoyance** — Discerning of things not normally present to senses.

11. **Coven** — A community of witches: 6 males, 6 females, 1 High Priest.
12. **Crystal Gazing** — Fortune telling by means of Ball, Mirror, Crystal Gazing.
13. **Cosmology** — Study of the order of the universe.
14. **Cartomancy** — Fortune telling by means of cards, related to Tarot.
15. **Chiromancy** — It is also called palmistry.
16. **Conjure** — In Necromancy
17. **Divination** — Another name for Fortune-telling.
18. **Excorcism** — Casting out of spirits.
19. **Epistomology** — Study of knowledge.
20. **Ectoplasm** — Unknown substance which oozes from body of a medium.
21. **ESP** — Extra Sensory Perception a sense or senses beyond the normal five (taste, touch, smell, sight, hearing) that give knowledge
22. **Fetishes** — Spiritual embodiment in a natural object, e.g. stone, tree, doll, etc.
23. **Gnostic** — Person/group who believes they have the only correct and accurate knowledge/data.
24. **Agnostic** — Neither for or against belief in God; man can never know, prove, or disprove the existence of God.
25. **Hypnosis** — Suggestion in hypnotic state or trance.
26. **Horoscope** — Refer to Observer of Times. Astrology, study of star at birth, by which they profess to tell events of a person's life.
27. **Hydromancy** — Divination by viewing images in water.
28. **Hepatoscopy** — Examination of liver or certain sacrificial animals then interpreting some meaning from them used as guidance.
29. **Incantation** — A spell or charm used in or as a part of magic ritual.
30. **Incubus** — A male demon that has sexual intercourse with humans.
31. **Succubus** — A demon assuming female form for purpose of sexual relations.
32. **Kabbalah** — Mystical body of law based on occult interpretation of Old Testament.
33. **Levitation** — The rising of physical bodies into the air, table floating; supernatural power that overcomes gravity.
34. **Magi** — Magi, Magic, Magician. Priestclass of Medes and Persians, offered sacrifices, interpreted dreams, and omens, and acquainted with all modern and ancient arts of spiritism.
35. **Magic** — a means of incantations, charms, witchcraft.
36. **Manifestation** — manifestation is a revealing of a demon.
37. **Meditation (Evil)** — A passive state of mind, open to spiritual forces, counterfeit, latent 'ego' within, and makes a self-savior.
38. **Mesmerism (Hypnotism)** — Essentially healing diseases by charms or rituals.
39. **Mind Awareness (Dynamics)** — New and higher levels of consciousness in passivity.
40. **Medium** — An occultist who is indwelt bodily as a dwelling place for spirits.
41. **Metaphysics** — Study of knowledge and order of the spirit world; forces beyond our normal five senses.
42. **Numerology** — An occult practice which interprets numbers for fortune telling.
43. **Ouji Board** — A board with letters of the alphabet on it — instrument designed to communicate with spirits of the dead.
44. **Omen** — An observable event or action pertaining to the future.
45. **Oracle** — "Speaking Place". A revelation or message from supernatural through a medium.
46. **Ontology** — Study of forces beyond the five senses — spiritual existence.
47. **Parapsychology (PSI)** — Especially study of demonic activity.
48. **Psychography** — Use of heart-shaped board with ouji board for spirit messages.
49. **Pendulum** — Divining-rod or fortune telling to locate objects unseen.
50. **Palmistry** — Divination by analysis of lines, shapes, etc., on the human hand.
51. **Pyramidology** — Mystic powers associated with models of the Pyramid.
52. **Psychoanalysis, Psychic** — Automatic writings, self-hypnotic, visions, dreams, trances, etc.
53. **Psychokinesis** — Moving objects by use of the mind and thought patterns; "mind over matter" Psychic: of the mind.
54. **Phrenology** — Divining/analysis based upon the bumps and structure of the skull.
55. **Parapsychology** — Branch of psychology dealing with investigation of psychic phenomenon, e.g. clairvoyance, ESP, telepathy, etc.
56. **Precognition** — Foreknowledge of the occurrence of events which cannot be inferred by present knowledge.

57. Phenomenon — An event or occurrence usually considered to be of an extraordinary nature.

58. Reincarnation — The belief that living beings possessing immortal spirits or souls are reborn i form of another living being. The belief that the soul, upon death of the body, comes back to earth i another body.

59. Rhabdomancy — Casting sticks into air — then interpreting omens from the manner in which the fall and land.

60. Stigmata — Wounds that may or may not bleed.

61. Seance — A meeting of spiritists or spiritualists.

62. Satanism — Worship of or religious allegiance to Satan. Satanic churches.

63. Sorcery — Form of magic which attempts to control or direct spirits.
  (a) Spiritism — belief that mediumistic phenomena is caused by spirits.
  (b) Spiritualism — Spiritism in a religious context.

64. Stichomancy — Fortune telling at random reference to books or the Bible.

65. Transmigration — Hindui doctrine similar to reincarnation, but believes that dead soul can retur to earth in body of a snail, crab, ant, man, etc.

66. Telepathy — Form of ESP: Greek "impressions across a distance". Thought reading, communica tion. Communicating to others at a distance, involving .mind reading.

67. Trance — Form of ESP: Greek "a condition in which consciousness and all natural senses ar withheld" the soul becomes susceptible only to a particular vision.

68. Transference — Process of an indwelling spirit leaving one body and entering another.

69. Talismans — Divining by charms.

70. Wizard — One devoted to black magic or sorcery.

71. Witch — A male or female who uses occultic powers for what they consider good or evil ends.

72. Warlock — A witch who is given to black magic and in pact with the Devil.

73. Yoga — physical exercises designed to enable one to gain control over bodily processes.

74. Zodiac — An imaginary belt of the heavens, which includes paths of the sun, moon and planet having 12 constellations.

These and others are all areas of demonic activity. The methods may vary but the same ends are i view. That is, communication by supernatural means with the spirit world. All these things profess t gain knowledge for man which is not available by mere natural means.

B. Warnings Against the Occult

The Bible is explicit in its warnings and judgements to all who get involved in the occult world. Whe man fails to respond to the Holy Spirit by whom he can be brought into contact with God, he ofte responds to evil spirits by which he contacts the god of this world, Satan. All such contact is forbidde by the Word of God and comes under divine judgement (Leviticus 19:31; 20:6; Deuteronomy 18:10 Many of the elements of the occult are Satanic counterfeits of the operations and manifestations of th Holy Spirit. As God moves by His Spirit in the supernatural realm, so Satan counterfeits by movin through his evil spirits. The purpose behind Satan's counterfeit is deception and enslavement Miracles wrought by the Spirit of God are designed to cause people to believe. Miracles of Satan ar designed to cause people to be deceived (Exodus 7:8-25; 8:1-19).

A believer does not have to be deceived. God has given certain means by which the source of supernatural manifestation may be tested. The Scripture tells us clearly not to believe every spirit, bu to try, prove and test them (I John 4:1). The following are the divine means of proving spirits.

1. The spirits must be tested by the Word of God. "To the Law and to the testimony: if they (the spirits speak not according to this Word, it is because there is no light in them" (Isaiah 8:19-20).

2. The spirit's utterance must be proven by fulfilment (Deuteronomy 18:21-22).

3. The spirit must be tested by the truth of Christ's coming in the flesh, both by His incarnation and i the Church, which is His body. (I John 4:2-3).

4. The spirits can be tested by the fruit they bring forth (Matthew 7:19-23).

5. The spirits can be discerned by the gift of the Holy Spirit in the discerning of spirits, which will expose what spirit is at work (I Corinthians 12:7-10; Acts 16:16-18).

From God's point of view, contact with the spirit world through the occult is: offering "strange fire" (Leviticus 10:1); burning "strange incense" (Exodus 30:9); and worshipping "strange gods" (Psalm 81:9). His judgement for seeking after demonic powers may include allowing a person's involvement in the occult to open the way for demon possession.

Any person who has been involved in the occult needs to genuinely repent of his sin, be cleansed by the blood of Jesus and verbally renounce his occult involvement. He must learn to depend on the Word and Spirit of God. If he is demon-possessed, his deliverance will have to include exorcism. Unless a person repents of this terrible sin and comes into complete deliverance from demonic forces, they will be cast into the Lake of Fire for all eternity, with the Devil and the evil spirits they have served in this life (Matthew 25:4; Revelation 21:8; 22:15).

V. CHRIST'S VICTORY

The Lord Jesus Christ in conquering Satan and all his hosts has made complete victory available for every believer. He is Lord over all principalities and powers. He is the "Strong Man" who has overcome. Satan has been stripped of his authority and now Christ is dividing His spoil with the Church (Luke 11:20-22; Psalm 19:5; Isaiah 53:12).

The victory of Christ is seen in three parts: in His life, death and resurrection.

A. In His Perfect Life

One of the greatest doctrines of the Christian faith is the fact that the Lord Jesus Christ overcame and conquered Satan and his evil hosts in two major realms. He conquered Satan personally, in the three major temptations in the wilderness, and representatively, for us, at Calvary in His death, burial, resurrection and ascension.

Jesus was tempted in the wilderness in the three areas of man's being: spirit, soul and body and in the three areas of sin: the lust of the flesh, the lust of the eyes, and the pride of life (Matthew 4:1-11; Luke 4:1-13; I Thessalonians 5:23; I John 2:15,16). As the last Adam and the second man, He was submitted to the attack and temptations of Satan and proved His complete mastery over the adversary. Satan had tempted the First Adam in these same areas (Genesis 3:1-6). The First Adam fell, thus bringing all of his unborn race under Satanic control and into the kingdom of sin, sickness and death. In the wilderness the devil sought to gain dominion over the Last Adam, Jesus Christ. He was tempted in:

1. Body — the lust of the flesh (Luke 4:2-4).
2. Soul — the lust of the eyes (Luke 4:5-8).
3. Spirit — the pride of life (Luke 4:9-12).

Thus, He was tempted in all points like as we are, yet without sin (Hebrews 2:18; 4:15). Though the First Adam was defeated, the Last Adam was victorious. He overcame by the Word of God. It was necessary for Christ to win His personal victory over Satan before He could gain a representative victory on behalf of all believers. Christ's power during His earthly ministry over sin, sickness. death and demons was founded upon this threefold victory over temptation.

Being the Head of the new creation race, Christ in his life personally conquered Satan. Having conquered the devil for Himself, He could conquer him for His people. No demon spirit could resist His perfect life and power.

B. In His Substitutionary Death

Christ's victory in the wilderness temptation was in His own behalf. The victory of Calvary's cross was in our behalf. This victory was actually begun in Gethsemane (Luke 22:53) and consummated on the Cross (Colossians 2:14-15; John 12:31; 16:11). In the cross He spoiled the principalities and powers, and made a show of them, triumphing over them in it.

Colossians 2:14-15 — Weymouth's translation — "And the hostile princes and rulers He stripped of from Himself, and boldly displayed them as His conquests, when, by the cross, He had triumphed over them".

Colossians 2:14-15 — Amplified New Testament — "God disarmed the principalities and power ranged against us and He made a bold display and public example of them, triumphing over them in Him and in the Cross".

Thus Christ utterly conquered all Satan's hosts and exposed them as defeated foes, captives over whom He had gloriously triumphed in His death on Calvary. When Jesus died and rose again, He defeated Satan in five realms.

1. He conquered him as the author of sin (I John 3:8; II Corinthians 5:19-21).

2. He conquered him as the author of sickness (Isaiah 53:4; Matthew 8: 16-17; I Corinthians 6:19-20 Acts 10:38).

3. He conquered him as the author of death (Hebrews 2:13-14; Revelation 1:18).

4. He conquered him as the ruler of the kingdoms of this world (Matthew 4:8-10; Revelation 11:15).

5. He conquered him in the realm of the heavenlies, over principalities and powers in heaven and earth (Ephesians 4:8-10; Philippians 2:9-11; Ephesians 1:19-23).

The victory of the Lord Jesus Christ on the cross has made Jesus Lord over all (I Peter 3:22). All things are now under His feet (Ephesians 1:22-23). He is indeed the "Strong Man" and has overcome Satan's palace and stripped him of his armour and now divides the spoils of His conquest with the Church, His Body.

C. In His Resurrection and Ascension
Not only did Christ's victory over Satan in the wilderness involve His personal victory, and Calvary His representative victory, it also ultimately includes that victory which is to be manifest in the heavenly realms (Luke 10:18; Job 1:6-12; 2:1-7; Revelation 12:9-12; Colossians 2:10; Ephesians 1:19-23; 2:2; Hebrews 4:12-14).

Sin brought discord, not only on earth, but also in heaven. Here in the heavenly places, Satan hurls his accusations against the saints, but with the resurrection, ascension and exaltation of the Lord Jesus to the right hand of the Majesty on high (Hebrews 8:1-2), we have a perfect man, the conqueror of Satan and his demonic hosts, representing us in heaven. The Scriptures declare that all principalities, powers and authorities are subject to His control (I Peter 3:22; Ephesians 1:21-23; 3:9-10; Matthew 28:19-20). He now has all power both in heaven and earth. The believer can rejoice in Christ's full and complete victory over Satan's entire kingdom of darkness. All are conquered. All are defeated. All are subject to Him. God has given Christ to be Head over all things to the Church. He must reign until all enemies are put under His feet (Psalm 110:1-2; I Corinthians 15:25-26). What Christ did on Calvary was for God, and for His Church.

VI. THE MINISTRY OF THE CHURCH
Involved in the purpose of God for the Church is that which is spoken of in Ephesians 3:10-11, "To the intent that now unto the principalities and powers in heavenly places might be known by the Church the manifold wisdom of God". In Romans 16:20 Paul told the Roman church that God would "bruise Satan under your feet shortly". God intends to use the Church, Christ's Body, to also subdue Satan. Christ has delegated His authority to the Church.

1. He delegated His authority to the twelve Apostles (Matthew 10:1-8; Luke 9:1; Mark 3:15; 6:7,13).
2. He delegated authority to the seventy disciples (Luke 10: 18-19).
3. He delegated authority to the Church corporately and to believers individually (Mark 9:38-39; 16:15-20; Acts 19:13-18; Matthew 24:14; Luke 22:26-30).

To proclaim the gospel of the Kingdom is to preach the Word, heal the sick and cast out devils. The Great Commission included the preaching of the Gospel with signs following. It was the Lord commissioning the Church, which is His Body, to continue His ministry on earth (Acts 1:1; Luke 4:18-20; Acts 26:18; Matthew 28:19-20; Luke 24:47-49). The Book of Acts demonstrates the power of this Gospel, proclaimed on the basis of Christ's complete victory over all the power of the enemy.

Since Christ has conquered Satan both personally and representatively, He has delegated His authority to the Church. The Church has been given power of attorney, the right to use His Name and to continue the ministry of Christ on earth. The ministry of the Church could be summarized in the Lord's commission to the Apostle Paul in Acts 26:18: "To open their eyes, and to turn them from darkness to light, and from the power of Satan unto God, that they may receive forgiveness of sins, and inheritance among them which are sanctified by faith that is in Me".

VII. THE BELIEVER AND THE KINGDOM OF DARKNESS

The believer needs to realize his position, his responsibility, his battleground and the spiritual armour that God has provided for complete victory over the powers of evil. He should neither be fearful (II Timothy 1:7), nor ignorant of Satan's devices but avail himself of the spiritual armour and weapons provided by Christ's victory (II Corinthians 2:11; 10:4-5).

The New Testament tells the believer of his position in Christ. On the foundation of all that Jesus Christ is, and all that He said and did, the believer stands firm on the grounds of victory. But, just as Israel had to battle to receive the land given them, so the believer has to do spiritual warfare to possess the promises of God (Joshua 1:2-3; Deuteronomy 1:8). Jesus, our heavenly Joshua, has already conquered our enemy so that we can move into a victory that is already won. This can only be known experientially as we recognize our complete identification with Christ.

A. The Believer's Position — Legally

1. We are in Christ (Ephesians 1:3-7). In Christ we are partakers of the divine nature (II Peter 1:4).
2. We are new creatures (II Corinthians 5:17; Galatians 6:15).
3. We are in the kingdom of light (Colossians 1:13-14; Romans 8:38; Acts 26:18).
4. We are seated in heavenly places with Christ (Ephesians 1:3; 2:2-8; 6:12).

B. The Believer's Responsibility - Experientially

1. The believer must live victorious over the sins of the flesh, giving Satan no ground to stand on (John 14:30. AMP. N. T.; John 16:31; Romans 6:7–8; Ephesians 4:27; Galatians 5:22–23).
2. The believer must keep himself in the love of God so that the Wicked One will not be able to touch him (I John 4:17–18; 5:18).
3. The believer must submit to God and then resist the devil (James 4:7; II Corinthians 2:11).

C. The Believer's Battleground - Personally

Satan seeks to attack the believer in the three areas of his being. He attacks the body and the soul to reach the spirit (I Peter 2:11). It is a spiritual battle. As the believer recognizes his position in Christ, and fulfills his responsibility, then there is no ground upon which Satan can work (John 14:30, AMP. N. T.; I Thessalonians 5:23; John 16:31; Amplified New Testament).

The following is a consideration of how Satan relates to the three areas of man's being.

1. Spirit

In that the believer is the temple of God, his spirit is the "holy of holies" or the "most holy place". It is God's inner sanctuary. The born again believer's spirit is regenerated, justified and indwelt by the Holy Spirit. It is one with the Holy Spirit. (I Corinthians 6:17; Romans 8:16; John 3:1-5). No truly born again believer can be possessed by demon spirits. The Holy Spirit comes to the believer's spirit to bring his spirit into total union with God, through Christ, and there is no room left for a demon to reside there.

2. Soul

The soul represents the Holy Place of the Temple of God, and includes the mind, will and emotions. The soul has to be renewed by the Word of God. This is referred to in Romans 12:1-2 where we find that the believer has to be transformed by the renewing of his mind. The mind, will and emotions have to be brought into full harmony with the Spirit and Word of God.

It is in the realm of the soul that the believer experiences the "fiery darts" of the enemy. Oppression, depression, fear, unbelief, evil thoughts, emotional and mental torment, Satanic accusations and deception, are some of the "fiery darts" that have to be recognized, resisted and quenched by the spiritual weapons of God. The battle for the mind is the major area of conflict (II Corinthians 10:3-5; Matthew 15:19-20; Proverbs 23:7).

It is important to recognize the three sources of all thoughts. In Matthew 16:15-23 we have a clear illustration of these sources; thoughts from man or one's self (verses 13-14), thoughts from God (verses 15-17) and thoughts from Satan, or evil spirits (verses 21-23). The believer must learn to recognize the source of his thoughts, He must learn not to entertain thoughts which are contrary to the Word and Spirit of God. No one can stop these "fiery darts" being sent at them, but he can quench them with the Word of God. He can put on the helmet of salvation which is for the protection of the mind.

Sin entered the mind when the serpent tempted Eve (II Corinthians 11:3). Peter allowed thoughts to enter in his mind from Satan (Matthew 16:22-23). Judas accepted thoughts of betraying Jesus which came from the devil (John 13:2,27). Thus, the mind has to be renewed (Romans 12:1-2); and the believer must allow the mind of Christ to be in him (Philippians 2:5-8). He must discipline his mind to think on divine things (Philippians 4:8-9). The carnal and fleshly mind must be crucified (Colossians 2:18; 1:21; Romans 8:7-9; Ephesians 4:17-23).

Every imagination and thought that would exalt itself against the knowledge of Christ must be cast down and brought into captivity to the obedience of Christ (II Corinthians 10:3-5).

3. Body

The body represents the Outer Court of the Temple of God (I Corinthians 6:19-20). Its faculties are the five senses of hearing, seeing, tasting, feeling and smelling. The body is the physical part of man through which he contacts the natural world around him. The attack of the enemy here is upon the appetites and instincts God has placed within man. Other "fiery darts" which attack the body are sickness, disease and infirmity. Afflicting spirits may attack the believer's body, but again, he is to take the Word of God and use the spiritual weapons God has given to conquer them.

D. The Believer's Spiritual Armoury — Practically

The Lord has given to the Church and the believer, spiritual weapons which are mighty through God. These are not carnal weapons but they come from the Lord's armoury (Jeremiah 50:25; II Corinthians 10:3-5).

1. The Word of God

It is essential to know the Word of God (John 8:32-34). In order to exercise our legal rights and privileges, we must know God's Word. Satan's power to deceive is on the ground of ignorance and God's people are often destroyed for lack of knowledge. It is the word which enlightens our ignorance. Jesus used the word ("It is written") to overcome Satan in his temptations (Matthew 4:1-10; Psalm 119:130; Ephesians 1:15-22; I John 2:12-14; Revelation 12:11; II Corinthians 2:11; Ephesians 6:17).

2. The Name of Jesus

Jesus gave the believer the legal right to use His name. His name represents our power and authority. He stands behind His name. There is no higher authority. The power is not in us but in Him whose name we bear (Matthew 10:1,8; Luke 9:1; Mark 3:15; 6:7,13; 16:17; Acts 16:18; Philippians 2:9-11; John 16:23-24; 14:13-15; Luke 10:17-20).

3. Christ in You
By new birth, the Holy Spirit indwells the believer. Greater is He that is in the believer than he that is in the world (I John 2:14; Galatians 4:6; Colossians 1:27; Ephesians 1:17-23; John 1:12; I John 4:17; I Corinthians 6:17; I John 4:4).

4. The Blood of Jesus
The sinless and incorruptible blood of Jesus is the cleansing power in the believer against sin (I John 1:5-6). The blood of Christ is our redemption ground. It is our justification and it keeps us clean before God (Romans 3:25; Revelation 12:11).

5. The Power of the Holy Spirit
The believer who is Spirit-filled is given equipment also to contend with and withstand all the power of the enemy. Jesus cast out spirits by the power of the Holy Spirit. As a man He utterly depended upon the Spirit (Matthew 12:28). The Holy Spirit, who resides within us, is God; omnipotent, omniscient, omnipresent and greater than every other spirit in the world (Acts 1:5,8; Luke 24:49).

6. The Gifts of the Spirit
Another spiritual weapon is the gift of the discerning of spirits. This is a protective gift, enabling the Church to discern what spirit is at work in a supernatural manifestation (I Corinthians 12:9-11; I John 4:1-3; Isaiah 8:19-20).

7. The Whole Armor of God
God has provided all the armor needed by the believer in spiritual warfare. Each piece of this spiritual armor is important (Ephesians 6:10-18; Romans 13:12; II Corinthians 6:7; Romans 10:6-17).

It is by the spiritual weapons which God has given to the Church that all believers may be able to war a good warfare and be part of that victorious Church against which the gates of hell shall not prevail (Matthew 16:18-19).

Chapter 8

DOCTRINE OF MAN

The Scriptures clearly teach that the original man was the direct result of a creative act of God. Being the masterpiece of creation, man was created in the image and likeness of God as a tripartite being, consisting of spirit, soul and body. God created man to have a relationship with Him, to be made into His image and likeness, to share in His function of dominion and to be fruitful and reproduce Himself. Though the entrance of sin seemed to frustrate God's purpose for man in creation, this purpose will be accomplished through redemption.

CHAPTER OUTLINE

I. THEORIES CONCERNING THE ORIGIN OF MAN

A. Atheistic Evolution
B. Theistic Evolution
C. Theistic Creation

II. WHAT MAN IS

A. Man is a Created Being
B. Man is a Dependent Being
C. Man is an Intelligent Being
D. Man is a Moral Being
E. Man is a Love Being
F. Man is a Triune Being

III. GOD'S PURPOSE FOR MAN

A. Relationship
B. Character
C. Function
D. Reproduction

THEORIES CONCERNING THE ORIGIN OF MAN

The study of the doctrine of man has also been called Anthropology. This word comes from two Greek words; "anthropos" meaning "man" and "logos" meaning "word, or discourse". One of the chief areas of concern is the inevitable question of the origin of man. Mankind wants to know where he came from and where he is going. Three theories concerning man's origin will be treated briefly here.

A. Atheistic Evolution

The Atheistic Evolutionist holds the theory of spontaneous generation—that all forms of animal life evolved from more primitive forms of life. The evolutionary theory holds roughly that cell matter evolved into life forms, and then to fish, birds, animals, apes and finally man. It remains a theory, not a proven fact, because the "missing links" in the transitional stages have never been found. The evolutionary theory is built on supposition, and literature with an honest representation of it abounds in the use of terms like "maybe, we suggest, perhaps, it could be, we assume, it is possible, it is feasible, and, it may be presupposed". Atheistic Evolution is based on the survival of the fittest, but it cannot account for the arrival of the first. It fails to adequately account for the origin of matter and life because it rejects God the originator of matter and the source of all life.

B. Theistic Evolution

This theory also holds that higher forms of life evolved from lower forms, but that the lower forms were created by God. This is partly the truth in that God is acknowledged as the creator of part of creation. However, it is also partly false in that the Bible teaches the creation of the species, not their evolution. All fish, birds, animals and man were created in their order to reproduce "after their kind", not to evolve to some higher form. A reptile can only produce a reptile, a horse can only produce a horse, and a monkey can only produce a monkey, never a man.

C. Theistic Creation

Theistic Creation holds to the Scriptural fact that God is the life-source, the originator and maintainer of all forms of life, and the one who created all to reproduce "after their kind". God created the heavens and the earth, the universe of worlds and the galaxies(Genesis 1:1). God created the archangels and the angelic hosts (Colossians 1:16-17; Revelation 4:11). God created the fish of the sea, the fowls of the air, the beasts of the field and every living creature (Genesis 1:21-25; John 1:1-3). The final creative act of God was man, the highest creation of God on this earth (Genesis 1:26-31).

The original man was the direct result of a creative act of God. Man is a divinely created being, the crowning glory and masterpiece of God's creation. The unity of the human race points to the creative act of God of the original pair, man and woman (Acts 17:26; Romans 5:12,19; I Corinthians 15:21-22; Hebrews 2:16). All the nations are of one blood for all were "in Adam" when he was created. The only true answer to the questions concerning the origin of man is God's answer as found in the Bible. Man is a created being.

II. WHAT MAN IS

The Psalmist in beholding the glory of the heavens, asked the question, "What is man..." (Psalm 8:4 with Job 7:17-18; Psalm 144:3; Hebrews 2:6). The following outline answers this vital question.

A. Man is a Created Being

(Genesis 1:26-28; 2:7; Job 33:4; Revelation 4:11; Psalm 139:14-16; 104:30; I Corinthians 11:9; Isaiah 45:12) God said "Let us **MAKE MAN** in our image, after our likeness ..." (Genesis 1:26-27). There are two words used in the Genesis account of creation that are worthy of consideration. These words are "created" and "made" (Genesis 1:26; 2:1-3). The word "create" means "to make something out of nothing, to bring into existence". The word "make" means to fashion or form as a potter forms a vessel of clay. Thus God created man as to his spirit and soul (Zechariah 12:1) but God made man as to his body (Genesis 2:7). Man is a created being. He owes his existence to God, the creator and sustainer of all things.

B. Man is a Dependent Being

The fact that man owes his existence to a creator, makes him a dependent creature. He is not self-existent and thus cannot be independent. Whether realizing it or not, he is totally dependent on God for his very breath. It is in God that "we live, and move and have our being" (Acts 17:23-31).

C. Man is an Intelligent Being

Man is a being having reason, intelligence, imagination, and the ability to express his thoughts in language. This is far superior to the animal creation who are simply creatures of habit and instinct. (Genesis 2:15; 1:26-28; 2:19-20; Isaiah 1:18; Matthew 16:7; Genesis 11:6; 8:21; Job 35:11; Romans 1:21).

D. Man is a Moral Being

God created man with a free-will, the ability to choose. It is this which makes man a moral and therefore responsible creature. Just as God created the angelic hosts as beings with free will, having the power of choice, so God created man with the power of choice. Man was not created as a robot, a machine, or a will-less creature. God desired a creature that would respond to Him willingly and freely. This necessitated man having a free will.

Some deny the fact of man's free will, but the Scriptures support it by often appealing to man's will to respond to God's will. It will be admitted that man's will is weakened because of sin, but nevertheless it is still existent. Though man's will is subject to his corrupt nature and evil heart, he can still respond to the influence of the Holy Spirit. This is not to say that man can save himself. God must do that, but man can respond to God's call. These Scriptures illustrate how God appeals to man's will (John 7:17; Hebrews 3:7,8,15; 4:7; John 1:12,13).

God placed within man a conscience which gives him a moral sense, distinguishing right from wrong. Conscience means "a knowledge of self in relation to a known law of right and wrong". It is a faculty that no animal has. Though man was created in a state of innocence, purity and uprightness, he was ignorant of evil. In this upright state, his conscience was inactive until he sinned. The moment he sinned, his conscience began to work, and his thoughts began to accuse and excuse him.

Strong, in "Systematic Theology" (p.497) says concerning man's moral powers, "These powers are intellect, sensibility, and will together with that peculiar power of discrimination and impulsion, which we call conscience". The intellect enables man to discern between what is right and wrong; sensibility appeals to him to do one or the other; and will decides the issue. Conscience involves them all. It applies God's moral law to man.

A. A. Hodge in "Outlines of Theology" (p. 285) states "Conscience, like every other faculty of the soul, is undeveloped in the infant, and very imperfectly developed in the savage; and, moreover, after a long habit of inattention to its voice and violation of its law, the individual sinner is often judicially given up to a carnal indifference; his conscience for a time lying latent. Yet it is certain that it is never destroyed". Conscience is indestructible, and it is this which consititutes man's torment as "the worm that never dieth" in Gehenna in eternity (Mark 9:46-48; Isaiah 66:24).

Conscience, however, is fallible, for since man's knowledge has been perverted through sin, it does not form a perfectly sound basis of judgment. Conscience is not a perfect moral standard. Thiessen in "Lectures in Systematic Theology" (p.229) says "The only true standard for conscience is the Word of God as interpreted by the Holy Spirit" (John 8:9; Acts 24:16; Hebrews 9:14; Romans 2:15; I Corinthians 8:7; Titus 1:15; I Timothy 4:2). The Holy Spirit has to bring the conscience into line with the infallible Word (Romans 9:1). (Refer to the section on the conscience in "The Doctrine of Sin".).

E. Man is a Love Being

In this fact we come to the very purpose and reason for the creation of man. God is love and love must not only have an object but must have that which can reciprocate that love (I John 4:16-19). The created universe with all of its glories cannot respond to the love of God. The brute creation cannot enjoy or reciprocate God's love. If God, who is love, desires a creation upon whom He can bestow His love, then it must be able to respond and reciprocate it. Such a creature would be unresponsive, unaffectionate and will-less, affording God no pleasure at all. The answer to the heart cry of God was the creation of man. Man is a being with a will and intelligence; capable of choosing to love. He was created by love, for love, and to reciprocate love. Without such love man's heart remains empty and void.

F. Man is A Triune Being

There are two basic theories concerning man's being.

1. The Dichotomous Theory

This theory holds that man is a dual or bi-partite being, consisting of a spirit/soul (two terms which are synonymous and interchangeable) and a body.

2. The Trichotomous Theory

This theory holds that man is a tripartite being, consisting of spirit, soul and body. Spirit and soul are distinguishable but indivisible, and these are housed in a physical body. This seems to be more consistent with the whole of Scripture.

God is triune in His being, and so man, created in the image and likeness of God, was created a triune being, consisting of spirit, soul and body (I Thessalonians 5:23; Hebrews 4:12; Genesis 2:7; I Corinthians 2:14-3:4). These are the three centers of consciousness within the total personality of man.

There are three different words both in Hebrew and Greek pertaining to man's tripartite being.

In Hebrew: 1. "Ruach" — Spirit
2. "Nephesh" — Soul
3. "Beten" or "Geshem" Body

In Greek: 1. "Pneuma" — Spirit
2. "Psueche" — Soul
3. "Soma" — Body

Let us consider the triunity of man, which speaks of three centers of consciousness within man's being.

a. **Spirit:** The God-conscious part of man, capable of knowing God. When God created man, He formed the spirit of man within him (Zechariah 12:1). Thus God is the God of all spirits (Numbers 16:22; 27:16; Hebrews 12:9). The spirit is the eternal part of man that is able to worship God who is Spirit (John 4:24). It is referred to as the candle of the Lord (Proverbs 20:27; Job 32:8; Ecclesiastes 12:7; 3:19-21; I Corinthians 2:11). The faculties of the spirit are intuition, conscience and communion.

When man fell, his spirit lost its contact with God. This can only be restored through regeneration. In the new birth, it is man's spirit that is born again, or renewed. "That which is born of the Spirit, is spirit (John 3:6 with Romans 8:16; Titus 3:5; Ezekiel 11:19-20; 36:25-27; John 3:1-6; 20:22; Colossians 3:10; Ezekiel 18:31; Psalm 51:10; Malachi 2:16). The believer's spirit, when joined to the Lord, becomes one with the Holy Spirit (I Corinthians 6:17).

b. **Soul:** The self-conscious part of man, capable of knowing one's self. Moses, in the account of creation tells how God formed man's body out of the dust of the earth, and then breathed into man "the breath of life", or more literally, "the breath of lives" (Genesis 2:7).

Man received his spirit and soul as God breathed into his body formed of the earth. The breath of lives included both spirit life and soul life. The first man then became a living soul (I Corinthians 15:45-47; Ezekiel 18:4; Matthew 10:28; Leviticus 17:11; Revelation 6:9,10). The soul is the central or the mediatorial part of man connecting the spirit and the body together in triunity. It can influence spirit and . .or body because of its centrality. There are basically three theories as to the origin of the soul.

The Theory of Pre-existence: this theory states that all souls have previously existed and then enter the human body at some point after conception. However, this theory has absolutely no foundation in Scripture.

The Theory of Creation: this theory holds that every soul is created by God some time after conception. It teaches that the person only receives their body from the parents, but the soul from God. However, Bible revelation and human experience shows that the sinful nature of Adam and character traits and likenesses of the parents are seen in every child born.

The Theory of the Traducianists: this theory holds that the human race was created "in Adam" as pertaining to soul and body and that both are the result of natural reproduction. This theory seems to be most consistent with the Word of God.

The Bible is clear that all the human race was representatively "in Adam" and that when he sinned and fell, the whole human race fell with him. Both Scripture and human experience shows the sinful nature and character traits of parents to be in their offspring. Adam, the first soul came into being as a result of God's creative power. All souls since come into existence by the co-operation of Creator and parents. God is the "Father of spirits" (Hebrews 12:9), and the soul and body come from the parents according to the laws of human reproduction. It is this that seems to balance out the views concerning Creationism and Traducianism.

Creationism holds the view concerning that the soul is transmitted from the parents, as seen in traits, characteristics of the parents in the child. God does not create sinless souls every time a child is born, nor is the soul pre-existent, but God gives the spirit and the child receives soul and body from the original parents via the laws of human reproduction. This would account for the sinful nature, and character traits from parents (Job 14:14; 15:4; Psalm 51:5; 58:3; John 3:6; Ephesians 2:3; Psalm 139:13-16; Job 10:8-12; Ecclesiastes 11:5).

We will consider how the word "soul" is used in Scripture and then consider its various associations.

(1) It is Used of Persons in General

There is a general use of the word "soul" with reference to persons. When we say "there are 70 souls present", we mean that there are 70 persons present. Following are some Scriptures which illustrate this point (Genesis 12:5; 46:15,18, 22-27; Exodus 1:5; Joshua 10:28-39; Acts 2:41-43; 7:14; I Peter 3:20; Revelation 20:4; Ezekiel 22:25-27). Thus when God breathed into man the breath of life, man became a living soul, that is a living person (Genesis 2:7).

(2) It is Sometimes Used Interchangeably for Spirit

Sometimes the words "soul" and "spirit" are used interchangeably or synonymously. It is for this reason that some expositors hold to the dual being of man, or follow the Dichotomous theory. In the bodily resurrection of the child under Elijah's ministry, the Scripture says that the child's soul came again (I Kings 17:17-23). In the bodily resurrection of the child under Christ's ministry, the Scriptures say that "her spirit came again" (Luke 8:49-56). Hebrews speaks of the dead believers as being "the spirits of just men made perfect" (Hebrews 12:23). Revelation speaks of "the souls under the altar" in heaven appealing to God for vengeance (Revelation 6:9-11). When it is understood that the spirit and soul are distinguishable but indivisible then the interchangeable or synonymous use of both does not produce any conflict. The Scriptures given illustrate this statement. In the bodily resurrection, the child's soul could not come again without the spirit, nor the spirit without the soul. The spirits in heaven are souls and the souls are redeemed spirits.

(3) It is Used to Denote Soul-Faculties

The faculties of the soul are basically three; mind, will and emotions. It is for this reason that the word is used of the following:

God has Soul: Though God is a Spirit, yet He is spoken of as having soul and His soul is grieved over man. Spirit and soul are associated with God; distinguishable but indivisible (Leviticus 26:11; Joshua 10:16; Isaiah 1:14; Hebrews 10:38).

Christ has Soul: Several times Scriptures speak of the soul of Christ (Psalm 16:10; Acts 2:27-31; Isaiah 53:11-12; John 12:27; Matthew 26:38). As perfect and complete Man, He has spirit, soul and body. Christ's mind, will and emotions were absolutely one with God the Father.

Man has Soul: The Scriptures not only show man has a soul, but that man is a living soul.

Man is spirit, soul and body. (I Thessalonians 5:23; Hebrews 4:12). The word "soul" is used of man about 400 times in the Bible. Man is a spirit being, yet he has a soul with mind, will and emotions.

Animals have Soul: The Hebrew word "nephesh" for "soul" is also translated "living creature" and is used to refer to "animal soul". It is used of beasts several times in the Word of God (Genesis 1:21,24; 2:19; 9:10,12,15,16; Leviticus 11:46; Ecclesiastes 12:7). However, there is a definite distinction between animal soul and human soul. The soul life of man is manifested in mind, will and emotions, as well as in bodily instincts. Human soul is now sinful. Animal soul is not. Animals do not have spirit, nor are they able to know and commune with God. They do not have a conscience, nor are they able to sin and thus be accountable to God. Man was made in the image and likeness of God; not the animals. Man's blood is of higher value to God than animal blood. Some of the major differences between man and beast are that man has a spirit, capable of knowing God, that man is a moral being having a conscience and that he is responsible and accountable before God. This is not so of animals. Animals cannot be born again, walk with God, love God nor worship Him intelligently, as can man made in God's image. Man also has the capacity for immortality. The animals do not.

(4) Associated with Other Parts of Man's Being.

(a) Spirit, soul and body: This is significant of the whole personality of man (I Thessalonians 5:23; Hebrews 4:12).

(b) Spirit and soul: This is significant of the eternal and invisible parts of man's being; involving the God-conscious part, the self-conscious part of man, with mind, will and emotions. (Isaiah 57:15-16).

(c) Spirit and Body: This involves the God-conscious and the sense-conscious part of man (Daniel 7:15; I Corinthians 14:14)

(d) Body and Soul: This speaks of the self-conscious and sense-conscious parts of man. (Matthew 10:28; Luke 12:4)

(e) Soul and Blood: This speaks of the soul-life that is in the blood (Leviticus 3:17; 17:11; Isaiah 53:10,12). Blood is the source and holder of physical life. The heart is the pump causing the blood to carry life to the whole body. The blood of man has become the seat of corruption, sickness, disease, and death. Blood speaks of the life of man, thus God could take the blood of Jesus, which is precious and incorruptible, and make atonement for man's sin. Blood has value. The blood of animals is of lesser value than the blood of man (Genesis 9:6). The blood of martyrs is valuable to God (Matthew 23:35; Revelation 6:9,10; Genesis 4:10; Hebrews 12:24; Job 24:12). The blood of Christ is of infinite value because it is the blood of God (I Peter 1:19; Hebrews 9:12). Thus when soul and blood are associated in Scripture it speaks of the soul-life which is in the blood—that is, conveyed by the blood, giving a person consciousness physically. In death the blood perishes, but the soul with its faculties continue to exist.

(f) Soul, Heart, Mind and Strength: The soul, heart, mind and strength are used to set forth man's faculties (Matthew 22:37; Mark 12:30; Deuteronomy 6:11, 4:29).

(5) It is Used of the Human Soul
The human soul has the faculties of mind, will and emotions.

(a) The **mind** includes the thoughts, imaginations, understanding, memory, reason and intellect. Heart and mind are connected in Scripture. "As a man thinketh in his heart, so is he" (Proverbs 23:7). It is out of the heart that thoughts proceed (Mark 7:20-23). This is not referring to the physical heart but to the soul faculty (Psalm 46:2; Ezekiel 27:25-27; Exodus 15:18; Matthew 12:39-40; Genesis 6:5; 8:21; 17:17; Exodus 23:9; Deuteronomy 4:9, 29,39; II Kings 10:30-31).

(b) The **will** is the ability to choose and to make decisions. The heart and will are also connected in Scripture (I Chronicles 29:9; Exodus 35:5,29; Psalm 9:11).

(c) The **emotions** involve the feelings, good or bad, which are the result of good or bad behavior, or good or bad attitudes. The emotions of joy (Isaiah 65:14), exultation (Acts 2:46), pain (Proverbs 25:20), sorrow (Psalm 14:1; 102:4), anger (Proverbs 23:7), and fear (Jeremiah 32:40) all center in the soul.

c. Body:

The sense or world-conscious part of man; capable of knowing and receiving things from the world around him. God made and formed man's body out of the dust of the earth, as a potter forms a clay vessel (Genesis 1:26-27; 2:7; Job 10:9; Genesis 3:19; I Timothy 2:13). It is the physical part of man which is similar to the brute creation. The Scripture gives the following designations and information concerning the human body.

(1) The Human Body is a House (II Corinthians 5:1)
As a house is built to be indwelt by someone, so man was built to be indwelt by the Spirit of God. Jesus spoke of unclean spirits that desire to live in man's body, as a house (Matthew 12:43-45).

(2) The Human Body is a Tabernacle (II Corinthians 5:1-4; John 1:14; II Peter 1:13).
A tabernacle is a tent. Christ's body, as well as our human bodies are likened to tents. It is significant of the fact that we are pilgrims. At physical death the tent is taken down and dissolved, as the spirit and soul depart.

(3) The Human Body is a Temple (John 2:21; II Corinthians 5:19; I Corinthians 3:16; 6:19-20; I Kings 8:27-28).

The body of Jesus was likened to a Temple. So is the believer's body. It is to be a habitation of God by the Spirit, teaching the same truth as that of the tabernacle (Ephesians 2:21-22). We are to present this purchased body to the Lord and keep the temple clean, pure and holy for His dwelling (I Corinthians 6:20; Romans 12:1; Hebrews 10:22).

(4) The Human Body is a Sheath (Daniel 7:15 margin).
The human body is likened here to a sheath in which the spirit is placed like a sword. At death, the sword of the spirit is withdrawn from the sheath and the sheath decays.

(5) The Human Body is Earthy (I Corinthians 15:47; Psalm 103:14; Genesis 2:7; 3:19).
The First Adam had a natural and earthly body prepared and placed upon him. It is from the dust of the earth and at death it returns to dust. The human body has the same ingredients in it as the dust. Its whole substance comes from earth and all that pertains to it.

(6) The Human Body is a Body of Humiliation (Philippians 3:21; Job 19:25-27).
The body is spoken of as being "our vile body" in Philippians. It is literally "the body of our humiliation". This is particularly true since the fall of man. Sin has subjected man's body to sickness, disease infirmity, corruption and death (I Corinthians 15:33). Mankind groans in this mortal or death-doomed body (II Corinthians 5:2). It is indeed the body of our humiliation and because of this God gave Israel very strict laws for the governing and cleanliness of bodily life, as seen especially in Leviticus.

(7) The Human Body is Governed by Senses
The body, being the instrument of the soul, and being the world-conscious part of man is governed by five senses; seeing, hearing, smelling, tasting, and feeling. By these five

faculties, man acquires knowledge of the external world, communicates with mankind and cares for his physical and mental wellbeing.

In due time God will redeem the believer's body from all corruption and mortality and make it like Christ's glorious body (Philippians 3:21; I Thessalonians 4:15-18; I Corinthians 15:51-57; II Corinthians 5: 1-5).

God's order for man to find fulfilment as man is to maintain proper order of spirit, soul and body, subject to the Word and Spirit of God. Any violation or corruption in these areas of man's being brings chaos. Man was created by God, for God, to be filled with God. Apart from God, man finds neither purpose or fulfillment in life. Thus man becomes self-willed, frustrated, self-centered, confused and a continual vacuum; spiritually, psychologically and physically. The man who finds completeness and fulfilment in life is the man who knows God. It is God's purpose that man's whole being be redeemed. Redemptive power will perfect man's spirit, cleanse and purify his mind, will and emotions, and ultimately redeem his body.

II. GOD'S PURPOSE FOR MAN
God has a reason for everything He does. He moves with definite purpose. Careful forethought and planning goes into all His works. The following Scriptures speak of God's purposes:

Isaiah 14:26 — God has a purpose that involves the whole earth and all the nations on it.

Isaiah 14:24,27 — If God decides to do something no one can stop Him.

Isaiah 46:11 — God will follow through and accomplish His purposes.

Romans 8:28 — God has invited us to fulfill His purpose

II Timothy 1:9 — God's purpose was fixed before creation, is centered in Christ and is not beyond the means of His grace.

Ephesians 1:9-11 — Our destiny has been pre-determined according to His purpose (our lives were pre-planned to fulfill it).

Ephesians 3:9-11 — God's eternal purpose is centered in the church.

All of God's purposes proceed from His person. What He does is always consistent with who He is. The kind of person He is dictates the kind of things He does. Of all the descriptions of God in the Bible, perhaps the most all-inclusive one is the title "Father". God's Father-heart compels Him to have a family that He can be a Father to. His purposes are easily illustrated centering around this theme.

The only way that man will be able to find fulfillment in life is to discover the reasons why he was created and fulfill them. Just as using a saw to hammer nails or trying to use a car to fly are inconsistent with the law of purpose and will not be successful, so man living for reasons other than those God intended will only lead to frustration and failure. Man should be endeavoring to discover and fulfill the reasons God had in mind for creating him. The Bible reveals God's purpose for man which is summarized here as being four-fold; (1) Relationship, (2) Character, (3) Function and (4) Reproduction.

A. Relationship
The first reason God created man was for the purpose of relationship. God the Father wanted a family of children to share life with to get to know in a personal way. Throughout Scripture God's desire for fellowship and communion with man is revealed. From the time that God sought Adam "in the garden in the cool of the day" God has been seeking fellowship with man (Genesis 3:8). However, the sin which caused Adam to hide from God has been hindering man's relationship with God ever since (Isaiah 59:1,2). It is only through the New Covenant that God's purpose of relationship with man is fully accomplished. Now God indwells each believer making fellowship constantly available (John 14:16-20,23).

B. Character

The second reason God created man was to reproduce His nature and character. God the Father wanted His children to look like Him on the inside. He wanted them to bear the family "image and likeness" (Genesis 1:26). Character is one of the main thoughts in the word "image". In Hebrews 1:3 Jesus is described as being "the express image" of His father's person. The Greek word translated image in that verse is pronounced CHARACTER and it is the word from which our English word "character" is derived. God wants man to partake of His divine nature (II Peter 1:4-7), to be conformed to the image of His Son (Romans 8:28,29), and to be changed into His image by the Spirit (II Corinthians 3:18; 4:4). Since it was a corruption of character (disobedience) that broke man's relationship with God, it is necessary that man's character be changed, restored and made just like God's own nature. The sinful, self-centered element in man's nature must be replaced by the holy, loving and self-giving nature of God.

C. Function

The third reason God created man was to have someone share in His function of ruling the universe. God the Father wanted His children to be involved in the family business. He not only purposed that man be something (character) but also that he do something (function). God wanted man to share in His dominion (Genesis 1:26). To do this God told man to subdue, which means to conquer an enemy (Genesis 1:28). At that time the only enemy there was to conquer was Satan and in man's first encounter with him, he lost (Genesis 3). Man lost his dominion and came under bondage to Satan, sin, sickness and death. Now, only through Christ, who has conquered all, can man's dominion be regained.

D. Reproduction

The fourth reason God created man was to share some of His creative powers. God the Father wanted His children to reproduce more children to be in the family. He told Adam and Eve to "be fruitful, and multiply, and replenish the earth" (Genesis 1:28). This certainly speaks of reproduction by natural birth, but there is more to it than just bringing babies into existence. There is the factor of reproducing "after our kind". The seed of sin in Adam was reproduced in his first-born son Cain. This necessitates the new spiritual birth in which those who have been "born-again" and have become the children of God by redemption, reproduce "after their kind". Thus the New Testament exhorts us to "be fruitful" (Colossians 1:10; John 15:16) and records that the disciples of Jesus "multiplied" (Acts 6:1,7).

This four-fold purpose of God is both progressive and interdependent. Relationship with God is essential for character development to occur, character is to be the basis for function, and when these three are in order, reproduction will be the natural result. This purpose of God for man has never changed and will yet be fulfilled through the church of Jesus Christ.

Chapter 9

THE DOCTRINE OF SIN

Human history and man's conscience bear testimony to sin's reality. The Scriptures show that sin entered the universe through Satan and then into the human race with the fall of Adam and Eve. The Bible reveals the essence of sin to be self-centeredness and its tragic result to be death, but it also reveals God's redemptive plan in Christ to make an end of sin for eternity.

CHAPTER OUTLINE

I. THE FACT OF SIN

    A. Creation declares it
    B. Human History declares it
    C. Human Logic declares it
    D. Human Conscience declares it
    E. Human Experience declares it
    F. Human Religions declare it
    G. Believers declare it
    H. Scriptures declare it

II. THEORIES CONCERNING SIN

    A. False Theories Concerning Sin
    B. False Religious Theories Concerning Sin
    C. Other Theories Concerning Sin

III. BIBLE DEFINITIONS OF SIN

    A. Scriptural Definitions
    B. Hebrew Words for Sin
    C. Greek Words for Sin

IV. THE LAW OF GOD IN RELATION TO SIN

    A. The Necessity of Law
    B. The Transgression of Law

V. THE ORIGIN OF SIN

    A. The Entrance of Sin into the Universe
    B. The Entrance of Sin into Humanity

VI. THE LAW OF SIN

VII. A BRIEF SYNOPSIS OF THE LAWS OF GOD

    A. The Law
    B. The Law of Conscience
    C. The Law of Works
    D. The Law of Faith
    E. The Law of Ten Commandments
    F. The Law of Sin and Death
    G. The Law of the Spirit of Life
    H. The Law of Righteousness
    I. The Royal Law of Love

The Doctrine of Sin is called Hamartiology, which comes from two Greek words, Harmartia meaning sin and Logos meaning word or discourse. Thus Harmartiology is the Biblical teaching concerning sin, its origin, definition, expression and final end.

There are certain questions concerning sin's origin that finite man cannot answer. The word of God to Israel in Deuteronomy 29:29 was "The secret things belong unto the Lord our God: but the things which are revealed belong unto us and to our children forever, that we may do all the words of this law." Man must satisfy himself with the measure of truth concerning the doctrine of sin that is revealed in the Scriptures, not seeking to go beyond it, knowing that God will answer the questions in His own time.

I. THE FACT OF SIN
It is evident that there is something wrong in the universe, with both the earth and its inhabitants. The source of all chaos, disharmony and strife in the world can be traced back to the existence of sin.

We will now consider several evidences of the fact of sin.

A. Creation Declares It
All of nature declares that something is wrong. The contrast between life and death, harmony and discord, beauty and ugliness, light and darkness, declare the fact of sin. Planet earth and the forces of nature seem to be turned against mankind. Sometimes blessing and sometimes blighting, nature seems to be double-minded in its treatment of man. The earth which was meant to bless man seems to be under some form of a curse. And this is exactly so, for when sin entered the human race, all nature fell with its king and turned against him (Genesis 3:17; 8:22).

B. Human History Declares It
The briefest view of human history with its chaos and confusion, war and bloodshed, the spirit of hate and murder, covetousness, moral corruption and dominance indicates that something is wrong in the nations of the earth. Where do the wars and fightings among the nations of the world come from? The answer is found in the existence of sin (James 4:1-4).

C. Human Logic Declares It
To deny the fact of sin in the human race would be an insult to all logic. Man knows that something is wrong inside of himself. He knows that he is out of harmony with himself, that discord reigns within his being. It is the fact of sin that explains it. Educated mentality would seek to deny the fact of sin but deep within every person's being he knows that when he would do good, evil is present with him (Romans 7:14-21). Man does wrong because he is wrong. Any one who exercises any measure of intellectual honesty will admit that sin is a fact.

D. Human Conscience Declares It
This is closely linked with human logic, but conscience is a further witness to the fact of sin. The moment a person does something wrong, his conscience smites him and his thoughts begin to accuse or else excuse him (Romans 2:14-15). The law of conscience gives abundant evidence of sin's reality.

E. Human Experience Declares It
When one reads the list of horrible sins in Scripture such as Romans 1:21-32 and Mark 7:20-21 in the light of the news of today, there is abundant evidence of sin's expression in human experience. Immorality, crime, violence, perversion and all forms of lawlessness abound. Sin desires to express itself and the corruption of society in modern civilization is evidence of the fact of sin. Scripture indicates that this will increase in the last days (Matthew 24:12; II Timothy 3:1-5).

F. Human Religions Declare It
In every nation there is belief in a god or gods. Nearly every nation has developed some form of religion involving priesthood and sacrifices of appeasement. They seek to appease the gods because of the inner sense of sin and as a realization of their need of redemption. Religion itself is another witness of sin's reality. However, it is only true Christianity which has God's answer to the sin problem as dealt with in the person of Christ.

G. Believers Declare It
The believer who knows Christ as His Lord and Savior becomes more accutely aware of the fact of sin.

The believer is more conscious after salvation of two laws of conflict within him; the law of sin and death and the law of the Spirit of life. Paul's words in Romans 7 testify to this fact. No believer is sinlessly perfect yet, but is vitally aware that sin is a reality and must be cleansed and overcome by the Word and Spirit of God (Romans 3:20 with 7:7-25).

H. Scriptures Declare It

The highest court of appeal is the Word of God. The Bible declares the universality of sin, that all men are sinners in God's sight, needing salvation (Psalm 14:1-3; 53:1-3; Romans 5:12). Romans 3:23 — "All have sinned and come short of the glory of God". The Scriptures show that there are two major mysteries at work in the universe and all other mysteries referred to in the Word of God find their place under these two. These two mysteries are called "The Mystery of Godliness" and "The Mystery of Iniquity" (I Timothy 3:16 with II Thessalonians 2:7). Thus, good and evil, light and darkness, life and death, godliness and iniquity are at work in the universe. All created beings, angelic or human, will make their choice and take their place under one mystery or the other. Their choice will settle their eternal destiny.

II. THEORIES CONCERNING SIN

A proper conception of sin is absolutely necessary to a correct understanding of practically every other Bible doctrine. This is a fundamental issue in theology. Spiritually speaking, there comes a "chain reaction" in the fundamental doctrines of redemption. False concepts of the holiness of God arise out of false concepts of sin, which lead to a lack of conviction and a lack of repentance.

What is sin? Wrong convictions and answers with regard to this question affect one's understanding and experience of the plan of redemption. In fact it will be seen that those who hold false theories concerning sin also hold false theories concerning Christ and His atoning work as the Savior from sin.

A. False Theories Concerning Sin

1. Atheistic Theory

In denying the existence of God, Atheism indirectly denies the existence of sin. If there is no God to sin against, then there is no sin, and if there is neither God nor sin, then man is not accountable for anything he is or does. It is for this reason that men today seek to deny the existence of God and to destroy all Biblical absolutes.

2. Deterministic Theory

This theory believes that man's free will is a delusion. It holds that man cannot help himself from doing the things he does, whether good or bad, and therefore is not to be blamed. It is a fatalistic view that seeks to excuse man for what he is and does.

3. Evolutionary Theory

This theory holds that sin is not sin, but seeing that man evolved over countless ages from fish to bird, to beast, to ape, to man, that "sin" is simply the "animal" in us. It holds that man is only an animal having animal instincts and fulfilling his animalistic tendencies should not be termed sin. This ignores the Biblical truth of man being a moral being made in the image and likeness of God, higher than the animals.

4. Hedonistic Theory

The root of the word "hedonistic" means "pleasure", and it suggests the theory that a person should be free to do whatever brings pleasure and fulfilment. It is the philosophy of self-expression, proclaiming: "if it feels good, do it". Justifying sin on a seemingly positive philosophic base it has become quite popular in modern society.

These theories may cause one to defile his conscience and eventually sear it by the habitual rationalization of sin (Hebrews 11:25; Titus 1:15). Once a person sears his conscience, he falls beyond the conviction of sin by the Holy Spirit (I Timothy 4:2).

B. Cult Theories Concerning Sin

False cults seek to advance theories which deny, pervert or minimize the doctrine of sin. Whether secular or false religious philosophies, all are attempts of evil and deceived men to either justify or excuse sin and all are endeavours to make man irresponsible and unaccountable to God for what he is, and what he does (II Timothy 3:13). The following are statements gathered from the various writings of these religious cults concerning sin.

1. Christian Science

Christian Science says that "man is incapable of sin, that sin is an error of mortal mind. Man only thinks there is sin and when his thinking is corrected, then sin will not exist. Sin, sickness and death are not realities but illusions. Man cannot sin in as much as he derives his essence from God and possesses not a single original and underived power."

2. Spiritism

Spiritism says, "Man never had a fall. Whatever is, is right. Evil does not exist. Evil is good. No matter what man's path may be, good or bad, it is the path of divine ordination and destiny. A lie is the truth intrinsically; it holds a lawful place in creation, it is a necessity."

3. Russellism

Russellism or Jehovah's Witnesses, say concerning sin: "Death, extinction of being, is the wages of sin. During the millennium, the spirit will be resurrected and given a second chance or trial for everlasting life. Each does not die now for his own sin, but for Adam's sin, thus in Adam all died. The day in which every man shall die for his own sin is the millenniel or restitution day."

4. Theosophy

Theosophy teaches "All thought, good or bad, leaves its traces on the thought body and reappears as tendencies in future incarnations. No escape from this sequence of cause and effect is possible. Our past must work itself out. Man's spirit is transmigratory and its good or bad conduct determines the body it will have in each successive birth. The only freedom from sin is to become entirely lost in meditative contemplation.

5. Unity

Unity teaches "There is no sin, sickness or death. God, who sees and understands perfectly, sees no evil because there is no evil. Eventually we shall see clearly the unreality and futility of appearances of evil, to which, through misunderstanding, men now attribute substance and reality. Sin is falling short of demonstrating our divine nature. I do not accuse the world or myself of having lustful passions or sensual appetites, for God is all. The sins of ancestors cannot reflect upon us in any way."

6. Mormonism

Mormonism teaches "It was necessary for Adam to partake of the forbidden fruit or he would not have known good or evil here, neither could he have had mortal posterity."

In the light of these concepts which contradict the Biblical revelation concerning the doctrine of sin, it is no wonder that each of these also hold false views concerning Christ and His atoning work.

C. Christian Theories

Other theories have been proposed by men, being a mixture of truth and error. They center around the imputation of sin to all mankind. A. H. Strong in "Systematic Theology" (pp.597-628) presents six major views concerning the imputation of sin and its racial consequences.

1. The Pelagian Theory — The Theory of Man's Natural Innocence.

Pelagius was a British monk, born about 370 A.D. He taught the theory that Adam's sin affected himself only. He held that every human soul is immediately created by God, innocent and free from depraved tendencies as Adam was. He further taught that God only holds man responsible for the sinful acts he consciously performs. He interprets Romans 5:12 concerning "death passed upon all men, for that all have sinned" as referring only to physical death which passes upon men after they sin, following Adam's example. This view plainly contradicts Scripture as will be seen under the universality of sin. The Scriptures show that all are born in sin and shaped in iniquity, and that this sinful nature is inherited from Adam (Romans 5:12; Psalm 51:5; Job 14:4).

2. The Arminian Theory — The Theory of Voluntarily Appropriated Depravity.
Arminius was a professor in Holland (1560-1609). His theory is also called Semi-Pelagianism. It holds that man, as a result of Adam's sin, is indeed born destitute of righteousness and any ability in himself to attain to it. However, man is not counted guilty of Adam's sin, he is only accountable for his own conscious acts of sin. Romans 5:12 concerning "death passed upon all men, for that all have sinned" is interpreted to mean that man suffers the consequences of Adam's sin. Because of this, God is obligated by His very nature to send the influence of the Holy Spirit to man to counteract the evil tendencies inherited by Adam's fall.

This view, however, is inadequate for the Scriptures show that all sinned "in Adam", that all are therefore born sinful and guilty, and that God is under no obligation to save anyone. Physical death is the penalty for sin. Any saving influence of the Holy Spirit upon sinful man is all of free grace.

3. The New School Theory — The Theory of Uncondemnable Depravity.
This theory is very similar to the Arminian theory. It holds that men are only responsible for personal acts, even though all are born with a sinful disposition. This theory holds that Adam's sin is not imputed to men, only their own acts of transgressing known law. Death is not a penalty on man, but a consequence of God's displeasure with Adam's transgression. Romans 5:12 is interpreted to mean that "spiritual death passed on all men, because all men have actually and personally sinned." It also teaches that each soul is immediately created at birth, and because the will has no moral character at birth, it does not need the influence of the Holy Spirit to make right choices. It is this latter statement that is the only difference between this theory and the Arminian theory. The same refutation is applicable to both views.

4. The Federal Theory — The Theory of Condemnation by Covenant.
According to Thiessen who follows Strong (p.262) this theory originated with Cocceius (1603-1669), professor in Holland and was more fully developed by Francis Turretin (1623-1687), also a professor in Holland.

It holds that God made a covenant with Adam as the federal head of the human race, promising eternal life to him and his posterity upon obedience, and death and corruption if he disobeyed. Because Adam sinned, all his descendants are sinners. God condemns all because of Adam's transgression. It holds that each soul is created by God with a corrupt and sinful nature as a punishment upon Adam.

However, this theory does despite to the just and righteous character of God, for it represents Him as immediately creating every person with a corrupt nature leading them to sin.

5. The Theory of Mediate Imputation — The Theory of Condemnation for Depravity.
This theory originated with a man by the name of Placeus (1606-1655), a professor in France. Initially he taught that Adam's sin was in no way imputed to his descendants, however, after this doctrine was condemned, he changed the theory by saying that all men are born physically and morally depraved and this is the source of all sin in man. This theory holds that the physical depravity comes from Adam by natural propagation but the soul immediately created by God becomes corrupt the moment it is united with the body. He interprets Romans 5:12 to mean that all sin by having a sinful nature.

This view is opposed to Scripture also. It denies the fact that all were in Adam and sinned when he sinned, and thus came under condemnation, depravity and the penalty of death in their federal head.

6. The Augustinian Theory — The Theory of Adam's Natural Headship.
A. H. Strong (p.619) notes that this theory was first expounded by Augustine (354-430), the great opponent of Pelagius, though its central feature is found in the writings of Tertullian. The Reformers generally held this view. It holds that Adam's sin was imputed immediately to all his unborn generations, because of the organic unity of all mankind who were "in Adam". All humanity was in him, in his loins, as yet unborn. Adam's will was the will of all mankind. As the federal head and representative of the human race, he did what we all would have done under similar probation. Romans 5:12 thus means that "death passed upon all men for that all have sinned" or "in whom (Adam) all have sinned". This means physical, spiritual and eternal death as all were seen in Adam's natural headship. The principle of representative headship is also seen in Hebrews 7:9-10 where Levi

paid tithes "in Abraham" as yet unborn and in his loins, Abraham being the representative head of the chosen nation. The same is true of Adam's headship.

It is this theory of Natural Headship which is the most Scriptural theory of all mentioned and gives the clearest understanding of original sin. It brings together what partial truths there may be in the other religious theories. The sin of Adam is the immediate cause and ground of the inborn depravity, guilt and condemnation of the whole human race. Hence, instead of all being tried as individuals, all were tried in Adam, their natural head. They all sinned in him and thus come under guilt and judgement. This is developed more fully in the following divisions of this chapter.

III. BIBLE DEFINITIONS OF SIN

A. Scriptural Definitions
There are six major Scriptures which define sin and all are seen in their embryonic form in the original sin of Satan and Adam.

1. The thought of foolishness
Proverbs 24:9 — "The thought of foolishness is sin". When Satan and Adam entertained the thought of being "as gods" it was indeed foolishness and this covetous thought itself was sin.

2. Transgression of Law
I John 3:4 — "Sin is transgression of the law." Transgress means "to pass across", "to go across a forbidden boundary line. Adam also transgressed God's law.

3. Unrighteousness is Sin
I John 5:17 — "All unrighteousness is sin". Unrighteousness, or injustice, is sin. Adam committed an injustice to God and man by selling himself out to Satan.

4. Not doing good is Sin
James 4:17 — "To him that knoweth to do good and doeth it not, to him it is sin".

Satan knew good and did it not. Adam knew good and did it not. Both knew God's law and what would please Him.

5. Doing good may be Sin
Proverbs 21:4 — "...the plowing of the wicked, is sin". Plowing was considered to be an honorable activity in Oriental culture. It was a good deed. However, the Scriptures declare that anyone that is not rightly related to God cannot do anything that is good and acceptable in the sight of God. A sinner can do nothing but sin. Even charitable and religious deeds though beneficial to others, may still be sin. Adam's self-righteous attempt to cover himself with fig leaves proved inadequate. As Isaiah said, "...all our righteousnesses are as filthy rags; and we all do fade as a leaf" (Isaiah 64:6). Another illustration of this is the righteousness of the Pharisees (Matthew 23:13-33; Philippians 3:4-9).

6. Unbelief is Sin
Romans 14:23 — "Whatsoever is not of faith is sin". Adam and Eve knew the good and perfect will of God, yet sinned. They did not believe the Word of God, but instead believed the word of the serpent. They fell from faith in the Word of God to unbelief.

B. Hebrew Words for Sin
There are various words used for sin in Hebrew, but we note the major four words used in the Old Testament.

1. Sin — Heb. "chattath" means "an offence, sometimes habitual sinfulness, and its penalty, occasion, sacrifice, or expiation". It also means "to miss, to sin, by inference to forfeit, to lack" (Leviticus 4:2-3,25-35; Psalm 32:1,5; 51:2-5; Isaiah 53:10,12).

2. Transgression — Heb. "pawsah" or "pehshah". This word means "to break away from just authority; trespass, apostasize, quarrel, a revolt (national, moral or religious)". It is translated by the words

"offend, rebel, revolt, transgression" (Exodus 34:7; Numbers 14:18; Psalm 19:13; 32:1; Isaiah 53:8; Daniel 9:24).

3. Iniquity — Heb. "avon, or avown". It means "perversity, evil" translated "do amiss, bow down, make crooked, commit iniquity, pervert, fault" (Psalm 52:3; Leviticus 16:21,22; Psalm 103:3,10; Isaiah 53:5,11; Daniel 9:24).

4. Trespass — Heb. "asham", meaning "to be guilty" or "a fault", also "a sin offering" (Leviticus 6:2,5-6; 7:1-7).

C. Greek Words for Sin
There are nine different Greek words used for "sin" in the New Testament, each having its own distinct shade of meaning.

1. HAMARTIA — this word is used 174 times in the New Testament and is always translated "sin" or "sins" (except in II Corinthians 11:7 — "offence"). It means literally "to miss the mark, or to seek to attain results which lie beyond the limits of one's capabilities." In the New Testament it became the general term for sin, referring to both the inner principle of sin and its outward expression; to both the power of sin and its fruit (Matthew 1:21; Matthew 26:28; Luke 11:4; Luke 24:47; John 1:29; John 8: 34; Acts 2:38; Romans 3:20; Romans 5:12; Romans 6:10-23; Romans 8:2; Romans 14:23; II Corinthians 5:21; James 1:15; James 4:17; I John 1:9; I John 5:17).

2. HAMARTEMA — this word is used only four times in the New Testament and is always translated "sins" or "sin". It only differs in meaning from the word above in that its meaning is limited to the outward expression of sin. Thus it denotes an actual act of disobedience against the divine law (Mark 3:28; Mark 4:12; Romans 3:25; I Corinthians 6:18).

3. PARAKOE — this word is used only 5 times in the New Testament. The noun form is translated "disobedience" 3 times and the verb form of it is translated "neglect to hear" two times in Matthew 18:17. It means literally "to hear amiss" and thus it refers most likely to a refusal to listen to God speaking or possibly an imperfect hearing of His voice. Both of these display a carelessness in attitude toward the Word of God (Romans 5:19; II Corinthians 10:6; Hebrews 2:2).

4. ANOMIA — this word is used 15 times in the New Testament and is always translated "iniquity" (except in II Corinthians 6:14 — "unrighteousness" and in I John 3:4 — "transgression of the law"). It literally means lawlessness and in the New Testament is used similarly to #1 above in that it refers both to the inward opposition of the heart to the law of God and to the outward acts of violating that law (Matthew 7:23; Matthew 23:28; Matthew 24:12; Romans 4:7; Romans 6:19; II Thessalonians 2:7; Titus 2:14; Hebrews 1:9; Hebrews 8:12; Hebrews 10:17).

5. PARANOMIA — this word is used only once in the New Testament and is there translated "iniquity". Its meaning is essentially the same as that of #4 above and it refers to a breaking of the law (II Peter 2:16).

6. PARABASIS — this word is used 16 times in the New Testament. The noun forms are translated "transgressor" and "transgression" (except in Romans 2:23 "breaking" and Romans 2:25 "breaker") and the verb form is translated "transgress" or "transgresseth". It means literally to step beyond as when crossing a line or boundary. Thus in the New Testament it refers to a direct action of violating God's law. This word, as does #4 and #5, necessitates that there be a law in existence in that unless there is a boundary line drawn, there can be no stepping across such (Matthew 15:2,3; Romans 4:15; Romans 5:14; Galatians 2:18; Galatians 3:19; I Timothy 2:14; Hebrews 2:2; Hebrews 9:15; James 2:9,11, II John 9).

7. PARAPTOMA — This word is used 23 times in the New Testament and is translated "trespasses", "offences", "offence", "fall", "fault", "faults" "sins". It means literally to fall aside to fall away, to blunder. In the New Testament it refers to a deviation or falling away from uprightness and truth (Matthew 6:14,15; Romans 4:24; Romans 5:15-20; Romans 11:11;12; II Corinthians 5:19; Galatians

6:1; Ephesians 1:7; Ephesians 2:1; Colossians 2:13; James 5:16).

8. AGNOEMA — This word is used only once in the New Testament and is there translated "errors". It means literally an act of ignorance and refers to a sin of ignorance. It regards sin in the mildest light possible without making excuses for it. It refers to sins not especially meant to occur rather than open outright acts of rebellion (Hebrews 9:7).

9. HETTEMA — this word is used only twice in the New Testament and is translated "diminishing" in Romans 11:12, and "fault" in I Corinthians 6:7. It means literally a lessening or a loss and it refers in I Corinthians 6:7 to a defect, a flaw (the loss of their unity).

In summary, consider how that sin is set forth in the New Testament in these various images: the missing of a mark; the disobedience to a voice; the non-observance of a law; the crossing of a boundary line; the falling away from uprightness, the ignorance of what should have been known, and the diminishing of what should have been full.

V. THE LAW OF GOD IN RELATION TO SIN

That the doctrine of sin and the subject of law are vitally connected is evident from the Scriptures. It is the relationship of law and sin that Paul deals with in the Epistle to the Romans, especially as he answers the objections raised by the Jews of his time.

Romans 3:20—"For by the law is the knowledge of sin" Romans 7:7—"I had not known sin, but by the law" I John 3:4—"Sin is the transgression of the law" Romans 4:15—"Where no law is there is no transgression"

A. The Necessity of Law

When the Apostle Paul dealt with the relationship of the law and sin in Romans 7, it is evident that he anticipated some reaction, especially from the Jews who knew much about the subject of Law. In verses 7-11, he states how it was the Law that gave him the knowledge of sin — "I had not known sin but by the law". He continues to say that "without the law sin was dead" and that when the commandment or law of God was given it caused sin to come alive. In other words, if there was no law to violate, then sin would not have taken place, for "sin is not imputed when there is no law" (Romans 5:13). Paul anticipated the reaction that the law of God must be the real problem. "What shall we say then? Is the law sin? God forbid" (Romans 7:7). He further adds that the law is holy just, good and spiritual (Romans 7:12,14).

The problem therefore is not the law of God but in the creature who transgresses it. God is not the author of sin and He does not need sin to exist to glorify Himself. It is this that brings us to the absolute necessity of law in the universe as well as the created beings, whether angelic or human.

1. In the Universe

God is the Creator and Lawgiver of the universe (James 4:12; Isaiah 33:22). When God created the universe of worlds, He created them to be regulated by certain orbital laws. All the universe is governed by the laws of God. Without such there would be absolute chaos, worlds in collision. There can be order and harmony in the universe only as the planets move in the orbit of God's will for them. A lawless universe would be chaotic. Of course, planets are inanimate and without will, therefore they must be under the sovereign will of God, subject to His unchanging laws.

2. In the Creature

God is also the Creator of angels and man. When it comes to the creation of the universe of worlds, God does not have any problem, for these are inanimate and will-less creations. God places them all in the universe of worlds to move in the orbit of His will, under universal law. The first law of the universe is order, which produces harmony. God has no fear that the worlds will rise in rebellion against His law and sovereign will for them. However, when God decided to create the angels, and in due time, man, He could not create them as will-less, and therefore unresponsive creatures. God is love and desires to give Himself to a creation that could choose to freely reciprocate and respond. Hence God chose to create a creation with free will, having the power of choice, a moral and therefore responsible creature. A. H. Scherling in "The Origin of Sin and its Characteristics" (pp.7-12) gives the following excellent comments on the occasion of sin, which we condense and arrange here for the purpose of this text.

a. A moral being is a "free being made in the image and likeness of God". If not free, he would not be made in His image.

b. A moral being must be conscious that he is free. He cannot be free without being conscious of it.

c. A moral being must love to exercise this freedom in the way of independent action, which means mainly that he must love to seek and obtain whatever he pleases, to seek his own personal gratification without restraint. He cannot have this freedom without loving to exercise it — in common language, without loving to have his own way.

d. However, can a moral agent, conscious of free will, be safely allowed to have his own way? Absolutely not! For, in that case, each one acting out his natural inclinations would set up for himself, and there would be as many independent wills as there are individuals, each acting for himself, and with no regard for the general good. The resulting collision, strife, discord and suffering would be uncontrollable and dreadful. The universe itself would become a moral wreck.

e. Therefore, the only security for the harmony and happiness of the universe is the submission of all individual free wills to the controlling will of God."

Thus we see the absolute necessity that God exercise control over free-will moral creatures and give them some law or laws that will prevent the possible collision of the individuals themselves, as well as the resultant chaos in the universe. God must, by the very nature of His own being, and the absolute necessity of maintaining order and harmony in the universe, place the free will moral creature under some law. Otherwise all created beings would be lawless, becoming a law to themselves. Law may be defined as "a decisive rule of action for moral creatures".

If God is the Lawgiver, then He must see that this law is obeyed under His authority. He must also judge any violation. If God is to give a law to free-will moral agents, then what law should be given? The answer is, the law of His own being, the law of love. This is the law of God's own being. God Himself, the Lawgiver, is governed by the law of self-giving love. Hence, the creature must be governed by this same law in its twofold requirements; love for God, the Creator, and for other creatures as Himself.

In God's government, the law of God demands voluntary and unconditional submission of the free moral agent. It asks the creature to give up his independence of action and submit his will to God's will. It involves self-denial, asking the creature not to seek his own way and will, but God's way and will, with the reward being eternal life and joy. In order for there to be harmony among the created beings, as well as in the universe, it means that all free will must be submitted to the one controlling will of the Creator. It means accepting the restraints of the law of love, the law of God's own being. It means the giving up of self-will and consenting to be guided and governed by God's just, holy and loving will.

Thus, God created first the angelic hosts, and then man. Both orders of creatures were created with free will, each having the power of choice. The choice was simply self-will or God's will; independence or dependance; love of God or love of self; self-gratification or self-denial; rebellion or submission; law or lawlessness; good or evil.

B. The Transgression of the Law
In the light of the absolute necessity of law both for the universe and created beings, it can be seen that any violation of law would be sin. God, the Lawgiver, must of necessity give His creatures a law to be governed by. Law would also act as a restraint on free-will agents in their relationships with God Himself and other free-will agents. The language of law is "Thou shalt" and "Thou shalt not".

Thus when God created the angels, He created them as spirit beings, freewill moral agents, having the power of choice. They could voluntarily choose to submit their free wills to God's will, or exercise their free wills in self-will with its results. The one and only law or commandment given to angelic hosts was the law of loving obedience to God's good and perfect will. Perhaps the law of God to angels could be defined as "Thou shalt lovingly obey the good and perfect will of God thy Creator", or, to use the words of Scripture in Matthew 4:10, "Thou shalt worship the Lord thy God and Him only shalt thou serve...". To violate this would be sin, for "sin is transgression of the law", and this principle is true whether the law be given to angels or men (I John 3:4).

V. THE ORIGIN OF SIN

A. The Entrance of Sin into the Universe
The Apostle James, in dealing with the birth of sin, gives us some vital insight into the origin of all evil. The principle he sets forth is applicable both to angels and men. It helps to answer such questions as "Who tempted Lucifer?" and "Did Lucifer's temptation come from within or without?"

James 1:13 — "Let no man (and we can rightly say 'let no angel') say when he is tempted, I am tempted of God, for God CANNOT be tempted with evil, neither tempted He any man (or angel)." Thus God did not and could not tempt angels or man to sin. This would violate His moral attributes. God did not create or decree sin. He does not approve of it nor incite His creatures to sin. To charge God with such is an attack on His holiness and moral attributes.

The Scriptures clearly show that the first moral beings created were the angelic hosts and that Lucifer and his angels were the first and original sinners. Sin therefore began in heaven among the angelic order. It then came to earth in the being of the tempter, Satan.

1. Lucifer, the Original Sinner
Under the figure of the King of Tyre and the King of Babylon, we have a description of Lucifer, who, as most expositors believe, became the devil (Isaiah 14:12-14; Ezekiel 28:11-19).

The prophecy here has a twofold or dual application, as is evident. The language used here could not, in its full sense, apply to a human king, such as the Prince of Tyre or of Babylon. This principle of Scriptural interpretation is seen throughout the Word. In Genesis 3:14-15 where God speaks to the serpent, He is also speaking to the devil behind the serpent. The serpent in Eden became the mouthpiece and vessel of the serpent, the devil. Matthew 16:16-23 also illustrates the same truth, for when Jesus spoke to Peter, He was speaking to Satan behind Peter's utterance. So in Isaiah and Ezekiel, God, in speaking of the Princes of Tyre and Babylon, is referring also to the prince behind these earthly princes, even Satan himself. Thus these prophecies have a dual application. In these passages we have a description of Lucifer before his fall, which we note in outline form.

   a. He is called Lucifer, the Day Star, the Shining One, the Light-bearer.
   b. He is called Son of the Morning because of his brightness.
   c. He was full of beauty and wisdom. Nothing could be hidden from him.
   d. He was in Eden, the Garden of God.
   e. Every precious stone was his covering, as the colors of the rainbow for beauty.
   f. His ministry was in the area of music for the workmanship of his pipes and tabrets was in him from the day he was created.
   g. He was the anointed Cherub and guardian of the throne of God.
   h. He was in the Holy Mountain of God and given a high position in heaven as a created being.
   i. He walked up and down in the midst of the stones of fire, the fire of God's holiness.
   j. He was perfect in all his ways from the day that he was created.

Thus this angelic being, Lucifer, was clothed with wisdom, light and beauty. He was given leadership in the ministry of worship. He was the anointed Cherub guarding the throne of God. He was created as a free-will moral agent, a dependent being. He was created for God's glory and pleasure.

It was in this created archangel that "the mystery of iniquity" began (II Thessalonians 2:7). How did this happen? What was the sin of Lucifer? What was the cause of Lucifer's fall? Who tempted Lucifer to sin? Did God create Lucifer to be the devil? In seeking to answer these questions, it is recognized that certain answers God has reserved for Himself (Deuteronomy 29:29), but enough has been revealed in the Bible to enlighten us in measure. Ezekiel 28:15 tells us that the Prince of Tyre was perfect in all his ways from the day he was created until iniquity was found in him. Other Scriptures speak also of the devil as a sinner.

I John 3:8 — "The devil sinneth from the beginning".
Ezekiel 28:16 — "Thou hast sinned..."
John 8:44 — "The devil was a murderer from the beginning and abode not in the truth, because there is no truth in him; when he speaketh a lie, he speaketh of his own, for he is a liar and the father of it".

Evil originated in the heart of Lucifer himself. He is the author, the originator of all sin, the beginning of sin, sin personified, the first and original sinner. The mystery of iniquity began its work in the universe, in this fallen Archangel. Lucifer became corrupted in his entire nature and being and became the devil. Many names are used to describe the fallen nature of this Archangel, as seen in "Doctrine of Satan and Demonology".

As a fallen spirit being, sinning in the blazing light of God's holiness, he became an unredeemable being. Though his God-given wisdom and beauty became corrupted, twisted and perverted, God did not divest him of it. The wisdom that he had became earthly, sensual and devilish (James 3:15). God did not create this Archangel to be the devil.

God did not create a wicked creature, but He created a free-will being who had the power of choice and became evil by choice. When God said in Isaiah 45:7, "I form the light and create darkness, I make peace and create evil, I the Lord do all these things", He did not mean that He was the Creator of sin and iniquity. To interpret this Scripture that way charges God as being the originator of sin and attacks His moral attributes. God cannot and will not do anything that is inconsistent with His own righteous character. The "evil" spoken of both in Isaiah 45:7 and Amos 3:6 refers to those acts of judgement God brings on sinners who trangress His laws.

2. The Nature of Lucifer's Sin

Having shown that the original sinner in heaven was Lucifer, and that this is how sin entered the universe, we now consider in detail the nature of his sin. The essence of sin is self-centredness. From this origin its progression is threefold, or what may be called the triunity of sin, consisting of pride, covetousness or lust, and self-will exercised against God's will.

a. Pride

The word "pride" means "inordinate self-esteem, conceit, vanity, self-exaltation" or "to be lifted up in smoke". The opposite character quality is humility, modesty, lowliness and meekness. We note several Scriptures pertaining to pride and its subsequent fall.

Proverbs 16:18 — "PRIDE goeth before destruction and an HAUGHTY SPIRIT before a fall". Certainly applicable to Satan and the angels which fell.

Proverbs 18:12 — "Before destruction the heart of man is haughty, and before honor is humility."

Isaiah 14:12 — "How art thou fallen from heaven, O Lucifer (Day Star), Son of the Morning!"

Luke 10:18 — "And He said unto them, 'I beheld Satan as lightning fall from heaven' ".

The prophet Ezekiel speaks of this pride and self-assertion in Ezekiel 28:1-19. In verses 2,4,5,17 he speaks of Lucifer's heart being "lifted up" because of riches and beauty. In verses 2,6,9 he "lifted himself" up to be a god, to sit in the throne of God, and set his heart as the heart of God. Pride turned this Archangel into a devil! Lucifer's God-given beauty, wisdom and anointing became a temptation to lust after that worship which only belonged to God. He beheld himself and turned in upon himself. This is in direct contrast to the Word, Jesus Christ, who came down from heaven and humbled Himself to the death of the cross, and was "lifted up" to do the Father's will on Calvary (John 3:14; 8:28; 12:32). After this He was exalted. Lucifer sought to ascend, but was cast down. Jesus humbled Himself and was exalted.

b. Covetousness or Lust

Lust is unlawful or inordinate desire and is synonymous with covetousness. Lucifer's temptation came from within. Pride led to an unlawful desire, a coveting of something that was forbidden. Paul tied lust to covetousness in Romans 7:7 "... for I had not known lust, except the law had said 'Thou shalt not covet'", by referring to the tenth commandment (Exodus 20:17). God had forbidden any angel to worship other than the only God and Creator. Angels were to lovingly do the will of God and direct their worship to Him. Lucifer coveted the worship and praise that belonged only to God (Psalm 103:19-22; Revelation 4:11; 5:11-14). This was the inordinate desire that rose within his being. History has proven this fact. His temptation to Christ, as well as that seen in the Book of Revelation shows that the devil covets worship. He said to Jesus in Matthew 4:9, after showing Him the glory of the kingdoms of this world, "All these things will I give thee, if thou will fall down and worship me." Jesus replied that all creatures were created to worship the Lord God and serve Him only (Matthew 4:10; Revelation 13:11-18).

Lucifer stated this lustful desire when he said "I will be like the Most High" (Isaiah 14:14). He coveted the position of God and the worship that was due Him. It has also been suggested that Lucifer rose up against the Word, the eternal Son, when the Father said in Hebrews 1:6 "And let all the angels of God worship Him". Lucifer envied the position and worship given to The Word, coveted His place and rose up against The Word. It was for this reason that The Word humbled Himself and took upon Himself flesh in order to deal with the original sinner and all sin (John 1:13, 14-18; Hebrews 2:14-16).

c. Self-will

As pride led to covetousness, so covetousness led to self-will. Lucifer's pride and inordinate desire prompted him to turn the freewill God had given him against God's will, in self-will. Lucifer's act was a deliberate act of the will, as all sin is.

The prophet Isaiah, in speaking of Lucifer's fall, lists his five expressions of self-will (Isaiah 14: 12-14).

I will ascend into heaven

I will exalt my throne above the stars of God

I will sit also upon the mount of the congregation in the sides of the north.

I will ascend above the heights of the clouds.

I will be like the Most High.

Let us consider further what was involved in these five "I will's" of Satan.

(1) Self-ascension
"I will ascend into heaven". Ascend means to go up, to be lifted up from a lower realm to a higher realm.

(2) Self-exaltation
"I will exalt my throne above the stars of God". This was to set his seat above the other angelic stars and take the position of leadership.

(3) Self-enthronement
"I will sit also upon the mount of the congregation in the sides of the north." This self-enthronement on the mount of the congregation involved the desire for the worship of other angelic beings. This is inferred in Psalm 48:1-2 where the congregation of Israel would gather to worship the Lord in Mt. Zion situated in the sides of the north. Satan sinned at the very throne of God.

(4) Self-dependence

"I will ascend above the heights of the clouds". This not only involves self-ascension, but a seeking for a position of independence above the clouds. All beings were created and thus were to be dependent upon God. Satan sought to be independent, to imitate and counterfeit God. He repudiated dependence upon God, believing that he was self-sufficient and could get along without God. However, the Most High alone is the self- dependent one, the all-sufficient one. All creatures depend on Him for their existence and the maintenance of it. Dependence upon God involves faith. Independence therefore is sin.

(5) Self-deification

"I will be like the Most High". He did not want to be "like God" as to character, but "like God" as to independence and being worshipped by other creatures. The devil has ever since sought to be God. He is the god of this world order (II Corinthians 4:4). He closes this age by receiving the worship as God that he has always sought (Revelation 13 with Matthew 4:9-10).

Thus, the devil, an angelic spirit being, a created moral and freewill being, rose up against God the Creator, in rebellious pride and self-will. But, instead of ascending, he fell. In seeking to gain something that was not rightfully his, he lost even that which was his. Self-will became the seed-sin of all sin. All the fruit of sin was in that seed form. No creature could conceive the full implication of that seed-sin when it would come to its maturity in the universe, among both angels and man.

Self-centredness is ego-centric. It is ego-theistic,when self is lifted up as God. From being God-centred, Lucifer became self-centred, self-directing, self-reliant, and self-supporting. He became selfishness personified. He turned in upon himself. Beholding his own beauty, wisdom, anointing and ministry, he was lifted up in pride, forgetting that all he had was God-given. He then coveted a higher position, even God's. With this, he set his will against God's will and fell.

3. The Sinning Angels

The Scriptures indicate that other angels sinned with Lucifer. They transgressed a given law and, like Lucifer, became totally apostate and unredeemable.

II Peter 2:4 — "God spared not the angels that sinned, but cast them down to hell (Greek: Tartarus) and delivered them into chains of darkness to be reserved unto judgement...".

Jude 6 — "And the angels which kept not their first estate (principality) but left their own habitation, he hath reserved in everlasting chains under darkness unto the judgement of the great day."

Many expositors believe that the devil drew a third part of the angelic hosts with him in his original sin and fall (Revelation 12:3-4).

God created all beings, archangels and angelic hosts, to do His will. God's will was to be the supreme joy of their existence. God did not create them as mere machines who would obey without reason, intelligence, affection or will. He created each with a free will, capable of choosing either to obey God's will or that of another. Lucifer and the angels chose self-will and thus crossed God's will.

The angels which did not respond to Satan's will but submitted to God's will, are known as the "elect angels" (I Timothy 5:21). Their reward was sinless perfection from which it is impossible to fall and which made them eternally secure. However, the devil and his angels will be punished in the Lake of Fire for all eternity (Matthew 25:41; Revelation 20:11-15).

In summary, Satan was the original sinner, responsible for the entrance of sin into the universe. He then led an angelic rebellion and eventually caused the fall of man through Adam.

B. The Entrance of Sin into Humanity

The foregoing conclusions on the entrance of sin into the universe among the angelic order helps us to understand the entrance of sin into the human race, for it involves the same basic principles.

1. The Creation of Man

The Book of Genesis gives the account of the creation of man as a free-will, morally responsible and intelligent creature (Genesis 1:26-28; 2:7,15-25). As considered under the Doctrine of Man, this creation was made in the image and likeness of God; a triune being composed of spirit, soul and body. Adam's sinlessness was an untested perfection. He and Eve were placed in the Garden of Eden, a perfect earthly environment, and were in unhindered fellowship with their Creator.

2. The Probation of Man

As with the angelic creation, it was necessary that man be placed under a period of probation. Man, though a freewill creation, had to be placed under the law of God, especially because of the whole human race yet to come. Adam and Eve had to make their choice between God's will and their own; to be dependent upon God or independent; to be self- giving or self-gratifying. Thus God gave them one law, with a penalty attached if violated. This commandment is recorded in Genesis 2:17, "But of the tree of the knowledge of good and evil thou shalt not eat of it, for in the day thou eatest thereof thou shalt surely die." In principle this was the tenth commandment which says "Thou shalt not covet..." (Exodus 20:17).

3. The Temptation of Man

In Genesis 3:1-6 we have God's account of the temptation of man and of the entrance of sin into the human race. The word "temptation" simply means "to test, to try, to prove". The test centered around a particular tree which was in the Garden of Eden; the tree of the knowledge of good and evil. More particularly it involved obedience to the one commandment of God given in Genesis 2:17. Man was permitted to eat of all the trees of the garden which included the tree of life. Only one tree was forbidden, the tree of the knowledge of good and evil. Man was confronted with a choice; obedience or disobedience to God's will. He also knew the consequences of his choice would be either life or death. As a freewill creature, he had the power of choice. Deuteronomy 30:19 could well have been spoken to Adam, as it was to Israel: "I call heaven and earth to record this day against you, that I have set before you life and death, blessing and cursing, therefore choose life, that both thou and thy seed may live...".

In the testing of man, God permitted the devil, the original sinner, to tempt him (Matthew 4:3; I Thessalonians 3:5). As noted previously, Lucifer's temptation came from within himself, pride leading to lust, but for man the temptation came from without, lust leading to pride. It should be remembered that temptation is not sin. It is yielding to temptation that is sin. We will now analyze the things involved in the temptation of man.

a. Tempted in Body, Soul and Spirit

God permitted Adam and Eve to be tempted by the serpent, to prove whether they would make the supreme consecration of their freewill to the will of God in loving obedience or stoop to self-will. The temptation of Satan was to all parts of man's being, spirit, soul and body (I Thessalonians 5:23). His approach was body, soul and spirit from without to within.

(1) Temptation to the **body,** the lust of the flesh. The tree was good for food.

(2) Temptation to the **soul,** the lust of the eyes. The tree was pleasant to the eyes.

(3) Temptation to the **spirit,** the pride of life. The tree was desired to make one wise, making them as gods,knowing good and evil.

Thus man in his triune being was tempted according to the three things mentioned in I John 2:15-17. When man fell, he fell in body, soul and spirit, committing sins of the body, sins of the soul and sins of the spirit. It produced total depravity.

b. Tempted to Lust, Pride and Self-will

Lucifer, being an angelic spirit being, was tempted to sin from within himself. Sin began in him when he became lifted up in pride, while viewing his God-given attributes. Thinking more highly of himself than he should he coveted God's position and set his will against God's in rebellion. The beginning of sin in man was slightly different in that the temptation to sin came to him from without. Lucifer appealed first to the external part of man's being, enticing him to covet what was not rightfully his. This lust led to pride which led to self-will against God's will. Thus, for Lucifer it was pride, lust and self-will while for man it was lust, pride and self-will.

(1) Covetousness or Lust

The serpent's temptations were aimed at God-given instincts within man. Satan always seeks to exploit and pervert these basic laws of man's being. God has given man five basic instincts, which are as follows:

(a) The Law of **Self-Preservation**: enabling man to take care of himself.

(b) The Law of **Self-Acquisition**: which enables man to acquire the necessities of life for self-support.

(c) The Law of **Self-Sustenance**: the food seeking instinct.

(d) The Law of **Self-Propagation**: the sex instinct by which man can be fruitful and multiply in the earth.

(e) The Law of **Self-Assertion**: whereby man can subdue and have dominion over the earth.

Satan's initial temptation was aimed at the body when he showed the woman that the tree was good for food. It was an appeal to the desire of the flesh which was a God-given and lawful appetite. This desire could be satisfied on any other tree but not on the fruit of the tree of knowledge of good and evil. The temptation therefore was designed to make man covet or lust for the forbidden fruit (Exodus 20:17; Romans 7:7). The temptation was an exploitation or perversion of a God-given instinct, a law of man's very being. The serpent kept enticing the woman to break God's one commandment.

(2) Pride

The temptation also involved that which arises out of inordinate desire, even pride. Satan's statement, "Ye shall be as gods, knowing good and evil" was an appeal to the ego. It was an appeal of pride, exploiting the law of self-assertion. Lucifer himself desired to be "like the Most High", to be "as God" and now his appeal to the man was to be "as Gods". The temptation appealed to man to gain wisdom and knowledge which he did not have and which was forbidden by the law of God.

(3) Self-Will

Enticed by the serpent's appeal, the final step was an independent and deliberate act of the will. This was the whole purpose of Satan's temptation. Though all temptation is aimed at spirit, soul and body (or the "all points" of man's being), the act of sin being self-will, Satan's aim was to get to the will of man. He wanted to get man to exercise self-will against God's will, to exercise his will independently of God. Satan fell through self-will and so did Adam.

Thus man exercised his freewill; he made the choice to disobey God's will, God's law and God's Word. God's Word is His will and His will is His Word. His Word is also law. Man chose to be independent of God, to be selfish, to be a law to himself, to deify himself, to follow self-will and thus chose death for himself and for the entire unborn human race in his loins (Romans 5:12,21; Psalm 51:5; Romans 7:14,24). Adam did not originate sin but fell into it, by a deliberate choice. There was a response in him to the principle of sin. The seat of sin is in the will.

c. Tempted in Relation to the Law

Another important thing to observe in the temptation in Eden, as well as in temptation ever since, was the attack on the law of God. The one prohibition given by God to men in Genesis 2:17 was God's law, commandment, word and will. The temptation was a direct attack by the devil, the "lawless one", on the law of God that man was placed under. To break that one law was to break all laws, as is stated in James 2:10, "For whosoever shall keep the whole law, and yet offend in one point, he is guilty of all". Adam sinned when he and his wife transgressed the one law. As I John 3:4 declares, "Sin is transgression of the law".

The serpent had to undermine God's law to lead man to exercise self-will. He had to attack that law before he could entice man to transgress it. We note the successive steps involved in this.

(1) The Serpent put a doubt into the mind of the woman concerning the word or law of God. He questioned, "Hath God said?". It was a doubt as to the authority of the spoken word. It was the beginning of unbelief.

(2) The woman added to the Word by saying that they were not to touch the tree.

(3) The woman also adulterated the Word by watering it down, taking away its full effect, when she said "lest" ye die (compare Genesis 3:3 with 2:17).

(4) The serpent lied against the Word by saying "ye shall not surely die".

(5) The serpent slandered the Word by attacking God's intentions, suggesting that He was withholding from them the privilege of being as gods to know good and evil.

(6) The woman was then deceived and believed the lie of Satan instead of the Word of God, thus falling from faith to unbelief. (I Timothy 2:13-15). Adam sinned knowingly. He was not deceived, therefore this sin was charged to the man as the seed-bearer of the entire human race (Romans 5:12-21; 14:23).

4. The Fall of Man and its Effects

Adam's sin was a deliberate choice, a deliberate act of the will against a given law. It was high treason against God and open rebellion. Not only did the fall affect Adam, but all of his unborn descendants. We outline the immediate and the far-reaching effects of the fall.

a. Immediate Effects of the Fall

(1) **Forfeited Purity** (Genesis 3:7 with 2:25).
"They knew they were naked". A sense of shame fell upon Adam and Eve after their disobedience. Undoubtedly they were clothed with garments of light before the fall (Psalm 104:2). Those redeemed from the fall will have a glorified body like Christ's in eternity which will be a divine covering for the spirit (Philippians 3:21; II Corinthians 5:1-5).

(2) **Knowledge of Good and Evil**
A dual knowledge of good and evil entered their minds, but though they knew good and evil, they could only do evil. (Romans 7:18-24). It is interesting to note that the tree of the knowledge of good and evil found in Genesis is not found in Revelation, but the tree of eternal life is there restored through Christ.

(3) **Law of Conscience at Work**
The moment man sinned, the law of conscience began to work, "their thoughts the mean-

while excusing and accusing" them (Romans 2:14-15). Conscience produced guilt.

(4) The Law of Works
A guilty conscience drove them to works, to make themselves presentable to God in the cool of the evening. They sewed fig leaves together to make aprons to cover themselves (Genesis 3:7).

(5) The Fear of God
Sin and their guilty conscience drove them to hide themselves from the presence of God. Sin brought fear instead of love. When God came, they hid themselves among the trees of the garden (Genesis 3:8).

(6) The Blame of Others
When the Lord came on the scene and called them, Adam and Eve were in hiding. God sought a confession of sin from them. However, each blamed other than themselves for their sin. Adam indirectly blamed God: "The woman thou gavest me..." Adam also blamed the woman: "The woman gave me to eat...". The woman blamed the serpent: "The serpent beguiled me and I did eat...". This was an endeavor to balance out their guilt by blaming others (Genesis 3:19-13).

(7) Man's Nature Corrupted
When sin entered man, it corrupted his entire human nature; spirit, soul and body. Man became totally depraved.

(a) Man's spirit
Man's spirit, which is the lamp of the Lord (Proverbs 20:27) was thrown into darkness, losing its contact with God.

(b) Man's soul
Man's soul and its faculties of mind, will and emotion, were also affected. The mind became self-centered, the emotions uncontrolled and the will bent away from God's (Ephesians 2:1-3; 4:17-19; II Timothy 2:25-27; Genesis 6:5,12; Romans 1:18-31; 8:7,8). Sin brought moral and mental discord. Man's affections were defiled (Titus 1:15).

(c) Man's Body
Man's body with its senses became subject to perverted instincts, sickness, and death.

Instead of God's order being spirit, soul and body, it was reversed so that man's body and soul controlled his spirit. He now had the sin principle operating in his being. Sin is an intrusion into man's nature and was never meant to be there, which explains why man seeks to be rid of it. It should be remembered that sin is not a physical thing, but a spiritual law, though expressed physically. (Galatians 5:19-21; Romans 8:7; Mark 7:21-23; Genesis 6:5; Jeremiah 17:9). Sin as a spiritual law within man desires expression in sins of the spirit, sins of the soul and sins of the flesh.

It should be noted also that the seven-fold immediate effects of the fall are included in the long range effects of the fall on all men.

b. The Long-range effects of the Fall
The full effects of the fall were not evidenced immediately in Adam and Eve but were to follow in his offspring, the human race. We summarize under two headings the longrange effects of the fall upon mankind.

(1) Sin Passed Upon All Men
Romans 5:12 clearly explains that by one man sin entered the world and all have sinned in Adam. When Adam sinned, all men sinned, for they were as yet in his loins. All were made or constituted sinners in Adam as the federal head and representative of the entire human race

(Romans 5:19). In this sense, sin is both hereditary and universal. All of Adam's posterity are born in sin. All are born with sinful and depraved natures. Thus all need to be born again.

Romans 3:23 — "All have sinned and come short of the glory of God".

Romans 3:9-18; Psalm 53:1-3 — "There is none righteous, no, not one, there is none that understandeth, there is none that seeketh after God, they are all gone out of the way, they are together become unprofitable".

I Kings 8:46 — "There is no man that sinneth not".

Galatians 3:22 — "Scripture hath concluded all under sin".

Isaiah 53:6 — "All we like sheep have gone astray".

Romans 5:12 — "By one man's disobedience many were made sinners.

(Read also Psalm 14:1-3; Jeremiah 17:9; Mark 7:21-23; Matthew 15:18-20; Isaiah 1:5-6; Psalm 51:5; Job 14:4; Ephesians 2:1-5; I John 1:8-10; 5:19; Romans 6:17; 7:14; I John 3:8-10; John 8:44).

Adam sold his unborn generations into slavery in Satan's kingdom of darkness, and all became children of the devil. They all came under the curse of the law (Galatians 3:10). Though all sin is primarily against God (Psalm 51:4) Adam also sinned against the entire human race. His breaking the law brought all of mankind under the wrath of God (Romans 4:15).

Man became a sinner both in original and actual sin. Original sin is inherited from Adam. Actual sin is that which man commits. Because man is sinful in nature, he is also sinful in acts. He does what he does because of what he is. He is not a sinner because he sins, but sins because he is a sinner. Man is also accountable to God for his sins, though not the sins of his fathers (Jeremiah 31:29-30; Ezekiel 11:21; 18:4,20).

The progression of sin as seen in both Lucifer and Adam became active in man. As sin began in Lucifer from within, pride leading to lust and self-will, and began in Adam from without, lust leading to pride and self-will, so man is now subject to sin coming both from within and without. In that fallen man now has self-centeredness and pride resident within him, he has lusts that arise within him and lead him to exalt his will against God's. This is similar to the progression seen in Lucifer. But, having the nature of Adam, man is also subject to lusts being stirred up from without that cause him to rise up in pride and set his will against God's.

(2) Death Passed Upon All Men
As sin entered the world by one man, so also the penalty of sin. This penalty is death (Romans 5:12-21; Genesis 2:17; Romans 6:23). All sinned and all died "in Adam", the father and representative of the human race (I Corinthians 15:21-23; 45-50). Death was also foreign to man. Man was created with a capacity for immortality and did not need to die. The tree of life was available to man but as sin became universal, so also did death (Genesis 3:22).

c. Divine Judgement Pronounced and Executed

(1) Judgement on the Serpent
The serpent was cursed with an irrevocable curse. In the midst of this pronouncement, the promise of Messianic deliverance was given. The Seed of the woman would bring about the crushing of the serpent's head in due time (Romans 16:20; Luke 10:18; Genesis 3:14-15; Revelation 20:1-3,10).

(2) Judgement on the Woman
Sorrow and pain in childbearing, under the headship of the husband was the judgement

pronounced on the woman (Genesis 3:16 with I Timothy 2:13-15).

(3) Judgement on the Man
The judgement pronounced on man was that he would sweat in toil to earn his sustenance until death overtook him (Genesis 3:17-19).

(4) Judgement on the Earth
The earth was cursed with thorns and thistles. Instead of all the earth being as a Garden of Eden, it all came under the curse (Genesis 3:17-18 with 2:4-6,15). This also affected the animal creation which became wild, hostile and rebellious against man's dominion.

(5) Judgement on Sin by Death
Romans 6:23 declares "The wages of sin is death..." (James 1:15; Jeremiah 31:30; Ezekiel 18:20). God said to Adam "In the day that thou sinnest, thou shalt surely die". Or, more literally, "In dying thou shalt die" (Genesis 2:17). The death penalty touches three areas relative to man.

> **(a) Physical Death** — separation of the spirit from the body. Death began in Adam's body the moment he sinned and consummated 930 years later. (Ecclesiastes 12:7; Genesis 2:17; Numbers 16:29; 27:3; Psalm 90:7-11).

> **(b) Spiritual Death** — separation of the spirit from God. This speaks of man dead in trespasses and sins, out of fellowship with God (John 5:24; Romans 8:6; Ephesians 2:1,5; I Timothy 5:6; Romans 5:12-21).

> **(c) Eternal Death** — separation of spirit and soul from God for all eternity in the Lake of Fire. Death is not cessation of existence, nor annihilation, but eternal separation from God because of sin (Matthew 25:41; 10:28; II Thessalonians 1:9; Hebrews 10:31; Revelation 14:11; 20:11-15).

(6) Judgement by Expulsion from Eden
The final act of God in the Genesis account was to provide a substitutionary covering by death of an innocent victim, and then drive man out of the Garden of Eden. At the gate of Eden, God placed Cherubim and a flaming sword which turned every way to keep man from the tree of eternal life. Here He placed a manifestation of His presence where man could come for worship and sacrifice. In due time Christ would come, deal with sin, and open Paradise again, thus restoring the tree of life to man (Revelation 22:14). Sin separated man from God (Isaiah 59:2) and must be judged before perfect fellowship between God and man can be restored.

VI. THE LAW OF SIN
In this section the word "law" is being used to refer to a principle of action, or how a thing works (as with the "law of gravity", etc.) Thus, we will turn to the Scriptures relating to how sin works. The best Scriptural synopsis of the law of sin is to be found in James 1:15,16 "But every man is tempted when he is drawn away of his own lust, and enticed. Then when lust hath conceived, it bringeth forth sin; and sin, when it is finished, bringeth forth death".

There are four main elements in the outworking of sin as described by James. First, there is lust which is a wrong desire in the heart of man. Then, there is temptation which is an enticement preying upon the lust that is within man. When man responds to the tempting of his lust he is led to commit sin and when sin has run its course, it always produces death.

An important element to note in the statements of James is his use of reproductive language. Other Biblical writers also use the same imagery (Psalm 7:14; Acts 5:4; John 13:2,27; John 14:30 Amplified; Romans 7:7). Lust is viewed as being the female ovum that responds to and receives the male seed of temptation. Thus when a person responds to temptation, a conception of sin has taken place within him. This conception eventually leads to a birth of sin which is the wilful act contrary to God's will. According to James, when this infant called sin grows up, it turns out to be death.

VII. THE LAWS OF GOD

The relationship of the law to sin has been dealt with in a previous sub-section. However, in concluding the Doctrine of Sin, it will be profitable to have a brief synopsis of the various laws mentioned in Scripture, particularly as dealt with by Paul in the Book of Romans. It will be seen that man transgressed one law of God, thus bringing the whole human race under condemnation and death. The work of the atonement is to bring man back to the obedience from which Adam fell, to bring him back into harmony with the law of God, the royal law of loving obedience, which alone is eternal life.

We note these laws with a brief but suitable comment of clarification.

A. The Law (Romans 2:12)
This expression is often used in a broad and general sense to designate the will of God (I John 3:4; Romans 7:22).

B. The Law of Conscience (Romans 2:14-15)
The moment man sinned this law began to operate (Genesis 3:7-10). This is also called the law of our mind (Romans 7:23).

C. The Law of Works (Romans 3:27)
A guilty conscience drove man to operate in the law of works in self-effort to cover himself and make himself presentable to God (Genesis 3:7-10). Conscience drives men to seek to atone for their sins before God.

D. The Law of Faith (Romans 3:27)
The sacrificial victim which provided Adam and Eve with coats of skin necessitated an operation of the law of faith; faith in the substitutionary death of another to cover themselves acceptably before God (Genesis 3:21-24).

E. The Law of Ten Commandments (Romans 7:7)
This expressly speaks of the Law of God as contained in the Ten Commandments given to the nation of Israel (Exodus 20). Until this time, God dealt with man under the law of conscience. This is why Paul said that sin was in the world from Adam to Moses, but the law entered under Moses to give a more clear and full definition of sin (Romans 5:13,14; 3:20; 4:15; 7:7).

For the nation of Israel, the law was threefold:

1. The Moral Law (Deuteronomy 4:15; 5:6-22)
The Ten Commandments on two tables of stone were the moral law. It was actually given three times. First, it was spoken orally to the nation (Exodus 19-20; Deuteronomy 4-5; Hebrews 12:18-20). Then it was written on tables of stone, which were broken by Moses at the golden calf festival (Exodus 32,33,34). The commandments were written again on tbe second tables and these were placed within the Ark of the Covenant beneath the blood-stained mercyseat. (Exodus 34:1-9; 40:20-21) The first four commandments dealt with man's relationship with God; the last six dealt with man's relationship to man.

2. The Civil Law (Exodus 21-24; Deuteronomy 31:10-13, 24-26)
Written in a book called the Book of the Law, or the Book of the Covenant, the civil laws were simply amplifications of the moral law. This book was then placed in the side of the Ark of the Covenant.

3. The Ceremonial Law (Exodus 25-40; Leviticus 1-27)
These laws were also written in the Book of the Lord and involved the rituals of the feasts of the Lord, the priesthood, the sacrificial system and the sanctuary services.

The law gives the fullest and clearest definition of sin and this was partly the reason it was given. The Law gave a perfect, righteous and holy standard for man. It defined sin. However, being an external law it could tell man what he should do, and condemn him for not doing it, but it could give him no power to fulfil it. Hence it was used to drive man to God in Christ for redeeming grace (Romans 3:20; I John 3:4; Galatians 3:24; Romans 7:1-25).

A careful study of the various lists of sins given in the New Testament will show that all are violations of the commandments of God. (Read and compare these passages of Scripture with the Ten Commandments; Romans 1:18-31; Mark 7:21-23; Matthew 15:19-20; Ephesians 4:25-32; Revelation 22:15 with Exodus 20:1-17; Galatians 5:19-21)

F. The Law of Sin and Death (Romans 7:23; 8:2)
The law of sin entered man the moment he disobeyed God's law in his heart. The external act was only the outward evidence of an internal fall. The law of death followed as the subsequent penalty (Genesis 2:17).

G. The Law of the Spirit of Life (Romans 8:2)
This is opposite to the law of sin and death. It was symbolized in the tree of eternal life which man forfeited but it is restored in Christ by the power of the Holy Spirit (Genesis 2:9; Revelation 2:7; 22:14).

H. The Law of Righteousness (Romans 8:4; 9:31)
This law is also opposite to the law of sin. In Christ Jesus, the law of righteousness is put within man to overcome the law of sin and death. God's intention is to make an end of sin and bring in everlasting righteousness through Christ (Daniel 9:24).

I. The Royal Law of Love (Romans 13:8-10; James 2:8-10)
This is the highest law of God's being that redemption will bring man to. The grace of God in Christ will restore man back to the law of loving obedience to the will of God. Love is the fulfilment of the law. Against love there is no law (Galatians 5:23). The only answer to the sin problem is found in the Lord Jesus Christ. His redeeming grace deals with the law of sin, and brings man back to the law from which he fell.

Sin is lawlessness, selfishness and self-will. But through the redeeming work of the cross, God will have a people who will freely, willingly and lovingly submit their will to His good and perfect will. He will write His laws in their hearts and sin will be brought to an end in them. Law, order and harmony will prevail in the universe eternally upon the basis of the New Covenant (Hebrews 8:8-13; 13:20; Jeremiah 31:31-34).

The Scriptures close with the promise "Blessed are they that do His commandments that they might have right to the tree of life..." (Revelation 22:14). Adam forfeited the tree of life by disobedience to the one commandment. It is restored through Christ by obedience to His commandment.

Chapter 10

THE DOCTRINE OF CHRIST

Scripture reveals that the Lord Jesus Christ is the eternal Son of God, who always existed with the Father and the Holy Spirit, and who by His incarnation took upon Himself the form of man and became the God-Man. In the one person of Christ, there are two natures, human and divine, each in its completeness and integrity. They are distinguishable but indivisible, so that He is fully man and fully God. It is this sinless union of the divine and human natures which qualifies Him to be the only sacrificial mediator between God and man.

CHAPTER OUTLINE

I. INTRODUCTION

II. HERESIES CONCERNING THE PERSON OF CHRIST

A. The Ebionites
B. The Gnostics
C. The Arians
D. The Apollinarians
E. The Nestorians
F. The Eutychians
G. The Monophysites

III. ORTHODOX STATEMENT CONCERNING THE PERSON OF CHRIST

IV. OLD TESTAMENT PROPHECIES CONCERNING THE PERSON OF CHI

A. The Deity of Christ
B. The Humanity of Christ

V. THE INCARNATION OF CHRIST

A. The Fact of the Incarnation
B. The Necessity of the Incarnation
C. The Nature of the Incarnation
D. The Reasons for the Incarnation

VI. THE DEITY OF CHRIST

A. Divine Attributes
B. Divine Names
C. Divine Works
D. Divine Worship
E. Divine Claims
F. Divine Relationship

VII. THE HUMANITY OF CHRIST

A. The Humanity of Christ
B. The Sinlessness of Christ
C. The Example of Christ

VIII. THE MEDIATORSHIP OF CHRIST, THE GOD-MAN

A. Old Testament Revelation
B. New Testament Revelation
C. Maintaining Balance

INTRODUCTION
In the Gospels are presented two of the most important.questions relative to the Lord Jesus Christ. These questions were asked by Christ Himself of the religious leaders of His day, and by Pilate of the multitude seeking to bring about the crucifixion of Jesus.

Matthew 22:42 "What think ye of Christ; whose Son is He?"
Matthew 27:22 "What shall I do with Jesus which is called Christ?"

The plan of salvation, as revealed by God in Jesus Christ is dependent on the answers to these two questions. What a man believes about Jesus Christ will determine how he relates to Christ. This will in turn determine that man's eternal destiny. The Bible declares that Jesus Christ is the eternal Son of God, who by His virgin birth, sinless humanity, vicarious death, burial and resurrection, made the perfect sacrifice for sin, thereby making redemption available for fallen man. Apart from who He is and what He has done, there is absolutely no way of approach to the Father God (John 14:1,6; Hebrews 7:25).

The Doctrine of Christ has two major divisions:

1. The **person** of Christ — Who He is.
2. The **work** of Christ — What He has done

In this chapter, we will consider the person of Christ and in the following chapter the work of Christ. There are a full range of diverse views and heresies that center around the person and work of Christ. All religions may be tested in their doctrine by their view of Christ's person and work.

I. HERESIES CONCERNING THE PERSON OF CHRIST
All the basic heresies concerning the person of Christ were manifested in seed-form during the time of the early church and were dealt with in the Gospels and Epistles of the apostolic writers. There are actually no new heresies today, rather all are revivals of ancient ones. It was also due to these heresies that the various councils of the Patristic Church gathered together to formulate doctrinal statements and creeds to defend the Biblical Christology. The following are the most prominent heresies concerning the person of Christ, which the false cults in Christendom base their teachings upon.

A. The Ebionites
The Ebionites were Jewish believers that arose early in the second century. Their name is of Hebrew origin: "Ebion" which means "poor", "humble" and "oppressed". Because of their poverty, they regarded themselves as the only true disciples of Christ. The Ebionites believed that the Mosaic and Jewish ceremonies were still binding upon Christian believers. While upholding the teachings of Peter and James they disliked Paul's writings (e.g. Colossians 2:13-17 which refutes Jewish ceremonialism as being nailed to the cross and no longer binding to the believer in Christ). Before their influence had faded away in 135 A.D., they had divided into two groups: The Pharisaic Ebionites, who were successors to the Judaizers of Paul's days, and The Essenic Ebionites, who were more tolerant in their treatment of the uncircumcised Gentile believers that did not keep the Sabbaths nor other Jewish customs.

The major heresy of the Ebionites concerned the person of Christ. They denied that Christ had a divine nature, and discounted His supernatural conception. In denying Christ's deity, they viewed Him as merely a man. T hey rejected His deity because they believed it contradicted the fact of God's oneness. They taught that if Jesus were God, it would contradict monotheism, which is the belief that there is only one true God. There are modern cults which are counterparts of this heresy and deny the deity of Christ.

B. The Gnostics
The Gnostics appeared at about the same time as the Ebionites, though they went to the other extreme, denying the full humanity of Christ. The Gnostics were also called Docetae, meaning "to seem" or "to appear", because of their views of the person of Christ. There were basically three groups of Gnostics that held the same heretical views of Christ's humanity.

1. The Docetae — this group denied the reality of Christ's body, saying His body was a mere phantom appearance.

2. The Gnostics — this group taught that Christ had a real body but denied the fact that it was physical or material. They believed that since flesh was inherently evil, Christ's body could not have been a fleshly one.

3. The Cerinthians — a Gnostic by the name of Cerinthius taught that Jesus and Christ were distinct; that Jesus was an ordinary man, the son of Joseph and Mary, and that Christ was the spirit or power of God which descended upon Jesus at His baptism in the river Jordan. They taught that Christ departed from Jesus at His crucifixion leaving Him to suffer and die alone.

These Gnostic heresies are alluded to and dealt with in the Epistles of Colossians, I Timothy, II Timothy, I John, Jude and Revelation (read also John 20:31; I John 5:20; I John 2:1; Hebrews 2:14; I John 4:1-4; I Timothy 3:16; Colossians 1:19; 2:9).

C. The Arians
Arius was a presbyter of Alexandria in Egypt. The teaching of Arius relates more properly to the Doctrine of God rather than to the person of Christ. However, they cannot be totally separated from each other. The Arians taught that Christ did not pre-exist, that He was a created being and that by Him all other things were created. In His created state, He was called the Logos, the Son, the Only Begotten and the Beginning of the Creation of God (John 1:1-3,14-18; Revelation 3:14). Arius taught that though the Son was called God, He was not God in the fullest sense of the word, but was the highest of all created beings. He was divine, but not deity, a demi-god half-way between man and God. Arianism was condemned during the years 321-325 A.D. by Alexander, Bishop of Alexandria and Arius was dismissed from holding any church office as well as from communion. This heresy denies the eternity and co-equality of Christ's person with the Father and the Holy Spirit, making Him a created being only.

D. The Apollinarians
Apollinaris was a notable Bishop of Laodicea. He taught that Christ had a true body and animal soul but not a rational spirit or mind. Because of the difficulty in explaining the union of the two natures in the one person of Christ, he taught that the eternal Son supplied the spirit or mind of Christ Jesus. Thus the body and soul was the human part and the eternal Son was the divine or spirit part of Jesus. This teaching denies the completeness of Christ's human nature, teaching that He has only two parts instead of the full and total humanity of spirit, soul and body (I Thessalonians 5:23). Apollinarianism was condemned by the Council of Constantinople in 381 A.D. as being heretical.

E. The Nestorians
Nestorius, Bishop of Constantinople, taught concerning the person of Christ that there was a dual personality involved. He denied the real union of the divine and human natures in Christ, saying that the Logos (the divine personality) dwelt in Christ Jesus (the human personality), making two related persons. He presented Christ as a Spirit-filled man, a man filled with God, but without true deity and true humanity in the one person. Cyril of Alexandria opposed Nestorius' teaching and Nestorius was condemned and banished by the Synod of Ephesus in 431 A.D. Extreme forms of Kenoticism, which teach that when the Son of God became man, He emptied Himself of His divine attributes and thus as a man made intellectual errors and mistakes, are closely related to Nestorianism.

F. The Eutychians
In 451 A.D. the heresies concerning the person of Christ turned into another stream. Eutyches went to the opposite extreme of Nestorius, He held that Christ had but one nature and will, not two separate natures or wills. He taught that the divine and human natures were so mingled into one that it actually constituted a third nature. This teaching made Christ neither God nor man but a third person resulting from the mingling of the two, though different from either. It reduced Christ to a one "hybrid" natured person. Eutyches held that everything about Christ was divine, even His body and human nature.

G. The Monophysites
Eutychianism also flowed into several other smaller streams, which are briefly mentioned here.

1. Monophysites was another name for a branch of the Eutychians because they emphasized that Christ had but one nature, one will. This arose out of the difficulty to see the harmony and relationship of the two natures and wills in the person of Christ. In 680-681 A.D. the Council of Constantinople condemned their doctrine and held that Christ did indeed have two distinct natures, divine and human and that of necessity, possessed two intelligences and two wills. Both were in harmonious unity in which the human will was subject to the divine will.

2. **Adoptionists** were simply an offshoot of Eutychianism, Apollinarianism and Nestorianism. This heresy taught that the humanity of Christ was only by adoption. It denied the begotten and now eternal humanity of Christ.

Before defining and interpreting the orthodox view of the person of Christ we will summarize the major heresies dealt with thus far.

The **Ebionites** - denied Christ's deity.
The **Gnostics** - denied Christ's humanity.
The **Arians** - taught that Christ was a created being.
The **Apollinarians** - denied the completeness of Christ's human nature.
The **Nestorians** - denied the union of the two natures in Christ, reducing Him to a man filled with God.
The **Eutychians** - denied the distinction of the two natures of Christ, thus making a third or hybrid nature of the two.
The **Monophysites** - denied the two natures and wills in the one person of Christ.

III. ORTHODOX STATEMENT CONCERNING THE PERSON OF CHRIST

Because of the heresies which raged over the person of Christ, the various church councils gathered periodically to hammer out creeds on the anvil of truth in an endeavor to preserve and guard "the faith once delivered to the saints" (Jude 3). The apostles themselves never formulated any such creeds, but the truth was scattered in fragmentary statements throughout their writings. These needed to be brought together and studied carefully in order to formulate creeds that would best define the truths concerning the person of Christ. We note several of these creeds which best state the orthodox position concerning Christ's glorious person. The following Creed is that which was formulated by the Council of Chalcedon in 451 A.D. Because of its theological soundness it is quoted at length.

"Following the holy fathers we all with one consent teach and confess one and the same Son, our Lord Jesus Christ, the same perfect in deity, and the same perfect in humanity, truly God, and the same truly Man, of reasonable soul and body, of the same substance with the Father as to His divinity, of the same substance with us as to His humanity, in all things like to us, except sin, before the ages begotten of the Father as to His deity, but in the latter days for us, and for our redemption, begotten (the same) of the Virgin Mary, the mother of God, as to His humanity, one and the same Christ, Son, Lord. Only-begotten, manifested in two natures, without confusion, without conversion, indivisibly, inseparably. The distinction of natures being by no means abolished by the union, but rather the property of each preserved and combined into one person and one hypostasis; not one severed or divided into two persons, but one and the same Son and only-begotten, viz. God, Logos, and the Lord Jesus Christ". (Robert Clarke, in "The Christ of God" pp. 41-42)."

Henry Thiessen in "Lectures in Systematic Theology" (p.286), in quoting from Strong, writes:

"In the one person of Jesus Christ, there are two natures, a human and a divine nature, each in its completeness and integrity, and these two natures are organically and indissolubly united, yet so that no third nature is formed thereby. In brief (to use the antiquated dictum) orthodox doctrine forbids us either to divide the person or to confound the natures".

And further

"The redemption of mankind from sin was to be affected through a Mediator who should unite in Himself both the human nature and the divine in order that He might reconcile God to man, and man to God."

And finally, the statement of the writer of this text:

"The Lord Jesus Christ is the eternal Son of God, who pre-existed with the Father, and by His incarnation and Virgin Birth, took upon Himself the form of Man and was revealed as the God-Man. In the one person of Christ, there are two natures, human and divine, distinguishable but indivisible, qualifying Him to be the only true mediator between God and man. Jesus Christ was sinless, perfect, crucified, buried, resurrected, ascended, glorified and He will come again the second time in glory and judgement." The orthodox position concerning the person of Christ is that Christ is truly God and truly Man, and that because of the union in Him of two natures, He is the perfect mediator between God and man.

IV. OLD TESTAMENT PROPHECIES CONCERNING THE PERSON OF CHRIST
A consideration of Old Testament prophecies concerning the coming of the Messiah reveals that there were two streams of thought. One stream spoke of the deity of Christ, while the other spoke of the humanity of Christ. The Jewish interpreters of the Old Testament could not reconcile these streams. They could not understand how the Messiah could be divine, and yet also human. Thus they erred in understanding and missed the very Messiah that their Scriptures prophesied would come.

A. The Deity of Christ
The following Scriptures set forth the deity of Christ, showing that the Redeemer would be God incarnate.

1. "A virgin shall conceive and bear a Son ... and His name shall be called ... Immanuel" (Isaiah 7:1
2. "For unto us a child is born, unto us a Son is given ... and His name shall be called Wonderful, Counselor, the Mighty God, the Everlasting Father, and the Prince of Peace" (Isaiah 9:6-9).
3. "...the Lord our Righteousness" (Jeremiah 23:5-6).
4. From Bethlehem there was to come forth the "... Ruler, whose goings forth have been from of old (from the days of eternity)" (Micah 5:2).
5. "...What is His name, and what is His Son's name, if thou canst tell? (Proverbs 30:4).
6. "Thou art My Son, this day have I begotten Thee ..." (Psalm 2:7,12).
7. "...but unto the Son He saith, Thy throne, O God is forever ..." (Psalm 45:6 with Hebrews 1:8).

B. The Humanity of Christ
The following Scriptures indicated that the Redeemer would be a man, born of a woman. They set forth the humanity of the Messiah, even as the previous Scriptures set forth His deity.

1. The Redeemer was to be the "seed of the woman" who would bruise the serpent's head (Genesis 3:1 This is a prophecy of the Virgin Birth in enigmatic form.
2. The Messiah would also come from the Tents of Shem (Genesis 9:26).
3. The Redeemer would be the "seed of Abraham" (Genesis 22:18).
4. The Redeemer would be of "the seed of Isaac" (Genesis 26:2-4).
5. This promise was also confirmed to "the seed of Jacob" (Genesis 28:13-14).
6. The Messiah would come from the nation of Israel (Numbers 24:17-19).
7. The Lord also foretold that a prophet "like unto Moses" would be raised up out from the midst of his brethren (Deuteronomy 18:15-18).
8. Messiah was to come from the Tribe of Judah (Genesis 49:10-12).
9. Messiah would come of the family of Jesse (Isaiah 11:1-2).
10. Messiah would come out of the House of David (II Samuel 7:12-14).
11. The promise of Scripture was that "a virgin shall conceive and bear a Son...His name shall be called Immanuel" (Isaiah 7:14).
12. This Messiah would be "a man", whose name is The Branch" (Zechariah 3:8; 6:10-12; Isaiah 11:1-4).

All of these references show how God singled out a man, then a nation from the man, a tribe from the nation, a house from the tribe, a virgin from the house, and thus preserved the genealogy of the Messiah as to His humanity.

The Old Testament prophets foretold of the Messiah being both God and man, possessing both divine and human natures in one person. That it would be difficult to reconcile these two streams of Messianic prophecy is evident, for how could this Redeemer be both God and man at the same time? It is only in the

New Testament account of the historical fulfilment in the Gospels and then the doctrinal revelation in the Epistles that we can find the solution to the enigma and can see how God reconciled these two prophetic streams. The miracle of the incarnation is God's answer to the question. All men have been begotten of a human father and born of a human mother, since the creation of Adam and Eve, the first parents. This was not to be the case with the Messiah. He would be born of a human mother, a virgin. But He would not be begotten of a human father, for God would be His Father. This child would be "the seed of the woman" (Genesis 3:15), yet the "Son of God" by a virgin (Isaiah 7:14). This found its glorious fulfilment in the virgin birth of Jesus Christ by the power and overshadowing of the Holy Spirit (Matthew 1:18-23 with Luke 1:35).

Modernists may deny the virgin birth, scientific knowledge may not be able to account for it, and spiritual ignorance may state it is of no real consequence, but the Biblical importance of it cannot be over-estimated. It is upon the fact of the virgin birth that Biblical doctrine hangs. If Jesus Christ is not virgin born, He is not sinless, and if He is not sinless, then He Himself needs a Savior. If He Himself needs salvation, then He cannot be our Savior, Lord or King, and the entire redemptive plan falls powerless to the ground. Hence we need to understand and believe the foundational significance of the incarnation.

V. THE INCARNATION OF CHRIST

A. The Fact of the Incarnation

All of the New Testament writers attest to the truth of the incarnation. The birth of Jesus Christ is an historical fact and the Biblical writers under the inspiration of the Holy Spirit give us the details of this miraculous event. The word "incarnation" simply means "God taking on Himself human flesh". God took human form or clothed Himself with flesh in the virgin birth. The origin of the Christ-child, as to His humanity, is traced to the work of the Holy Spirit. God became man in Jesus, deity took upon Himself humanity. A.B. Bruce says "It is not deified humanity, but the descent of God into humanity. It is not man taking God into him, but God taking on manhood."

1. The Incarnation Historically

a. To Mary (Luke 1:26-35; Jeremiah 31:22)

The Angel Gabriel was sent to Mary, a young Hebrew virgin, to announce the birth of the Messiah. The word was clear. The Child would not be the product of the seed of men, but the Holy Spirit Himself would overshadow the virgin and place within her womb the seed of the Father God. This Child would be a sinless creation brought about by a miracle of God and the response of this pure virgin. There would be nothing unclean about the birth of this Child. God would bring forth a sinless, perfect, immortal creature out of a sinful, imperfect, mortal creature. This is the miracle of the virgin birth. It cannot be accounted for by purely human or natural means. Mary, in total faith, was willing to accept the responsibility and challenge of being the mother of the Christ-child (Luke 2:34-35).

b. To Joseph (Matthew 1:18-25)

Matthew, after listing the genealogy of Jesus breaks the pattern of common descent by introducing the miraculous birth of Jesus with "Now the birth of Jesus was on this wise..." This account says that Mary was found with child of the Holy Spirit. The Messianic genealogy was begotten of men, but the Messiah was born of Mary. Joseph, upon finding his espoused wife with child was ready to have her put away with a bill of divorcement, rather than have her stoned to death, which was the Law of Moses. However, the Angel of the Lord came to him and specifically told him that the child would be a Son whose name was to be called Jesus. This child was the product of the overshadowing of the Holy Spirit and would be Immanuel, "God with us". In faith, Joseph was willing to take the legal custody of the virginborn child, accepting the testimony of the Angel concerning the purity of his espoused wife, and accepting the miraculous fact of the virgin birth.

2. The Incarnation Personally

Jesus Himself gave abundant evidence of His own origin including the truth of His miraculous birth. Jesus said "I came out from God, I came forth from the Father..." (John 16:27 with 8:42). Jesus knew that He was David's Lord (as to His deity) and David's son (as to His humanity) (Matthew 22:42-46; Revelation 22:16 with Psalm 110:1). On numerous occasions He claimed God as His Father while never saying that Joseph was His father (John 2:16; 5:17; 18:47, 6:32-40; 8:42). The Father God also attested to the Son's miraculous birth. Three times He spoke from heaven, two of these times attesting to the fact "This is My Beloved Son in whom I am well pleased" (Matthew 3:16-18; 17:1-5; John 12:27-29). This was the Father's taking responsibility for the way His Son was born. It was the Father's way of acknowledging the virgin birth. Jesus knew of His pre-existence with the Father; His deity, and that He was virgin born as the God-Man. To deny the virgin birth is to reject Christ's own testimony, as well as the Father's witness.

3. The Incarnation Theologically
It has been contested by those who reject the virgin birth that the writers of the Epistles never speak of it. However, this is not so, for they clearly speak of both Christ's deity and humanity, but more so in the language of theology. The following brief quotations and references are the apostolic way of confirming the truth of the virgin birth.

a. To Paul
Paul the apostle has several unique expressions which speak of the incarnation. These attest to the foundational truth of the virgin birth.

(1) Jesus Christ our Lord was "made of the seed of David according to the flesh" (Romans 1:3-4).

(2) God sent forth His Son in the fulness of time, "made of a woman, made under the Law" (Galatians 4:4).

(3) In Christ "dwelleth all the fulness of the Godhead bodily" (Colossians 2:9 with 1:19).

(4) Great is the mystery of Godliness "God was manifest in the flesh" (I Timothy 3:16).

(5) The one mediator between God and men, "The Man, Christ Jesus" (I Timothy 2:5).

(6) "Forasmuch the children are partakers of flesh and blood, He Himself also took part of the same" in order to redeem man from death and the power of the devil (Hebrews 2:14).

(7) God sent forth His Son "in the likeness of sinful flesh" (Romans 8:3).

(8) Christ came of the fathers "as concerning the flesh" (Romans 9:5).

(9) Though Christ was originally in "the form of God", He made Himself of no reputation and took upon Himself "the form of a servant and was made in the likeness of men" (Philippians 2:5-8).

(10) When Jesus came into the world by the incarnation, He said "a body hast Thou prepared Me" (Hebrews 10:5). This body was prepared or fitted out perfectly to do God's will in the virgin Mary.

When God made Adam, He made a body out of the dust of the earth (Genesis 2:7). When God made Eve, He built a body out of the side of Adam (Genesis 2:21-22). All other human beings receive a body through natural processes including the union of a man and woman, but the body of the Son of God was not created this way but prepared in the virgin Mary's womb by the power of the Holy Spirit (Luke 1:30-33).

b. To Peter
The apostle Peter also acknowledged by revelation the truth of Christ's deity and virgin birth.

(1) Peter confessed that Jesus Christ was "the Son of the Living God" (Matthew 16:16). He was not just the Son of Man, as Jesus called Himself, but the Son of God. Jesus acknowledged that Peter had received this revelation from the Father of God. This is another way of acknowledging the virgin birth, and Christ's divine Sonship.

(2) Christ was foreordained as the Lamb of God before the foundation of the world but was

manifested in these last times for our redemption (I Peter 1:18-20). Pre-existence, incarnation and redemption are the truths Peter declares here.

c. To John
John also confirmed the deity and humanity of Christ.

(1) The Word was in the beginning with God, and the Word was God. This Word was made flesh and tabernacled among men (John 1:1-3, 14-18; I John 4:9-10). This is John's way of speaking of the virgin birth.

(2) False prophets deny that "Jesus Christ is come in the flesh" (I John 4:1-3).

(3) Deceivers and antichrists deny and "confess not that Jesus Christ is come in the flesh" (II John 7-10).

A consideration of these brief references all point to the foundational truth of the incarnation; Jesus Christ is God manifest in the flesh. He is the God-Man. The apostles confirmed theologically in the epistles the virgin birth as set forth historically in the Gospels.

In **Matthew** Jesus is presented as the Son of **David** (Isaiah 11:1; Matthew 1:1).
In **Mark** Jesus is presented as the Son of **Man** (Zechariah 3:8; Mark 8:38).
In **Luke** Jesus is presented as the Son of **Adam** (Zechariah 6:12-13; Luke 3:38).
In **John** Jesus is presented as the Son of **God** (Isaiah 4:2; 7:14; John 3:16).

It is upon the fact of the incarnation, or virgin birth, that the truths of Christ's pre-existence, deity, Saviorhood, Lordship, resurrection and the entire plan of redemption depend.

B. THE NECESSITY OF THE INCARNATION
There were two major things which necessitated the incarnation. The fall and sinfulness of man, and the covenant-making and keeping God. When God created man, it was upon the basis of the Edenic Covenant. The fact that God is a covenant-making and covenant-keeping God means that as the Creator He is obligated for the creature (Genesis 1:26-28). When man sinned God was still obligated by His own will to man, especially in the realm of redemption. This is to be fulfilled by the New Covenant (Jeremiah 31:31-34). In fact all of the covenants of God support this fact.

To state it more specifically, man sinned and therefore came under the death penalty (Genesis 2:16-17). He thus needed someone to redeem him from death. However, all those who would be born of Adam's race would be born in sin and need redemption from sin and death for themselves. None of Adam's race could by any means redeem his brother (Psalm 49:7-8; 51:5; 58:3). If man is to be redeemed, then a man must die for man, and if no man of Adam's race could do this then only God could redeem man, but by His own law, God could not redeem man as God, He had to become man. The fall of man necessitated the covenant-keeping God becoming man in order to redeem man back to relationship with Himself.

It was sin that necessitated the incarnation. However, if God was to become man, it must be without or apart from sin. Otherwise, He Himself would be a sinner unable to save others. God's answer was seen in the miracle of the virgin birth, in which God clothed Himself with human flesh, and was born of Mary into the human race. But He did not inherit a fallen, sinful or corrupt human nature. He took sinless human nature and united it with the divine nature.

When God foretold through the mouth of the prophet Jeremiah that the days would come when He would make a New Covenant with the House of Israel and House of Judah, He obligated Himself to die. This also necessitated the incarnation, for God could not die as God, but only as man (Jeremiah 31:31-34 with Hebrews 8:8-13; Hebrews 9:15-17; Matthew 26:26-28). A testament or covenant is only of force after men are dead. Thus the New Covenant could not come into effect until after the death of the testator, Jesus Christ. In summary:

1. Man sinned and therefore must die (I Corinthians 15:21; Romans 5:12-21; Genesis 2:16-17).

2. Only man could die for man, but no man born of Adam's race could qualify, as all are born in sin, shapen in iniquity. No-one born of Adam's race is clean (Job:14:4; 14:14; 25:4; Psalm 51:1-5; 58:3).

3. Only God could redeem man. But God could not redeem man as God,only as man. Thus God became sinless man by the incarnation to redeem man back to Himself (Galatians 4:4-5; I Peter 2:22; I John 3: II Corinthians 5:21). By the virgin birth, God brought forth a sinless being out of a sinful being

C. THE NATURE OF THE INCARNATION

The nature of the incarnation is given to us by Paul in the Philippian epistle in the seven-fol humiliation of the Christ of God. The seven steps of Christ's humiliation are noted in the followin outline of Philippians 2:6-8.

1. Who, being in the form of God
2. Thought it not robbery to be equal with God
3. But made Himself of no reputation
4. And took upon Himself the form of a servant
5. And was made in the likeness of men
6. And being found in fashion as a man, He humbled Himself
7. And became obedient unto death, even the death of the cross.

This seven-fold humiliation of Christ may be summed up in three major theological points: 1) His deity clauses 1 and 2; 2) His humanity; clauses 3,4 and 5; and 3) His crucifixion, clauses 6 and 7.

When Paul states that Christ "made Himself of no reputation" he is saying that Christ emptied Himself By being in "the form of God" and taking upon Himself "the form of man" there was a self-emptying process. This is spoken of as the Kenosis Theory. The expression "emptied Himself" comes from th Greek word "Kenoo" meaning "to make empty". Theologians in general accept the Kenosis Theory, that Christ did empty Himself in the incarnation, but there is much misunderstanding concerning thi theory. Common questions are, 'In what way did Christ empty Himself?' 'What did this self-emptying consist of?' and 'In becoming man did He cease to be God?'.

1. False Concepts

a. He Emptied Himself of His Deity
This theory holds that Christ in His self-emptying laid aside His deity, giving up His essential atributes when He took upon Himself humanity. It can be refuted in that Jesus was alway conscious of His deity. Deity could take humanity into union with itself but could never cease t be deity. Jesus was God manifest in the flesh.

b. He Emptied Himself of the Possession of Divine Attributes
This theory holds that in becoming man, Christ gave up the possession of certain essential attributes of deity, such as omnipotence, omnipresence, and omniscience. On the other hand this theory holds that Christ in becoming man did not empty Himself of His moral attributes such as love, truth, holiness and life. Also the essential attributes of self-existence, immutability and unity with the Father were not surrendered.

However, if Christ would have given up some of the divine attributes, which seems impossible then He would have ceased to be fully God.

c. He Emptied Himself of the Apparent Possession of Divine Attributes
This theory holds that Christ did not divest Himself of either essential or moral attributes, but simply acted as though He did not possess them. This theory introduces an element of decei that is totally uncharacteristic of the God of truth.

d. He Emptied Himself of the Use of Divine Attributes
This concept holds that Christ in His self-emptying, gave up the use of divine attributes. It hold that He did not give up the possession of the divine nature and attributes but only the use o them. However, the Gospels, as it will be seen, show that He did use or exercise divine attribute at times.

2. Proper Concepts

Christ in becoming man did not cease to be God, neither did He give up the possession or use of the divine attributes, whether essential or moral. It should be noted that God was not changed into a man, but rather assumed the nature of man without ceasing to be God.

What did this self-emptying then consist of? Christ surrendered the independent exercise of divine attributes. He laid aside His prerogatives as God to act as God, and became dependent upon the Father's will for any exercise, operation or manifestation of these attributes. A. H. Strong in "Systematic Theology" (p.703) says "His humiliation consisted in the continuous surrender, on the part of the God-Man so far as His human nature was concerned, of the exercise of those divine powers with which it was endowed by virtue of its union with the divine, and in the voluntary acceptance, which followed upon this, of temptation, suffering, and death."

a. Christ Was Always God

Before His incarnation, Christ was in the form of God (Philippians 2:6-8). In becoming man He did not cease to be God. The truth of His essential deity before His incarnation precludes that He could not cease to be God in becoming man. Jesus Christ was God before and during His incarnation. He never ceased to be God. He is eternally God, but now has taken humanity upon Himself. In taking humanity, He did not empty Himself of His deity. To deny this is to fall into the heresies of the early centuries and align with those who rejected the deity of Christ.

Herbert Lockyer in "All the Doctrines of the Bible" (p.45) says: "At His incarnation, Christ added to His already existing divine nature a human nature and became the God-Man. At our regeneration, there was added to our already existing human nature, a divine nature and we thus become partakers of the divine nature (II Peter 1:4). Thus, like Christ, every true Christian is divine-human."

In quoting Dr. Louis Berkhof, Lockyer continues to write "Christ has a human nature, but He is not a human person. The person of the mediator is the unchangeable Son of God. In the incarnation He did not change into a human person, neither did He adopt a human person. He simply assumed, in addition to His divine nature, a human nature, which did not develop into an independent personality, but became personal in the person of the Son of God."

b. Christ Always Possessed Divine Attributes

In becoming a Man, Christ did not empty Himself of any of His essential or moral attributes. We note this in the following Scriptures.

(1) Essential Attributes

(a) Omnipresence (John 3:13; Matthew 28:19-20; 18:20)

Jesus knew, as the Son of Man, that He was both on earth and in heaven. This is omnipresence. Only by this attribute can He also be with His people everywhere at all times.

(b) Omnipotence (John 6:36; 14:11; 10:25,37-38; 15:24).

The works of Jesus were divine works. Certain works only God Himself could do. Jesus forgave sins, declared the divine name, I AM, and exercised creative powers which only belong to deity. Jesus was all-powerful.

(c) Omniscience (John 2:24-25; 18:4)

Jesus knew all men. He also knew all that was in man. As to His deity, He was all-knowing. Nothing was hidden from His sight.

(d) Immutable (Hebrews 1:12; 13:8)

Jesus Christ is the same yesterday, today and forever. His character, love and life are unchangeable.

(ε) Self-Existence (John 8:58; John 1:4; 5:26)

Jesus offered men eternal life, saying that this life was in Himself. He that has the Son of God has eternal life. This is an attribute of deity (I John 5:11-13).

(f) Eternal (Revelation 1:8; John 3:16; 5:26)

Jesus is the eternal Son of God. He presents eternal life to all those who will believe on the Father through Him.

(2) Moral Attributes

The following moral attributes were also manifested in the Son of God. In becoming Man, He did not empty Himself of these moral attributes of deity.

(a) Holiness (Mark 1:24; Revelation 4:8; I Peter 1:15-16)

(b) Righteousness (I Corinthians 1:30; Jeremiah 23:4-5; I John 2:1-2)

(c) Love (John 3:16; Galatians 2:20; I John 4:16-19). Jesus Christ was perfect love manifested. This includes goodness, grace, mercy, compassion and kindness; all of which are qualities of God's love. (Ephesians 2:4,7; Titus 3:4-7).

(d) Faithfulness (John 14:6; I John 5:20; Hebrews 2:17). Jesus Christ is truthfulness personified.

Jesus was and is God, possessing both the essential and moral attributes of deity. He possessed the attributes of God because He was God. As the God-Man He could never cease to possess all the attributes of God. Jesus was conscious of His deity as well as His humanity.

c. Christ as God Became Dependent Man.

The self-emptying of Christ as God was in the fact that He humbled Himself, and from being in the form of God, took upon Himself the form of a servant. Though He was God and never ceased to be God in the incarnation, He became a subject, obedient and dependent Man upon the Father for the exercise of His essential attributes. Of His own free will He subjected Himself as the God-Man to the Father's will in total dependence upon the Holy Spirit.

The Son took upon Himself the limitations of a perfect humanity and exercised a continuous surrender of His will. He did not need to suffer hunger, thirst, weariness, sorrows, suffering or death, and He never used His divine prerogatives to alleviate these infirmities of human nature.

This self-humbling was not forced upon Him or against His will, but the love of the eternal Godhead compelled Him to bring about the redemption of fallen man. Christ delighted to do the Father's will (Psalm 40:6-7; Hebrews 10:5-10). As the subject and dependent God-Man He said that He could do nothing of Himself, only as the Father directed (John 5:30). Thus He never acted contrary to the will of the Father and any exercise or expression of essential or moral attributes was in accordance with the Father's will. As the perfect God-Man, He was totally dependent upon the Holy Spirit for all He said and did. In summary:

(1) In His Self-emptying He gave up the glory, the outshining majesty and outward expression of the Godhead that He had with the Father (John 17:5).

(2) In His Self-emptying He gave up the form of God and took upon Himself the form of a servant, without ceasing to be God. This He did in the virgin birth (John 1:14; Philippians 2:6-8; I Peter 1:16-18).

(3) In His Self-emptying He taught only what the Father told Him to say (John 5:30; 8:28,35; 12:44-50).

(4) In His Self-emptying He did only what the Father showed Him to do (John 5:36).

(5) In His Self-emptying He exercised only the authority the Father gave Him (John 10:18).

(6) In His Self-emptying He came into voluntary dependence upon the anointing and enabling power of the Holy Spirit (Acts 10:38; Luke 4:14-18; Matthew 12:38; Hebrews 9:14; Acts 1:2).

(7) In His self-emptying He laid aside the independent exercise of His divine attributes, only exercising them as the Father willed. This was self-subordination for a redemptive purpose. He never used any of His divine prerogatives for selfish purposes (John 14:28; 3:16; 10:18; I Corinthians 11:3; 15:27-28).

D. THE REASONS FOR THE INCARNATION
There are nine important reasons for the incarnation and they all find their fulfilment in the person and work of Christ.

1. To Confirm the Promises of Salvation made to the Patriarchs
God made covenants of promise with the patriarchs; Adam, Noah, Abraham, Isaac and Jacob. These covenants involved salvation for both Israel and the Gentiles through the seed of the woman, the Lord Jesus Christ. Christ came by the incarnation to fulfil these promises made to the fathers (Romans 15:8-9; Matthew 1:1; Isaiah 7:14; 9:6-9; Genesis 3:15; 22:18; Micah 5:1-2).

2. To Fulfil the Law, the Psalms and the Prophets

a. The Law

(1) To Fulfil the Law Morally
Jesus came to fulfil the demands of the Law and satisfy the claims of God's holiness. It was necessary that a man fulfil the Law before He could redeem those who had violated it. Man broke the Law and came under the death penalty. Jesus is the only man who has ever perfectly kept the Law of God.

(2) To Fulfil the Law Typically
The typical aspects of the Law involved the sanctuary services, the priesthood, the offerings and the festival seasons. This ceremonial law was typical of the coming priesthood ministrations of Christ. He came to fulfil the Law in every jot and tittle in His own person and work.

b. The Psalms
Many of the Psalms were Messianic. They foretold the sufferings of Christ and the glory that was to follow (I Peter 1:10-12). Christ came to fulfil these things.

c. The Prophets
The Law, the Psalms and the Prophets pointed to the coming Christ, the coming Redeemer. They typified and prophesied of His person and work. Jesus specifically stated that He came to fulfil all that was in them (Matthew 5:17-18; Luke 16:16; Romans 2:21; Hebrews 10:5-8; Luke 24:27,44-46; Galatians 4:4-5; Psalms 16:8-10; 22:1-18; 41:9-11).

3. To Give a Complete Revelation of the Father God
The Old Testament saints and prophets gave but fragmentary revelations of God and were not able to give a full or perfect revelation. Only the Son of God, who was God incarnate could do this. In Christ God was clothed with the flesh of man. The distinctive revelation of God in the New Testament is that of the Father. Jesus Christ was the fullest and clearest revelation of the Father and Son relationship that God desires the redeemed to come into by the new birth (John 1:14-18 Amplified Version; 14:9; 16:27; Matthew 6:8; 5:45; Psalm 103:13; John 3:1-5; Matthew 11:27; I John 3:1-2).

4. To Destroy the Works of the Devil and His Kingdom

The devil's kingdom is a kingdom of darkness and all his works are from that realm. Sin, sickness disease, death and bondage are the works of the devil. Jesus came to destroy them all and bring mankind out of the kingdom of darkness into the kingdom of light (I John 3:5,8; Romans 13:12 Ephesians 5:11; Galatians 5:19; Hebrews 2:14-15; John 12:31; 14:30; Revelation 20:10-15).

5. To Live a Perfectly Sinless Human Life

Jesus came to live a perfect and sinless life as God intended man to be on this earth. Adam fell from this life, but Jesus lived it. Though the Bible writers gave infallible teaching under inspiration o the Spirit, none of them were infallible in character. Jesus alone had no sin, no imperfections in His character. He had no fallen or carnal human nature. He is therefore our only perfect exemplary man (I John 2:6; I Peter 2:21; Matthew 11:29).

6. To Put Away Sin by the Sacrifice of Himself

The wages of sin is death and the only way sin could be dealt with was through the death of a sac rifice. When Adam fell, God introduced substitutionary sacrifice for sin until Christ came to offer Himself as the perfect sacrifice. Every Old Testament sacrifice pointed to Christ's perfect once-for all sacrifice. This was the supreme purpose of the incarnation. Only a perfect sinless man could atone for sin. Christ fulfilled and abolished all animal sacrifices (Leviticus 16:10-22; Isaiah 53:6 Hebrews 10:1-10; II Corinthians 5:21; Hebrews 2:9-14; Hebrews 9:26; Mark 10:45; I John 3:5; John 1:29,36).

7. To Bring Into Effect the New Covenant

Christ came to fulfil in Himself all Old Testament utterances including all the covenants. He came to bring into effect the New Covenant as foretold by the prophet Jeremiah. Only upon the basis of the death of the testator could the New Covenant promises of blessing come into effect and be av ailable for all the world (Jeremiah 31:31-34; Hebrews 8; Matthew 26:26-28). The New Covenant is the fulfilment of all previous covenants and brings redeemed mankind into the purposes of the co venant made in the counsels of the Godhead in eternity before sin began (Hebrews 13:20).

8. To Fulfil Old Testament Offices

There were primarily four Old Testament offices which shadowed forth the ministry of Christ and which He came to fulfil.

a. The Office of the Judge

The judges were deliverers and saviors of God's people, Israel. Each of them in their office were types and shadows of Christ as The Judge, Deliverer and Savior. Their chief function was to deliver Israel from the bondage of servitude and oppression of their enemies and bring them back into relationship with the Lord God. This is also Christ's ministry to His people (Judges 2:14; Nehemiah 9:27; John 5:19-20; Acts 17:31; Isaiah 33:22; Revelation 20:11-15; Acts 5:31) The Gospel of John particularly presents Christ as the Judge and Savior.

b. The Office of the Prophet

Moses in particular shadowed forth Christ as The Prophet, The Word of God to man. The prophets of Israel were God's spokesmen to the people. They came from God representing Him to man. In this they foreshadowed Christ who came from God, and represented God to man, as the final Word, the perfect revelation of God to mankind (John 1:17-18; Luke 10:16; Hebrews 1:1-2; Acts 2:22-23; 7:37; Luke 13:33; Matthew 13:57; Hebrews 12:25; John 6:14; John 7:40; Luke 7:16; Exodus 4:14-16; 7:1; Deuteronomy 18:15-18). Christ is the infallible teacher and prophet of God. The Gospel of Mark particularly presents Christ as the Prophet.

c. The Office of the Priest

As the prophet represented God to man, the priest represented man to God. Aaron the High Priest and all subsequent priests in their office typified Christ in this office. The qualifications anointing and consecration of priests to their function typified Christ in this office. The qualifications, anointing and consecration of priests to their function typified the qualifica tions, anointing and consecration of Christ as our Great High Priest to His function. He was a priest not after the "order of Aaron" but after the "order of Melchisedek" (Leviticus 21:16-24

Exodus 28-29; Leviticus 8:23-26; Hebrews 1:9; Zechariah 6:12-13; I Samuel 2:27-35). The Church is also called to be after the order of Melchisedek (I Peter 2:5-8; Revelation 1:6; 5:9-10).

This office is vitally connected with the sacrificial system of the offerings for sin. Christ, as High Priest, offering Himself combines both offerer and offering in His one person. He is the propitiation, the Advocate, the Intercessor, the High Priest in behalf of the sins of the people (Hebrews 2:10, 17-18; 4:15-16; 5:1-5; I Timothy 2:5; Isaiah 53:10-12; John 1:29,36; I John 2:1-2; Psalm 110:4).

Christ as a priest on earth offered at Calvary's altar His own body and blood as the supreme sacrifice for sin. Christ as a priest in heaven makes intercession in the heavenly sanctuary for His own people. This is on the basis of His resurrection and ascension and fulfills that which was typified in the great Day of Atonement ceremonies as set forth in Leviticus 16 (Hebrews 7:26-27; Romans 3:25; Hebrews 8:1-2; 9:24; Romans 8:34). The Gospel of Luke particularly presents Christ as our Priest.

d. The Office of the King

The kings of Israel and Judah, though imperfect in character and deeds, shadowed forth the Lord Jesus Christ who would be King of Kings and Lord of Lords, the Son of David. The incarnation was also for the fulfilment of the Davidic Covenant which promised Messiah the King to be the ultimate ruler of the world (Psalm 89; Psalm 2; Psalm 45; Psalm 72; Psalm 110; John 18:36; II Samuel 7:8-17; Revelation 15:3; 19:16). The Gospel of Matthew particularly presents Christ as King.

As King-Priest Jesus combined in Himself that which was set forth in the order of Melchisedek (II Timothy 4:18; Jeremiah 23:5-6; Genesis 14:18-19; Hebrews 7:1-29; Zechariah 6:12, 3:8; Hebrews 1:8; Luke 1:30-33; Genesis 17:6,16; 49:9-10; Isaiah 11:1; 9:6-9; Numbers 24:17; Matthew 2:2; John 1:49; I Timothy 1:17; 6:5).

Jesus Christ combines in Himself all of these Old Testament offices. As Judge, Christ is God's Savior and Deliverer to us. As Prophet, Christ is God's word to us. As Priest, Christ is God's Mediator, Advocate and Intercess. As King, Christ is God's Ruler and authority over us.

9. To Consummate the Redemptive Plan in His Second Coming

The first coming of Christ by the incarnation was but preparatory for the second coming of Christ. The first coming and all that was involved in the redemptive plan made way for the second coming. The first coming was the inauguration of redemption's plan, and the second coming is the consummation of it. In the first coming we were saved from the guilt and penalty of sin and in the second advent we will be totally redeemed from the power and presence of sin. The second coming completes that which was begun in the first coming; each is incomplete without the other (Daniel 9:24-27; Romans 8:18-25; Hebrews 9:27-28; Philippians 3:21; I Corinthians 15:25-28; I Thessalonians 4:15-18).

VI. THE DEITY OF CHRIST

As noted earlier, heresies concerning the deity and humanity of Christ arose in the early centuries of Church history. The pendulum swung back and forth in its extremes. However, there was more denial of His deity than of His humanity. The deity and humanity of Christ need to be kept in delicate balance, as evidenced by the New Testament writers, to avoid heresy.

Following are the Scriptures which confirm the deity of Christ. The strongest proofs that the Lord Jesus Christ is God are the divine attributes, divine names, divine works, divine worship, divine claims and divine relationship ascribed to Him.

A. Divine Attributes Ascribed to Him

1. Essential Attributes

a. Eternity of Being
The sonship of Christ is an eternal sonship in the eternal Godhead. His name is I AM and expresses eternity of being. Jesus knew that He pre-existed with the Father and came down from heaven (John 1:1-3; Proverbs 30:4; Romans 1:20; John 17:3-5; Matthew 3:11; 16:16; Hebrews 7:1-4; Isaiah 7:14; 9:6-9; Proverbs 8:23-31; Revelation 1:8,11; John 6:33, 41, 50, 51, 58, 62; 8:56-58; Exodus 3:14; Micah 5:2)

b. Pre-existence of Being
Jesus Himself witnessed to His own pre-existence. He knew that He dwelt in the bosom of the Father. Eternity of being involves pre-existence of being. Jesus existed before He was born of the virgin Mary (John 1:1-3,27,30; 16:26-28; 17:1-5; Luke 12:49-51; Matthew 10:40; Proverbs 8:13-36; John 6:38-57; 8:28,38,58; Mark 1:38; Micah 5:2).

c. Self-existence
The Son existed with the Father and the Holy Spirit. The Son is the life-source and has power to give eternal life to all who will believe. He lives in the power of an endless life. Such language can only apply to deity, to the self-existent God. (John 1:4; 5:21-26; 14:16; Hebrews 7:16; I John 5:11-12).

d. Deity
The testimony of scriptures witness to the deity of Christ.

(1) He existed in the beginning as the Word, as God (John 1:1 with Genesis 1:1; Philippians 2:6; Revelation 19:13).
(2) He was with God, the Father (John 1:1).
(3) He was God, the Son (John 1:1; Romans 9:5; Hebrews 1:8,10; I John 5:20; Titus 2:13).
(4) He is God manifest in the flesh (John 20:28; I Timothy 3:16; Colossians 2:9; 1:19; Acts 20:28; Hebrews 1:8).
(5) He is the Mighty God (Isaiah 9:6; Psalm 45:6).
(6) He is Immanuel, God with us (Isaiah 7:14; Matthew 1:23).
(7) He is The Word made flesh (John 1:14-18).
(8) He is the True God (I John 5:20 with Titus 2:13; Romans 9:5).
(9) He is the great God (Titus 2:13).
(10) He is our God and Savior (II Peter 1:1).
(11) He existed in the form of God before His incarnation and was equal with God the Father (Philippians 2:5-7).
(12) He is the only wise God (Jude 25).

e. Omnipotence
The Son is all-powerful. He is the Creator and sustainer of the universe of worlds. (Colossians 1:17; Ephesians 3:9; Hebrews 1:10; Revelation 3:14; John 1:3,10; I Corinthians 8:6).

(1) He has power in heaven (Matthew 28:18).
(2) He has all power in earth (John 17:2).
(3) He has power over all nature (Matthew 8:23-27).
(4) He has power over all demonic hosts (Luke 4:35-41).
(5) He has power over all the angelic hosts (I Peter 3:22; Ephesians 1:20-22).
(6) He has power over all things (Hebrews 1:3).

f. Omniscience
The Son is all-knowing as to His deity. Nothing is hidden from His sight (John 16:30; 2:24-25; Colossians 2:3; John 14:16-19; 21:17; Hebrews 4:12-13; Revelation 2:23).

g. Omnipresence
The Son is everywhere present at all times. Because of this attribute, He is able to gather with His people wherever they meet in His name (Matthew 18:20; 28:20; John 3:13; Ephesians 1:23; I Corinthians 1:2; 5:4). For this reason He could say that He was in heaven as well as on earth.

h. Immutable
The Son is unchanged and unchangeable, the same yesterday, today and forever as to His character and attributes (Hebrews 1:12; 13:8; Psalm 102:26-32; Malachi 3:6).

i. Infallible
The Son is infallible. That is, not able to err or to make mistakes. Only deity is infallible. All men are fallible. He never spoke a wrong or erring word, for His words were the Father's words (John 12:44-50; 14:6). He is the truth.

j. Sovereign
Every knee shall bow to the Son of God and confess His Lordship; that is, confess His deity (Philippians 2:9-11; Isaiah 9:6; Revelation 19:16; Matthew 25:31-46) He is King of Kings and Lord of Lords.

2. Moral Attributes

a. Perfect Holiness
The Son of God is holiness personified. The only perfectly holy person who ever walked this earth (Luke 4:34; Acts 4:27-30; I Peter 2:22). (This is dealt with more fully under the sinlessness of Christ.)

b. Perfect Righteousness
The Son of God is the Lord our Righteousness. Jehovah Tsidkenu. This is only applicable to deity (Jeremiah 23:5-6; I Corinthians 1:30; Hebrews 1:9; I Peter 2:22).

c. Perfect Love
The Son of God is perfect love. This is the very nature and character of deity. Men may have love, but God is love (John 15:9-10; I John 3:16; I John 4:7-8; 15-16). This includes the qualities of mercy, grace, compassion and goodness.

d. Perfect Faithfulness
The Son of God was perfectly faithful (Revelation 1:5).

B. Divine Names Applied To Him

1. He is the Everlasting Father, or Father of Eternity (Isaiah 9:6).

2. He is called Lord (Joel 2:32; Acts 2:21; Romans 10:13; Acts 9:17). It was blasphemy to call any man "Lord" to the Jewish mind, as this was the name of deity.

    a. He is the Lord of Hosts (Isaiah 8:13-14; I Peter 5:15; 1:7,8).
    b. He is the Lord our Righteousness (Jeremiah 23:5-6).
    c. He is the Lord (Matthew 22:43-45; Psalm 110:1; Luke 2:11).
    d. He is the Lord Jesus Christ (Acts 2:34-37; 16:31; I Corinthians 12:3; Philippians 2:11; Romans 10:9; Matthew 1:21; Luke 2:11).

3. He is called Jehovah (Genesis 19:24; Hosea 1:7; Zechariah 12:10; Psalm 83:18; Isaiah 12:2).

4. He is Alpha and Omega (Revelation 1:7,8,11; 22:13,16).

5. He is the First and the Last (Isaiah 44:6; 41:4; 48:12; Revelation 1:17-18).

6. He is the eternal Word (John 1:1,14; Revelation 19:13; Hebrews 1:1-2).

7. He is the I AM (Exodus 3:14-15; John 8:56-58; Leviticus 24:12-16). (Note all the I AM's of Jesus in the Gospel of John) It would be blasphemy to use this name of deity unless Jesus were God.

8. He is the root and offspring of David. He is David's Son and David's Lord, by pre-existence, deity and incarnation. He is root and Lord, as to His deity. He is offspring and Son, as to His humanity

(Revelation 22:16; Matthew 9:27; 21:9; Matthew 22:41-46).

9. He is the Angel of Jehovah (refer to Old Testament theophanies or Christophanies). (Genesis 16:7-14; 22:11-18; 31:11-13; Exodus 3:1-5; 14:19; Judges 6:11-23; 13:2-25; I Chronicles 21:1-27; Numbers 22:22-35; I Kings 19:5-7; II Kings 19:35; Zechariah 1:11; 6:12-15). The Hebrews recognized this manifestation as a manifestation of deity.

10. He is the Son of God. This Sonship is an eternal Sonship, and is acknowledged by all realms.

   a. By the Father God (Acts 13:33; Hebrews 1:5; Matthew 17:5).
   b. By demon spirits (Matthew 8:29).
   c. By the angel Gabriel (Luke 1:35).
   d. By the apostles (Matthew 16:16-17; Romans 1:1-3).
   e. By the Lord Himself (Mark 1:61-62; Luke 22:70; John 5:25; 11:4; Psalm 2:7; Proverbs 30:4; Isaiah 7:14; 9:6-9).

11. He is the Holy One of God (Mark 1:24).

12. He is the truth (John 14:6). He spoke the truth, He was and is the truth. He is the truth personified. This is inapplicable to any man.

C. Divine Works Attributed to Him
Divine works were done by the Son of God (John 14:11; 10:37; 5:36).

1. He was the creator of the universe of worlds (Hebrews 1:3; Genesis 1:1-5; John 1:1p-4,10; Hebrews 1:10; Colossians 1:16-17).

2. He was the creator of angels and man (Genesis 1:26; Proverbs 8:30; Colossians 1:16-17).

3. He forgave sins (Acts 5:31; Luke 5:21-14; Matthew 9:6; Mark 2:5-7; Colossians 3:13). It is the prerogative of God only to forgive sins as all sin in primarily against God Himself (Psalm 51:4).

4. He raised the dead and will change the vile bodies of believers at His coming by reason of who He is (John 5:28- 29; 11:25; Philippians 3:21; II Timothy 4:1).

5. He will judge the whole world in righteousness. All judgement has been given to Him by the Father. He could only judge the entire world in perfect justice by reason of divine attributes (John 5:22-29; Acts 17:31; II Corinthians 5:10; II Timothy 4:1; Matthew 25:31-46).

6. He upholds and maintains the universe by His mighty word of power (Hebrews 1:3; Colossians 1:17).

7. He is the giver of eternal life to all who trust the Father through Himself (John 10:28; 17:2).

8. He will bring about the regeneration of the heavens and the earth (Hebrews 1:10-12; Revelation 21:5; Matthew 19:28).

D. Divine Worship Given to Him
Divine worship was given to and received by Jesus. Jesus never refused such worship. This is in great contrast to other men of God who absolutely refused worship of other men, as did the elect angels. Only self-deified men accepted worship of others as seen in Roman Emporers (Acts 10:26; 14:15; Revelation 22:9). To worship Jesus as God would be blasphemy and idolatry if He were not deity. For Jesus to accept worship which alone belongs to God His Father would have been robbery, blasphemy and idolatry.

1. He is worshipped by angels (Hebrews 1:6; Isaiah 6:1-5; Revelation 5:12-14).
2. He is worshipped by men (Matthew 8:2; 15:25-28; 28:17; Luke 24:51-52; Acts 1:24; 7:59-60; I Thessalonians 3:11; John 9:38; Philippians 2:9-11; Psalm 45:11; I Corinthians 1:2).
3. He is worshipped by all creatures (Revelation 5:13).

4. He is prayed to as praying to God (Acts 1:24; 7:59-60).
5. He is honored equally with the Father God (John 5:23; Revelation 1:5-6; Hebrews 1:6-8).

E. Divine Claims Made by Him
Jesus made claims which could only have been made by God. If these claims are not so, then Jesus was either self deceived or a liar and imposter.

1. He claimed to be one with God (John 10:30,38; 5:23; 14:10.
2. He claimed God as His Father (Luke 2:41-52; Matthew 12:48; Mark 3:33-34). He never acknowledged Joseph as His father
3. He claimed to love as God the Father loves (Matthew 10: 37-38; Luke 14:26).
4. He claimed to be the I AM, denoting eternal existence (John 8:56-58; 18:1-5 with Exodus 3:14-15).
5. He claimed divine Sonship, making Himself God (John 5:25; 11:4; Mark 12:6; Proverbs 30:4).

F. Divine Relationship Spoken of Him
The Son is associated with the Father and the Holy Spirit in covenantal relationship both in eternity and time. This could not be so unless the Son was divine, co-equal in the Godhead.

1. Baptism is administered in the name of the triune God, the Son being centrally involved (Matthew 28:18-20; Acts 2:34-36).

2. The apostolic benediction involves the eternal Godhead, the Son being the revelation of the grace of God (II Corinthians 13:14).

(Read also Matthew 28:18-20; John 14:1,6; 10:28-30; 17:21; 5:17-18; Matthew 11:27; Colossians 1:19; 2:9; I Corinthians 8:6; Ephesians 4:8-10; I Timothy 1:15-16; John 14:9; Colossians 1:15; I John 2:23; I Thessalonians 3:11; I Corinthians 12:4-6; Luke 22:29; Psalm 2:7; 45:6-7; 110:1-4; and Isaiah 53:10-11.)

It is impossible to deny or reject the truth of the deity of the Son of God in the light of these Scriptures. For Jesus to accept such claims, worship, names and works as ascribed or attributed to Him, if He were not God, would be utter blasphemy. No saint ever made such claims or accepted homage, which would have been presumptuous sin and worthy of death. But Jesus accepted and demonstrated the claims of deity. Jesus, the Son of God is indeed deity; God manifest in the flesh. The true believer can only exclaim with Thomas "My LORD and my GOD" (John 20:28 with Isaiah 25:9).

VII. THE HUMANITY OF CHRIST
The Scriptures present the incarnate Christ as having two natures. He is God and man yet one person. Great is this mystery of godliness; God was manifest in the flesh (I Timothy 3:16; Colossians 2:2-3). In this section we will consider the evidences of Christ's perfect and sinless humanity, and His supreme example to all believers.

A. The Humanity of Christ

1. He had a human birth

   a. He was born of a woman, as to His humanity (Matthew 1:18-23; 2:11; Luke 1:30-33; Galatians 4:4). The virgin Mary was the chosen one to be the mother of Christ's humanity.
   b. He is spoken of as being the Seed of David according to the flesh (Romans 1:3; Matthew 1:1).
   c. He was the promised Seed of the Woman (Genesis 3:15 with Matthew 1:23; Isaiah 7:14).
   d. He came of the nation of Israel as pertaining to the flesh (Romans 9:5).
   e. He was recognized as the Son of David (Matthew 15:22; Acts 13:22-23; Hebrews 7:14). His genealogy could be traced through His mother Mary back to David the King of Israel.
   f. He was the Word made and manifest in the flesh (John 1:14; Romans 1:3; I Timothy 3:16).

2. He Had Human Ancestry
The genealogy of Christ after the flesh is traced back to David and Adam in Luke's Gospel through His

mother Mary, and back to David and Abraham in Matthew's Gospel through His assumed father, Joseph (Luke 3:23-38 with Matthew 1:1-17). However, although others said Jesus was the son of Joseph, Jesus Himself never acknowledged Joseph as His human father. He did claim that God was His Father, and acknowledged Mary to be His mother (Luke 3:23; 4:22; Matthew 13:55-56; John 1:45; 6:42). As far as the Jews in Christ's time were concerned, He was a real man, of flesh and blood as other men were. He was not a phantom or apparition but truly a man.

3. He Had Human Names and Titles Applied to Him

a. He was named Jesus before His birth by the angel Gabriel, both to Mary and Joseph (Matthew 1:21-23).
b. He was called the Son of David (Matthew 1:1; 9:27; 12:23; 20:30-33).
c. He was called the Son of Abraham (Matthew 1:1).
d. He is called the Son of Man over 80 times in the New Testament (Matthew 16:28; 26:64-65; Acts 7:56; Revelation 1:13; 14:4).
e. He is called the Mediator, the man Christ Jesus (I Timothy 2:5).
f. He is called a Jew as to His nationality (John 4:9; 8:57).
g. He is called the last Adam (I Corinthians 15:45-47).
h. He is called a man (John 8:40; 1:30; Acts 2:22; Philippians 2:8; I Corinthians 15:21,47).
i. He is still a man in heaven, though now glorified (John 20:15; I Timothy 2:5; Acts 17:31).
j. He will come as the Son of Man the second time to judge the world (Matthew 16:27-28; 25:31 26:64-65).

4. He Had Complete Human Nature
The Son of God had all the essentials of human nature even as God created man in the beginning. Jesus was a complete man having spirit, soul and body. (I Thessalonians 5:23; Hebrews 4:12) This truth refutes the heresy of Apollinarianism which denied the completeness of Christ's humanness (I John 4:3).

a. Jesus had a human spirit (Luke 23:46; Mark 2:8; 8:12; John 13:21).
b. Jesus had a soul (Matthew 26:38; Luke 23:43; John 12:27; Acts 2:27-31; Isaiah 53:10; Mark 14:34). This involved mind, will and emotions (I John 1:1-2).
c. Jesus had a human body, of flesh, bones and blood (Hebrews 2:14; John 1:14; Matthew 26:12; Luke 22:19; John 2:21; Luke 23:52-56; Hebrews 10:5,10). After His resurrection He had a body of flesh and bones (Luke 24:39). In His human body He was limited locally and geographically, and limited by sinless infirmities.

5. He Experienced Human Development
As to His humanity, Jesus grew and developed normally and naturally like any other human being. This is seen in the following references and comments.

a. He grew as a child (Luke 2:40).
b. He increased in wisdom and stature (Luke 2:52).
c. He learned obedience by the things He suffered (Hebrews 5:8).
d. He worked hard as a man following Joseph's trade as a carpenter (Mark 6:3; Luke 3:23).
e. He suffered human limitations (Hebrews 2:10).
f. He experienced human temptations (Matthew 4:1-11; Hebrews 2:18; Mark 1:35; Luke 22:28; Hebrews 4:15).
g. He learned to live in dependence upon the Father by continual prayer (Matthew 14:23; Hebrews 5:7; Luke 6:12; 22:39-46). There are about 25 references to Jesus praying in the New Testament.
h. He learned to depend upon the Father and the power of the Holy Spirit continually. He could do and say nothing of Himself but only what He was given (Mark 1:35; John 6:15; Acts 1:2; Hebrews 9:14; Acts 10:38; Hebrews 5:7).

i. He was a man approved of God (Acts 2:22).

j. He was limited in His human knowledge (Matthew 24:36 with Mark 13:32; Luke 7:9).

k. He desired human sympathy in the Garden (Matthew 26:36-40).

6. He Had Sinless Infirmities of Human Nature

As a man Christ suffered the limitations and infirmities of human nature, which are not sinful in themselves, but are part of man's lot since the fall. The glorified human body will not have these sinless infirmities (Philippians 3:20-21).

a. Jesus grew weary (John 4:6).

b. Jesus had normal appetites and was hungry (Matthew 4:2; 21:18).

c. Jesus was also thirsty (John 4:7; 19:28).

d. He also enjoyed natural sleep (Matthew 8:24).

e. He was limited in human knowledge (Mark 11:13; 13:32; 5:30-34; John 11:34).

f. He groaned in Himself (John 11:33).

g. He also wept over people (John 11:35; Matthew 23:37; 26:38).

h. He needed to be strengthened for the suffering of the cross by an angel (Luke 22:43).

7. He Suffered Human Death

Death has belonged to man since the fall in Eden. When Jesus took our sin upon Himself, in His own body on the tree, He suffered the wages of sin, which is death (I Peter 2:24; Genesis 2:17; Hebrews 9:27; Luke 23:33; Hebrews 2:9). His death was the supreme purpose of the incarnation, to be followed by His resurrection.

8. He Experienced Human Resurrection

He was raised from the dead and still possesses that virgin-born, crucified, buried, resurrected and now glorified body. The body of Jesus was sinless, immortal and incorruptible. He laid down His life, as the Father commanded Him (Luke 23:39; John 20:27; Acts 7:55-56). His resurrection as a human being is the sample of all other resurrections. He, in His ascension, has taken manhood into the Godhead. He is still the man Christ Jesus in his glorified position at the throne on high (I Timothy 2:5; Hebrews 8:1-5).

The humanity of Christ is an irrefutable fact. Jesus, the eternal Son of God became the Son of Man. He was deity and humanity united in one person. His human birth, genealogy, names, titles, limitations, suffering, death and resurrection all attest to the reality of His full and complete humanity. This same humanity is now glorified and when He comes again the second time it will be "this same Jesus" who will so come in like manner as He went to heaven (Acts 1:11).

B. The Sinlessness of Christ

That Christ had a perfectly sinless and incorruptible humanity is the testimony of the Old and New Testament Scriptures. It was necessary that Christ be sinless in order to be the Savior of the world. If He had not been sinless He would have had to die for His own sin and would have needed redemption Himself. Christ could not be the perfect, full and final revelation of God to man if He was sinful. Without the sinlessness of Christ the redemptive plan falls to the ground, for the Redeemer of sinners cannot Himself be a sinner.

Sinlessness is complete conformity to the will of God in thought, word and deed. Sinfulness is lack of conformity to the will of God in thought, word and deed. Thus Christ, as a perfect man, perfectly fulfilled the Father's will. He never committed a sin in thought, word or deed. His perfection was a sinless perfection.

1. Theories Concerning the Sinlessness of Christ

a. Sinful Flesh Theory

This theory holds that Christ had "sinful flesh" and that He had to overcome sin by the power of the Holy Spirit, as all believers do. This is based upon a misunderstanding of Romans 8:3 where

Paul states that Christ was "made in the likeness of sinful flesh".

b. Sinful Potential Theory

This theory holds that Christ, though God incarnate, could have sinned but would not sin. He was able to overcome sin. It states that the fact that Christ was tempted proves He could have sinned. The argument is presented that a temptation in order to be valid presupposes that the person tempted can possibly sin. It also teaches that Christ could not be a merciful and sympathetic High Priest to us in our temptations unless He could have sinned.

c. The Sinless Perfection Theory

This school of thought holds that Christ was incapable of sinning because of who He is. This is the view held by the present text. Before considering the reasons for this view, we must note the common ground of faith held by most all evangelical believers, in the following statements:

The Son of God possessed a perfect human nature and a divine nature.

The Son of God suffered temptations in all points as we do and these were valid temptations.

The Son of God did not sin in thought, word or deed.

The Son of God is able to sympathize and succour those who suffer like temptations.

(I John 3:5; I Peter 2:22; II Corinthians 5:21; Hebrews 4:15; 7:26; 2:18).

The disagreement between these theories is over the following statements:

Christ could have sinned but would not and did not sin.

Christ did not sin because He could not sin.

The questions therefore arise, "Was it possible for Christ not to sin or was it possible for Christ to sin?" These questions have stirred the minds of Christians for centuries. However, it should be kept in mind that whether Christ could or could not have sinned, the fact remains that He did not sin. Thus He alone can be the Savior of sinners.

2. The Sinless Perfection of Christ

a. Major Questions and Objections Considered

(1) If it was impossible for Christ to sin, then what was the purpose in His being tempted? Wouldn't this make His temptation unreal and therefore invalid? Why tempt a sinless being? Angels sinned when tempted. Adam sinned when tempted. Why could not have Christ sinned when tempted? Doesn't there have to be some inward desire for the temptation to appeal to?

(2) If it was impossible for Christ to sin, then it means that He did not have the power of choice, the will to choose between good and evil. Could He not have done His own will and not His Father's will, as the temptation in Gethsemane seems to indicate? (Matthew 26:39)

(3) If it was impossible for Christ to sin, then He did not truly identify with the human race, and cannot fully understand our human and sinful nature. Doesn't this automatically place a gap between the Savior and sinner that can never be bridged?

(4) If it was impossible for Christ to sin, then how would temptation be a cause of suffering to Him and how could He sympathize with us in our temptations?

(5) If it was impossible for Christ to sin, then don't His temptations differ from those that we, as sinful men, go through?

We will proceed to answer these questions and objections by dealing with several main arguments concerning the temptations of Adam, Jesus and all men, the nature and meaning of temptation, and finally the testimony of the sinlessness of Christ.

b. The Temptations of Adam, Jesus and all Men

There were only two men in Scripture whose temptations were unique, Adam and Jesus. Both were Sons of God in a unique sense, Adam being the created son of God, and Jesus the begotten Son of God (Luke 3:38; John 3:16). Both had a sinless human nature, not having any sin principle within their being. They were tempted from without by the Devil. Adam responded to the temptation, while Jesus did not. Adam and Jesus are the federal heads or representative men of the old creation race and the new creation race. God sees all men either "in Adam" or "in Christ" (I Corinthians 15:46-47). All these facts place the temptations of Adam and Jesus in direct distinction from the temptations of all men born of Adam since the fall. All other men, born of Adam's race, are tempted as sinners born in sin. None of them know what it is to experience temptation in a state of sinlessness. The temptation of Adam and Jesus was unique in that neither were tempted from within, but rather from without. All other sinful men are tempted both from without and within. All men are tempted when drawn away of their own lust and enticed. Then when lust has conceived it brings forth sin and sin, when it is finished, brings forth death (James 1:13-14).

Sin was an intrusion into Adam's humanity. Only Adam and Jesus had a sinless human nature, thus their temptations were distinctive. However, there was also a great difference between Adam and Jesus. Adam was only a man but Jesus is both God and man. Though both Adam and Jesus were sinless, Adam was a created being and Jesus was not. Adam had only one nature, human, while Jesus had two natures, human and divine.

The statement in Romans 8:3 that Christ was "made in the likeness of sinful flesh" must not be misunderstood. This verse does not say Christ had "sinful flesh" but He was "made in the likeness of sinful flesh". Here the "likeness" is the sinless infirmities of human nature. Christ indeed had real flesh, but it was sinless. There was no original sin or sin-principle in Him as the eternal and begotten Son of God. Sin is not essential to human nature, but an intrusion. Christ had sinless human nature as did Adam before the fall. However, He also had "the likeness" of Adam's flesh after the fall, that is, human nature with sinless infirmities. Though certain Gnostics taught that flesh was inherently sinful, this is contrary to the Word of God. Christ had flesh that was free from the law of sin, but that was "made in the likeness" (and likeness only) of sinful flesh. A comparison and contrast of the temptations of Adam and Jesus, unbelievers and believers, will help to bring these facts into sharper focus.

ADAM	JESUS
The First Adam	The Last Adam
The First Man, Earthy	The Second Man, Lord from Heaven
No evil tendency originally	No evil tendency within Him
Liability to sin	Two natures, divine and human
One nature, human nature	No liability to sin
Tempted from without in spirit soul and body	Tempted from without in spirit soul and body
Response to sin	No response to sin
Now fallen human nature	Unfallen sinless human nature
A creation of God	The incarnation of God
A created Son of God	The begotten Son of God
A human being	A divine-human being

UNBELIEVERS	BELIEVERS
"In Adam" - sons of men	"In Christ" - sons of God
The natural birth	The spiritual birth
Fallen human nature	Fallen human nature - partakers of divine nature
Sinful tendencies	Sinful tendencies - to overcome

Sin principle prevailing within	Sin principle to be eradicated in due time
Tempted from within and without in body, soul, spirit	Tempted from without and within in body, soul and spirit, yet strengthened to overcome by the Holy Spirit
Born in sin	Born in sin, yet born again
No good thing in the flesh	Christ in you, the hope of glory
Old creation, of parents	New creation in old creation
Sinful human beings	Redeemed human beings
Sin will destroy unto death	Sin to be overcome unto life

c. The Meaning and Nature of Temptation

The New Testament uses two particular Greek words which have the meaning of "testing" in them, for temptation has to do with testing, either by God, Satan or others.

(1) The Greek word "Dokimazo" means "to prove a thing whether it is worthy to be received or not, to test (lit. or fig.); by implication, to approve, allow, discern, examine, prove, try". (Luke 14:19; Romans 2:18; 12:2; 14:22; I Corinthians 3:13; 11:28; Galatians 6:4; Hebrews 3:9; James 1:12; I Peter 1:7; I John 4:1) It is used in the following ways in the New Testament. People proved oxen; believers are to prove what is the good will of God; believers have their faith tried and approved. God proves His saints. All believers are tested and tried by the circumstances of life, by the weaknesses and infirmities of human nature. The purpose of this type of temptation is to prove and approve. It is a temptation that expects a positive result. In this manner, God "tried" Abraham (Hebrews 11:17 with Genesis 22:1). This word is used about 25 times in the New Testament and is never used of Satan trying to prove anyone.

(2) The Greek word "Peirazo" translated "tempt" means "a putting to proof (by experiment (of good), experience (of evil); solicitation, discipline or provocation; by implication, adversity". This word is used about 40 times in the New Testament, and conveys the idea of testing and making trial of someone. It is used in the following ways:

(a) Man Tested God
That is, man put God to the test to discover whether He would do good or evil to them. Thus Israel "tempted God" in the wilderness (Hebrews 3:9). The legalistic teachers "tempted God" by desiring to put a yoke on the neck of the Gentiles (Acts 15:10). Ananias and Sapphira "tempted the Holy Spirit" in their act of deceit (Acts 5:9). Man is exhorted not to "tempt (put to test) the Lord God" (Matthew 4:7).

(b) Man Tested by God
God at times tests or tempts man; that is, never to evil, but with a view of proving what is in man and to expose to man his inward need (James 1:2,12). But God cannot be tempted with evil, neither does He tempt any man to sin (James 1:13-14). As noted, Abraham was tested by God in the matter of offering up his only son, Isaac (Hebrews 11:17 with Genesis 22:1). The Old Testament saints were tried and tempted by persecutions, opposition and thus proved themselves faithful to God in all things (Hebrews 11:37; read also Galatians 4:13-14; I Corinthians 10:13; John 6:6; Matthew 6:13).

(c) Man Tested by Satan
Satan also tempts and tests man. This temptation however is always an enticement to sin, a solicitation to do evil. These temptations do not come from God (James 1:13-14). They come from Satan or from man's sinful nature. Thus Satan tempted the angels, tempted Adam and tempted Jesus. He also tempts all sinful men born of Adam's race (Genesis 3:1-6; Matthew 4:1).

d. The Nature of Christ's Temptations
The nature of Christ's temptation is better understood in the light of the preceding definitions. The Gospel writers and the writer to the Hebrews dealt specifically with the temptations of

Jesus, the God-Man (Matthew 4:1-11; Mark 1:13; Hebrews 2:18; 4:15).

(1) Jesus was tested by His Father God
These testings first involved the sufferings that Jesus endured in His sinless humanity by having sinless infirmities. He was tested by opposition, persecution, weariness, the contradiction of sinners, contrary circumstances, the Jews, His own relatives, the religious leaders and His own disciples. In all these things He was tested and tried but was approved in all things by the Father. These things were part of the "temptations of Christ" (Luke 22:28).

(2) Jesus was tempted by Satan
Jesus was tempted to do evil by Satan, that is, to do His own will instead of the Father's will. Satan sought to give the Father grounds to disapprove Jesus. This occurred throughout His whole life. The account of the forty days temptation was but a sample account of special seasons of trial that Jesus endured. The Scripture says that the devil left Jesus but for a season after His notable victory in these three major temptations (Mark 1:13).

(3) Jesus was not tempted by sinful nature
Jesus was not tempted by a sinful or carnal nature within. This is the eternal difference between the temptations of Jesus and all those born of Adam's race, whether believers or unbelievers. Jesus had no sinful or carnal nature within and thus He did not suffer inward temptations to sin, as all fallen men do. Nothing can alter or change this factual distinction. When it states that Jesus was "tempted in all points, like as we are, yet without sin" (Hebrews 4:15), it literally means "apart from sin". That is to say, He was tempted to sin, from without, but not tempted with sin, from within, because there was no evil in Him. He had no sinful human nature, no lust to sin within Him. There was no inner conflict as described in Romans 7:14-18 within His being (James 1:14). Hence He was tempted in all points, as we are, yet without lust within (Hebrews 2:18; 4:15; John 8:46; 14:30).

(4) Jesus was tempted in His Humanity, not His Deity
Jesus is God incarnate and God cannot be tempted with evil (James 1:13-14). Satan attacked the humanity of Jesus. Jesus suffered temptation in His humanity, not His deity. Jesus was thus "tempted in all points like as we", apart from sin. The points that Jesus was tempted in were:

   (a) Spirit - tempted to worship Satan

   (b) Soul - tempted to presume upon God's preserving power.

   (c) Body - tempted to satisfy a normal human bodily appetite by use of miracle power (Matthew 4:1-11 with I John 2:16-17).

Each of these temptations came from without, not from within. It was as man that He conquered by the power of the Word, declaring "It is written". As man, Jesus did not call upon His divine prerogatives to defeat Satan. He was tempted to by-pass the cross as Peter spake the thought Satan gave to him (Matthew 16:21-24). He was tempted in Gethsemane to bypass the agony of Calvary's cup but He submitted His will to the Father's will and was strengthened by an angel. His holy humanity naturally shrank from such an ordeal as being made sin. However, this was not a sinful feeling at all. He was also tempted on the cross when the religious Jews challenged Him to come down from the cross and to save Himself (Luke 23:35-37).

These were real temptations to His humanity and certainly His human nature suffered, dreading the agonies of the cross, both physically and spiritually. Being made sin and forsaken of the Father was the greatest agony and caused unspeakable suffering to His holy and sinless humanity. He did not have to be able to sin to validate the sufferings of these temptations. The sufferings of these temptations would be far more intense to His sinless humanity than sinful humanity could ever understand. Suffering the presence of sin is far more intense to the One who could not and did not sin than to sinful mortals. It should also be remembered that temptation is not sin, yielding is.

The teaching that God the Father and the angels in heaven were held in suspense during Christ's life on earth, fearful that the Son of God might fail and sin, belittles God's redemptive counsel and purposes. It minimizes the character of God in His essential and moral attributes. The plan of salvation was begotten in the counsels of the eternal Godhead and there was no possible chance of failure on the part of the eternal Son of God (I Peter 1:19-20; Psalm 40:5-8; Hebrews 12:1-4; 13-20).

e. The Reasons Jesus Suffered Temptation

We will now answer the objections concerning the purpose of Jesus suffering temptation if He could not possibly sin. Jesus did suffer temptation and therefore He is able to strengthen and succour all believers who are tempted.

(1) He suffered temptation for the development of a full and complete humanity.

As Jesus' humanity grew in wisdom and stature and in favor with God and man (Luke 2:52). He learned obedience by the things He suffered (Hebrews 5:8). He developed spiritually, mentally and physically. He suffered sinless infirmities, He suffered temptation in His human nature and proved Himself perfect. That which He suffered in His human nature added, in experience, a completeness to the divine nature, as the Creator was one with the creature, the divine one with the human.

(2) He suffered temptation to be approved of God His Father

Jesus of Nazareth was a Man approved of God. Thus the Father spoke from heaven and placed His approval on His beloved Son. The Son did not use His divine prerogatives apart from the Father's will, but was subject and obedient to His Father, by the Spirit, for all that He was, said and did.

(3) He suffered temptation to display to Satan's hosts a perfect humanity

Satan conquered Adam, the first man, through temptation, and has similarly conquered all men since. Jesus was the beginning of the "new creation" of God (Revelation 3:14). Satan used the mightiest of his temptations to entice Christ to sin. Satan and all his demonic forces were baffled by this creation, the God-Man. It was a creation in which there was no response to sin. It was a revelation of the coming defeat of sin, its author and his entire kingdom on the cross (Colossians 2:14-17). God was well pleased with His perfect Man, for He is the sample of many sons to follow (Romans 8:20-28).

(4) He suffered temptation in order to be a merciful High Priest

As a priest is taken from among men and ordained for men, he must be one who is touched with the feelings of the infirmities of the people He ministers for. Jesus Christ was taken from among men for the same purpose (Hebrews 4:14-16).

The expression "touched with the feelings of our infirmities" means that Christ can sympathize with us in our temptations and trials. Christ, as the God-Man, identified with man in His human nature, with its sinless infirmities. Whether Christ could sin or not, the fact is that He did not sin. If He had become identified with us in sin, He would have never been able to be our Savior. This is an eternal distinction between Christ and us. This was a limited identification of the God-Man with us, even as Creator/Creature and Savior/Sinner relationships have their distinctions and limits. He is eternally the God-Man and we are eternally redeemed men. The only way He became identified with us in our sin was when He took our sin upon Himself on the cross. In that Jesus did suffer temptation, trials and testings, He is able to be a merciful High Priest and sympathize with us. It should be remembered that He sympathizes with us in our temptations, not in our sinning.

The questions may be asked:
"Must a doctor himself have the same terrible disease before he can sympathize and help a sick person?"

"Does a person have to be an alcoholic or a harlot before they can help and sympathize with those in that bondage?"

"Does a judge have to be guilty of the same crime before he can truly judge it in others?"

Or, "Does Jesus have to sin or be able to sin before He can help and sympathize with the sinful?"

To say that it would make these persons more sympathetic if such was their case, is to say that Jesus would have been more sympathetic to us if He would have sinned. Jesus did suffer temptations and trials, and because He did He is able to strengthen and succour as well as sympathize with us in our trials and temptations.

(5) He suffered temptation in order to supply help to tempted believers.
Because He suffered temptation, He knows what we go through and can supply strength, grace and mercy to help us in our time of need. He has promised that He will not suffer us to be tempted above that which we are able to bear but with the temptation will make a way of escape that we may be able to bear it (Hebrews 2:18; 4:14-16; I Corinthians 10:13).

(6) He is now beyond all temptations as all believers will be.
Since His resurrection and the glorification of His sinless and incorruptible humanity, Christ is beyond all possible temptation. His glorified body is no longer subjected to sinless infirmities or the weaknesses of human nature. He never slumbers nor sleeps. He is never weary. He does not need to eat or drink. He lives in the power of an endless life. His body is the sample of what is to happen to the believer's body at the coming of Christ (Philippians 3:20,21; I Thessalonians 4:15-18; I Corinthians 15:51-57).

f. The Deity and Humanity of Christ
Another major factor that should be considered is the fact of the union of Christ's deity and humanity. As noted previously, the distinction between Adam and Jesus and all other men cannot be overlooked. Adam, as the created Son of God was a man, and was tempted as such, from without. Jesus, as the begotten Son of God, was the God-Man, and was also tempted from without. But Jesus was God incarnate, and in becoming man He never ceased to be God. The delicate balance between His deity and His humanity must be maintained.

As to His deity, "God cannot be tempted with evil, neither tempteth He any man" (James 1:13-14). As God incarnate, He was sinless and could not sin. As to His humanity, Jesus was tempted in all points like as we are (Hebrews 2:18; 4:15). As man, He is temptable and open to all kinds of external temptations. But because of who Jesus was, God made flesh, it was the divine nature in union with the human nature which carried the human nature through the temptations victoriously.

To hold the theory that Jesus could sin in His human nature, but could not sin as to His divine nature, is to destroy the unity of the person of Christ and collapse the redemptive plan of God. These two natures, though distinguishable, are indivisibly united in the one person of Christ. To have a sinful or potentially sinful humanity and a sinless divinity in the one person of Christ, God manifest in the flesh, is an impossibility. To say that Jesus could have sinned is to say that God could sin because He took on humanity. Such would limit the power of God Almighty.

3. The Testimony of Christ's Sinlessness
The Scriptures attest to the fact of Christ's sinlessness. Orthodox believers are all agreed that whether or not Christ could have sinned, He did not. There was ample opportunity for anyone in His time to convict Him of sin but none were able to do so. The following evidences give testimony to the truth of the sinlessness of Jesus Christ.

a. Testimony of Gabriel
Gabriel spoke of Jesus as being "that holy thing" (Luke 1:35). This was never spoken of any child ever born of Adam's race.

b. Testimony of Devils
Demon spirits recognized Jesus as "the Holy One" (Mark 1:24; Luke 4:34; Matthew 8:28-29). They never said this of any man, not even of the godliest of saints.

c. Testimony of Men

(1) He was called the Holy Child (Acts 4:27,30).
(2) Pilate found no fault in Him (John 18:38; 19:4).

(3) Pilate's wife testified that He was a "just man" (Matthew 27:19).
(4) The dying thief recognized Jesus as not worthy to die (Luke 23:41).
(5) The centurian recognized Jesus as "the Son of God" (Luke 23:47).
(6) Herod also said that He was not worthy of death (Luke 23:15).
(7) Judas realized that he had betrayed "the innocent blood" (Matthew 27:4).

d. Testimony of God
The Father also testified from heaven of His pleasure in His only begotten Son. No other man ever had such divine and heavenly approval (Matthew 3:15-17; 17:1-5).

e. Testimony of Christ

(1) Jesus challenged anyone to convince Him of sin (John 8:46)

(2) Jesus also said that the prince of this world was coming and that he had no claim on Him; nothing in common with him; that there was nothing in Him that belonged to Satan (John 14:30 Amplified New Testament). (Read also John 8:29; 15:10; 17:4) Either this testimony was true or Jesus was lying and self-deceived. No man has ever been able to make such claims.

f. Testimony of the Apostles

(1) Paul said "He knew no sin" (II Corinthians 5:21).
(2) Peter said "He did not sin" (I Peter 2:21-22).
(3) John said "In Him is no sin" (I John 3:5).
(4) Hebrews says that He was tempted in all points like as we are "yet without sin" or "apart from sin" (Hebrews 4:15).
(5) He is pure (I John 3:3).
(6) He that is born of God cannot sin for the Seed of God remains in Him (I John 3:9). If this is so of the believer, much more is it true of the sinless One, the Son of God.
(7) Jesus was "holy, harmless, undefiled and separate from sinners" (Hebrews 7:26-27).
(8) He was an offering "without spot" when presented in sacrifice (Hebrews 9:14; I Peter 1:19-20).

g. Testimony of the Law
The Old Testament sacrifices for sin shadowed forth Christ's sacrifice for sin. The sinlessness of Christ was emphatically set forth in the following thoughts.

(1) God took an innocent and sinless animal to die for guilty and sinful man. No animal has ever sinned, nor can sin.

(2) All sacrifices had to be "perfect to be accepted" (Leviticus 22:21). The word "perfect" means "without blemish, complete, full, perfect, sincere".

(3) The sacrifices had to be "without spot" to be offered to God (Numbers 19:2; 28:3,9,11 with Hebrews 9:14; I Peter 1:19-20).

(4) The sacrifices were to be "without blemish" (Exodus 12:5; 29:1; Leviticus 4:3,23,28,32).

(5) Even in the Sin Offering, God emphasized the fact that the sin offering was "most holy" (Leviticus 4; 7:1; with Luke 1:35).

However, animal nature could not atone for human nature. Animals could only be used as substitutionary sacrifices until the perfectly sinless human nature of Jesus could be offered in the atoning work of the cross. The sacrificial system of the law typified that Christ, though our sin offering, would be sinless.

h. Testimony of the Psalms
The Messianic Psalms speak of Christ as the righteous and holy one. These Psalms were prophetic of the coming Christ who would be the sinless Savior of Israel and the world. They also foretold how He would be offered as an offering for our salvation (Psalm 40:6-10; 16:8-11; 22:1-31).

i. Testimony of the Prophets
The prophets foretold the coming of the Redeemer, the one who would be "the Righteous Branch" the Davidic King who would make His sinless soul an "offering for sin", thereby making redemption available for all mankind. He would be "The Lord our Righteousness". This foretold the sinlessness of Christ. These prophecies reveal the foreknowledge of the Almighty God concerning Christ's incarnation and sinlessness (Jeremiah 23:5-6; Isaiah 53:10 Zechariah 3:8-9; 6:12-13).

j. Arguments from Christology

(1) Christ is God incarnate, God manifest in the flesh, God taking upon Himself manhood.

(2) In becoming man He did not lay aside His essential or moral attributes, but subjected Himself to the Father's will for all He was, all He said and all He did.

(3) The union of the divine and human natures in the one person of Christ made possible the sinlessness of Christ, even though tempted in all points like as we are.

The testimony of Scripture is complete. Though born of the virgin Mary, herself a sinner and in need of redemption, Jesus did not inherit sinful humanity. God brought forth "a clean thing" out of the woman (Job 14:4; 15:14; 25:4). The sinless humanity of Jesus was the product of a miracle.

Robert Clarke, in the contents of "The Christ of God" outlines his comments on the fact and implications of the sinlessness of Christ, a fitting summary of the truth of Christ's sinlessness.

The Fact of His Sinlessness

1. Christ claimed to be absolutely sinless.
2. He prayed, but He never prayed for forgiveness.
3. He interceded on behalf of His disciples but He never exhorted them to intercede for Him.
4. He prayed for His disciples, but He never prayed with them.
5. Although He called God His Father, He never called them His savior.
6. He was in the Temple, but He never offered sacrifice for Himself.
7. He was conscious of world sin, but He was never conscious of personal sin.
8. He allowed those nearest to Him to believe that He was sinless.
9. He was weary, but He was never ill.
10. He sorrowed for the sin of the world, but He never sorrowed for His own sin.
11. He taught that all need to be born again, but He never hinted that He was born again, or that He needed such a change.
12. He was explicitly declared by the apostolic writers to be sinless.
13. The sinlessness of our Lord is acknowledged by theologians of various shades and opinions.
14. His absolute sinlessness has been the faith of the Christian church for nineteen hundred years.

The Implications of His Sinlessness

1. Since He was absolutely sinless it follows that He felt suffering far more keenly than the sinful sons of men ever could.

2. Since He was absoutely sinless it follows that He felt temptation more keenly than sinful men.
3. Since He was absolutely sinless it follows that He was not liable to death.
4. Since He was absolutely sinless, it follows that the Holy Spirit could work through Him without hindrance.
5. Since He was absolutely sinless it follows that He had the highest possible fellowship with God.
6. Since He was absolutely sinless it follows that He had the fullest insight into divine things.
7. His absolute sinlessness was made possible through the miracle of the virgin birth.

Because of Christ's sinlessness, His human nature was therefore immortal. All men must die as a result of sin. The wages of sin is death (Romans 6:23). Christ, having no sin of His own, and conquering every temptation to sin, did not have to die. Sickness, disease or age could not have conquered Him. This makes His death unique, as was His birth and life. Jesus was sinless and therefore immortal. He voluntarily laid down His life for us. He died for our sins (John 10:18; 19:30; Romans 5:12-21). No sinful or mortal man could do this. Jesus was immortal because He was sinless; sinless because He was virgin born; and virgin born because He was God incarnate. Being the sinless God-Man He was the perfect revelation of God to man, and the perfect Mediator between God and man.

C. The Example of Christ

As a perfect man, being all that God intended man to be, Christ was totally dependent upon the Father for all He was, said and did. Christ was the perfect example for all believers to follow. Peter declared that Christ left "us an example, that ye should follow in His steps" (I Peter 2:21).

The Greek word "Hupogrammos" translated "example" means "an underwriting, i.e. copy for imitation". It comes from the custom of tracing letters for scholars to copy. So the believer is to follow Christ, He only is the copy for imitation. All other saints of Old and New Testament have various character qualities, which we may imitate, but the best of them had their imperfections. Christ alone is the perfect copy and He is the only one whom God has set forth for us to fully follow. We can follow others as they follow Christ, but when they fail to follow Christ we must cease to follow them (I Corinthians 11:1; Philippians 3:17; I John 2:6; Matthew 11:28-30). It is impossible for unregenerate men to imitate Christ. The believer receives the Holy Spirit in new birth and becomes a partaker of the divine nature thus enabling him to follow in the steps of Christ's example. What then is the example set forth in Christ's perfect manhood in which steps we are to follow?

1. He is our Example in Character — All He Was

The moral character and qualities of God were manifested in Christ as the perfect man. These moral attributes are to be manifested in the believer also, as he is conformed to the image of Christ. We list several of the main character qualities which are to be in the believer.

a. Holiness

Jesus was holy in nature and conduct. We are called to be holy even as He is holy. He is the example of sinless perfection and it is to this goal that God intends to ultimately bring His people (Matthew 5:48; Hebrews 6:1; I Peter 1:16; Luke 1:35; Acts 2:37; 3:14; 4:27; Hebrews 7:26; I Peter 2:21-23; John 8:29,46; 14:30; Hebrews 4:15).

b. Love

Christ is our example in love, which is the very nature of God and is to be revealed in the saints (Ephesians 3:19).

(1) He loved the Father God (John 14:31; 6:38).
(2) He loved the Scriptures (Matthew 5:17-18; Luke 4:16-21; 24:44-45; John 10:34-36).
(3) He loved His own disciples (John 13:1; 15:9; Romans 8:37-39).
(4) He loves the Church as His own bride (Ephesians 5:25-27).
(5) He loves all men regardless of race (Mark 10:21; Matthew 11:19; John 10:11; 15:13; Romans 5:8).
(6) He loved even His enemies (Matthew 5:43-48; Luke 22:51; 23:34; Matthew 26:50).
(7) He prayed that this love would be in us (John 17:26; 13:34-35).
(8) He was continually moved with compassion towards others (John 11:35; 6:5; Mark 6:34; Matthew 8:16 20:34; Luke 4:41; 5:12-15).

c. Faith

He is our example in faith in that He trusted His Father continually and never doubted. He is the author and finisher of our faith (Matthew 27:43; Psalm 22:8; Hebrews 12:1-4).

d. Meekness

He is our example in meekness and humility. No pride, harshness or arrogance ever manifested themselves in Him. From the cradle to the cross, gentleness characterized His dealings with the needy. Humility of mind was revealed and this mind is to be in us (Philippians 2:5-8; Matthew 11:28-30; II Corinthians 10:1).

2. He is our Example in Word — All He Said

Christ is the perfect example in all that He said. His words were always true and gracious. As the perfect man, His tongue was under full control. The words He spoke were His Father's words (James 3:2; John 8:55).

a. He is our example in word (John 12:47-50).

b. He is our example in prayer life (Hebrews 5:7; Luke 6:12; Matthew 14:23; Mark 1:35-38; Matthew 26:38-46; John 6:15; Luke 22:32,44; John 11:41- 42). If the Son of Man depended upon prayer to maintain communion with the Father God, how much more should the believer.

c. He is our example in teaching and preaching (Matthew 23:8; John 3:2; 7:16; 12:49; 3:34; Matthew 7:29; 11:28-29).

3. He is our Example in Deed — All He Did

Christ is our example in all that He did. He worked in secular life as a carpenter and in His Messianic work, doing His Father's will. He went about doing good. Jesus was a man of deeds as well as words. He fully obeyed the Father's will (Acts 1:1; John 6:38; Matthew 26:39; Psalm 40:8; John 4:31-34; 5:30).

Robert Clarke in "The Christ of God" (pp. 78-95) says that Christ is our example in faith, devotion, prayer life, self-abnegation, service, love, anger, patience, gentleness, meekness, courage, compassion, obedience, optimism and worship.

VIII. THE MEDIATORSHIP OF CHRIST

The summation of the doctrine concerning the person of Christ is that which pertains to the mediatorship of Christ as the God-Man. The Old Testament shadowed forth this truth and the New Testament shows its fulfilment in the Lord Jesus.

A. Old Testament Revelation

1. The Patriarch Job

The patriarch Job in his distress under Satanic attack expressed the heart cry of all men for a mediator between God and man. He cried "O that one might plead (i.e. reason, argue, decide as Daysman) for a man with God, as a man pleadeth for his neighbor" (Job 16:21. He reasoned, "For He is not a man, as I am, that I might answer Him, and we should come together in judgement. Neither is there any Daysman betwixt us, that might lay His hand on us both" (Job 9:32-33). (Read also Job 23:3-10; 19:25-27) A daysman is a judge, an umpire, an arbiter. He is a mediator. He is one who reasons, reproves, decides and acts as an umpire between two parties. Job's cry was really for the Messiah to come as the mediator between God and man.

2. The Mediator in Israel
The mediatorial work in Israel was typified first in Moses. He acted as the mediator of the law covenant when God spoke to him directly and then he in turn spoke to Israel. Moses in the mount stood between God and Israel as the mediator in the reception of the law covenant (Deuteronomy 5:1-29 with Galatians 3:19).

When the Tabernacle of Moses was established, God instructed Moses to take his brother Aaron and consecrate him to the office of High Priest in Israel. Aaron then became the mediator in Israel. All Israel had to approach God through this anointed and appointed High Priest. To bypass Aaron, the God-ordained mediator, was to bring divine judgement on oneself (Hebrews 5:1-5; Numbers 16-17).

Aaron represented in the twelve stones on the breastplate, the twelve tribes of Israel before God. The priestly ministrations of Aaron shadowed forth the mediatorial ministry of Christ. The Book of Hebrews sets forth Christ as being the one greater than Moses and Aaron in His mediatorial work (Hebrews 3:1-5; 5:1-10; 7:1-26).

B. The New Testament Revelation

1. The New Covenant Mediator
The New Testament brings to full revelation in the person of Christ that which was typified in the Old Covenant mediatorial ministry. The word "mediator" is used several times in the epistles, each of them referring to the Son of God. I Timothy 2:5 states "For there is one God and one Mediator between God and man, the Man Christ Jesus." In Hebrews 9:15 and 8:6, Jesus Christ is "the Mediator of the New Testament." Hebrews 12:24 declares that we are come "to Jesus the Mediator of the New Covenant." (Read also Galatians 3:19-20 Amplified New Testament)

The Greek word "mesites" translated "mediator" means "a go-between, i.e. simply, an internunciator, or (by implication) a reconciler, intercessor." A mediator is a "middle man" or "one that interposes between parties at variance, for the purpose of reconciling them". Thus Jesus Christ is the Go-between, Middle Man, Reconciler, Intercessor and Mediator between God and Man. He is the answer to the cry of Job and the fulfilment of all Old Testament mediators.

2. The God-Man Mediator
When we consider Jesus Christ as our New Covenant Mediator we discover that His mediatorial ministry far surpasses all that was typified in Old Covenant mediators. The following reasons confirm this.

a. A Sinless Mediator
Christ was a sinless Mediator. In contrast to Moses and Aaron, both of whom needed redemption from sin themselves, Christ needed no redemption. He was a sinless High Priest and therefore far superior to any Old Covenant mediator. He is indeed "better" than Moses and Aaron (Hebrews 5:1-5; 8:1-4; 10:1-11).

b. A Divine-Human Mediator
Not only was Christ a sinless Mediator, He was also a perfect Mediator as a divine-human person. A Mediator in the truest sense of that word must be able to understand perfectly the parties which need to be reconciled. He must be able to fully identify with both to effectively mediate between them. In other words, if Jesus Christ is to be a perfect Mediator between a holy God and sinful man, He must have the nature of God and the nature of man (sin excepted) to fully understand both and to effect the reconciliation between them. Moses and Aaron could never do this fully, because they only had one nature, sinful human nature. For this same reason, no priest in the Old Testament could ever be a perfect mediator.

Jesus Christ was the God-Man. He was God, having the nature of God, thus identifying with God and His absolute holiness. He also became man, taking sinless humanity upon Himself and thus identifying with man. The union of the divine and human natures in the one person of Christ qualifies Him to be a perfect mediator between God and man.

Hebrews 2:17 states "Wherefore in all things it behoved Him to be made like unto His brethren, that He might be a merciful and faithful High Priest in things pertaining to God, to make reconciliation for the sins of the people." Having divine nature, He was faithful to God and having human nature He was able to be merciful to man. However, it was not mercy at the expense of faithfulness to God. Sin had to be dealt with in a manner that would uphold God's holiness and righteousness. Only then could mercy and grace be extended to man in bringing about the reconciliation. It is in Christ that Job's cry for a Daysman "to lay his hand upon us both" finds perfect fulfilment (Job 9:32,33).

C. Maintaining Balance
In concluding this section, it must be pointed out that proper understanding and balance must be maintained concerning the divine and human natures in Christ to avoid heretical imbalance. The great mystery of Godliness is that "God was manifest in the flesh (I Timothy 3:15-16; Colossians 2:2-3). Christ is fully God and fully man.

1. Scripture Reveals His Deity
Jesus Christ is God. Divine attributes, offices, works and names are ascribed to Him. Worship is rendered to Him and what is said of the Father is said also of the Son. He knew that He was God incarnate. He is one in the eternal Godhead.

2. Scripture Reveals His Humanity
Jesus Christ is also man. Human nature, characteristics and qualities are attributed to Him. The Word attests fully to His perfect, real and sinless humanity.

3. Scripture Reveals the Union in One Person of Deity and Humanity
The scripture reveals clearly the union of deity and humanity in the one person of Christ. Christ has two natures, divine and human, each in its completeness and integrity, two natures are so united that they are distinguishable but indivisible, so as not to form a third nature.

a. False Views of This Union
The union of these two natures cannot be compared to:

(1) The marriage relationship of two persons, for these, though joined in one by marriage are still two distinct or separate persons.

(2) The relationship of the believer with Christ. For these, though one in spiritual union, are still two distinct persons.

(3) The believer filled with the Holy Spirit, which makes a person filled with God. Jesus was not merely a man filled with God, but God Himself who became a man.

(4) A dual personality, for Jesus Christ was not two persons. He was not God and man joined together as two persons; He was one person having two natures.

(5) A being as in Greek mythology: half-God and half- Man, or a demi-god or demi-man.

(6) God being converted into a man, nor was man converted into God. Deity was not humanized, nor was humanity deified.

None of these views are the Biblical view of the union of the divine and human natures in the one person of Christ.

b. Proper Views of this Union
The union of these two natures is spoken of as being "The Hypostatic Union", that is personal union, and is understood in the following manner.

(1) Christ Jesus was one Person, having in Himself the union of two natures; the nature of God and the nature of Man, thus constituting Him the God-Man. A. Hodge says "The Son of God did

not unite Himself with a human person, but human nature, thus one Person."

(2) The human nature was not the divine nature, nor was the divine nature human nature, bu Christ had two natures in His one person.

(3) These natures were distinguishable but indivisible; inseparably bound together so as t constitute the one personal Christ of God. The two natures existed in Christ, each in its ow perfection and maintaining its own identity.

(4) This union was the union of God and man in one Person, forming the "new creation (Revelation 3:14); having two centers of consciousness and two wills. Man did not becom God but God became Man. The incarnation joined two natures not two persons. The tw natures are inseparable though distinct.

Thiessen in "Lectures in Systematic Theology" (p. 305) says that Christ therefore had an in finite intelligence and will and a finite intelligence and will. He continues to write "Chris has a divine consciousness and a human consciousness. His divine will was omnipotent; Hi human will had only the power of unfallen humanity. In His divine consciousness He said ' and the Father are one"; in His human consciousness He said, "I thirst" (read John 10:3(14:28). Thus Jesus was conscious of His oneness with God and also His oneness with man

There are not two Christs, a human Christ and a divine Christ. There is but one Person havin divine and human natures. Jesus always spoke as a single person. The New Testament speak this way also. However, the attributes of both deity and humanity are ascribed to this on person.

Dr. Charles A. Ratz" in "The Person of Christ" (pp.81-82) comments on the precise differenc between "nature" and "person". He states how the English word "nature" is derived fror the Latin word "natura" and its Greek equivalent is "phusis" used in Romans 2:14; Galatian 2:15; 4:8; Ephesians 2:3 and II Peter 1:4). He then explains how the term "nature" has had varied usage in the history of Christian doctrine and says "today it is commonly used t designate the divine or human elements in the person of Christ. Theologically the term "nature" "substance" and "essence" came to be used interchangeably.

When speaking of "Nature and its Attributes" Ratz says "Divine substance or nature is th sum of all divine attributes. Likewise human substance or nature is the sum total of a human attributes. Attributes must be compatible to the nature which they correspond, an cannot be transferred to another substance or nature. Nature, as applied to the deity of Chris includes all that belongs to His deity." Thus we speak of the two natures of Christ, the divin and the human, each with their respective attributes.

Schaff (whom Ratz adapted) in "History of the Christian Church" writes concerning th words "nature" and "person"; "Nature or substance is the totality of powers and qualitie which constitute a being. The person is the ego, the self-conscious, self-asserting and actin subject... There is no person without nature, but there is nature without person as i irrational beings." Therefore in the mystery of the Incarnation, we say that the Son of Go "did not assume a human person, but assumed a human nature" (C.A. Ratz, p.82, in "Th Person of Christ"). Otherwise there would be two persons in the Christ of God. Theologicall there are two natures but only one person in the Son of God.

In speaking of the profound mystery of the union of the two natures in the one person o Christ, Edward W. A. Koehler in "A Summary of Christian Doctrine" (pp.90-92), expresses i with some elucidating statements: "When the Son of God assumed the human nature, He imparted and communicated to it divine majesty, glory and attributes. Thereby the majesty o the divine nature was in no wise lessened or divided, but remained fully intact in both natures ... In His divine nature the Son of God always did have divine glory and majesty (John 17:15) but to His human nature all this was given (Daniel 7:13-14; Hebrews 2:7-8)... While therefore, the divine attributes belong essentially to the divine nature, they belong by communication also to the human nature. But the human nature does not communicate anything to the divine nature because the divine nature is perfect, and nothing can be added thereto. Thus Christ has two distinct natures, a human and a divine, each of which has its own essential attributes, functions and activities. But as both natures belong to the same person, the attributes and properties of either may be ascribed to the person. Christ was begotten of the Father from eternity according to His divine nature (Psalm 2:7); Christ was born of the Virgin Mary in the fulness of time according to His human nature (Galatians 4:4). Jesus was 30 years old according to His human nature (Luke 3:23); according to His divine nature He could say 'Before Abraham was, I am' (John 8:58). Christ is 'equal to the Father as touching His Godhead, and inferior to the Father as touching His manhood'."

c. The Reason for this Union

The reason for the union of deity and humanity is in order that Christ might fulfil in His one person, that which was separate and distinct in Old Covenant mediatorial ministry.

In Old Covenant mediatorial ministry the offerer and the offering were distinguished. The High Priest and the sacrifice were separate. Moses and Aaron as mediators could never offer themselves, but they could offer a sacrifice for sin (Exodus 32:30-33; Hebrews 5:1-5). However, it was sinful human nature offering sinless animal nature to God as a sacrifice for sin. Thus there was always a separation between sacrifice and sacrificer, between priest and offering.

In Christ as the God-Man both are brought together in one. The union of the two natures in the one person was absolutely essential for an efficacious atonement for sin. Being real and proper God He could atone to God. This was the purpose of the incarnation — the divine nature bringing human nature into union with itself.

Edward W. A. Koehler in "A Summary of Christian Doctrine" (p.87) says: "Ordinarily a human nature exists as a human person, having its own and individual existence. The human nature of Jesus was from the moment of the incarnation assumed by the Son of God. "The Word was made flesh" (John 1:14). "God sent forth His Son, made of a woman" (Galatians 4:4). At no time did the human nature of Christ exist for and by itself, constituting in itself a person; but from the beginning it had its existence in the person of the Son of God. Nor were the two natures merged into one new person, but the eternal person of the Godhead, the Son, assumed the human nature, hence the impersonality of His human nature. The Son of God supplied the personality of the God-Man Jesus Christ."

The union of the two natures in the one person of Christ constitutes Him therefore as the one and only perfect Mediator between God and man; between a holy God and sinful man. Jesus Christ is the bridge between God and Man. He can stand with God above and with man below. He being the Son of Man (humanity) and the Son of God (deity) thus became "Jacob's Ladder" (John 1:51) bridging the gulf between God and man, and heaven and earth, that was brought about through sin.

Robert Clarke says "The eternal Son of God became the sinless Son of Man that the sinful sons of men might become the beloved sons of God." Christ is both offerer and offering, sacrifice and sacrificer, priest and gift, heavenly and earthly, spiritual and natural. In His deity, He is the offerer, sacrificer and priest. In His humanity, He is offering, sacrifice and gift. (Read also Ephesians 5:2,25; Hebrews 8:3; 10:1-14) Galatians 2:20 states; "...Who (the Priest) loved me and gave Himself (the sacrifice) for me". Titus 2:14 "...Who (the Priest) gave Himself (the sacrifice) for us".

On the cross it was the divine nature offering the sinless human nature to God for sin. It was deity presenting sinless humanity to God as a perfect sacrifice for sin. It was God atoning to God. It was a sinless man atoning for sinful men. Only the miracle of the incarnation and the union of the two natures in one person made this possible.

The First Adam had but one nature, human nature, and it had the liability to sin and did sin. Animal sacrifices were brought in as substitutes because animals had sinless animal nature. But animal nature could not atone for human nature; the lesser could not atone for the greater. God had to bring in a perfect human nature to atone for sinful human nature. But this could not be found among the best of the sons of men. So God did a miracle and divine nature assumed a perfectly sinless human nature in the miracle of the virgin birth.

The Last Adam, the Second Man, was the Lord from heaven and as the first of the new creation race had two natures, divine and human. His human nature was sinless as was Adam's before the Fall. Because it was the divine nature which assumed the human nature there was no liability to fall, no response to sin. Jesus was an incarnation, "God was in Christ" reconciling the world unto Himself (II Corinthians 5:18-21). Adam was a creation but he was not God incarnate. Thus Jesus, as Mediator and Priest (deity) was able to offer Himself, His own sinless body and blood as the sacrifice and oblation (humanity) and made possible the reconciliation between God and man.

For these reasons Christ is called a Theanthropic Person (Theos God; Anthropos Man). He does not possess a Theanthropic nature. His person is Theanthropic, not His nature. His person is one; His natures are two. He is eternally the God-Man. He does not have a divine-human or a human-divine nature, but He does have a divine nature, and a human nature, the qualities and attributes of each in union and total harmony, distinguishable but indivisible. He is truly God perfectly Man, one person, having two unconfused natures. He was not a humanized God or a deified Man. He was and is the God-Man.

The personality of Christ is unique; He is indeed only begotten. As to Adam, he was a real man yet not born of natural generation. Eve was a woman without a mother, not born, but made out of the side of her husband, Adam, the First Man. Christ, as to His deity had no mother, and as to His humanity had no father. Christ was God made flesh. He was not God because He was virgin born but He was virgin born because He was God.

The New Testament writers, under the inspiration of the Holy Spirit, set forth the delicate balance between the deity and humanity of Christ in their writings. We list a number of references as examples of this balance and the then set out in columns that which illustrates the balance between the deity and humanity of Christ, the divine and the human natures (I Corinthians 2:8; 15:47; Matthew 1:21; Luke 1:30-33; Hebrews 1:3; Romans 9:5; John 3:13; 6:62; Revelation 22:16; Acts 17:31; John 1:1-3,14-18; 11:25-26; 18:5-8).

ONE THEANTHROPIC PERSON

GOD	MAN
Truly God	Truly Man
Divine Nature	Human Nature
Lord from heaven	The Second Man
Immanuel	Jesus
The Eternal Word	Made flesh
Son of God	Son of Man
Son of the Most High	Christ come in the flesh
The Blood of God	A Body Prepared
Eternal	Begotten in time
Omnipotent	Dependent
Omnipresent	Localized
Omniscient	Grew in knowledge
Infinite	Finite
Sovereign	Servant
Immortality of life	Suffered death
Immutable	Sinless infirmities
I and the Father are one	My Father is greater than I
Divine Self-consciousness	Human Self-consciousness

Divine Will	Human Will:Not my will be done
God His Father	Mary His Mother
Root of David	Offspring of David
David's Lord	David's Son
Victor	Victim
The Son sent into the world	The Son made of a woman
The Priest, Sacrificer,	The Gift, Sacrifice,
The Offerer	The Offering, The Oblation
Divinity	Humanity
The Great I AM	Hungered, thirsted, weary
GOD	**MAN**

If we over-emphasize His deity, we obscure His perfect humanity. If we over-emphasize His humanity, we obscure His deity. If we deny His deity, there is no contact between God and man and the bridge is broken down from the divine side. On the other hand, if we deny His humanity, then the bridge is broken down on the human side. It is out of such imbalance that heresies have arisen concerning the blessed Son of God.

Dr. Charles A. Ratz in "The Person of Christ" quotes an old Latin inscription chiselled in marble, found in Asia, concerning the faith of the Lord Jesus Christ in the first century of Christianity. It reads:

I am what I was — God
I was not what I am — Man
I am now called both, God and Man

Truly Christ as the God-Man is the "Better Mediator" of a "Better Covenant".

Chapter 11

THE DOCTRINE OF THE ATONEMENT

The Doctrine of the Atonement comprises the redemptive work of Christ, involving His crucifixion, resurrection, ascension, exaltation, glorification, intercessory ministry, and second coming.

The plan of the atonement originated in the counsels of the eternal Godhead before the creation and fall of man. It is being accomplished in time through the work of Christ and the benefits of it that are realized by man on God's terms will continue for eternity. Such a plan is a revelation of the redeeming grace of the Almighty God.

CHAPTER OUTLINE

I. INTRODUCTION — THE WORK OF CHRIST

II. THE NECESSITY OF THE ATONEMENT

  A. Holiness of God
  B. Divine Law
  C. Sinfulness of Man
  D. Wrath of God

III. THE NATURE OF THE ATONEMENT

  A. Definition
  B. Wrath versus Love

IV. THE ORIGIN OF THE ATONEMENT

  A. Foreordained in Eternity
  B. Foreshadowed on Earth
  C. Foretold by the Law, Psalms and Prophets

V. THE WORK OF THE ATONEMENT

  A. Historically
  B. Doctrinally

VI. THE REALIZATION OF THE ATONEMENT

  A. Provision — Divine Sovereignty
  B. Application — Human Responsibility

VII. THE BENEFITS OF THE ATONEMENT

  A. Justification
  B. Regeneration
  C. Adoption
  D. Sanctification
  E. Perfection
  F. Glorification
  G. Salvation

INTRODUCTION — THE WORK OF CHRIST

Having considered in the previous section the person of Christ, we now proceed to a consideration of the work of Christ. The person of Christ deals with who He is, while the work of Christ deals with what He has done. As the person of Christ pertains to His eternity of being, incarnation and sinless life, so the work of Christ has to do more specifically with His crucifixion, resurrection, ascension, glorification, exaltation, intercession and finally His second advent.

Jesus was conscious of a particular "work" His Father sent Him to do, as is evidenced in these Scriptures.

John 4:34 - "My meat is to do the will of Him that sent Me, and to finish His work."

John 5:17 - "My Father worketh hitherto, and I work."

John 17:4 - "...I have finished the work which thou gavest Me to do." (Read also John 5:36; 9:4; 16:26-27; 19:30).

The Father, Son and Holy Spirit all worked in what has been called "The week of creation" and then rested (Genesis 1-2). When man was created, he began with rest. When he sinned, both his and God's rests were broken. God began to work again, this time in what has been called "The week of redemption". There could be no true rest while sin reigned, so the Father, Son and Holy Spirit had to work to redeem fallen man and bring about redemptive rest.

Jesus, the eternal Son, was given work to do the work of the atonement. All that Jesus did was the work of His Father. His work was to fulfill His Father's will. It is on the basis of Christ's work that the sinner is invited to enter into redemptive rest (Matthew 11:28-30; Hebrews 4:3,9-11).

I. THE NECESSITY OF THE ATONEMENT

The necessity of the atonement is understood when we realize the relationship between the holiness of God, His divine law, the sinfulness of man, and divine wrath.

A. Holiness of God

Under "The Doctrine of God" holiness was seen to be a fundamental moral attribute of God. Holiness describes God's inward character, His very essence. His holiness is absolute and underived. God is perfectly holy in all He says and does because He is holiness personified (Leviticus 19:2; Exodus 15:11; Isaiah 57:15; Exodus 28:36; Isaiah 57:15; Exodus 3:1-15; Joshua 5:13-15; Isaiah 6:3; Revelation 15:3-4; Psalm 33:5; 5:4-6; 47:8). Because God is absolutely holy, He can expect no less than holiness in His creatures (I Peter 1:1-6). He hates sin with a perfect hatred and cannot tolerate it. The righteousness of God demands that sin be exposed, judged and punished (Psalm 89:14; Romans 1:17).

B. Divine Law

When God created angelic and human beings with a free will, it necessitated that they all live within the boundaries of God's will. Thus God gave divine law as a standard of righteousness for all to follow. Without law there would be no order, and all would be chaos. God's will was His law and His law was His will. The laws governing God's own being were to be the laws which would govern all created beings. God gave Adam and Eve one law, the law of loving obedience (Genesis 2:17). To transgress this law was sin (I John 3:4).

C. Sinfulness of Man

Under "The Doctrine of Sin" it was seen that man fell into a state of sinfulness, becoming totally depraved in spirit, soul and body. Adam violated the one law God had given him and "Sin is the transgression of the law" (I John 3:4 with Genesis 2:17). Sin made man lawless, a rebel at heart. It separated him from God (Isaiah 59:2) creating a great gulf between them. Man is sinful by nature and therefore sins in thought, word and deed. He is not a sinner because he sins, he sins because he is a sinner. He does what he does because of what he is (Romans 3:23; Galatians 3:22; Psalm 51:5; Romans 7:7-21).

The holiness of God and the sinfulness of man are in direct opposition to each other. The holiness of God cannot tolerate the sinfulness of man; therefore God's holiness demands that man's sinfulness be exposed and judged. If God did not deal with man's sinfulness, then His law, His throne of holiness, His righteousness and justice would be in jeopardy.

D. Wrath of God

What happens then when the holiness of God comes into conflict with the sinfulness of man? The answer is, divine wrath is manifested. The reaction of God's holiness against man's sinfulness is wrath. The wrath of God is simply the righteous anger of a good and holy God against sin. Sin cannot be tolerated. It must be dealt with and come under divine judgment. Sin is essentially an attack on the honor and holiness of God. If it goes unjudged then God's law, holiness, righteousness and justice are violated. Only as sin is dealt with will God's character be vindicated, His throne established, the Law upheld and God's government of His creatures be maintained. We note several Scriptures which speak of the wrath of a holy God.

Romans 4:15 - "The Law worketh wrath".

John 3:36 - "...he that believeth not the Son shall not see life; but the wrath of God abideth on him.' (Read John 3:36 Amplified).

Romans 1:18 - "For the wrath of God is revealed from heaven against all ungodliness and unrighteousness of men..."

Revelation 6:16-17 - "...hide us from the face of Him that sitteth on the throne, and from the wrath of the Lamb, for the great day of His wrath is come..."

(Read also Psalm 78:31; 79:6; Romans 2:5-8; Ephesians 2:3; Revelation 14:9-11; 15:1; 16:1 19:15).

The progression evident here may be summarized in the following:

1. The Law of God
The Law of God is spiritual, holy, just, good and perfect (Romans 7:12; Psalm 19:7). God's law represents His holiness which is the law of His very being.

2. Transgression of the Law
Sin is lawlessness (I John 3:4). It is rebellion against God's will and law. Self-will is man being a law to himself. The sinfulness of man is his transgression of God's perfect and holy law.

3. The Wrath of God
The righteous reaction of a holy God against sin.

However, a full consideration of Scripture shows that divine wrath is not always executed immediately against sin, because of other moral attributes in the nature of God. God restrains immediate judgement so that man may be brought to repentance. This restrained wrath reveals to sinful mankind the wonderful attributes of God's grace, longsuffering and mercy (Ecclesiastes 8:11; Romans 2:4; II Peter 3:9; Revelation 2:21).

In summary then we see that God's holiness demands that man's sinfulness be dealt with; that wrath be executed upon it, but divine grace restrains immediate wrath waiting for God to provide a means for man to escape the wrath. These are the things involved which necessitated the atonement.

III. THE NATURE OF THE ATONEMENT

A. Definition
The Hebrew word "Kaphar" means "to cover"; figuratively "to expiate or condone, to placate or conceal". It is translated by these words: "appease, make an atonement, cleanse, disannul, forgive, be merciful, pacify, purge, reconcile". It comes from the Hebrew word "Kippur" meaning "expiation, atonement". The Old English word "atonement" means "to be made at one", "to reconcile, to bring

about agreement, or concord". Thus it may read "at-one-ment", the making at-one those that have disagreement. Further definition of the words "atone" or "atonement" are seen in the following:

1. To cover, or to expiate, condone.
2. To purge, to purge away.
3. To reconcile.
4. To answer or make satisfaction for, to expiate.
5. To appease, which is to make quiet; to allay; to satisfy, pacify, especially by giving in to the demands of someone, i.e. to appease wrath.
6. To make amends or reparation (for wrong-doing, a wrong-doer).
7. At-one; agreement; concord; reconciliation after enmity or controversy.

(Read Exodus 29:33-37; Leviticus 16:6-17)

Thus "atonement" is spoken of as the covering, the expiation, the satisfaction, the appeasement or the reconciliation. A consideration of the rich meaning of this word shows how vast and comprehensive a word it is. For this reason it has been chosen as the most suitable word to encompass all redemptive words.

Man broke God's holy law, violating the principles of righteousness by his wilful disobedience. This brought man under the power of sin and made his conscience laden with guilt. With the violation of the divine law also came the divine penalty of death (Genesis 2:17). Sin provoked God's wrath which then needed to be appeased. The law demanded a satisfaction and it could only be satisfied when its standard of holiness is upheld. Not until the death penalty had been executed (Romans 6:23) upon sin (Ezekiel 18:4,20; Hebrews 9:27) could the law be satisfied, God's holiness and righteousness upheld, and God's wrath be appeased. Sin had to be purged before there could be any reconciliation between God and man.
In summary we say then that the **holiness** of God against the **sinfulness** of man produced the reaction of divine **wrath**. It is this wrath that needed the appeasement before a holy God and sinful man could ever be reconciled. This appeasement is the **atonement.**

B. Wrath and Love
Meditation of the previous statements present to man an apparent problem. This has to do with the moral attribute of God, all of which are perfectly balanced in His being We specify these balancing attributes of the very nature and being of God as holiness and love. The Bible reveals that God is holy (I Peter 1:16) and God is love (I John 4:16).

As already noted, these attributes are in absolute and perfect balance in God. God in His love desired to save the sinner. God in His holiness must execute His wrath and judgement upon the sin. How could this be done? God could not manifest love at the expense of His holiness, and again, God could not save the sinner without judgement upon the sin. What was to be done?

Because of man's self-centeredness, the measure of these attributes in a believer's life, are generally out of balance and the pendulum seems to swing to either extreme bringing its attendant problems. It should be remembered that Calvary is not first a revelation of the love of God, but a revelation of the holiness of God. It is always holiness first, then love, for God's love can never be revealed at the expense of God's holiness. The same Apostle John who speaks of "the love of God" is the one who also speaks of "the wrath of God" (John 3:16,17,36). He speaks of "the blood of the Lamb" as well as "the wrath of the Lamb" and yet it is the same redemptive Lamb. (Revelation 5:9-10; 6:16-17). Saints in both Old and New Testaments experienced this order.

1. Moses received the revelation of the Lord God in the burning bush. There it was holiness first, then Israel's redemption (Exodus 3:5,9-10).

2. Joshua had to acknowledge God's holiness before he could receive the victory over the Canaanites (Joshua 5:13-15).

3. Isaiah received a revelation of God's holiness first, then the call to the prophetic office (Isaiah 6:1-8).

4. John, the apostle of love, spoke of the wrath of God as well as the love of God (John 3:16-17,36).

5. Paul spoke of the wrath of God against man's sinfulness before he even mentioned the love of God in Christ (Romans 1:18; 2:5,8; 4:15; 5:5). It is worthy to note that the theme of the Epistle to the Romans is that of justification and the reconciliation of man to God. However, in Romans chapters 1-3 the emphasis is on the wrath of a holy and righteous God revealed against all ungodliness and sin. The subject of love is not expressly brought up until Romans 5:5.

How can God in love save the sinner without violating His holiness and executing His wrath upon sin? The answer is found in the atonement, as typified in the Old Testament, prophesied of in the Law, the Psalms and the Prophets, and then fulfilled in the work of the Lord Jesus Christ. In the atoning work of the Lord Jesus Christ, God deals in holiness with sin, and in love with the sinner. In the work of the cross, holiness and love are seen in perfect balance, God judging sin and making provision for the sinner's salvation (Isaiah 53:3-6; II Corinthians 5:21; Romans 3:25).

IV. THE ORIGIN OF THE ATONEMENT

A. Foreordained in Eternity
The fall of man was foreknown by God. The covenant of redemption made in the counsels of the eternal Godhead before sin is evidence of this fact. The essential and moral attributes of God also attest to this. The very fact that God is all-powerful, all-knowing and ever-present confirms to us that God was not caught unawares by the entrance of sin into the human race by Adam's fall. Because God foresaw and foreknew He planned to deal with sin in His own wise way (Acts 15:18). God did not predestine sin, but foreknew it would enter.

In the counsels of the Godhead, the Father, Son and Holy Spirit made the Everlasting Covenant in the event of sin (Hebrews 13:20). This covenant was made in eternity, before the world began and before the creation and fall of man. The Godhead was not unprepared to deal with sin and its disastrous effects. This covenant of redemption was God's provision. The Son of God was foreordained before the world began to be the Lamb of God and take away the sin of the world. Scripture reveals that the Word would become flesh to deal with sin. In eternity past He was set aside for this redemptive work. Christ was set aside both before and from the foundation of the world.

1. Before the Foundation of the World
   a. The Father loved the Son before the foundation of the world (John 17:5,24).
   b. Christ was foreordained before the foundation of the world to be the Lamb of God (I Peter 1:19-20; Ephesians 1:4; Exodus 12:3-6; Acts 2:23).
   c. The redeemed were chosen in Christ before the foundation of the world (Ephesians 1:4).

2. From the Foundation of the World

   a. The Lamb was slain from the foundation of the world (Revelation 13:8).
   b. The Lamb's Book of Life had names written in it from the foundation of the world (Revelation 17:8).
   c. The Kingdom was prepared for the righteous from the foundation of the world (Matthew 25:34).
   d. The rest of God was provided for believers from the foundation of the world (Hebrews 4:3).
   e. The remedy for sin was prepared before it ever entered the world (Hebrews 9:26; Acts 2:23; Titus 1:2-3). (Read also Matthew 13:35; Hebrews 9:26; Romans 16:25-27).

The atonement was foreordained in eternity. The cross was ordained in heaven. Jesus was foreordained to die. As one writer has expressed it "Jesus was born crucified". Thus, the atonement historically was a manifestation in time of God's eternal purpose in Christ (Ephesians 1:4-12; 3:9-11). The Son of God knew that He was foreordained to die for the sins of the world (Matthew 5:17-18; 11:13; Isaiah 42:1; Isaiah 53; Mark 10:45). The sacrifice of Christ on the cross is an historical manifestation of God's eternal purpose.

B. Foreshadowed on Earth

1. Corrupted in the Gentile Nations

The moment man sinned, God set into motion the plan of redemption. Sin was judged in a sacrificial substitute, thus maintaining God's holiness and satisfying the broken Law of God. Man, the sinner, was clothed in the coats of skin provided through the death of an innocent victim, thus revealing the love and grace of God. In this act the atonement was foreshadowed. Both sin and sinner were dealt with as the holiness of God and sinfulness of man met together. The wrath and judgement of God fell on the innocent substitutionary victim (Genesis 3:1-24). The Gospel was condensed in the first Messianic promise given, Genesis 3:15, stating that the seed of the woman would bruise the serpent's head.

It is evident that God gave to the patriarchs, especially Adam, Noah and Abraham, a partial revelation of the atoning work needed for man's redemption from sin and Satan. The covenants made with these fathers are part of the Everlasting Covenant of redemption. Certain basic and fundamental principles of religion were disseminated through mankind, both in the Godly and ungodly lines.

Because of the corruption in the days of Noah, God judged the sinful world by means of the flood (Genesis 6-7-8). After the flood, mankind gathered together at the Tower of Babel under the leadership of Nimrod, the rebel. God again judged mankind, this time by confusing their tongues. Hence we have the origin of the nations as descending from the three sons of Noah; Shem, Ham and Japheth. God caused the earth to be divided with the confusion of tongues and the scattering of mankind. He set the nations in their own lands according to the nation of Israel (Genesis 10-11; Acts 17:26-27; Deuteronomy 32:8).

History shows how every nation in the world has certain similar principles of religion, which have been adapted according to their culture. Though the methods vary according to race and culture, the principles seem to be universally the same. Though this knowledge has been corrupted it still illustrates that man has an intuitive knowledge of a holy God, his own sinfulness and his need for redemption.

We list the basic principles of religion found in the nations of the earth, each of which show that man knows he needs the atonement:

a. All Nations believe in God
All mankind generally has an intuitive knowledge of the existence of some God or gods. All have this knowledge within (Romans 1:19-20). They seek God or they create their own gods of created things, and worship the creature more than the Creator. Idolatry itself is evidence of this intuitive belief in God. This knowledge did not come from without, it is within.

b. All Nations believe in Sin
The knowledge of sin is also universal even as the knowledge of God. All mankind has the law of conscience, convicting and accusing when it is violated (Romans 2:12-14). When evil befell various nations, they attributed such to the judgement of the gods upon their sins. Calamity was always due to their failure to please their deities. All men know that there is something wrong with man and that it needs rectification.

c. All Nations believe in Incarnation
It seems evident that the truth of God becoming incarnate had its beginning in Genesis 3:15 concerning the seed of the woman. With the scattering of mankind and the origin of all nations at Babel, the various nations took this enigmatic promise with them and developed a religion of their own from it. Various mythologies arose concerning the gods coming down to earth in the likeness of men. These gods were demigods, half-human and half-divine. Greek mythology is noted for its various forms of incarnation of the gods. Most all ancient religions believed in the incarnation of the gods. They also opened their own being to become incarnate with the spirit of the various gods they worshipped (Acts 17:18,23; 14:8-18; Daniel 2:11-28; 3:25; 4:8; 5:11,18).

d. All Nations believe in Sacrifice
Heathen nations had terrible fear of the deities they worshipped. This caused them to endeavor to appease the gods by offerings, sacrifices of all kinds, even to the sacrificing of their own sons

and daughters. They felt that some sacrifice of appeasement had to be made to the gods. They would sacrifice their dearest and best at times, in an endeavor to atone for sin, to reconcile themselves to the gods and to have peace with the deities. Sacrifice to Baal in the Old Testament evidenced this fact.

e. All Nations believe in Priesthood
Not being able to approach these deities or gods directly, the nations saw their need for a priesthood to act as mediators. They brought their offerings to their priesthood that held the secrets and mysteries of the mind of their god. In the Old Testament, the priests and prophets of Baal, Ashtaroth and other gods were supported by the gifts and sacrifices of the people. These priests could bring curses or blessings on the people through their prayers and mystical incantations.

f. All Nations believe in a Deliverer to Come
From the seed promise of Genesis 3:15 all nations saw that there would come some deliverer who would deliver from the curse of the gods. This child to be born would liberate their nation, make them rulers and restore man to his former state of glory. This deliverer was known under various names according to the particular nation holding the doctrine of a coming deliverer. The student is referred to "The Two Babylons" by Alexander Hislop for a comprehensive study of this matter.

g. All Nations believe in Life after Death
Deep within the heart of all men, regardless of nation or culture, there is a belief in life after death, a belief in some form of immortality. This is even seen in the various concepts of resurrection and re-incarnation which various nations hold. Man somehow knows that he will live again and that the life to come is determined upon the kind of life lived in the present. This knowledge, though often perverted is intuitive within man.

h. All Nations believe in Judgement to Come
Regardless of tongue, tribe or nation, man's conscience tells him that judgement is to fall upon him somewhere, somehow, sometime, for the deeds he does. Though sin often distorts it, man possesses an inbuilt knowledge of justice.

i. All Nations believe in Heaven and Hell
Concerning future states, all nations intuitively believe that there is some place of bliss and joy for those that do good and some place of torment and punishment for those that do evil. The Bible speaks of these two eternal states as heaven and hell.

In summary, mankind seems to know intuitively that there is a God, that he is under sin and needs an atoning sacrifice for sin. He knows he needs a mediating priesthood, a deliverer by incarnation. He knows that life does not cease with death and his eternal state is determined by this present life, whether good or evil.

Where did this knowledge come from? It is inbuilt by God Himself, and all man's religions are built upon these basic principles. The religions of ancient Egypt, Assyria, Babylon, Medo-Persia, Greece, Rome and many other nations, both ancient and modern, all fall short of the divine standard. While maintaining the basic principles, the methods were corrupted. Thus, there has always been the need for God to establish a purer foreshadowing of the atoning work that would be accomplished through His Son, He alone would fulfill all that is in the basic principles of religions.

2. Sanctified in the Nation of Israel
From Adam to Abraham, God preserved unto Himself a godly seed in which the divine principles of religion and method of approach to Himself were maintained. At the Tower of Babel, God called Abraham unto Himself and told him that He would make of him a great nation and that through his seed all the nations of the earth would be blessed (Genesis 12:1-3; 22:15-18). This same covenant of redemption was confirmed to Isaac (Genesis 26:3-5), and to Jacob (Genesis 28:13-15). In due time the nation of Israel was formed and after the Exodus, God, at Mt. Sinai entered into covenant relationship with this chosen nation (Exodus 19:1-6).

God took a nation from the midst of the nations to give His principles and methods whereby sinful man could approach a holy and righteous God (Deuteronomy 4:5-8, 31-40). At Mt. Sinai Israel received the revelation of the holiness of God and the sinfulness of man. Here they were given the Law, God's righteous standard. Here the moral, civil and ceremonial laws were given by revelation through Moses, the mediator of the Old Covenant. The ceremonial law was actually a revelation of the grace of God, though Israel as a nation did not seem to perceive this. This was seen in the mediating priesthood, the sacrifices for sin, the feasts of the Lord, and especially the great day of atonement. The operation of these things centered in the Tabernacle of Moses.

All that the Gentile nations had corrupted in their beliefs was given to Israel, God's chosen nation, in purity of revelation. It was illustrated in the whole of the Mosaic economy. All of this typified and foreshadowed the coming of Christ and his atoning work (Matthew 5:17-18; 11:13). It spoke of the fact that Christ would die "according to the Scriptures" (I Corinthians 15:1-3). The following is a list of those things which typified and foreshadowed the work of atonement which would be fulfilled in due time by Christ.

a. Patriarchal Age - Adam to Moses (Romans 5:14)

(1) Genesis 3:15. The Seed of the woman would bruise the serpent's head.
(2) Genesis 3:21. The Coats of skin.
(3) Genesis 4:14; Hebrews 11:4. The sacrifice of Abel.
(4) Genesis 8:20,21. Noah's altar and sacrifices of clean animals.
(5) Genesis 15:7-18. Abraham's altar and 5 offerings.
(6) Genesis 17; Acts 7:8. The Covenant of Circumcision.
(7) Genesis 22; Hebrews 11:17-19. The typical sacrifice of Isaac on Mt. Moriah.
(8) Genesis 26:25; 33:20; 35:1-7. The altars of Isaac and Jacob.

b. Law Age - Moses to Jesus (Matthew 11:13)

(1) Exodus 12. The Passover Lamb.
(2) Exodus 24. The altar and blood-sprinkled Book of the Covenant.
(3) Exodus 35-40. The Tabernacle of Moses and its ministrations.
(4) Exodus 28-29; Leviticus 8-9. The 5 Levitical offerings.
(5) Leviticus 1-7. The High Priestly ministry of Aaron and sons.
(6) Leviticus 16. The Great Day of Atonement.
(7) Leviticus 23; Numbers 28-29. The Feasts of the Lord; Passover, Pentecost and Tabernacles.
(8) Numbers 19. The sacrifice of the Red Heifer.
(9) Joshua 2. The scarlet thread of deliverance.
(10) Leviticus 25. The Kinsman Redeemer (Psalm 49:7-9).
(11) Judges 13:16-19. Manoah's sacrifice
(12) I Samuel 1:21. Elkanah's yearly sacrifice.
(13) I Samuel 7:9-10; 16:2-5. The offerings of the prophet Samuel.
(14) II Samuel 6:18; I Chronicles 21; II Samuel 24. David's altar and sacrifices.
(15) I Kings 18:38. Elijah's sacrifice and altar.
(16) II Chronicles 29. The renewal of the altar under King Hezekiah.
(17) Ezra 3:3-6; Nehemiah 10:32-33. The restoration of the temple and altar after the Babylonian captivity.
(18) Job 9:32-33; 19:25-27; 1:1-5. Job's sacrifices and cry for a daysman and redeemer.

The central thought of the Mosaic economy was that substitutionary sacrifice must be offered in approaching God. The sacrificial victims were distinctly the substitutes for the transgressors and suffered pain and death in their stead. The result was that the Israelite was forgiven the offense and received remission of the penalty. All this pointed to the Lamb of God who would die for our sins and die in our behalf (John 1:29,36; Romans 5:8; I Corinthians 15:3). However, because of the inadequacy and imperfections of the Old Testament priests and offerings, God foretold the coming of the Just One, the Son of God, who would die to bring about the reconciliation between the holy God and sinful man. No animal soul or life-blood could atone or make redemption for human soul (Hebrews 10:4; 9:13). Animal sacrifices were irrational, unwilling sacrifices. Being less than the man they died for, none could make a true atonement. A perfect man had to die for imperfect man. Thus animal sacrifices were but temporary and typical until the sacrifice and the oblation could come in the person of the incarnate Son of God (Daniel 9:24-27).

c. Foretold by the Prophets
Not only was the Law a schoolmaster pointing to Christ (Galatians 3:24), the Prophets also

pointed to Christ. The Law typified Christ, while the Prophets foretold Christ. The Law shadowed f
the atonement typically while the Psalms and the Prophets foretold the atonement prophetically. J
plainly declared that the Law, the Psalms and the Prophets typified and prophecied of Him (Matt
5:17–18; 11:13; Luke 24:27, 44–45; Hebrews 10:5–10).

While the Law majored on the offering of animal sacrifice, the Prophets pointed to a human sacri
The Prophets, when dealing with the sacrificial system dealt with several important things. T
showed the Israelites that along with animal sacrifices there had to be an inward corresponding sa
fice of a broken and contrite spirit. Without this inner sacrifice, all other sacrifices were vain, e
though God ordained them (Psalm 26:6; 50:12-14; 51:16; Proverbs 21:3; Amos 5:21-24; Micah 6:
Isaiah 1:11-17; 66:1-4). It may be summed up in the Proverb "The sacrifice of the wicked is
abomination to the Lord" (Proverbs 15:8).

The burden of the Prophets also was that there was to come a time when animal sacrifices would be a
ished, and for anyone to offer them after that time would be an abomination unto God (Isaiah 66:
Daniel 9:24-27; Hebrews 10:1-10). The prophets further showed that the Messiah was to come and fu
and abolish all animal sacrifices by offering Himself as the supreme and perfect once-for-all sacrifice
sin. They showed that all the sacrifices under the Law pointed to Messiah. The following is a brief
of some of the major prophecies from the Psalms and Prophets concerning the sacrifice of Messia

(1) The Psalms

(a) Psalm 2. The Psalm of the King in Zion, the begotten Son.
(b) Psalm 22. The crucifixion of Messiah.
(c) Psalm 23. The Shepherd Psalm.
(d) Psalm 24. The King of Glory Psalm.
(e) Psalm 40:6-8. The Burnt Offering Psalm (cf. Hebrews 10:1-10).
(f) Psalm 41 and Psalm 69. The Betrayal Psalms.
(g) Psalm 89. The Davidic Covenant Psalm of Messiah.
(h) Psalm 110. The Psalm of Christ's Priesthood after Melchisedek.

These Psalms, along with others; foretell Christ's sufferings, betrayal, death, resurrection and ascension to glory.

(2) The Prophets

(a) Isaiah 7:14. The Messiah's virgin birth.
(b) Isaiah 9:6-9. The Messiah's everlasting kingdom.
(c) Jeremiah 31:31-34. The Messiah makes the New Covenant (Hebrews 8).
(d) Daniel 9:24-27. Messiah's crucifixion.
(e) Isaiah 53. The sufferings of the Messiah on the cross.
(f) Zechariah 3:8; 6:12-13. Messiah sits as King-Priest on the throne.
(g) Zechariah 13:6-7. The smitten Shepherd.
(h) Zechariah 11:12-13. Messiah sold for 30 pieces of silver.

(Note: refer back to "Prophecy and Fulfilment" under the section concerning proofs of
inspiration for a fuller list of Messianic prophecies from the Law, Psalms and Prophets.)

God chose the nation of Israel and gave them His education under the Law Covenant. The priest
and sacrificial system under the Tabernacle economy pointed to the Messiah. All this was a sc
master to bring the nation to Christ (Galatians 3:24). The Prophets pointed to the real and spir
meaning behind the animal sacrifices, they foretold the coming of Jesus, the God-Man, who woul
for man, and abolish animal sacrifices. They pointed out that these sacrifices were indeed tempo
imperfect and could never take away sin. How could animal soul atone for human soul? How c
sinless animals atone for sinful man? How could animal atone for man? How could the out
cleansing of defilement bring the inner cleansing from a heart defilement? These foreshadows
good for "the time then present" (Hebrews 9:8-9,22) but they could not accomplish what only C
could.

It should be remembered that the Old Testament saints of the true Israel of God exercised faith in the coming Messiah each time they presented the animal sacrifice in sincerity, as their substitute for sin. The Old Testament saints were saved by looking forward in faith to the Messiah's death through this typical death (Hebrews 9:15). The New Testament saints are saved by looking back to the Messiah's death. Both Old and New Testament saints are saved and redeemed by the same sacrifice of Jesus Christ. Jesus died for the transgressions of those under both the Old and New Covenants.

. THE WORK OF THE ATONEMENT

A. Historically
The work of the atonement will now be considered historically. As noted earlier the work of Christ viewed historically includes His death, burial, resurrection, ascension, glorification, exaltation, session, second coming and final judgements.

1. His Atoning Death

a. Introductory:
It is important to understand that the death of Christ is an absolutely unique death. All the combined deaths of mankind cannot be compared with the death of Christ, for His death is an atoning death. The work of the cross sets forth Christ's death in its uniqueness because it is the only death which makes redemption possible. The whole structure of Christianity is founded on this death. It is a pivotal point in time. Many will accept Christ as a leader, an example, as a prophet, or teacher, that which is set forth in His life, but they reject His atoning death as priest and sacrifice for sin. However, it is not His ethics, life or example, but His death which saves man. His perfectly sinless life, like the perfect Law, simply condemns man. It is like the unrent veil. It stands between God and man, condemning and excluding man from any approach to God. It is His life, His risen life that saves men (Romans 5:1-10). God's order is first His saving death and then His saving life.

b. False Theories of His Death
Theologians deal with false and inadequate views of the death of Christ. We give but the briefest view of these theories as suggested by Henry Thiessen in "Lectures in Systematic Theology" (pp.315-320), and E.H. Bancroft in "Christian Theology" (pp.107-116). One writer suggests that there are over 40 different views of the death of Christ. The following are six of the major theories adapted from the above authors.

(1) The Accident Theory
This view sees no significance in the death of Christ. It holds that Christ's principles and methods did not appeal to the people of His day, so they killed Him. It was unfortunate that such a good man had to die that way, but His death is meaningless apart from this. His death is counted as an unfortunate accident.

(2) The Martyr Theory
This theory is related to the previous one. It teaches that Christ died as a martyr for the principles He was faithful to. It teaches that His death was an example for all of being willing to die for the things they believe. It denies that Christ's death was a substitutionary and propitiatory death. Christ is held up as any other martyr is held, dying for a good cause.

(3) The Moral Influence Theory
This theory holds that Christ's death was just the mere natural consequence of His taking human nature upon Himself. His death is likened to the missionary who lives, suffers and dies for those he wants to minister to. This theory holds His death up as an example of meekness and humble suffering for others. However, it fails to accept that God must be propitiated before He can forgive sins.

(4) The Governmental Theory
This theory follows the same thought as all previous theories, teaching that Christ's death

was not propitiatory. It holds that, in Christ's death, God made an example of His hatred for sin. God punished Christ to maintain respect for His holy law. It teaches that God accepted the measure of suffering Christ endued as a substitute for our penalty. It also holds that Christ's death is an example of the death all will suffer who hold to their sin and do not repent. However, this view is inadequate when it comes to the Biblical interpretation of Christ's death, for it fails to understand the fundamental truth of His death in its propitiatory meaning.

(5) The Commercial Theory

This theory holds that sin violates the honor of God. Therefore God's honor requires Him to punish sin, while His love pleads for the sinner. The theory teaches that the ransom price was paid to Satan in an agreement between him and Christ in order to release all men who were Satan's prisoners. It holds that Christ purchased souls from Satan, and deceived him by entering his domain to loose the captives by resurrection. This theory neglects the holiness of God and misses the substitutionary aspect of Christ's death. Also it is false in the matter of the ransom price, for Christ paid nothing to Satan. It was God's holy Law and God's justice which demanded the ransom price.

(6) The Eradication Theory

Bancroft (p.113) mentions the "theory of Gradually Extirpated Depravity" which Strong deals with in "Systematic Theology". This theory holds that Christ in the incarnation took sinful human nature as Adam had after the fall, with all of its inborn corruption and depravity. By the power of the Holy Spirit, He restrained any manifestation of sin and completely purified it through suffering and death, thus eradicating original depravity and reuniting it to God. This theory denies the sinlessness of Christ, which would make His death of no avail for mankind.

Each of these theories are inadequate and have erroneous elements in them. They are the natural mind endeavoring to explain the unique death of Christ and thus fall short of the truth. Christ did die as a result of loyalty to the truth He taught and believed. He did die as an expression of the love of God. He did die to maintain the truth of divine government. He died to pay the ransom price for sin. But all these are only partial aspects of His death. They all miss the major purpose of His death which is atonement. To miss the atoning work of Christ's death is to miss the fundamental truth of the work of Christ.

c. Scriptural Views Concerning Christ's Death

Paul aptly summarizes the view of Christ's death when he says: "Christ died for our sins according to the Scriptures" (I Corinthians 15:3-4).

"Christ died" - this is the historical fact of the atonement.

"For our sins" - this is the doctrinal interpretation of the atonement.

His soul was made an offering for sin, or a sin-offering (Isaiah 53:5-3,10; II Corinthians 5:21; I Peter 2:24; 3:18). To understand this is to understand the atonement. We note a number of the most important scriptural facts concerning the unique death of Christ.

(1) The Death of Christ was part of God's Eternal Purpose
(Revelation 13:8; I Peter 1:18-20; Acts 2:22-23).

(2) The Death of Christ was foretold under the Law, Psalms and Prophets.
(Luke 24:27, 44-45; Matthew 5:17-18; 11:13)

(3) The Death of Christ was the chief purpose of the Incarnation.
(Mark 10:45; Hebrews 2:9,14; 9:26; I John 3:5; Matthew 20:28) He was born to be crucified.

The incarnation was not an end in itself but the means to an end.

(4) The Death of Christ is the major theme of the Gospel of Grace.
(I Corinthians 15:1-4; Romans 5:5-10, 12-21) Christ died for our sins. The death penalty was paid. This is God's good news to a sinner.

(5) The Death of Christ is prominent in the New Testament Writings.
(I Corinthians 2:2; 15:1-4; Galatians 1:4; 2:20; 6:14; Romans 5:6; I Thessalonians 4:14; Philippians 3:10; Ephesians 2:13; Colossians 1:14; I Timothy 2:6; I Peter 1:11-12; I John 3:1-4; Hebrews 9:26; Revelation 5:1-13) The last 3 days of our Lord's earthly life is said to occupy about one fifth of the contents of the four Gospels. Although His 3-1/2 years ministry is covered, the details of His death and the 3 days and 3 nights of Calvary are given the most detail. His death is mentioned about 175 times in the New Testament; that is, one out of every 53 verses mentions it. The apostles Peter, John and Paul are the major interpreters of the death of Christ.

(6) The Death of Christ is the burden of the Law and the Prophets.
(Luke 9:30-31; Revelation 5:8-12; Matthew 16:21-25) When Moses and Elijah, representing the Law and the Prophets, appeared on the Mount of Transfiguration, they spoke to Jesus about His coming decease. He was to be the Kinsman Redeemer of a lost race.

(7) The Death of Christ is essential to Christianity.
All other world religions are built upon the teachings of their founders, who are dead, or will die. Christianity alone is built upon the death and **resurrection** of Jesus Christ, its founder. As the rod of Aaron budded to life, attesting to the fact that he was God's ordained and anointed High Priest, so the resurrection of Christ from the dead attests to His divine priesthood. Without the death of Christ, Christianity is reduced to the level of other religions.

(8) The Death of Christ is essential to our Salvation. (John 3:14-15; 12:24; Romans 3:25-26; Matthew 16:21; Mark 8:31; Luke 9:22; 17:25; Acts 17:3; I Peter 3:18; Matthew 20:28; 26:28; Luke 22:19; I Timothy 2:6; II Corinthians 5:14; I Peter 2:24; Hebrews 8:28; I John 3:5) It was necessary that Christ die, for God cannot pardon sinners unless sin is dealt with. In order for God to pardon the sinner and remain consistent with His holiness Christ must pay sin's penalty. The wages of sin is death.

(9) The Death of Christ was a Voluntary Act. (John 10:17-18; Matthew 26:53-54; Isaiah 53:12) The cross was His deliberate choice, not His fate. He offered Himself as a freewill or "voluntary offering" as shadowed forth in the voluntary burnt, meal and peace offerings in Leviticus 1-3. His seeming tragedy was God's triumph.

(10) The Death of Christ was an Atoning Sacrifice.

The following words relative to Christ's atoning death will be dealt with more fully under the doctrinal aspect of the atonement, but they are noted here as part of the atoning death of Christ.

   (a) A Redemption (Titus 2:14).

   (b) A Ransom (Matthew 20:28; Mark 10:45).

   (c) A Substitution (Romans 5:5-10; II Corinthians 5:18).

   (d) A Reconciliation (Romans 5:10; Hebrews 2:17).

   (e) A Propitiation (Romans 3:25-26; I John 2:1-2).

   (f) An Atonement (Leviticus 16:16-20).

(11) The Death of Christ was a necessary Penalty for Sin.
(Isaiah 53:4,6; Micah 5:1-3) Jesus suffered at the hands of a righteous and holy God. I
pleased the Lord to bruise His Son. Jesus was smitten with the rod of God for our sins. The
death penalty which Christ suffered satisfies the justice and law of God.

(a) It satisfied the Justice of God.

State criminals have to be penalized for their crimes. Man sinned against God's
government. Divine justice can be satisfied only when the penalty has been executed on
the criminal.

(b) It satisfied the outraged holiness of God. God is holy, therefore sin must be judged. Calvary
is a revelation of the holiness of God, and His holy hatred against sin.

(c) It satisfied the violated Law of God. The wages of sin is the death penalty. Any violation o
the law is worthy of death (Genesis 2:17; Romans 6:23; Ezekiel 18:4,20). Once death ha:
been executed, the Law can do no more. Its claims have been satisfied.

Thus His death was necessary. It vindicated God's holiness, upheld His justice, and satisfied
the demands of His broken law.

(12) The Death of Christ was a manifestation of Divine Love.
(John 3:16; I John 3:16; Romans 5:8; Psalm 85:10) Holiness hates sin, and deals with it. Go
is love and loves the sinner, and thus died for him. God could not manifest love at the
expense of holiness, nor save the sinner without judging sin. The death of Christ then is a
manifestation of both holiness and love (John 15:13; I Peter 2:21; I John 4:9-10).

(13) The Death of Christ was for the Whole World.
(John 1:29; 3:16; Isaiah 53:6; I Timothy 3:5-6; I John 2:2)

(a) Christ died for the whole world (John 3:16; Romans 8:32; Titus 2:14; I Corinthians 15:22
45; John 1:29,36).

(b) Christ died for the Church, His Bride (Ephesians 5:26-27; I Timothy 4:10).

(c) Christ died for the unjust (I Peter 3:18); for the sinner (Romans 5:8); for the ungodly
(Romans 5:6). He tasted death for every man (Hebrews 2:9).

(d) Christ died for the elect out of every kindred, tongue, tribe and nation (Revelation 5:9;
Timothy 2:6; Matthew 20:28).

(14) The Death of Christ was Incomparable to all other Deaths
Because of the uniqueness of Christ's death it makes His death incomparable with all the
deaths of mankind. All others die for their own sin. Jesus alone died for the sins of others
His death was attended by supernatural signs. No other man has ever had his death with
signs as Jesus had (Matthew 27:51-53).

(15) The Death of Christ is of Infinite and Eternal Value.
Because of who Jesus is and what He was to accomplish in His life and death, the death o
Christ is of infinite and eternal value. Jesus was God incarnate; the eternal Son of God and i
is this which makes His death of eternal and therefore infinite value. His death conquered
all other deaths.

(16) The Death of Christ was an Accomplishment, not an Accident.
Jesus Himself spoke of the things that He should "accomplish" at Jerusalem (Luke 9:31; 12:50; 18:31; 22:37; John 19:28). His death was neither an after-thought nor an accident but a divine accomplishment.

(17) The Death of Christ was the Conquest of Satan's Kingdom.
(Colossians 2:15; Hebrews 2:14-16; John 12:31-32) Satan held the power of sin, sickness, disease and death, as well as control over his own kingdom of principalities, powers and wicked spirits of this world system. At Christ's death, He disarmed the princes and powers of Satan, stripping Satan of the keys of death and hell. He turned what seemed to be the greatest defeat into the greatest victory. He spoiled principalities and powers, making a show of them openly, and triumphed over all in the cross. The death of Christ was the conquest of the whole of Satan's realm.

(18) The Death of Christ was both Retroactive and Retrospective.
Christ's death looked backward to those under the Old Covenant who had faith for redemption, and also looked forward to those under the New Covenant who would have faith for redemption. Christ died for all the faithful of both Old and New Testament eras. The Old Testament saints are saved by faith looking forward to Calvary while the New Testament saints are saved by faith looking backward to Calvary, as well as upward to Jesus in heaven (Hebrews 9:11-14; Romans 3:25).

(19) The Death of Christ was Complete and Final.
(Hebrews 10:12; Ephesians 5:2; I Thessalonians 5:10; John 19:30; Matthew 20:28; Hebrews 9:25-28)

Christ's death took place once, and "once-for-all". It was a finished and complete work. There is no need of continual sacrifices, as were offered under the Law. Christ sat down after He offered an acceptable and perfect sacrifice, for it is a finished work (Hebrews 10:10-18).

(20) The Death of Christ became the Foundation of Eternal Worship.
(Revelation 5:9-13) The revelation of the redeemed gathered around the throne, out of every kindred, tongue, tribe and nation, shows that all worship to the Father God is through The Lamb. This designation of the Savior is used about 24 times in Revelation. He is eternally "The Lamb" and the worship of the saints in eternity will always pass through him. The atonement will be eternally fresh, and the redeemed of earth will never forget the cost of their eternal salvation.

The testimony of the Scriptures is overwhelming as we consider the importance and meaning of Christ's death. It indeed makes His death unique, incomparable, infinite and of eternal value.

Herbert Lockyer, in "All the Doctrines of the Bible" (p.50) shows how Christ viewed His own death, and we adapt his comments here as a fitting summary of the importance of Christ's death.

(21) Christ's View of His Own Death.

    (a) He predicted the fact and manner of His own death (Matthew 9:15; 16:21; 17:22,23; 20:18, 19; 21:33-39; Luke 9:22; 18:31-33).

    (b) He taught that His death had a universal significance (John 3:16; 12:32-33).

    (c) He affirmed that His death had a definite bearing upon the spirit-world (John 12:31).

    (d) He linked His incarnation and crucifixion together (John 12:27).

    (e) He declared that His death was vicarious and substitutionary. (Matthew 26:28; Mark 10:45; Luke 22:19; I Corinthians 5:21; Galatians 2:20).

(f) He died by His own volition. His life was not taken, but given (Matthew 27:50; John 10:18).

(g) He prayed that His death would glorify God (John 12:27-28; 13:31; 17:1).

Christ alone of all men was able to view and understand the significance of His own death. He often spoke of "His hour" in which He would fully accomplish the purpose of the Father's will in His incarnation (John 2:4; 7:6; 8:20; 17:1). He knew He "ought to suffer" these things (Luke 24: 25-27). He established the Lord's Table with the bread and wine as the covenant symbols of His atoning death, and every time a believer has the communion, he is "showing forth the Lord's death till He come" (Matthew 26:26-28; I Corinthians 11:23-32; Luke 22:19-20).

d. Tasting Death for Every Man
The writer to the Hebrews says that Christ "tasted death for every man" (Hebrews 2:9-10). The Prophet Isaiah tells us that the Messiah "made His grave with the wicked and with the rich in His death" (Isaiah 53:9). The Hebrew word "death" has the thought of plurality and the marginal reading in the Authorized Version reads "with the rich in His deaths". The Scripture does reveal or speak of three aspects of death as pertaining to man; spiritual, physical and eternal death. Death is not annihilation or a state of sleep or non-existence. It is a state of separation as the following definitions show.

(1) Spiritual Death
Adam died spiritually the moment he sinned (Genesis 2:17). Mankind is spiritually dead in trespasses and sins. That is, man's spirit is separated from God in this sinful state. This is referring to the spirit and soul being cut off from God (Ephesians 2:1-6).

(2) Physical Death
Physical death has to do with the body. Adam died physically 930 years after his spiritual death (Genesis 2:17). Thus God said "In dying thou shalt die". Physical death has to do with the separation of the spirit and soul from the body.

(3) Eternal Death
Eternal death has to do with the spirit and soul being separated from God eternally because of unregeneracy. This is spoken of as being "the second death". When a sinner rejects Christ, the only hope of eternal life, he can only suffer eternal death. This second death is eternal separation from God. It is the final Hell (Revelation 20:11-15).

Christ "tasted" each of these deaths for us. When He was made sin He experienced spiritual death (II Corinthians 5:21). When He suffered the scourging and crucifixion and died, He suffered the scourging and crucifixion and the agonies of physical death. His head, hands, side and feet were pierced for our sin. He suffered the curse of the broken Law (Galatians 3:13). No physical agony can compare with the sufferings and agonies of a crucified man. None can deny the reality of His death.

When He was forsaken of the Father God, He "tasted" the agonies of the damned; He "tasted" for a short while that which those who experience the second or eternal death will suffer. To be forsaken of God is hell indeed. This suffering exceeded all other.

Jesus indeed tasted death for every man. He experienced the three aspects of death that we might have eternal life. He says of Himself that "I am He that liveth and was dead, but behold I am alive for ever more" (Revelation 1:18). How can any despise such a miraculous death?

e. The Crucifixion and the Atonement
In concluding our thoughts on the death of Christ, it is important to understand the difference between the crucifixion and the atonement. In the atoning work of Christ there is that which is God-ward, and that which is man-ward. There is something which is historical; there is something which is doctrinal. There is that which is physical and there is that which is spiritual. The following columns will show the inter-relatedness and yet the differences and distinction between the crucifixion and the atonement.

Robert Clarke in "The Christ of God" (p.115) makes this distinction which we adapt and set out here in contrast and comparison.

THE CRUCIFIXION	THE ATONEMENT
The Christ after the flesh	The Christ after the spirit
What man did to Christ	What God did in Christ
Physical and mental	Spiritual
Temporal	Eternal
The Act of Man	The Work of God
The sin and hatred of Satan	The holiness and love of God
Took place in time	Pertains to eternity
Manward aspect of the cross	Godward aspect of the cross
Historical	Doctrinal
The Gospels - external	The Epistles - internal
The supreme crime of the ages	The masterpiece of the ages

Thus in the crucifixion and the atoning work of Christ on the cross, God bridged the great gulf between Himself and man which had been brought by sin.

As expressed by the writer in a verse of a hymn:

"Could all the world-wide suffering compare with that of thine,
Forsaken by the Father, as 'sin' in wrath divine,
When deaths untold, unnumbered,
    upon that cross you died,
And Paradise was opened — my Jesus crucified?"

2. His Exodus

The word "exodus" means "a going out" or "departure" and it is used in connection with Christ's death, when His spirit departed from His body and went to be with the Father God. On the Mount of Transfiguration, Moses and Elijah spoke to Jesus about His 'decease'', that is, His exodus, which He should accomplish at Jerusalem (Luke 9:30-31). The Apostle Peter also spoke of his own decease (or exodus) which he knew he was soon to experience (II Peter 1:13-15). The putting off of the human body in death was the putting off of the earthly tabernacle. Thus with the death of Jesus Christ, a period of 3 days and 3 nights elapsed before His bodily resurrection, or before He again put on His tabernacle in resurrection. What took place in this period of His exodus or departure has been a matter of much enquiry.

a. Three Days and Three Nights

Jesus expressly said that He would be in the heart of the earth for a period of 3 days and 3 nights, thus fulfilling the sign of the prophet Jonah when he was 3 days and 3 nights in the heart of the great fish (Matthew 12:39-40; Jonah 3:3; Mark 8:31; John 2:18-21; Matthew 27:63; Mark 14:58; 15:29; Ephesians 4:8-10).

This period of 3 days relative to the death and burial of Christ was shadowed forth in Old Testament times as a consideration of these Scriptures show. (Joshua 1:11; 2:16-22; 9:16; Esther 4:16; Jonah 1:17; Numbers 10:33; Genesis 22:1-14; Exodus 3:18; 10:22; 15:26; Genesis 40:12-19).

These 3 days act as a bridge between Christ's crucifixion and His resurrection.

b. Descent and Ascent

As to the body of Jesus being in Joseph's new tomb for 3 days and 3 nights, all are generally agreed. But what happened to His spirit during this time is a matter of controversy. Three main views are held and these are considered in brief.

(1) His Descent to Hades

This view teaches that Christ descended to Hell (Greek: Hades) or Sheol (Hebrew) and preached to the spirits in prison during the 3 days that His body was in the tomb. At either the beginning or end of these 3 days, He stripped Satan of the keys of death and Hades and led the host of captive saints up to heaven. This view holds that Christ transferred Paradise, the section in which all the righteous dead of Old Testament times were imprisoned, to the third heaven. Those who hold this view base it on a misunderstanding and therefore a misinterpretation of the following Scriptures (I Peter 3:18-22; 4:6; Ephesians 4:8-10).

However, a proper understanding of these passages show that it was the Spirit of Christ preaching through Noah while the Ark was in preparation, not a preaching going on during the 3 days and 3 nights of Calvary's experience. It was in the time of Noah that 8 souls were saved and the rest perished with water. There is no second chance or Gospel preaching in Hades. The "time element" is the key to a proper interpretation of these passages.

(2) His Ascent to Heaven

This view teaches that Christ ascended to His Father and was with the Father during the 3 days and nights of Calvary. He took the repentant thief with Him to Paradise, which is the third heaven. At the end of the 3 days His spirit returned to earth and He experienced the resurrection of His incorruptible body. Then after 40 days with the disciples, He ascended bodily to heaven to begin His High Priestly intercessory ministry. This view is based upon the following passages of Scripture (Luke 23:46; II Corinthians 12:1-4; John 13:36; 14:1-6). It holds that the Old Testament saints went to heaven at death; not a righteous section of Hell or Hades. When interpreting Christ leading "captivity captive" (Ephesians 4:8-10) it is said that this refers to sin, sickness and death, which are the things which held the human race captive to Satan. It was this captivity that Christ led captive. This view seems to be far nearer the teaching of Scripture than the previous.

(3) His Ascent and Descent

The third view is between the previous two views. It teaches that Christ did go to heaven, or Paradise, and was with the Father during the 3 days and nights of Calvary. It rejects the teaching that Christ preached during this time to the spirits in prison. However, it holds that the spirits of the Old Testament righteous were in a division of Hades and were released by Christ either at the beginning or close of the 3 days period, and taken to the the third heaven which is Paradise. After this, Christ descended to the tomb and His physical resurrection took place.

The following outline of Scriptures is used to support this theory and it appears to be the most consistent.

    (a) Jesus promised the repentant thief that he would be with Him in Paradise that day (Luke 23:39-43). Paradise is spoken of as being up, being the third heaven (II Corinthians 12:1-4). Paradise has the Tree of Eternal Life (Revelation 2:7; 22:2). These passages show that Paradise could not be Sheol or Hades, nor was the Tree of Life ever in Hell.

    (b) At His death, Jesus committed His spirit to the Father God (Luke 23:46).

    (c) Jesus, before His death, clearly told the disciples that He was going "unto the Father" not to Hades (John 13:1,36; 14:1-6,28; 16:5,16-22; 17:11,13). These references very clearly show that Jesus went to be with the Father.

    (d) The Scriptures also say that Christ descended into the lower parts, or the lower down divisions of the earth and then led captivity captive (Ephesians 4:8-10). In ancient times, victorious kings, after returning from the battle, led their captives in a triumphant march into the city and then threw out as gifts the spoils of the battle to the citizens. So Christ led captivity captive after His triumphant victory of the cross and gave gifts to men (Colossians 2:14; Hebrews 2:9-15). Two aspects of "leading captivity captive" are seen in the following:

DOCTRINE OF THE ATONEMENT

(i) Christ conquered Satan, and spoiled principalities and powers. He conquered sin, sickness, disease, the curse, demons and death, all of which hold man captive. Thus Christ led this "captivity captive" (Judges 5:12; Job 42:10; Psalm 68:18; 126:1).

(ii) Christ also led "a host of captives" to heaven. Various translations read as follows:

"He re-ascended on high: He led captive a host of captives" (Weymouth).

"He led a host of captives" (Goodspeed)

"He led captivity captive, He led a train of vanquished foes" (Amplified).

The Old Testament tells us that the saints were "gathered to their people" when they died (Genesis 25:8; 35:27-29; 49:29,33). Old Testament saints knew that they would be delivered from Sheol, the place of departed spirits (Genesis 37:35; Psalm 49:14-15; Hosea 13:14).

Jesus also knew that His soul would not be left in Hades (Psalm 16:8-11; Acts 2:29-31). It is evident that because of the work of the cross, all "the spirits of just men made perfect" are in the Heavenly Zion, the Heavenly Jerusalem (Hebrews 12:22-24; Luke 16:19-31). Read also I Samuel 28:3-20 in connection with these comments, for Samuel was "brought up" from his place of rest when God intervened to judge King Saul for seeking a woman who had a familiar spirit.

In summary, it is seen that the Lord Jesus, at His death, ascended in spirit to the Father and was with the Father during the 3 days and nights that His body lay in the tomb. The spirit of the repentant thief, as well as the spirits of the Old Testament saints who died in faith, and were waiting in Sheol, were taken to heaven to be with the Father also. This was the triumphant entry of the King of Glory into the gates of the heavenly Jerusalem with a host of captives (Psalm 24). At the close of the 3 days and nights, Jesus returned to earth by the power of the Holy Spirit and re-entered His incorruptible body. From this point on we see the Lord Jesus appearing to His own disciples in His resurrected and glorified body.

Thus the 3 days and nights that His body lay in the tomb covers the period of His exodus between His death and resurrection, giving us insight as to what took place in this period of time.

3. His Resurrection

The resurrection of Christ is one of the great fundamental doctrines of the Christian faith. There are about 104 references to the resurrection of Christ in the New Testament. Many believe in the death of Christ, yet reject His resurrection, yet both of these facts are declared by the same writers (Acts 26:8).

Christ was "delivered for our offences and raised for our justification" (Romans 4:25). The death and resurrection of Christ should never be separated for one preceded the other, and the one completes the other. A balanced Gospel always includes His saving death and His saving resurrection life. We are saved first by His death, and then we are saved by His life (Romans 5:10). The resurrection was the foundation for Apostolic preaching and practically every sermon in the Book of Acts refers to it. The Apostle Peter speaks much of it (Acts 1:21-22; 2:24,32; 3:15; 4:10,33; 5:30). The Apostle Paul also speaks of it much (Acts 13:30,34; 17:31; Philippians 3:21; Acts 17:18; 23:6). The great resurrection chapter is found in the Epistle to the Corinthians (I Corinthians 15).

The resurrection of Jesus Christ took place after 3 days and 3 nights. His body saw no corruption. God raised Jesus from the dead, by the power of the Holy Spirit, immortal and incorruptible, to live in the power of an endless life (Hebrews 7:16). The resurrection of Jesus Christ was God's sign and seal of an accepted atonement of His only begotten Son (Romans 1:4; Acts 3:13-15; Mark 16:16; I Corinthians 15:3-4). The resurrection of Christ answers the age-long question of Job — "If a man die, shall he live again?" (Job 14:14).

a. The Necessity of His Resurrection

(1) The Old Testament Prophets Foretold His Resurrection.
It was necessary that Christ be raised from the dead in order to fulfil the Old Testament prophecies concerning it. His resurrection, as well as His birth, life, ministry and death had been foretold both in type and prophecy.

(a) In Type

(i) Isaac, the only begotten son of Abraham was raised from the dead after 3 day journey to Mt. Moriah. This was resurrection in a figure, or type (Genesis 22 with Hebrews 11:16).

(ii) Jonah was raised from the dead, typically, after 3 days and nights in the heart of the fish, and Christ used this sign to shadow forth His own resurrection after 3 days and nights (Jonah 1:17 with Matthew 12:39-40). (Read also Exodus 3:14-16 with Matthew 22:31-32; Romans 4:17-25).

(b) In Prophecy
The Psalms and the Prophets clearly foretold Christ's resurrection (Psalm 16:8-11; 21: Psalm 110:1; Psalm 89; Psalm 72; Genesis 3:15; Isaiah 53:10-12). The Scriptures tell th God would not suffer His Holy One to see corruption, but would raise Him up to sit upo the throne as His King in Zion, begotten by the resurrection of the dead (Acts 3:29-36 Christ's bodily resurrection was in a unique sense the day He was begotten (Psalm 2 with Acts 13:31-37).

(2) The Character of Christ necessitated His Resurrection.
Because Jesus Christ was the holy and sinless one, and death really had no power over Him, was not possible that death should hold Him (Acts 2:24). God's Holy One would not se corruption which is always the result of sin (Psalm 16:10).

He voluntarily laid down His life; it was not taken from Him (John 10:15-18). Sin and deat could lay no claim to Him because He was sinless, uncorrupted and therefore incorruptibl Because of His voluntary sacrifice in taking our sins and our death penalty upon Himself, necessitated that the Holy One be justified. The resurrection of Christ was God's justifica tion of His Son (I Timothy 3:16). His resurrection was necessary because of who He was an what He had done.

(3) Christ Foretold His own Resurrection.
It was necessary that Christ be raised from the dead in order to confirm the truthfulness of Hi own statements, for He Himself declared that He would arise from the dead.

(a) He spake of His body being a temple destroyed, as in death, and then raised up again i resurrection after 3 days and nights (John 2:18-22). The disciples did not understan this until after His resurrection took place.

(b) He used the sign of Jonah as a sign of His resurrection after 3 days and nights. As Jona came out of the mouth of the fish, so Christ would come forth from the mouth of th tomb (Matthew 12:39-40).

(c) He also said that He would lay down His life in death and then take it again i resurrection as His Father had commanded Him to do (John 10:15-18).

(d) He also clearly foretold His death and resurrection to His disciples (Matthew 16:21 17:22-23; 27:62-64; Mark 8:31; 10:45).

The resurrection proved that Christ was not a liar or imposter, but the very truth of God, for no man could naturally foretell His exact death and time of resurrection (Matthew 27:62-66). He who was "the resurrection and the life" and raised others from the dead said He had power to raise Himself from the dead (Matthew 9:18-26; Luke 7:11-18; John 11:1-44; 10:15-18).

(4) Redemption's Plan necessitated the Resurrection
The resurrection of Christ was absolutely necessary in order to complete the redemptive work of Christ. If Christ is not raised from the dead, then all are yet in their sins (I Corinthians 15:16-20). His death alone does not save men. It is His death and His resurrection that brings salvation to mankind (Romans 5:8-10). If He was to be our Redeemer then He must conquer sin, sickness, disease and death. Death could only be conquered by resurrection (Hebrews 2:9-14). The redemptive plan of God for the fallen race necessitated the resurrection of Christ. He is the conqueror of death and now has the keys of death and hell (Revelation 1:18; Hosea 13:14; Isaiah 26:19). In the redemptive plan we see the eternal Godhead involved in Christ's bodily resurrection.

(a) He was raised from the dead by the glory of the Father (Ephesians 1:19-20; Romans 6:1-4).

(b) He was given power and commandment by the Father to lay down His life and to take it again (John 10:15-18).

(c) He was raised from the dead by the power of the Holy Spirit (Romans 8:11). The Holy Spirit is the Spirit of the resurrection.

b. False Theories Concerning His Resurrection
The bodily resurrection of Christ is one of the most documented facts in the New Testament Gospels and most often confirmed in the epistles. The four Gospels all give account of the resurrection. The sermons in the Book of Acts all speak of the resurrection. The epistles continually refer to this fact. The whole of Christianity is built upon the historical fact of the resurrection of its founder. Following are some of the false theories concerning the resurrection story.

(1) The Swoon Theory
This theory holds that Christ fainted on the cross, and then, in the coolness of the grave regained consciousness. It holds that the disciples believed He was dead, but He was not.

(2) The Theft Theory
This theory teaches that the disciples came and stole the body of Jesus and thus claimed a resurrection story. However, neither foes nor friends could produce the body (Matthew 27:62-66; 28:11-15).

(3) The Hallucination Theory
This theory holds that the disciples imagined that they saw Jesus and thus believed a resurrection took place. However, the disciples were very slow to believe even when they did see Jesus (Luke 24:11,25; John 20:25).

(4) The Ghost Theory
This theory teaches that Christ did not really physically arise from the dead, but that His spirit appeared to the disciples. But Jesus ate and drank with His disciples which is something a spirit does not do (Luke 24:36-43).

(5) The Fraud Theory
This theory holds that the resurrection story was a fabrication of the forlorn disciples, and that it was a deliberate imposture. Would the disciples live and die for such a hoax and at the same time purport to be preachers of the truth of God? (Acts 5:41; 7:56; II Corinthians 11:23-27).

(6) The Myth Theory

This theory holds that the story of the resurrection began like any myths do until it came to be accepted as a fact. However, the evidences of the resurrection refute any such mythical origin.

The account of the resurrection of Jesus is too well documented by honest witnesses to even consider as factual, any of these theories. How could a fainting Christ deceive His disciples that He had never died, and how could He escape from a sealed tomb? Why would the disciples be willing to live and die for a deliberate lie, or a myth, and base all their hopes of eternal salvation upon a fraudulent story? These theories are the result of the sin of unbelief in the resurrection power of God.

c. The Fact of His Resurrection

(1) Witnesses of the Resurrected Christ

Although there were no exact witnesses of the resurrection, there were numerous witnesses of the resurrected Christ. The post-resurrection appearances of Christ took place at different times and to different persons.

(a) Post-Resurrection Appearances

(i)   The two messengers in the tomb (Mark 16:6; Matthew 28:6; Hebrews 2:2; I Timothy 3:15-16).
(ii)   To Mary Magdalene (Mark 16:9; John 20: 11-18).
(iii)   To other women who told the disciples (Mark 16:1-3; Luke 23:54-56; 24:1; Matthew 28:9).
(iv)   To Peter (Mark 16:7; Luke 24:34; I Corinthians 15:5).
(v)   To two disciples on the Emmaus Road (Mark 16:12-13; Luke 24:16-24,34).
(vi)   To ten disciples, Thomas being absent (Luke 24:33,36-48; John 20:19-24; Acts 1:23-26).

(vii)   To eleven disciples, Thomas now present (John 20:25-28).
(viii) To seven disciples at Galilee (John 21:1-24).
(ix)   To eleven disciples at a mountain in Galilee (Matthew 28:16-17).
(x)   To over 500 brethren (I Corinthians 15:6).
(xi)   To James (I Corinthians 15:7).
(xii)   To disciples at Bethany at the Mount of Ascension (Luke 24:49-50; Acts 1:3-5; Mark 16:9).

These disciples saw His body, ate and drank with Him, and beheld the wounds in His hands, feet and side (John 20:27; Luke 24:37-39). They handled Him as the Word of Life (I John 1:1-3).

(b) Post-Ascension Appearances

(i) To Stephen at his martyrdom (Acts 7:54).

(ii) To Paul (Acts 9:1-7; 22:9; 26:16-18; I Corinthians 15:8; Galatians 1:11-18).

(iii) To John (Revelation 1:7,10-16).

The witness of the disciples concerning the resurrected Christ is full and complete. It would be incredible to say that all of these hundreds of witnesses were liars who concocted the resurrection story at the risk of their own lives, and did so without any contradiction. Their testimony and evidences would stand up in any court of enquiry today.

(2) Infallible Proofs of His Resurrection
Besides the testimonies of the witnesses of Christ's resurrection, there are other irrefutable evidences to this stupendous miracle. They are spoken of by Luke as being "infallible proofs" (Acts 1:3). None can account for these evidences apart from the fact of Christ's resurrection. Josh McDowell, in "Evidence that demands a Verdict" (pp.185-270) lists a number of evidences, several of which we mention here.

(a) The Empty Tomb
(Matthew 27:57-60; Mark 15:42-45; Luke 23:50-53; John 19:38-41). Jesus' body was actually placed in Joseph's tomb in a garden after being wrapped in spices. When his friends came to the tomb on the first day of the week, it was empty. The disciples were as surprised as anyone. Such would not be the case if any of them had stolen the body, as the soldiers were bribed to say. Only the resurrection explains the empty tomb.

(b) The Roman Seal
The tomb was sealed with the official Roman seal, thus making the body of Jesus Roman property. For any one to touch or attempt to break the seal of Rome and to steal the body of Jesus was to come under the danger of death. None dare tamper with the seal of Rome. The seal was a very important sign of ownership in all nations of antiquity. It was the Angel of the Lord who broke the seal on the tomb and rolled the stone away, not some fearful disciples.

(c) The Rolled-Away Stone
The tomb was closed by a stone door. Even the women, in their innocency, when they went to wrap the body in more spices, wondered who would roll away the stone. However, when they arrived at the garden tomb, the stone had already been rolled away. The stone was rolled away, not to let the risen Lord out, but to let the disciples in. The rolled away stone was another resurrection evidence.

(d) The Surprised Guard
The Temple Guard was appointed to watch the sealed tomb for the 3 days. This was due to the fear that the disciples would steal away the body of Jesus and propagate a false resurrection story. The guard was surprized and shocked by the earthquake and the Angel of the Lord who rolled the stone away and sat on it. Thus the story that was concocted by the religious leaders for the guards to tell was false and ironical. For, if, as they were taught to say, the disciples came and stole the body of Jesus away while they were asleep, the guard was self condemned. Sleeping on duty as Punishable by death. Also, if they were asleep, how did they know for sure that the disciples stole away the body? And why pay the guards large sums of money if the resurrection story was a hoax? The guards knew that something unnatural happened, and no amount of money or lies could ever alter that fact.

(e) The Missing Body
As far as the body of Jesus was concerned, there are several things worthy of consideration. The disciples were Jews and very much bound to the Laws of God, moral, civil and ceremonial. One of the ceremonial laws concerned the touching of dead bodies or bones. Any who did so were ceremonially defiled (Numbers 19:11-22). The disciples would have had to fulfil the ceremonial laws for handling the dead body of Jesus.

But far greater than this was the disappearance of the body of Jesus. The disciples were fearful of all the events relative to the crucifixion. How could they muster up enough courage to break the sealed tomb, overpower the Temple Guard, and then steal the mangled body of Jesus? What would they do with the body if they did steal it but bury it in some other place? The disciples themselves were amazed at the disappearance of the body of Jesus. They themselves did not understand nor yet believe His prophecied resurrection. His body was not stolen by the disciples but raised by God from the dead and neither friends nor foes could produce it. The body of Jesus was preserved incorruptible by the power of God. All other human bodies are corrupted in death (Acts 2:24-32).

(f) The Empty Grave Clothes

One of the most startling and convincing evidences of the resurrection was the empty grave clothes of Jesus. The body of Jesus had been wrapped in spices in the linen grave-clothes. Peter and John went into the tomb and saw the graveclothes still there, but not His body. The peculiar thing was that the napkin which had been around His head was folded in a place by itself. The clothes that had been around His body were lying in their place, apparently in the cacoon shape, still unwrapped. Who would be able to take the body out of the clothes? And why leave the clothes? The miracle of the resurrection is the answer to the empty graveclothes. It is another of those "infallible proofs" (Acts 1:3).

(g) The Transformed Disciples

Added to all the previous evidences we have the amazing transformation of the fearful disciples to bold and courageous men. The Book of Acts reveals that the resurrection of Jesus was the foundation and center of every sermon preached in Acts. His death and His resurrection were like two sides of the one coin and became the foundation of the Gospel.

It is incredible to think that these disciples were willing to live and die to maintain a deliberate lie if the resurrection were not a fact. The disciples hardly believed, let alone understood the resurrection. Hence it was most unlikely that they would concoct a lie and die as martyrs for it (Luke 24:11; John 20:24). Any court would accept such valid witness of two or three, but here we have over five hundred witnesses. It was the fact of the resurrection which changed the timid, fearful and unbelieving disciples into bold men.

(h) The Christian Church

The true Christian Church itself is an evidence of the resurrected Christ. Christianity is the only religion founded on a resurrected Man. The resurrection is unique to Christianity. All other religions are founded on dead men (Acts 2:24,32; 3:15,26; 4:10; 13:29-37; 17:31; Romans 4:24-25; 6:4,9; 7:4; 8:11; 10:9; I Corinthians 6:14; II Corinthians 4:14; Galatians 1:1; Ephesians 1:20; Colossians 2:12; II Thessalonians 1:10; II Timothy 2:8; I Peter 1:21).

(i) The Lord's Day

Another evidence of the resurrection is the Lord's Day, celebrated since the early Church as the day of the resurrection (Acts 20:7; I Corinthians 16:2; Revelation 1:10; Matthew 28:1-2). No Jew would change the Sabbath Day and make the first day of the week the day of special worship. It was the resurrection of Christ that changed the calender for the whole world.

(j) The New Testament Books

There would be no New Testament books apart from the resurrection of Christ. The Gospels record the historical evidences of His birth, life, ministry, death and resurrection, while the epistles interpret the same. How incomplete the New Testament would be if we had books that recorded only His death but not His resurrection. Every New Testament book speaks of the doctrine of resurrection, and thus becomes another evidence of its truth.

It is worthy to note also that the last the world saw of Jesus was on a cross, that is, His death. Only chosen witnesses ever saw Him alive, that is, in resurrection life (Acts 10:39-41). Truly there are many "infallible proofs" of the risen Lord and Christ (Acts 1:3; I Corinthians 15:1-4; Revelation 1:17-18).

d. The Nature of Christ's Resurrection Body

A brief consideration of the body of Jesus in His resurrection is profitable because His resurrection body is the sample of what the resurrected bodies of all believers will be like (Philippians 3:21). The resurrection of Jesus was the resurrection and glorification of His actual physical body which had been virgin-born, crucified and buried (Luke 24:39; John 21:1-5). It was:

(1) A body of flesh and bone, not flesh and blood (Luke 24:39; I Corinthians 15:50).

(2) A spiritual body, no longer a natural body (I Corinthians 15:42-54).

(3) A heavenly body, no longer an earthly body (I Corinthians 15:44-47).

(4) A glorified body, no longer veiling the glory inside His flesh (Matthew 17:1-9; Revelation 1:10-16).

(5) An immortal body, no longer able to die but to live in the power of an endless life (Hebrews 7:16).

(6) A powerful body, no longer subject to sinless infirmities of hunger, thirst, weariness. It could pass through doors, vanish and appear at will (John 20:19; Luke 24:31,51; Acts 1:9).

(7) A real and actual body, not a phantom appearance, but the same virgin-born, crucified, buried and now resurrected body. The blessed nail-prints are eternally in this glorified body (John 20:19-25; I John 1:1-3).

(8) A firstfruit and sample body of the coming harvest of resurrection bodies of the saints (I Corinthians 15:20-23,35-38).

(9) An incorruptible body, because of its sinlessness (Acts 2:31-32; 13:34-37; Psalm 16:8-11).

(10) An ascending and returning body. He will so come in like manner the second time as He ascended to heaven; that is, visibly, personally, actually and bodily (Acts 1:10-11; Revelation 1:7; Philippians 3:21).

e. Divine Reasons for the Resurrection

The importance and significance of the resurrection of Christ cannot be over-estimated for it is indeed the cornerstone of the Christian faith. Paul argued that all faith and preaching is vain and the disciples were false witnesses if Christ is not risen. He also said that we are yet in our sins and there is no hope for the dead if there is no resurrection (I Corinthians 15). The resurrection of Christ is the foundational confession unto salvation for all who would be saved (Romans 10:9-10).

(1) God raised Him from the dead because of His perfect obedience to His will (Philippians 2:9).

(2) God raised Him from the dead in order to justify Him (I Timothy 3:15-16).

(3) God raised Him to attest to His deity (Romans 1:4).

(4) God raised Him from the dead for our justification (Romans 4:25).

(5) God raised Him from the dead to be the saving life of all who believe (Romans 5:8-10).

(6) God raised Him from the dead to fulfil the sign of the 3 days concerning Jonah and the temple (Matthew 12:38-40; John 2:18-22).

(7) God raised Him to be a Prince and a Savior (Acts 5:31).

(8) God raised Him from the dead to be Head of the Church (Ephesians 1:19-23).

(9) God raised Him to be the Baptizer in the Holy Spirit (John 1:33; Acts 2:32-33).

(10) God raised Him to be a great High Priest (I Timothy 2:5-6; Hebrews 8:1-4).

(11) God raised Him to be our Advocate and Intercessor (Hebrews 7:26-28; I John 2:1-2; Romans 8:34).

(12) God raised Him to show Him as the bruiser of the serpent's head (Genesis 3:15; Romans 5:11-21; Ephesians 1:19-20; Hebrews 2:9-14; Romans 16:20).

(13) God raised Him from the dead as a seal to His perfect atoning sacrificial death and work (Romans 1:4; 4:25).

(14) God raised Him to be the dispenser of gifts to men for the church (Ephesians 4:8-16; I Corinthians 12:1-12; Romans 12:1-6).

(15) God raised Him as the guarantee of all coming resurrections (Romans 8:11; John 5:28-29; I Corinthians 15:20-23; II Corinthians 4:4; I Thessalonians 4:15-18; I Corinthians 15:51-57). He is the sheaf of firstfruits of the coming harvest.

(16) God raised Him to be the appointed Judge of all mankind (John 5:30; Acts 10:42; 17:31).

(17) God raised Him to be the crowning glory of the work of redemption. By one man came death and by one man came the resurrection of the dead (Romans 5:12-21).

4. His Ascension

The ascension of Christ to heaven was the next significant step in His redemptive ministry. It fulfilled the cycle of the Father's will that Jesus came to do (John 16:27-28). The ascension was the crowning culmination of His ministry on earth. The Son of God became the Son of Man in the incarnation, taking upon Himself a body of flesh and blood and then He returned to heaven with this same virgin-born, crucified, resurrected and glorified body. He came from heaven to earth as God becoming man, and then returned to heaven as the God-Man. In descending from heaven in the incarnation He did not cease to be God, and in ascending to heaven in the ascension, He did not cease to be man. Thus we have a man in the Godhead today (I Timothy 2:5-6). He is the surety of what we will become. He has gone ahead as the forerunner within the veil (Hebrews 6:20).

Between Christ's resurrection and actual ascension there were 40 days of post-resurrection and pre-ascension ministry. It is difficult to establish a precise order of events for this period but we note some of the major things which took place.

a. The 40 Days Post-Resurrection Ministry

Jesus spoke of the sign of the prophet Jonah which was given to the great city of Ninevah (Matthew 12: 39-40). This sign involved a time period of 3 days followed by another time period of 40 days (Jonah 1:17; 3:1-4). The Lord Jesus wonderfully fulfilled this sign at Jerusalem in His 3 days burial, followed by 40 days post-resurrection and pre-ascension ministry (Acts 1:3).

We list a suggested order of events which took place during this period of time.

(1) His bodily resurrection at the close of 3 days and 3 nights began His post-resurrection ministry (Acts 1:3).

(2) Christ presented Himself as the sheaf of the firstfruits in the heavenly sanctuary on His resurrection day, thus fulfilling the Old Testament type (Leviticus 23:9-15; I Corinthians 15:20-23).

(3) The presentation of Himself also as the perfect and once-for-all sacrifice for sin, presenting His own body and blood at the Father's throne. As Aaron entered within the veil on the Day of Atonement, so Christ entered within the veil of the true and heavenly sanctuary (Leviticus 16; Hebrews 9:12-15; 6:11; John 20:11-18 with 20:22-23).

(4) The various appearances of Christ to His own (Acts 10:38-41; John 21:1,14). The Lord Jesus showed Himself alive to His own by many infallible proofs (Acts 1:3). Refer to list of the witnesses of the resurrection during the 40 days.

(5) The opening of the disciples understanding of the Old Testament scriptures. The risen Lord gave spiritual insight and illumination on the Law, the Psalms and the Prophets. He interpreted in all the Scriptures the things concerning Himself (Luke 24:27,44-45).

(6) The teaching and instruction of Jesus to His disciples concerning the Kingdom of God took place during this 40 days. Jesus expounded to them His truth concerning the Kingdom. The Church in Acts always preached the Gospel of the Kingdom. His kingdom would be after the order of Melchisedek (Acts 1:3,6; Matthew 21:41-44; 16:15-20; I Peter 2:5-9; Revelation 1:6; 5:9-10; Hebrews 7).

(7) The Great Commission given to the disciples as the final charge before His bodily ascension to heaven (Matthew 28:18-20; Mark 16:15-20; Luke 24:45-50; Acts 1:8).

b. The Ascension to Heaven

The ascension of Christ simply means His going back to heaven to the Father, but this time with His resurrected and glorified body. A study of the Scriptures pertaining to the "descending and ascending" ministry of Christ shows that Christ descended from heaven to earth and ascended from earth to heaven, both in spirit and also in His body (read Genesis 28:12 with John 1:51; Proverbs 30:4; Psalm 68:18; Romans 10:6-10; Ephesians 4:8-10; John 20:17). His ascension defied the law of gravity because He was moving in a higher law. His resurrected body was glorified and therefore adapted to the terrestial abode. The bodily ascension of Christ is another important article of faith because it is foundational to His bodily return, for He is to come back again in like manner (Acts 1:8-10). We note that Christ's ascension was:

(1) Foretold by the Prophets
(Psalm 68:18; Psalm 110:1).

(2) Foretold by Christ Himself
(John 16:27-28; 20:17; 6:61-62).

(3) Recorded by the New Testament writers.
There are many witnesses to His ascension and the New Testament writers use various expressions to describe His bodily ascension to heaven.

(a) Mark says that He was "received up into heaven" (Mark 16:19).

(b) Luke says that He was "parted from them" and carried up into heaven as He lifted His hands in priestly blessing (Luke 24:50-53).

(c) Luke also says that He was "received out of their sight" by a cloud (Acts 1:9).

(d) Jesus said that He would "ascend" up where He was before, that He would "depart" from this world and go back to the Father (read John 3:13; 6:62; 13:1; 14:1-4,26-28; 16:10,16,17, 28; 17:11; Luke 9:51). Jesus also spoke of His ascension in parabolic form.

    (i) His ascension was like a man going into a "far country" (Matthew 21:33; Mark 12:1; Hebrews 11:13-16).

    (ii) His ascension was like a man in a far country "receiving for Himself a kingdom" and in due time He would return to reward His servants (Luke 19:11-27).

    (iii) Jesus also spoke of His ascension as "going back to the Father" (John 14:12,28; 7:33; 16:27-28; 20:17).

(e) Stephen saw the Son of Man standing in heaven when he was being stoned (Acts 7:55-56).

(f) John saw the risen and ascended Lord in the heavens also (Revelation 1:10; 4:2).

(g) Peter said that He had "gone into heaven" (I Peter 3:22; Acts 2:30-36; 5:31).

(h) Paul also in His writings speaks of the risen and ascended Lord (Ephesians 4:8-10; Philippians 2:9; I Timothy 3:16; Colossians 3:3; Ephesians 1:20).

(i) The Epistle to the Hebrews tells us that Jesus has "passed into the heavens" within the veil of the heavenly Sanctuary (Hebrews 4:14; 8:1; 9:24; 10:12).

The apostles believed in His ascension and looked for His coming again. Jesus passed through the heavens, through all principalities and powers and wicked spirits in heavenly places and right into the presence of the Father (Ephesians 6:10-18). There is an actual place where the risen and glorified Lord is bodily and from which He will come again. Stephen (Acts 7:55-56), Paul (Acts 9:3-5) and John (Revelation 1:13-17) saw the Lord in heaven after His ascension. The ascension was preached by the apostles as part of the Gospel of Christ (Acts 2:33-34; 5:31).

c. Translation and Ascension
The difference and relationship between translation and ascension should be noted. The bodily ascension of Jesus, passing into the heavens into the presence of the Father was a miracle. It should be distinguished from the translation of Old or New Testament saints. Scripture intimates that three Old Testament saints are in glory, translated from earth to heaven by the power of God.

(1) Enoch, the seventh from Adam, representing the patriarchs, was translated from earth to heaven without dying (Genesis 5:24; Hebrews 11:5).

(2) Moses, apparently was buried and then raised by the Lord and taken to heaven, for he appeared on the Mt. of Transfiguration with Elijah to talk to Jesus (Deuteronomy 34:5-6; Jude 9; Matthew 17:1-9). Moses represents the Law.

(3) Elijah, the prophet and representative of the prophets, was translated from earth to heaven without dying. He was taken up in chariots of fire. He also appeared on the Mt. of Transfiguration with Moses (Matthew 17:1-9 with II Kings 2:11-18).

These translations shadow forth the resurrection, and translation of the saints at the coming of Christ (I Thessalonians 4:15-18; II Thessalonians 2:1; I Corinthians 15:51-57; Revelation 12:5). The ascension of Jesus from the Mt. of Olives stands unique among all men. In contrast to these Old Testament saints, and the translation of the saints at Christ's coming, Jesus ascended to heaven by His own right, because of who He is and what He had done. These Old Testament saints were translated by the power of God, not their own power or right. Jesus ascended by His own right and power as the God-Man (John 3:13; Psalm 24:1-4; 68:18; 110:1-4).

The ascension was a necessary step. It is the closing act of His earthly ministry and the initial act of His heavenly ministry. This was the last glimpse of the Christ on earth that the disciples would see before He returned again (II Corinthians 5:16). The Gospels show the disciples walking by sight of the man Christ Jesus on earth. The Acts and the Epistles show these same disciples walking by faith in the man in heaven. So all believers since that time must live by the same faith (II Corinthians 5:17; John 20:29).

The bodily ascension of Jesus is a historical fact, attested to by the mouth of many witnesses (Acts 1:9-11; I Corinthians 15:1-7). It was expedient in order to complete His earthly work and to make way for the Holy Spirit to come (John 16:7). Jesus has entered heaven as the forerunner and will continue His work in heavenly ministry until He comes again for His own (Hebrews 6:20; 9:24; Acts 1:1).

5. His Glorification
Relative to His ascension was the glorification of Christ by the Father. The Lord Jesus spoke of this coming glory and His disciples wrote of it. The word "glory" and other synonymous expressions signify "majesty, brightness, outshining, beauty and honor". In the incarnation the Son of God laid aside the glory that He had with the Father and humbled Himself to take

manhood upon Himself. Upon the completion of this perfect work Jesus was entitled to receive back the glory that He had laid aside in His humiliation. However, this glorification, though being the same eternal glory He had with the Father, pertained to His humanity. It was as Man, the perfect God-Man, that He was glorified. It was by right of who He was and what He had done. It also exemplifies the coming glorification of the saints. Not by virtue of their own righteousness, but by virtue of faith and obedience to God through their risen and ascended Lord. The following are a number of the most important references of Scripture which speak of Christ's glorification.

a. The Sufferings and the Glory to Follow

(1) The prophets foretold the sufferings of Christ and the glory that was to follow (I Peter 1:10-12; Luke 24:26-27; Matthew 16:15-28).

(2) Jesus laid aside His glory in the humiliation of the incarnation for the sufferings of the cross (Philippians 2:5-8; John 1:14-18).

(3) Jesus prayed in His High Priestly prayer that the Father would glorify Him with the glory that He had with the Father before the world began (John 17:1-5). This prayer was based on the finished work.

(4) Jesus also told His disciples that the Holy Spirit could not be given until He was glorified (John 7:37-39; 1:33; 14:16; 16:7; Acts 2:33).

(5) The Lord Jesus spoke much to the disciples of His coming glorification (John 12:23-32; 13:31-32).

(6) In His ascension the Lord Jesus was "received up into glory" (I Timothy 3:16).

b. The Glorification of Christ

The glorification of Christ involved the following things.

(1) The glorification of His resurrected body. On the Mt. of Transfiguration Christ's perfect body shone with light and glory (Matthew 17:1-8; Luke 9:26-32; II Peter 1:17-18). Now His body shines and eternally radiates such glory, which no mortal eye can stand unless strengthened. This glorified body now has no sinless infirmities. The glory can be veiled or unveiled as He pleases (Revelation 1:16-18; 10:1; 18:1; Ezekiel 43:1; Mark 9:1).

(2) The glory that He had with the Father in eternity is now bestowed upon Him as Man (John 17:1-5; I Peter 1:21; Isaiah 22:24; II Timothy 2:10).

(3) The Father God crowned Him with glory and honor before all heaven and all the angelic hosts as the God-Man (II Peter 1:17; Hebrews 2:7-9).

(4) Jesus will come in the brightness of the Father's glory (Mark 8:38; Matthew 16:17; 24:30-31; Titus 2:13).

(5) The everlasting kingdom will be the revelation and manifestation of the glory of the risen Christ (Daniel 7:14; Mark 9:1; II Thessalonians 1:9-10; Matthew 13:43; Numbers 14:21).

Thus Jesus, the God-Man, has been glorified by "the Father of Glory" (Ephesians 1:17) and He is now "the King of Glory" (Psalm 24:7-10). His glorious body is the sample of that glory which the saints will experience at His coming and for all eternity (I Corinthians 15:40-44; Philippians 3:21).

6. His Exaltation

Vitally connected with the glorification of Christ was His exaltation. The exaltation of Jesus Christ involved His enthronement and the reception of His exalted Name.

a. His Enthronement

With His ascension and glorification, Christ was exalted by the Father to sit in the throne with Him. "Sit Thou on My right hand until I make thine enemies thy footstool" (Psalm 110:1). The New Testament emphasizes the exaltation of Christ because it fulfills the main offices of Old Testament times.

(1) Seated Prophet

During His earthly ministry Jesus often taught people from a seated position. As the prophet He was the mouthpiece of God. As the seated prophet in heaven His ministry is to dispense the knowledge of God to His people. This He does by the ministry of the Spirit.

(a) As the Word He speaks to men in behalf of God (Jeremiah 26:12; John 12:49-50; 6:26-51; Deuteronomy 18:12-19; John 1:21).

(b) As the Word He speaks the truth of God (John 14:6; Acts 3:22; 7:37; John 7:40; 9:17; 14:10:24).

(c) As the Word He confirms the Word of the Gospel by signs and wonders in earth (Deuteronomy 18:15-18; Mark 16:15-20).

(d) As the Word He speaks with authority and anointing (Matthew 7:29; Mark 1:22; Matthew 21:11,46; Luke 7:16; 24:19; Isaiah 61:1; Luke 4:18).

(e) As the prophet and Word of God He predicts the events of the future, showing the Church things to come (Matthew 24-25; Luke 21; Mark 13; John 16:9-16).

Thus Jesus Christ, as the exalted prophet, speaks the word and will of God to the Church, His body, by the Spirit (Hebrews 1:1; 2:1-4; Luke 13:33; He is God's oracle).

(2) Seated Priest

Jesus in His exaltation was seated at the Father's right hand as a Great High Priest who had accomplished a "finished work" (John 17:1-4; 19:30).

In the Tabernacle of Moses there was no seat for the priest to sit upon. The lid of the Ark of the Covenant was the Mercy Seat upon which was the glory of God. The writer to the Hebrews takes up priestly ministry and their daily standing as being significant of a work never finished. But when He speaks of Jesus he says that "this Man sat down from henceforth expecting His enemies to be made His footstool". Christ accomplished a finished work and in His exaltation was seated at the Father's throne as a priest (Hebrews 10:11-13; 1:3; 8:1; 12:2; John 19:30; Psalm 80:1; 99:1).

(a) As Priest He speaks to God in behalf of men, where as Prophet He spoke to men in behalf of God (Hebrews 5:1-10; 8:1).

(b) As Priest He was chosen from among men (Hebrews 5:1).

(c) As Priest He was appointed and anointed by God (Hebrews 5:4,10).

(d) As Priest He makes sacrifice for sin (Hebrews 5:1-5; 7:8-10; 8:1-5; Romans 3:25-26).

(e) As Priest He makes intercession (Hebrews 4:15; 7:25; 9:11-28; 10:19-22). He is the New Covenant advocate (Luke 22:20; Hebrews 7:22).

(f) As Priest He can be faithful to God, yet merciful to His own people (Hebrews 5:2,7; 2:17-18).

(g) As Priest He can be the Mediator between God and man (I Timothy 2:5-6; Zechariah 6:12-13; I John 2:1,9). He is our Advocate.

(h) As Great High Priest He can direct the church as His priestly body in earth in the ministry of reconciliation (II Corinthians 5:19-21).

Thus Jesus was exalted and enthroned as Priest in the throne of God. He began His priestly ministry at the cross (The brazen altar ministry) and He continues His priestly ministry at the throne (The Ark of the Covenant ministry) in heaven (Hebrews 9:13-14; 7:25; 10:1,14). He offered His own body and blood and performed a finished work. Now He can be seated within the veil in heaven's sanctuary (Hebrews 6:20).

(3) Seated King

Christ is not only Prophet and Priest, but also King. He combines all offices in Himself. He is a King-Priest which constitutes Him in the Order of Melchisedek. The Kings of Judah sat upon the throne of David. Christ as the greater Son of David was to sit on the throne for ever. There was to be no end to His kingdom. The right hand is symbolic of a place of honor, power and authority. The Father gave this place to His Son (Zechariah 3:1; Revelation 12:10; Psalm 110:1; Genesis 48:13-19; Psalm 110:5).

This enthronement fulfills the prophecy of Zechariah that the Man whose name was The Branch would "sit and rule upon the throne; and He shall be a priest upon His throne; and the counsel of peace shall be between them both" (Zechariah 6:12-13).

(a) As King He sits enthroned with the Father God (Revelation 3:21; 22:1).

(b) As King He exercises authority over all things in heaven and earth (Matthew 28:19-20).

(c) As King all enemies are to be placed beneath His feet, He will reign until the last enemy, death, has been destroyed (I Corinthians 15:24-28).

(d) As King all creatures are subjected to Him (I Peter 3:22).

(e) As King He rules and reigns in righteousness, and peace and joy (Romans 14:17; Isaiah 32:1).

(f) As King all kingdoms of this world are to be subjugated by Him (Daniel 7:14; Psalm 72:11; 22:28; Ezekiel 21:27; Revelation 11:15-19).

(g) As King He rules in the Church, His Body, which is also after the Order of Melchisedek, and order of king-priests unto God (I Peter 2:5-9; Revelation 1:5-6; 5:9-10). God has given Him to be head over all things to the Church (Ephesians 1:20-22).

Jesus Christ as King-Priest has been given all power and authority. All things are under His feet. The last enemy to be destroyed will be death. He rules and reigns as King now. He executes the rule of God's kingdom in heaven and earth. He takes the highest place in the universe because He took the lowest place (Psalm 2:4; 93:1; 96:10; 97:1; Isaiah 16:5; Isaiah 32:1; I Corinthians 15:24-28,54-57; Mark 16:19-20; Matthew 22:41-46; Hebrews 4:14; 6:20; 7:1-3; Revelation 3:21; Ephesians 1:20-23; Colossians 3:1).

He is King of the saints (Revelation 15:3). He is King of Kings and Lord of Lords (Revelation 19:16). He is the King of Glory (Psalm 24:7-10; Matthew 26:64). He is King-Priest and is the one who was to sit in the Tabernacle of David, judging, hasting righteousness and exercising mercy (Isaiah 16:5).

(4) Seated Judge

Christ is Prophet, Priest, King and also Judge. All the Old Testament judges were types and shadows of His ministry as deliverer and judge of all men.

(a) As Judge, the Father has committed all things to His Son (John 5:19-30).

(b) As Judge, He has perfect insight and discernment and is able to be a perfect judge of all mankind. His moral perfections and attributes qualify Him to be the true Judge of all men's thoughts, words, deeds and motives. There is nothing hid from His eyes. God has therefore appointed Him as the Man to judge all mankind in an appointed day (Acts 17:31).

(c) As Judge, He will judge and reward all saints and sinners according to their works. The saints will be judged and rewarded at His second coming, and the ungodly will be judged at the Great White Throne judgement (I Corinthians 3:10-15; II Corinthians 5:10; Romans 14:10; Revelation 20:11-15).

b. His Exaltation

The exaltation of Christ not only involved His enthronement to exercise His offices, but also included the reception of the exalted name, whereby His lordship as the man Christ Jesus is forever settled. As to His deity, He was always Lord (Luke 2:11; I Corinthians 15:47). As to His humanity He was made Lord. This act of exaltation was the Father's bestowal of His name upon His Son making Him the Lord Jesus Christ. He was raised from the dead to be "Lord both of the dead and the living" (Romans 14:9).

The first revelation and declaration of His Lordship was given by Peter on the Day of Pentecost when Peter declared to the Jews that Jesus had been exalted to the right hand of God. He said "...God has made this same Jesus whom ye crucified both Lord and Christ" (Acts 2:32-36). Paul said "God also has highly exalted Him, and given Him a name which is above every name... that every tongue should confess that Jesus Christ is the Lord to the glory of God the Father" (Philippians 2:9-11). Confession of the Lordship of Jesus is necessary for salvation (Romans 10:9-13; I Corinthians 12:3; Acts 9:1-6).

Numerous scriptures could be listed concerning the Lordship of Jesus Christ. There is no higher name in the universe (Ephesians 1:20-22). The Father bestowing His own incomparable name upon the Son is the highest honor possible for it makes the Son of Man equal with the Father. Here "The Lord (the Father) said to my Lord (the Son); Sit thou on My right hand..." (Psalm 110:1-5; Genesis 19:24; Acts 2:34; 10:36; Revelation 3:12; Mark 16:15-20).

The triune name of the Lord Jesus Christ is therefore the greatest redemptive name ever to be revealed. It comprehends in itself all of the redemptive names of God. (Refer to "Doctrine of God" and The Names of God) At the name of Jesus every knee shall bow and every tongue will confess His Lordship and thus acknowledge this exalted name (Phillipians 2:9-11).

Because Jesus left the throne for the cross, He could return to the throne. He came down as God in the incarnation, He returns as the God-Man in the exaltation. He left His former glory, He now has greater glory. His exaltation is unique and deserved, because of His perfect humility, His perfect life, and His perfect sacrifice.

In Summary:

As **Prophet** He is the word and truth of God.

As **Priest** He is the reconciler, mediator, advocate and intercessor.

As **King** He is the ruler, governor of the universe.

As **Judge** He is the discerner, and rewarder of all mankind.

As **Lord** He is the enthroned and exalted God-Man, worthy of all praise, adoration and worship.

He came in His first advent as Prophet. He rules and reigns now as Priest and King, and He will return the second time as Judge.

7. His Session

The word "session" refers to "the act of sitting" or "the sitting together or meeting of a group; an assembly, as of a court, or a council". It is also used of a continuous, day to day series of such sittings. It speaks of a court in session, or some governing board or council, fulfilling official function and carrying out official business.

When it is used of Christ, it refers to His official function in heaven in behalf of His own, as well as in world affairs. The period of time in which Christ is in session reaches from His ascension to His second advent.

a. The Basis of His Session

One of the most neglected areas of truth specifically dealt with in the Scriptures is that which pertains to the sacrificial body and blood of Jesus. The body and blood of Jesus are the most holy things in the universe. They provide the basis of Christ's session and official function in heavenly ministry.

How the eternal Word, the Son of God obtained body and blood has been dealt with under the incarnation. In His incarnation He partook of flesh and blood (Hebrews 2:9-14). The purpose of this was the crucifixion. where this holy body and blood could be offered to God as the supreme sacrifice for sin.

However, this was not to be the consummation of Christ's work of atonement. He came down from heaven to earth to obtain body and blood and this same body and blood has been taken from earth back to heaven. In fact. He dare not enter into the heavenly sanctuary without such, for this alone is the basis of His heavenly ministry. It is His sacrifice which gives His session power. The body and blood of Jesus were incorruptible because of His sinlessness.

(1) Old Testament Sacrifices

A study of the Old Testament sacrificial system given to Israel indicates how particular God was when it came to the details concerning the body and blood of the victims.

(a) The body of the **burnt offering** had to be wholly burnt on the altar; the blood had to be sprinkled according to God's command (Leviticus 1).

(b) The body of the **peace offering** had to be disposed of in a special way also. Certain parts were given to the priests. The blood had to be sprinkled on the altar (Leviticus 2).

(c) The bodies of the **trespass** and **sin offerings** also were disposed of in certain ways. Sometimes the bodies were burnt on the altar, sometimes outside the camp. The blood also had to be sprinkled as God ordained (Leviticus 4-5).

(d) On the great **Day of Atonement** the body of the sin offering had to be taken outside the camp, but the blood had to be sprinkled within the veil. Aaron dared not enter the Holiest of All without sacrificial blood or he would have been slain (Leviticus 16).

(e) The body of the **red heifer** had to be burnt outside the camp and the blood sprinkled before the sanctuary (Numbers 19).

(f) When God made covenant with **Abraham,** He told him to order the sacrificial victims (Genesis 15).

(g) All **covenants** established by God were founded upon body and blood sacrifices. These ratified the covenants (Genesis 8:20; II Samuel 7; Deuteronomy 27-30; Genesis 15).

(h) Numerous sacrifices were offered at the **Feasts** of Passover, Pentecost and Tabernacles (Exodus 12; Numbers 28-29; Leviticus 23).

(i) Beside these special sacrifices there were always **"the morning and evening"** sacrifices. This was called "the daily sacrifice" (Exodus 29:38-46; Daniel 8:11-12; 11:31; 12:11).

Sufficient references have been given to show the importance of the body and blood of the sacrificial victims. These sacrifices all foreshadowed the perfect, once-for-all sacrifice of the Lord Jesus Christ. All covenants pointed to the New Covenant which Christ established. If God was so particular and exacting concerning the body and blood of animals under the type and shadow, how much more so concerning the body and blood of His only begotten Son? (Genesis 3:21; 4:1-16; 8:20; 12:7; 13:4,18; 15:9-21).

(2) New Testament Sacrifices

All the Old Testament sacrifices were shadows of the sacrifice of Christ. The New Testament writers jealously guarded the truth concerning Christ's sinless sacrifice. They emphasized Christ's body and blood. Some of the major passages are listed here.

(a) Jesus took bread and wine as symbols of His own broken body and shed blood. By this act He established the covenant table for all believers (Matthew 26:26-28; Luke 22:19-20; Hebrews 9:17-23).

(b) His body and blood were offered on Calvary as the sinless sacrifice and oblation fulfilling and abolishing forever all animal sacrifices (Daniel 9:24-27; I Peter 1:18-20; Hebrews 10:1-3).

(c) Paul received a special revelation of that which is symbolized in the New Covenant table of the Lord, concerning discerning the body and blood of Jesus (I Corinthians 11:23-32).

(d) Christ's body and blood fulfilled all the sacrifices used in the feasts of Israel (I Corinthians 5:6-8; Hebrews 10:19-20; 13:10-13).

(e) The body and blood of Christ is now the believer's "daily sacrifice". Not that which the Roman Church presents in the "daily sacrifice of the Mass", but that ever-fresh sacrifice of Christ available daily for the needs of cleansing for all believers.

(f) The writer to the Hebrews devotes two chapters to the body and blood of Jesus in heaven for us. Hebrews 9 deals with the blood of Jesus, the word "blood" being used over 10 times. Hebrews 10 deals with the body of Jesus, showing its supremacy over the bodies of animal sacrifices.

Apart from the body and blood of Jesus there is no salvation for sin. Christ has no ministry apart from His sacrifice. His resurrection, ascension, glorification, exaltation and session are all because of His crucifixion. Calvary's cross was the New Testament altar where His body and blood were offered.

The foundation scripture for blood atonement is found in Leviticus 17:11-14. "For the life of the flesh is in the blood: and I have given it to you upon the altar to make an atonement for your soul: for it is the blood that maketh atonement for the soul". The Lord also said "And the blood shall be to you for a token... and when I see the blood, I will pass over you..." (Exodus 12:12-13). Untold thousands of animal sacrifices were offered in Old Testament times, but Jesus offered one perfect, sinless, human sacrifice, once-for-all (Hebrews 10:11-14). The evidence of this sacrifice is in heaven. The body and blood of Jesus are incorruptible and therefore eternal. These will be the eternal evidences in heaven of our salvation, both having been supernaturally taken to heaven. Jesus would not have entered heaven without His blood. It is the blood which makes atonement for the soul. His blood and body did not perish at Jerusalem, nor did they see corruption. They are in heaven for us now and have been accepted of the Father as the basis of Christ's session. What then is the significance of the body and blood of Jesus being in heaven as far as God and the redeemed are concerned? The following outline gives insight to this question.

(3) The Body and Blood of Jesus in Heaven

(a) His Body

(i)   His body in heaven is the result of the miraculous incarnation. It is His virgin-born body, prepared of the Holy Spirit in the Virgin Mary on earth (Hebrews 10:5-8; Luke 1:30-33; Matthew 1:18-21).

(ii)   His body in heaven once experienced sinless infirmities, sufferings and death, but now it is resurrected, glorified, and no longer subject to sinless infirmities or death.

(iii)   His body in heaven is the surety of our entrance to heaven (Hebrews 7:22).

(iv)   His body in heaven will be the eternal evidence of His perfect sacrifice, for it still has the wounds, though glorified, in His hands, feet and side (John 20:24-29).

(v)   His body in heaven is the guarantee that the bodies of the saints will be raised and glorified. His body is the sample, the first-fruits of the harvest of the resurrected and immortalized redeemed (I Corinthians 15:51-57; Philippians 3:21).

(vi)   His body originated in earth and was taken to heaven, thus transcending natural laws, moving in higher and spiritual laws. The saints will also have bodies like Christ's that are adapted to the celestial realms for all eternity.

(b) His Blood
The blood of Christ is the most precious thing, and the only cleansing agent from sin in the universe (I Peter 1:18-20). It is the blood of God (Acts 20:28). It is far more valuable than animal blood, and sinful human blood, for it is the divine life, the blood of God. It speaks to God in our behalf (Hebrews 12:22-24). All true believers have faith in the blood of Jesus (Romans 3:23-25). Some of the benefits which the believer receives by reason of the blood of Jesus being in heaven are noted here.

(i)   Cleansing from sin by the blood (I John 1:7).

(ii)   Justification available by the blood (Romans 5:9).

(iii)   Redemption through His blood (Ephesians 1:7; Romans 5:9-10).

(iv)   Reconciliation through the blood (Colossians 1:20; Romans 3:25).

(v)   Peace through the blood (Colossians 1:20).

(vi)   Access to God by the blood (Ephesians 2:13).

(vii)   Conscience purged by the blood (Hebrews 9:13)

(viii)   Sanctification by the blood (Hebrews 13:12)

(ix)   Communion through the blood (I Corinthians 10:16).

(x)   Covenant relationship through the blood (Hebrews 13:20).

(xi)   Kingship and Priesthood unto God through the blood (Revelation 1:5; 5:9-10).

(xii)   Overcome Satan by the blood (Revelation 12:11).

(xiii)   Eternal life through the blood (John 6:53-57,63). All that the believer receives from God through Christ is because of the efficacious blood of Jesus which is in heaven before the Father's face, sprinkled upon the throne.

b. The Function of His Session
What official function does Christ fulfil in heaven? The sitting of Christ is not a period of idleness but of universal administration. Things involved in Christ's session have been covered more fully under His exaltation. They are mentioned briefly again here along with other things which are part of the function of His session from His ascension to His return. The Session involves Christ:

(1) Appearing in the presence of God on our behalf (Hebrews 6:20; 9:24).

(2) Sitting on the Father's right hand as King-Priest (Zechariah 3:1; Psalm 110:1,5). He acts as

mediator, intercessor, and advocate, handling the accusations that Satan would charge against the believer (Revelation 12:10-11).

(3) Filling the universe with His presence, no longer being limited to a local or geographical place (Ephesians 4:10; Matthew 18:20).

(4) Exercising His authority in heaven and in earth (Matthew 28:18-20).

(5) Directing the affairs of the Church, His body in earth, as the heavenly head (Ephesians 1:22; Colossians 1:15-19; 2:9-10; Revelation 1-2-3).

(6) Bestowing gifts and ministries upon the Church, both individually and corporately (I Corinthians 12:4-11, 28-30; Ephesians 4:8-10; Romans 12:1-6).

(7) Pouring out His Spirit on all flesh, Jew or Gentile (Acts 2:33; John 16:7; 14:16; I Corinthians 12:13; John 7:37-39).

(8) Leading the worship of the redeemed both in heaven and in earth to the Father God (John 4:20-24; Hebrews 12:22-24; Revelation 5).

(9) Bringing conviction, repentance and faith to man by the power of the Holy Spirit (Acts 5:31; 11:18; II Timothy 2:25).

(10) Receiving into Paradise all the saints who die (Philippians 1:23; II Corinthians 5:6-8; John 14:1-3; Hebrews 9:21-24).

(11) Administering the affairs of the Kingdom of God in the nations of earth, restraining the work of Satan and his kingdom, until the Church is completed and has finished her work (Ephesians 1:20-23; 6:10-18).

(12) Remaining in heaven and in session until the restoration of all things spoken by the prophets has taken place, after which He will return (Acts 3:20-21).

Thus the session of Christ is seen to be one of full activity and administration. Once the period of grace has ended, and the dispensation of the Holy Spirit has come to a close, then Jesus will leave the throne to return for His own. This will be the time of His second coming, and will usher in the next phase of God's redemptive plan.

8. His Advent

As seen previously, the period of time when Christ is in session reaches from His ascension to His second coming. As the risen Lord ascended bodily to heaven, two men stood by in shining garments and said: "This same Jesus, which is taken up from you into heaven, shall so come in like manner as ye have seen Him go into heaven (Acts 1:9-11). The early Church held strongly to the doctrine of the Lord's return. The watchword of the early believers was "Maranatha", or "The Lord cometh" (I Corinthians 16:22); or, "Come, Lord Jesus" (Revelation 22:20). The doctrine of the Lord's coming almost faded into oblivion during the period of Church history known as "The Dark Ages", but the recovery of this truth has been especially evident the last century.

Although there are several major schools of thought relative to the actual details and order of events pertaining to the coming of Christ, all are agreed on the fact that Christ is coming again. Christians today would do well to learn from what happened to the Jews in relation to Christ's first coming. The religious leaders, and more especially the Scribes, as the official interpreters of the Old Testament scriptures, had developed some set ideas concerning the first coming of the Messiah. However, when Christ did come, it was not exactly in the way they had planned on and therefore the nation missed His coming and crucified Him. The Church should be careful not to make the same mistake concerning Christ's second coming. The New Testament reveals certain events which are to take place relative to the Lord's return. Dogmatism and intolerance on exact details is not always wise, for it is only history which proves prophecy. For this reason this text deals with a basic outline concerning those things that the major schools of eschatology agree on. There are several erroneous views concerning the nature of Christ's coming which need to be dealt with briefly before setting out the Biblical view.

a. The Erroneous Views of Christ's Coming

(1) Some hold that the coming of the Holy Spirit at Pentecost was the coming of Christ, basing this view on John 14:15-26; 16:7-12,16. It is true that the Lord Jesus did 'come" to His disciples by the Holy Spirit, but this was not the second coming. After the Holy Spirit had come to the disciples, they still spoke of a future coming of Jesus Himself (James 5:8).

(2) Some hold that every time a person is converted Christ "comes" to them. However, this is very similar to the first view and it certainly does not fulfil the Biblical view of the coming of Christ.

(3) Some hold that the destruction of Jerusalem in A.D.70 was the "coming" of Christ in that He came in judgement on the Jews. They hold that it was similar to the Old Testament prophets when they spoke of "The Day of the Lord cometh" as this was often fulfilled in a local and national judgement (Joel 2:1-2; Luke 19:41-44; Matthew 16:28). This was indeed a "coming" of the Lord in judgement but does not fulfil that which is meant by the Lord's return.

(4) Some hold that, when the believer dies, Christ "comes" for him at death and receives him to glory and that this is what is meant by the coming of Christ. However, death is an enemy and at death we go to the grave physically. At Christ's coming, death is conquered and we leave the grave in bodily resurrection (I Corinthians 15:25-26,51-57; I Thessalonians 4:16-17; Revelation 1:7; Matthew 16:27-28; John 21:21-23; Titus 2:13; John 8:51).

(5) Some hold that a spiritual awakening or revival is the "coming" of the Lord to His Church (Revelation 2:5,16; Malachi 3:1-3; Hosea 6:1-2). This also is a spiritual coming of the Lord but it is not the coming the Lord speaks of that is to take place at the close of the present age.

The major weaknesses of each of these views is that it limits Christ's coming to a spiritual coming and does away with His bodily and visible coming, which is the Biblical teaching concerning Christ's return.

b. The Biblical View of Christ's Coming

The doctrine of the second coming is mentioned about 318 times in the 216 chapters of the New Testament. That is, one in every twenty-five verses refer to it. Some entire chapters are given to it and at least three New Testament writers wrote books concerning it (i.e. Matthew 24; Mark 13; Luke 21; I Corinthians 15; I Thessalonians and II Thessalonians; Jude; Revelation). Not one New Testament writer fails to speak of the Lord's coming. There are actually more references to the coming of Christ than any other New Testament doctrine. The reason for this is evident in that His coming consummates all other doctrine. It consummates that which was begun in the first coming. Often the Bible writers linked the first and second comings together in one verse. However, history has proven that there is about 2,000 years between these comings (Job 19:25-26; Zechariah 14:4; Malachi 3:1-2; Daniel 7:13-14; Genesis 49:10).

The coming of Christ is foretold in both Old and New Testaments. As the burden of the Old Testament writers was particularly the first coming, so the burden of the New Testament writers is the second coming. The New Testament shows the detailed historical fulfilment of the first coming, so the Old and New Testament together speak in detail about Christ's second coming. We note some of the men who foretold this great event.

(1) The Old Testament

(a) Enoch, the seventh from Adam spoke of His coming (Jude 14-15).
(b) Jacob the patriarch foretold Christ's coming (Genesis 49:10).
(c) Balaam, the soothsayer, spoke of it also (Numbers 24:7,17-19).
(d) Isaiah foretold His coming (Isaiah 59:20; 63:15; 13:6-9).
(e) Jeremiah foretold His coming (Jeremiah 23:5,6; 25:30-33).
(f) Ezekiel spoke of Christ's coming (Ezekiel 34:23-29; 43:7).
(g) Daniel, the statesman and prophet spoke of His coming as the smiting stone and the Son of Man (Daniel 2:44-45; 7:13-14).

(h) Joel spoke of Christ's advent also (Joel 2:28-3:21).

(i) Micah the prophet foretold it (Micah 2:12-13; 4:1).

(j) Nahum foretold His coming (Nahum 1:5-6).

(k) Zechariah the prophet spoke of it (Zechariah 12:4-14; 13:1-9).

(l) Malachi the final prophet spoke of it (Malachi 3:1; 4:6).

Many other Old Testament references could be given. The Old Testament spoke of both comings, the one to precede the other, and the latter to consummate the previous (Psalm 37:9-20; Proverbs 2:21-22).

(2) The New Testament

(a) The two men in shining garments spoke of Christ's coming again (Acts 1:10-11).

(b) Jesus Himself foretold His coming again (Matthew 16:27; 24:1-25:46; Luke 17:22-37; 21:1-33; John 14:3; 21:22-23; Matthew 24:27; Revelation 1:7; 16:15; 22:20).

(c) The Apostle Peter spoke of His coming (Acts 3:19-21; II Peter 3:3-10).

(d) The Apostle Paul spoke of it also (I Thessalonians 4:15-17; Titus 2:13; II Thessalonians 1:7-10; Hebrews 9:28; I Corinthians 11:26; I Corinthians 15:22-23).

(e) James the Apostle spoke of Christ's coming (James 5:7).

(f) John, the beloved apostle, wrote an entire book about it, and also spoke of Christ's coming in each of the other books he wrote (John 14:3; I John 2:28; 3:2-3; Revelation 1:7; 22:7,12,20).

(g) Jude refers to Christ's coming when he quotes the prophecy of Enoch concerning it (Jude 14-15).

Every New Testament writer speaks in some way of His coming. Every time a believer celebrates the Lord's Table, he is "showing forth the Lord's death until He come" (I Corinthians 11:26). The Lord's Table involves both the first and second comings of Christ.

c. The Signs Preceding Christ's Coming

Although the major schools of eschatology vary much as to the exact order and details of Christs' coming, they are in general agreement as to the following basic events which are to take place. We list these events in a reasonable order without details. These things are certainly important signs of the Lord's coming and call all true believers to be prepared for this momentous event. The Scriptures show two streams of prophetic events relative to the time of Christ's coming; things which are negative, and things which are positive. Darkness and light, the mystery of iniquity and the mystery of godliness run parallel together from the beginning until the end of time.

(1) Negative Signs of Christ's Coming

a) Perilous times are to come in the last days (II Timothy 3:1-7).

(b) The days of Noah and the days of Lot are to be repeated as to the evil and judgements (Luke 17:20-37).

(c) Wars, famines, pestilences and earthquakes are to increase (Matthew 24:6-7; Revelation 6:1-17).

(d) Wealth is to increase in the last days (James 5:1-9).

(e) Intense persecution and tribulation is to come upon the saints in the last days (Matthew 24:9-10,21).

(f) Great deception with the rise of the occult will abound (Matthew 24:4,5,11,24; I Timothy 4:1).

(g) False prophets and antichrists are to be manifested in these times (Matthew 24:5,11, 23-26; II Thessalonians 2:1-12; Revelation 13).

(h) Great apostacy from the Church will take place (II Thessalonians 2:1-3; Matthew 24:12; Hebrews 6:3-8).

(i) World kingdoms will arise in conflict with each other, and the kingdom of antichrist will be a universal kingdom (Daniel 2; Daniel 7; Daniel 18; Daniel 11; Revelation 13; Revelation 19:11-21).

(j) The Babylonian system will prevail through the whole world (Revelation 17-18; Zechariah 5; Isaiah 47-48).

(k) A one-world religious Church will be manifest (Revelation 17).

(l) A one-world dictatorship and government will arise and be under the rule of the antichrist at the coming of Christ. It will be a ten-kingdom world power (Revelation 13:17; Daniel 2,7). (Read also II John 2:18,22; 4:1-3).

(m) There will also be special judgements of God in the earth as symbolized under the opening of the judgements of Revelation under the Seven Seals, Seven Trumpets and Seven Vials of Wrath (Revelation 6-16).

The evidence of all these things surround us today in an increasing manner. The generation alive at the coming of Christ will see these things in intensity and consummation at Christ's coming.

(2) Positive Signs of Christ's Coming

(a) A universal outpouring of the Holy Spirit on all flesh will take place before Christ's coming (Joel 2:28-32; Acts 2:17; James 5:7-8). This began on the Day of Pentecost and will consummate in the final days. It will be upon all flesh, whether Jews or Gentiles and will graft all into the olive tree by faith (Romans 11).

(b) The Gospel of the Kingdom is to be preached to all nations for a powerful witness before the end comes (Matthew 24:14).

(c) A recovery of Bible truths to God's people will take place (Hebrews 6:12; John 16:12-13; Ephesians 4:9-16).

(d) The Church of the latter days is to be restored to its early glory (Acts 3:19-21; Ephesians 5:23-32). The Lord is going to present to Himself a glorious Church without spot or blemish. It will be a victorious Church (Matthew 16:15-20).

(e) The prayer of Christ for the unity of His Church will come to fulfilment, in order that the world will see such a witness before Christ returns (John 17).

(f) The Church will bring in the final harvest of souls into the Kingdom of God, as symbolized under the harvest festivals in the Feasts of Passover, Pentecost and Tabernacles (Leviticus 23).

As seen above, the Scriptures show that there are two prophetic streams pertaining to Christ's coming at the end of this age. The one stream shows the darkness increasing, and the other shows the light increasing (Proverbs 4:18-19; Isaiah 60:1-3). The wheat and the tares will grow together until the end of the age. The same rain that ripens and matures the wheat does the same for the tares. The same Gospel net brings in the good and the bad fish. At the coming of Christ there will then be a great separation (Matthew 13:24-30, 36-43, 47-50).

d. The Nature and Value of the Doctrine of Christ's Coming

(1) Nature of Christ's Coming

The Scriptures show that Christ will return literally, visibly, bodily and personally in the same manner as He went away (Acts 1:9-11).

    (a) It will be "this same Jesus" who will come again, not another Jesus (Acts 1:11 with II Corinthians 11:4).

    (b) Jesus said that He would personally come again and receive His saints unto Himself (John 14:3).

    (c) He will come again "in like manner" as He went away into heaven, that is, personally, bodily, and visibly (Acts 1:11; I Thessalonians 4:16-17).

    (d) He will return unexpectedly, like a thief in the night, especially to those who are not watching for His coming (Matthew 24:36-51; 25:1-3; Mark 13:32-37; Revelation 3:3; 16:15; II Peter 3:10; I Thessalonians 5:1-11).

    (e) He will return suddenly (Mark 13:36).

    (f) He will come back quickly (Revelation 22:7,12,20).

    (g) He will return in great glory, even the glory of His Father (Matthew 16:27; 19:28; 25:31).

    (h) He will return with the angelic hosts accompanying Him (Matthew 16:27; 25:31).

    (i) He will return for and with His saints and the saints will be with Him forever (I Thessalonians 4:15-18; II Thessalonians 2:1; John 14:3; Zechariah 14:4-5; Revelation 1:7; Jude 14-15; Revelation 19:11-16). The dead saints will be resurrected and all saints will be immortalized (I Corinthians 15:51-57; Hebrews 9:28; Philippians 3:20-21). Enoch, Moses and Elijah pre-figure the resurrected, translated and immortalized saints at Christ's return.

    (j) He will return in flaming fire, taking vengeance on them that know not God and do not obey the Gospel of the Lord Jesus Christ. These will be punished and banished from the presence and glory of the Lord when He is glorified in the saints (II Thessalonians 1:7-10; 2:3-12).

    (k) He will return in the Father's appointed and set time. No one knows the exact day or hour, though believers should know the times and seasons (Matthew 24:36; Mark 13:32; Acts 1:7; I Thessalonians 5:2, II Peter 3:10, Acts 3:19-21).

Those who presume to set dates for the coming of Christ bring reproach on the doctrine and cause people to mock it (II Peter 3:4). Truth often suffers at the hands of its friends more than its enemies.

(2) Practical Value of the Doctrine

Often the doctrine of Christ's coming is challenged as to its practical value. The end of all doctrinal teaching is practical godliness. The proper application of the truth concerning Christ's return is one of the greatest challenges to godly living. This will be especially true for the generation which will be alive at that coming. The New Testament writers also applied this doctrine practically to the lives of the believers in their day.

(a) The doctrine of Christ's coming is a comfort and purifying hope which encourages the believer to holy living (I John 3:2-3; Acts 23:6; 26:6-8; Romans 8:20-25; I Corinthians 15:19; Galatians 5:5; Titus 2:13; II Peter 3:9-13). It is the hope of the Church.

(b) The doctrine of Christ's coming is called to remembrance every time a believer partakes of the Table of the Lord. The Church is to do this "until He come" (I Corinthians 11:23-32; Matthew 26:26-29).

(c) The doctrine of Christ's coming challenges the believer to watchfulness and prayer (Matthew 24:42-44; 25:13; Luke 21:34-36).

(d) The doctrine of Christ's coming challenges the believer to:

    (i) Be supplied with the oil of the Holy Spirit and watch for the coming of Christ, the Bridegroom (Matthew 25:1-13).

    (ii) Be faithful and use the talents the Lord has given him as he will give an account at Christ's return (Matthew 25:14-30; Luke 19:11-27; II Corinthians 5:10-11; I Corinthians 3:1-15).

    (iii) Be awake and not fall into a condition of spiritual sleep and lethargy (Mark 13:32-37; Romans 13:11-12; I Thessalonians 5:1-10).

(e) The doctrine of Christ's coming encourages the believer in times of trial and persecution (Hebrews 10:32-37; II Timothy 2:12; James 5:7-8).

(f) The doctrine of Christ's coming also serves as a warning to the ungodly (II Thessalonians 1:7-10; Matthew 25:31-46). It stirs the Church to evangelism as the harvest is the end of the age. (Matthew 13:24-30,36-43).

(g) The doctrine of Christ's second coming consummates that which was begun in His first coming.

As the believer and the Church applies the truth of the "blessed hope" of Christ's return, it will have a practical purifying effect and thus prepare the Church as His Bride for the Lord's coming.

9. His Final Judgements

The final phase of the redemptive work of Christ is judgement. This work may be summed up under the Doctrine of Eternal Judgement as set forth in the first principles of the doctrine of Christ (Hebrews 6:1-2; II Timothy 4:1). The very fact that God is just, righteous and holy in His being demands that He judge all unrighteousness and sin in His creatures (Acts 24:25). The purpose of Christ's resurrection was also the judgement of all men in due time. This will come after the period of probation for all men on earth has ended (Acts 17:30-31). A judge is one who speaks with authority because of his ability to discern right and wrong. He is one who hears, sees, perceives, discerns and on the basis of all these facts, is able to render a verdict. With God there is no possible chance of deception or mistaken judgement. Because of His essential attributes all things are open and naked before His eyes. He sees all things. He knows all things. He understands and perceives all things. His justice and judgements are perfect. He is able to deal perfectly with His creatures. God will not do anything with His creatures which is inconsistent with His holy and righteous character.

The eternal Godhead is involved in the work of judgement, as the following indicates:

a. The Godhead in Judgement

(1) God the Father is the Judge
As a God of law and order, His ways and commandments must be upheld. Violation of His law that remains unrepented of must come up for judgement (Psalm 50:6; 75:7; Isaiah 33:22; Psalm 110:6; Romans 3:6; Revelation 6:10; Isaiah 30:18; Malachi 3:1-6).

(2) The Son of God is Judge
The following Scriptures clearly teach that the Father has now committed all judgement to the Son (John 5:22-30; 8:15-16,26,50; 12:47-48; Isaiah 11:1-10; James 5:9; Micah 5:1; 4:3; II Timothy 4:1,8). Jesus Himself said that the Father judges no man but all judgment is committed to the Son. The Son judges by the Word the Father gave Him to speak. God has set Christ to be the Judge of all men (Acts 17:31; Romans 2:16; I Peter 4:5-6; I Corinthians 4:4; Revelation 19:11; Isaiah 9:6-9; 42:1-4; John 9:39; Hebrews 9:27). Christ will not judge by His natural senses but by the spirit.

(3) The Holy Spirit is Judge
The Holy Spirit is not only the "Spirit of Grace" but He is also spoken of as being the "Spirit of Judgement and Burning" (Isaiah 4:4; John 16:7-11). The Holy Spirit comes to convict the world of sin, of righteousness and of judgement (Acts 24:24-25). The judgement of the Spirit is according to the word of the Son, which is also the word of the Father.

Thus the Scripture teaches that God is the Judge of all men and must eventually bring all men to judgement. God's justice would be insulted if He did not bring all unforgiven sinners to judgement, and also reward the saints who have served Him faithfully.

b. The Times of Judgement

(1) Judgement Past

(a) God pronounced judgements of the Serpent, and Adam and Eve and the ground after the entrance of sin (Genesis 3:1-24).
(b) God judged mankind in Noah's days by the flood (Genesis 6-8).
(c) The Tower of Babel was a judgement on mankind also (Genesis 10-11).
(d) God judged the cities of Sodom and Gomorrah by fire and brimstone as a sample of coming judgement (Genesis 19; Jude 7).
(e) The nation of Egypt was judged by the plagues (Exodus 6:6; 7:14; 12:12).
(f) God also judged Korah and the rebels in Israel (Numbers 16; Psalm 106:30).
(g) Cain was judged for murdering his brother after rejecting the blood of the lamb (Genesis 4).
(h) Achan and his family were judged in Israel for sin (Joshua 7).
(i) God judged Sapphira and Ananias for their sin of lying to the Holy Spirit (Acts 5).

Other examples could be given. God judged sin both individually and corporately as Bible history shows. God judged His own chosen people, Israel and Judah for their sins by the various captivities and curses of the law which came upon them.

(2) Judgement Present
In present history God still reveals His judgements in the earth. These judgements are in the form of the curses of the law as set forth in Deuteronomy 27-28. These chapters show blessing upon obedience and curses upon the disobedient. These laws are still operative today. The Prophet Isaiah said "When Thy judgements are in the earth, the inhabitants of the earth will learn righteousness" (Isaiah 26:8-9). It should be noted that all of God's judgements in this present time are two-fold in purpose.

(a) Judgement unto Restoration
This aspect of judgement is corrective. It is divine discipline having restoration as the end in view. God desires to restore man back to Himself through redemptive processes. Thus He punishes, chastises, corrects and judges, even as a father does his children (I Corinthians 5:1-13; 11:31-32; I Peter 4:17; Job 33:13-33). Christ was judged for our sin on

Calvary that we might not come up for judgement, but when we are judged we are chastened of the Lord that we should not be condemned with the world (John 3:18-21; Romans 2:2-3; 5:16).

(b) Judgement unto Damnation

This aspect of judgement is punitive, final, and unto damnation. If man refuses God's judgement in this world and continues to sin wilfully, there is only one alternative; eternal judgement unto damnation in the world to come. This judgement is eternal and fixed. It is unchangeable when executed by God through His Son (I Peter 4:17-18; John 5:24-29; I Corinthians 11:31-32; John 3:36; Revelation 14:9-11). This judgement may be executed in this present life but the final verdict and penalty is rendered on the Day of Judgement.

Thus judgement, both of the believer and the unbeliever, is going on now in this present life. It is either unto restoration or unto damnation, according to the attitude of the person involved. As to the ungodly and the sinner, there is a measure of judgement taking place in this present life. As to the godly and the believer, there is also judgement taking place. Church discipline is also a part of judgement unto restoration (Matthew 18:15-20; I Timothy 5:17-20; Luke 12:41-48; Galatians 6:1; Romans 16:17-18; Luke 12:58).

(3) Judgement Future

It is clear from both Scripture and experience that many things seem to escape the judgement of God or man. This very fact necessitates a coming Day of Judgement, a final retribution. If God did not come to judge the deeds of men, His throne of justice and holiness would tremble at the wickedness of men. The Scripture speaks of a coming Day of Judgement (I John 4:17; I Peter 4:17). It is this aspect of judgement which the Son will execute when He comes in the glory of His Father. We will consider the future work of Christ in His final judgements on the sinner, the saint and the angelic beings.

(a) Judgement of Satan and His Hosts

(i)   Satan will be judged at Christ's coming, as the author of sin and rebellion in the universe, He will be judged by being cast into the bottomless pit for 1,000 years. Then, after a short release, he will be eternally judged by being cast into the Lake of Fire (Revelation 20). The student is referred back to the judgement of Satan under "The Doctrine of Satan and Demonology."

(ii) Fallen Angels will also be judged (II Peter 2:4-9; Jude 6; John 12:31; 16:11; I Corinthians 6:1-3).

(iii) Demon spirits also will be judged (Matthew 8:28-34; Mark 5:1-20; Luke 8:26-39). In Christ's day they did not want to be tormented or sent to the abyss before "the time."

Thus at Christ's coming one phase of the judgement on Satan and his hosts will be executed and then the final and eternal judgement will take place at the Great White Throne. Here all the hosts of Satan will be cast into the Lake of Fire for all eternity.

(b) Judgement of Sinful Mankind

At the coming of Christ there is a judgement which takes place on all the ungodly (Jude 14-15).

(i)   All sinners and ungodly will be destroyed by the brightness of Christ's coming, for He comes in flaming fire taking vengeance on all them that know not God and that obey not the Gospel (II Thessalonians 1:7-10). The world at this time will be under the control of the Antichrist and will be worshippers of the Devil, under the leadership of the false prophet. (Revelation 13-19 provides the details of the condition of the ungodly at the coming of Christ.)

(ii) Antichrist and the false prophet are also judged. They are actually the first ones to be cast alive into the Lake of Fire because of the deception of the whole godless world under their control (Revelation 19:11-21 with Revelation 13).

Thus all unbelievers will come up for judgement. They will be judged not only for their sins, but especially for the great damning sin of unbelief. The greatest sin, the unpardonable sin, is to reject Jesus Christ as Savior and Lord. He died for all other sin. He was judged for the sin of the world. None need come up for this judgement if they accept Christ as the Savior of the world. The final and eternal judgement of all unbelievers and fallen angels will be the eternal Lake of Fire.

(c) Judgement of Redeemed Saints

At the coming of Christ there is also a judgement for all the believers. This judgement is not pertaining to their salvation, but to their works and service.

(i)   The believer was judged at Calvary when Christ was judged, as to his sins. He does not come up for judgement on sin in the future (John 3:16,18,36).

(ii) The believer is being judged now and must judge himself. If he will judge himself here and now, he will not be judged. If he fails to do this, then the Lord will judge and chasten him (I Corinthians 11:23-32; Hebrews 12:5-11; I Timothy 5:24; Hebrews 10:30-31; Psalm 50:4-5; Deuteronomy 32:36; I Peter 4:17).

(iii) The believer will be judged in the future as to his works and service for the Lord (II Corinthians 5:10-11; I John 4:17; Matthew 12:36-37; Romans 14:10-12; John 12: 47-48; II Timothy 4:1,8; Revelation 11:18; I Corinthians 3:11-15).

The believers, whose works will stand the divine fire-test, will be rewarded. This judgement takes place at the Judgement Seat of Christ, not at the Great White Throne Judgement which is for the unredeemed. The Greek word for the Judgement Seat of Christ was used to refer to a seat in ancient Greece where the Judge rewarded the winner of the games or various events. So Christ will award His own for their faithful service in His kingdom. These things will determine their place and position in the Kingdom of God. The rewards that are presented to the believers are crowns:

(i)   **The Crown of Life** (James 1:12; Revelation 2:10). This is especially the martyrs crown.

(ii) **The Crown of Glory** (I Peter 5:2-4). This is especially the shepherd's crown.

(iii) **The Crown of Rejoicing** (I Thessalonians 2:19-20). This is especially the soul-winner's crown.

(iv) **The Crown of Righteousness** (II Timothy 4:8). This is especially the crown for holy living for all believers.

(v)   **The Crown of Incorruption** (I Corinthians 9:25-27; I John 2:28). This crown is for all the redeemed, resurrected, immortalized and made incorruptible forever.

Other Scriptures speak of the saints being rewarded for their faithfulness in the work of Christ (Daniel 7:10,22-26; Revelation 20:4; 11:18; Acts 24:28; Matthew 25:14-30,31-46).

The Lord often spoke of the rewards that He will give to His saints. He uses this as a motivating force and encouragement to all believers who run in the race of faith, and who work faithfully in His Kingdom (Matthew 5:12; 6:18; 10:41-42; 16:27; Mark 9:41; Luke 6:23,35; I Corinthians 3:8,14; Colossians 2:18; 3:24; Hebrews 10:35; 11:26; II John 8; Revelation 22:12). At the coming of Christ and the establishment of His Kingdom, the saints will shine in their various glories, be rewarded according to their works, and be placed in the Kingdom of Christ accordingly. At the close of this period, the Son will then deliver the Kingdom back to the Father God, and be subject to the Father, that God may be all in all (I Corinthians 15:35-57; 22-28; Matthew 13:43). This act of the Son brings us into the eternal state, completing His total redemptive work.

B. Doctrinally

Having considered the work of Christ historically, it is now appropriate to consider the work of Christ doctrinally. Paul says that "Christ died (that is historical) for our sins" (that is doctrinal) (I Corinthians 15:3).

The great words of theology, such as grace, redemption, ransom, substitution, propitiation, reconciliation and atonement, together constitute that which is involved in the work of Christ doctrinally.

1. Grace

a. Definition
Grace has been defined as "that which is freely bestowed with no expectation of return. It is an act which finds its only motive in the good-heartedness of the giver". The best theological definition is "the undeserved, unearned and unmerited favor of God bestowed upon sinful men."

It is: (1) Undeserved for man deserves wrath (Romans 9:22).

(2) Unearned for man cannot earn this grace by works (Ephesians 2:1-9; Titus 3:4-7).

(3) Unmerited for there is nothing in man that deserves it (Romans 3:23-25; 11:32).

b. Amplification
The word "grace" has basically the same meaning in Hebrew and Greek. The Hebrew word "Chen" translated "grace" means "graciousness, kindness, favor (Genesis 6:8; 32:5; Exodus 33:12,13). The Greek word "Charis" translated "grace" means "graciousness, of manner or act; especially the divine influence upon the heart, and its reflection in the life". The definition of grace arises out of a Greek custom. When the Greeks wanted to give a gift out of pure generosity of heart, without any thought of reward, the word they used for "gift" was "grace".

c. Illustration
The first demonstration of grace is that which was evidenced in the Garden of Eden at the fall of man. The moment Adam and Eve sinned, they came under the wrath of God. However, God came in grace and provided a substitute victim to atone for their sin. Note that God sought man; man did not seek God. Grace is not man coming to God but God coming to man. It was the grace of God which provided salvation for Adam and Eve (Genesis 3:1-24). Grace is the love of God in manifestation and operation. God could have restrained love and displayed His wrath when Adam fell, but instead He manifested grace. This was indeed the lovingkindness, favor and mercy of God extended toward sinful man. Adam did not and could not deserve, earn, nor merit it. Noah found grace in the eyes of the Lord (Genesis 6:8). So did every Old Testament saint. We note some special verses concerning the grace of God, because it is the foundation of the whole redemptive plan. All the provision, application and benefits of the atonement arise out of God's amazing grace.

(1) Grace originates in the heart of God the Father (Romans 1:5,7).

(2) Grace flows to us through the Son of God, the Lord Jesus Christ. "The Law was given by Moses, but grace and truth came by Jesus Christ" (John 1:17).

(3) The believer is justified by grace (Romans 3:24).

(4) The believer is saved by grace through faith, not of works lest boasting should arise (Ephesians 1:6,7; 2:4; Titus 3:4-7).

(5) The Holy Spirit is the Spirit of Grace and ministers the grace of God to us (Hebrews 10:29).

(6) The believer is not to frustrate the grace of God in his life (Galatians 2:21; 5:4; Hebrews 12:15).

(7) The believer has to beware of those teachers who would abuse the grace of God and turn it into lasciviousness (Jude 4).

Even under the Law of Moses, or the dispensation of Law, the grace of God was manifested and typified. This is especially seen in the Tabernacle of Moses, the Feasts of the Lord, the Aaronic Priesthood, and the Sacrifices and oblations of the ceremonial law. The sacrificial blood upon the mercyseat of the Ark of the Covenant, covering the tables of the Law, was actually a revelation of grace under the period of the Law. Though Israel did not generally recognize it, there was a faithful remnant who did perceive God's grace in this manner. Many of the Psalms of David show the insight he had into God's Law and grace (read also Acts 4:33; 11:23; 13:43; 18:27; 20:24,32; Romans 5:2,15-21; I Corinthians 15:10; Ephesians 1:6-7; 3:2; II Timothy 2:1; Hebrews 4:16).

2. Redemption

a. Definition
The word "redemption" in its simplest definition means "to buy back, to purchase with a price out of the market place". It refers to "the act of bringing back from slavery, captivity or death by the price of judgement."

b. Amplification
The Hebrew mind was particularly saturated with the concept of redemption. The thought carries over also into the Greek language. There are several Hebrew and Greek words used which speak of the redemptive act and the work of a redeemer. We note the most important words in these languages.

(1) Hebrew

(a) Gah-al meaning "to redeem (according to Oriental law of kinship), to be the next of kin, and as such to buy back a relative's property, marry his widow, etc." Translated "redeem, redeemed, kinsman redeemer, ransom, deliver, purchase, avenger of blood, revenger, redeemer" (Exodus 6:6; 15:13; Ruth 3:13; Jeremiah 31:11; Psalm 119:154; Leviticus 25:33; Numbers 35:12,19-27; Isaiah 44:6,24; Job 19:25; Hosea 13:14; Genesis 48:16).

(b) Pad-dah meaning "to sever, i.e. to ransom, to release, preserve." Translated "redeem, redeemed, delivered, redeeming, rescued, ransom" (Leviticus 27:27; Deuteronomy 9:26; 21:8; Psalm 78:42; Exodus 13:13,15; I Samuel 14:45; Hosea 13:14; Isaiah 35:10; 51:11).

(c) P'Dooth meaning, as Pad-dah. Translated "distinction, deliverance, division, redeem, redemption." (Exodus 8:22,23; Psalm 111:9; 130:7; Isaiah 50:2).

(d) Pah-rak meaning "to break off, to deliver" Translated "break off, deliver, redeem, rend (in pieces) tear in pieces" (Genesis 27:40; Psalm 136:24; 7:2-3; I Kings 19:11).

Thus redemption in the Old Testament meant "to ransom, deliver, purchase, avenge, rescue, make a division, to break off or tear in pieces."

(2) Greek

(a) Lutreo meaning "to ransom, literally or figuratively." Translated "redeem" (Luke 24:21; Titus 2:14; I Peter 1:18; Luke 1:68; 2:38; Hebrews 9:12). Translated "ransom" (Matthew 20:28; Mark 10:45)

(b) Apolutrosis meaning "the act of ransom in full; riddance, or specially Christian salvation" Translated "deliverance, redemption" (Luke 21:28; Romans 3:24; 8:23; I Corinthians 1:30; Ephesians 1:7, 14; 4:30; Colossians 1:14; Hebrews 9:15; 11:35).

(c) Agorazo meaning "to go to the market, to purchase" Translated "buy, redeem" (Matthew 13:44,46, I Corinthians 6:20; 7:23; II Peter 2:1; Revelation 3:18; 5:9; 14:3-4).

(d) Exagorzao meaning "to buy up, to rescue from loss, improve opportunity" Translated "redeem" (Galatians 3:13; 4:5; Ephesians 5:16; Colossians 4:5).

Thus redemption in the New Testament means "to ransom, to deliver, to loose by a price, to purchase out of the market place, or acquire out of a forum."

c. Illustration
Undoubtedly the richest illustrations of redemption are those furnished in the Old Testament, given to Israel in the laws of redemption. All were prophetic foreshadowings of the redemptive work of Christ.

(1) Israel as a nation was redeemed by the blood of the Passover lamb. It was the blood that made the redemptive division (Exodus 8:22,23; Exodus 12).

(2) The Israelites were also redeemed with silver and gold at times and this was called "redemption money" (Exodus 30:11-16; Numbers 3:44-51; I Peter 1:18-20).

(3) The Israelites experienced the laws of redemption as seen in the function of the Kinsman Redeemer. This involved the redemption of a wife, a slave, or forfeited land inheritance (Leviticus 25; Jeremiah 32:6-15; Ruth 4). The Kinsman Redeemer had to have three qualifications to have three qualifications in order to fulfil this function.

(a) He must be a near kinsman, a relative.
(b) He must be willing to redeem to the lost inheritance, or to buy back the relative.
(c) He must be able to pay the full price of redemption.

All of these laws of redemption shadowed forth the Lord Jesus Christ as our Kinsman Redeemer, fulfilling the laws of redemption as set out by the Lord God.

(a) Christ became our near Kinsman Redeemer by the incarnation and virgin birth (Hebrews 10:5-8).

(b) Christ was willing to redeem the human race and the inheritance forfeited through sin (Hebrews 10:5-10; Psalm 40:7-8).

(c) Christ was also able to pay the full redemptive price (Revelation 5:9; 14:3-4; Galatians 3:13; Titus 2:14; I Peter 1:18-20; Matthew 20:28; Ephesians 1:7; Colossians 1:14; Romans 3:24-25).

(4) The Israelites also were given the revelation of the redemptive name of Jehovah (Exodus 3:14-15; 6:1-6). The New Testament shows how all of these things find fulfilment in the Lord Jesus Christ and His person and work. He is the Lord Jesus Christ. His name is now the greatest redemptive name comprehending in itself all Old Testament redemptive names. He is Jehovah our Redeemer (Exodus 3:14-15).

d. Summary
Christ had redeemed us as sinners out of the slave market of Satan, even as the Romans also had a custom to buy slaves out of the market. We summarize the glorious truth of redemption with Scripture references concerning our redemption in the Redeemer.

(1) He is our Kinsman Redeemer (Revelation 5:9-10; Romans 3:24).

(2) He redeems us from all iniquity (Titus 2:13-14; Psalm 130:8).

(3) He redeems us from the curse of the Law (Galatians 3:13; 4:5).

(4) He redeems us from the kingdom of darkness (Colossians 1:13-14).

(5) He redeems us from all evil, distress, adversity and bondage (Exodus 6:6; Deuteronomy 15:15; Genesis 48:16; Psalm 25:22; I Kings 1:29; II Samuel 4:9).

(6) He will redeem us from death and hell. The final redemptive work will be the redemption of our bodies (Romans 8:22-23; Philippians 3:20-21; I Corinthians 15:52; Ephesians 1:14; 4:30; Job 19:25-27; Hosea 13:14; Psalm 49:15).

(7) He will avenge our enemy and His enemy as the Revenger of Blood. Satan will come under His final judgements and thus the Kinsman Redeemer will avenge the blood of His saints (Psalm 106:10; 107:2; Jeremiah 15:21; Psalm 136:24; Revelation 6:9-11; 16:4-7; 18:20).

The redemptive work of Christ covers the past, present and the future. For this reason the believer can sing the song of redemption, a song which the angels cannot sing (Revelation 5:9-10). The Psalmist exhorts us by saying "Let the redeemed say so..." (Psalm 107:2).

3. Ransom

a. Definition
The word "ransom" refers to the price actually paid in the transaction of redemption, the price paid to release the slave. The distinction and relationship between redemption and ransom may be defined as follows. Redemption is the act of purchasing the one out of the slave market, while ransom is the price paid in the redemptive act.

b. Amplification

(1) Hebrew
Kopher (or Kaphar) meaning "to cover" figuratively "to expiate, condone, to placate or conceal". Figuratively "a redemption price". Translated "bribe, pitch, ransom, satisfaction, sum of money" (Exodus 30:12; Job 33:24; 36:18; Psalm 49:7; Proverbs 6:35; 13:8; Isaiah 43:3; Hosea 13:14).

(2) Greek

(a) Lutron meaning "something to loosen with a redemption price (figuratively atonement). Translated "ransom" (Matthew 20:28; Mark 10:45).

(b) Antilutron meaning "a redemption-price." Translated "ransom" (I Timothy 2:6).

Thus ransom in both Hebrew and Greek simply means the actual price paid in the act of redeeming a person or thing.

c. Illustration
The concept of ransom is abundantly evidenced in the Old Testament revelation of redemption, as previously seen. It may be illustrated by several Scripture references.

(1) The The half-shekel of silver was the ransom money paid for the price of an Israelite soul (Exodus 30:12). This ransom price was to prevent the plagues falling on Israel when numbering the people (note II Samuel 24 with I Chronicles 21).

(2) Even though this was the price of a soul, God said that no amount of money can really ransom the soul of man (Psalm 49:7; Proverbs 6:35).

(3) Job said that God Himself would provide and be the ransom (Job 33:24).

(4) God gave the Egyptians as a ransom price to redeem Israel from the house of bondage. (Isaiah 43:3).

(5) The saints are to be ransomed from the power of the grave and to be redeemed from death (Hosea 13:14).

Man is in bondage to sin and Satan. He needs deliverance and emancipation from Satan's dominion, into which he was sold by Adam. He cannot redeem himself. There is no price man can pay to free himself. The Lord Jesus Christ paid the price of redemption. Christ's death on the cross provided the ransom price. That price is the precious blood of Jesus. We have been purchased with the blood of God. Jesus gave Himself as the ransom price and fulfilled in His death all that was typified in the Old Testament concerning the redemption of the soul. He gave "His life a ransom for many" and this was testified in "due time" (Matthew 20:28; I Timothy 2:6). (Read also Acts 20:28; Ephesians 1:14; Matthew 26:28; Luke 22:19)

4. Substitution

a. Definition
The word "substitution" means "to put in the place of another, or in behalf of another, to exchange, or interchange."

b. Amplification
The Latin word "substitute" was used as a military word, where a person was engaged to serve in the room of another; or one delegated by Law to act for another. A synonym is the word "vicarious" which means "deputed, acting or suffering for another, substituted."

These words are not used in the Scriptures, but the truth of these words is evidenced in both Old and New Testaments. The Greek word which supplies the thought and truth of "substitution" is "Huper" which is translated "for". It is generally accepted that it means "on behalf of, for the sake of."

M.R. Vincent in "Word Studies in the New Testament" says that "In the great majority of passages the sense is clearly for the sake of, or on behalf of. The true explanation seems to be that, in the passages principally in question, those namely relating to Christ's death, as here, Galatians 3:13; Romans 14:15; I Peter 3:18, Huper characterizes the more indefinite and general proposition Christ died on behalf of leaving the peculiar sense of in behalf of undetermined, and to be settled by other passages. The meaning 'instead of' may be included in it, but only inferentially."

c. Illustration
As noted, although the words "substitution" and "vicarious" are not used in Scripture, the truth of these words is abundantly illustrated. The Old and New Testaments teach the fact of substitutionary or vicarious sacrifice for sinners.

(1) Old Testament

(a) The animal which died to provide the coats of skin for Adam and Eve was a substitute victim, dying in their stead, on their behalf (Genesis 3:21 with 4:4).

(b) The sacrificial victims on Noah's altar illustrated the truth of substitution (Genesis 8:20-21), as did also the victims ordained of God on Abram's altar (Genesis 15:7-17).

(c) The ram caught in the thicket by its horns and offered by father Abraham "in the stead of" Isaac, his only begotten son, illustrates wonderfully the doctrine of a substitutionary sacrifice (Genesis 22:13-14).

(d) Every sacrifice and oblation offered upon the altar of brass in the Tabernacle and

Temple taught the offering Israelite the doctrine of substitutionary or vicarious sacrifice. The Israelites were accepted by the Lord in the death of the victim (Exodus 27:1; Leviticus 1-7; Numbers 19,28-29; Leviticus 16).

The innocent victim suffered for, or in behalf of, the offerer. All these foreshadowed the substitutionary sufferings and death of Christ. It was the truth of substitution in the victims which restrained the wrath of God and the immediate death penalty being executed on the guilty sinner, giving all a period of grace in which they could repent and turn to God through vicarious sacrifice.

(2) New Testament

The New Testament writers also attest to the doctrine of Christ's substitutionary sacrifice. Christ's death was vicarious. He suffered for us, in our behalf. He had no sin of His own. He had no need therefore to die. His death was for us, for our sake, in behalf of the guilty sinner.

His substitutionary death fulfills all Old Testament types and prophecies. His cross was the altar. He was the priest. He also was the substitute victim, dying in our place.

(a) Christ died for the ungodly (Romans 5:8).
(b) Christ loved us and gave Himself for us (Galations 2:20).
(c) Christ suffered for sins, the just for the unjust (I Peter 3:18).
(d) Christ died for the people (John 18:14).
(e) Christ gave Himself a ransom for all (I Timothy 2:6).
(f) Christ was made a curse for us (Galatians 3:13).
(g) Christ gave Himself for us as a sweet-smelling savor and sacrifice (Ephesians 5:2,25).

(Read also II Corinthians 5:19-21; Romans 5:6-8; I Corinthians 15:3; Isaiah 53:5-6; I Corinthians 5:7; I Peter 3:21; Mark 10:45; John 10:11; Hebrews 10:1-4; Matthew 26:28) Christ was chosen to die in our stead and in our behalf. Just as Christ was chosen instead of Barabbas, the thief and murderer, and died in his place, whether he recognized it or not, so Christ died in our behalf. The believer knows and accepts that he is a sinner, guilty and condemned and under the death penalty. Christ stepped into the human race by incarnation and took our sin and died in our stead as our substitute, in our behalf. The New Testament writers confirm that Christ's death was indeed substitutionary and vicarious.

5. Propitiation

a. Definition

The word "propitiation" means "to appease, to render favorable." It is also defined as "the offering of a gift or sacrifice or sufficient value in order that the wrath of another might be appeased", or "to appease the righteous wrath of a holy God by the offering of an atoning sacrifice."

b. Amplification

Several Greek words relative to the truth of propitiation are used in the New Testament.

(1) **Hilaskomai** meaning "to conciliate, i.e. to atone for sin, be propitious. Translated "be merciful, make reconciliation for" (Luke 18:13; Hebrews 2:17).

(2) **Hilasmos** meaning "atonement, i.e. an expiator." Translated "propitiation" (I John 2:2; 4:10).

(3) **Hilasteerion** meaning "an expiatory place or thing, i.e. an atoning sacrifice, or specifically the lid of the ark in the Temple." Translated "propitiation, mercy-seat" (Romans 3:25; Hebrews 9:5).

(4) **Hileos** meaning "cheerful, i.e. propitious, and by Hebrew "God is gracious, i.e. in averting some calamity." Translated "Be it far, merciful" (Matthew 16:22; Hebrews 8:12).

Thus "propitiation" involves "conciliation, atonement for sin, expiation of sin, by a sacrificial victim at a specific place." W.E. Vine in "An Expository Dictionary of New Testament Words" (pp. 223-225) comments on these Greek words, which we adapt for our purpose here. The Greek verb "Hilaskomai" was used among the Greeks with the significance to make the gods propitious, to appease, propitiate, in as much as their good will was not conceived as their natural attitude, but something to be earned. This use is foreign to the Greek Bible, with respect to God, whether in the Septuagint or in the New Testament. It is never used of any act whereby man brings God into a favorable attitude or gracious disposition."

The prophets of Baal endeavored to "appease the gods" they called upon by sacrifice and self-mutilation (I Kings 18:21-29). Jacob tried to "appease" his brother Esau, fearing his wrath, by sending ahead a large present, hoping to effect reconciliation (Genesis 32:20). However, man cannot appease God as he has nothing to offer to God which will appease His wrath. It is God in Christ who brought about the appeasement. This was through the vicarious and expiatory sacrifice of Christ. When sin was judged in Christ, God's holy and righteous character was vindicated. Because sin has been dealt with, God's wrath has been appeased and now He can show mercy to the believing sinner in the removal of his guilt and the remission of sins.

c. Illustration
The Old Testament sacrifices for sin, as noted in other theological words, illustrate the truth of propitiation.

(1) The Hebrew word "Kaphar" in connected with "Kopher" a covering, which was the mercy-seat, and is used in connection with the Burnt, Meal, Peace, Sin and Trespass offering (Leviticus 1-7). All point to the appeasement, the propitiation (read also Ezekiel 45:15,17; Exodus 29:33; Leviticus 14:20; 16:20). (The student is referred to the word "atonement" for a fuller development of this truth.)

(2) Christ in His sacrificial offering, in His broken body and shed blood, fulfilled all that was shadowed forth in the Old Testament atonement, as the New Testament writers clearly show.

(a) God set forth Christ and His shed blood to be a propitiation in which our faith must be placed (Romans 3:25).

(b) Christ was the propitiation for the sins of the believer and of the whole world (I John 2:2; 4:10). Sin had to be judged by death. Christ was the sacrifice offered to God to avert wrath on man and secure mercy.

(c) Christ as a merciful and faithful High Priest made reconciliation, or atonement for the sins of the people (Hebrews 2:17).

(d) Christ is the mercy-seat personified. All that was typified in the blood-sprinkled mercy-seat, the lid of the ark of the covenant, pointed to Christ and finds fulfilment in Him and His incorruptible blood. As the wrath of a holy God was appeased while He gazed upon the blood on the mercy-seat, covering the Law of God, the ministration of death, so God gazes on Christ the Mercy-Seat with His shed blood and His wrath is appeased and He is rendered favorable to us. (Romans 3:25; Exodus 25:22; Hebrews 9:5).

(e) It is because Christ died that God's wrath has been appeased and He can now be gracious to us and avert the calamity that was to come upon us (Hebrews 8:12; Luke 18:13). It has been said "propitiation is an act of God whereby He frees Himself to act in love towards the sinner." In summary we may say:

"**Hilaskomai**" (verb) refers to "the **act** of appeasement" Christ's death.

"**Hilasmos**" (noun) refers to "the **one** or thing which appeases" Christ and His shed blood.

"**Hilasteerion**" (noun) refers to "The **place** of appeasement". The Mercy-Seat, or now Throne of God, as the blood is taken from the cross to the throne.

(The student is referred to the Hebrew word for "Atonement" for a fuller development of this truth.)

6. Reconciliation

a. Definition
To reconcile means "to make friends and bring together those who are at variance, or at enmity" or "to cause to be conformed to, or adjusted to, a specified norm or standard."

b. Amplification
The words "reconcile" or "reconciliation" as translated from Hebrew in the Authorized Version (7 times) would more correctly be translated "atonement" (to which the student is referred). The word "reconcile" in the Greek language has its own particular meaning, different from the Hebrew word.

(a) Katallaso meaning "to change mutually, i.e. to compound a difference." Translated "reconcile" (Romans 5:10; I Corinthians 7:11; II Corinthians 5:18,19,20).

(b) Katallegeo meaning "exchange, fig., adjustment, i.e. restoration to the (divine) favor." Translated "atonement, reconciling, reconciliation" (Romans 5:11; 11:15; II Corinthians 5:18,19).

(c) Apokatallaso meaning "to reconcile fully." Translated "reconcile" (Colossians 1:20-21; Ephesians 2:16).

(d) Diallasso meaning "to change thoroughly; to conciliate" Translated "reconcile" (Matthew 5:24).

The Greek thought of reconciliation is "to exchange mutually, to compound a difference, to exchange, to adjust, to conciliate, or to restore to favor." The English word is often used in dealing with errors in bank statements. When an account is out of balance, it needs adjustment, it needs to be conciliated, or sometimes there has to be an exchange from the debit column to the credit column. When the differences on both sides have been adjusted then it is said the statement has been reconciled.

With regard to the relationship between God and man, sin brought an estrangement and thus there needs to be a reconciliation. It is not that God has to be reconciled to man. It is man who needs to be reconciled to God. But how can the reconciliation take place? How can the enmity and hostility in man's heart brought about through the entrance of sin be removed?

It is God who took the initiative in effecting the reconciliation. This He did in Christ. Before sin entered, God and man stood face to face with each other. When sin entered, man turned his back on God. This caused God to turn His back on man. (Hosea 5:15; 6:1-3; Isaiah 59:1-2; Genesis 4:13-14). The holiness of God and the sinfulness of man were at enmity. How can a holy God and sinful man be reconciled? God's answer was the substitutionary and atoning death of Christ on the cross. In Christ's death sin, which brought the enmity, was dealt with, God's righteousness and holiness were upheld, His wrath was appeased. His holy law was vindicated, and the effect of the atonement was reconciliation.

Christ's death satisfied the demands of God and now God has turned His face toward man. It remains now for man to turn around and face God. Man can do this because Christ Jesus stands between him and God. William Evans says concerning Christ's death, "God is propitiated and man is reconciled". In Christ man is adjusted, conciliated, restored to favor. In Christ God has balanced the account. This is the reconciliation.

c. Illustration

The several uses of the word by the New Testament writers, especially Paul, supply sufficient illustration of the doctrine of reconciliation.

(1) A wife and a husband that have been estranged need to be and can be reconciled (I Corinthians 7:11).

(2) In the case of two brothers at variance with each other there has to be reconciliation. The Greek word here has the thought of mutual hostility and thus there needs to be mutual conciliation (Matthew 5:24).

(3) Man has to be reconciled to God for the wrong is on man's part, not God's. The reconciliation has been effected in the atoning death of Christ.

    (a) Man is reconciled by the death of God's Son (Romans 5:10-11). Note: the word "atonement" in verse 11 should be translated more correctly "the reconciliation."

    (b) Man is reconciled by the work of the cross (Ephesians 2:16).

    (c) Man is reconciled in Christ (Colossians 1:20-22).

    (d) God was in Christ reconciling the world unto Himself. Because of this the church has been given the word and ministry of reconciliation. As the Body of Christ in earth, the Church stands in Christ's stead to beseech men to be reconciled to God (II Corinthians 5:18-21).

7. Atonement

a. Definition

The word "atone" means "to cover, to expiate, or to make at one". Atonement has the meaning "to harmonize, expiation, satisfaction or reparation given for an offense."

b. Amplification

We note some of the relative Hebrew words concerning the atonement.

(1) Kaphar meaning "to cover; fig. to expiate or condone, to placate or conceal." Translated "appease, make an atonement, cleanse, disannul, forgive, be merciful, pacify, pardon, purge away, put off, make reconciliation (Exodus 30:10; Leviticus 4:20,26,31; Genesis 32:20; Ezekiel 16:63; 45:15,17,20; Leviticus 8:15; 6:30; 16:6-33; Daniel 9:24; Psalm 65:3; 78:38).

(2) Kippur meaning "expiation." Translated "atonements, atonement" (Exodus 29:36; 30:10:16; Leviticus 23:27,28; 25:9; Numbers 5:8; 29:11).

(3) Kapporeth meaning "a lid" used only of the cover of the sacred Ark. Translated "mercy-seat" (Exodus 25:17-22; 26:34; 30:6; 31:7; 35:12; 37:6-9; 39:35; 40:20; Leviticus 16:2,13-15; Numbers 7:89; I Chronicles 28:11).

(4) Kopher meaning "to cover, i.e., literally a village as covered in bitumen as used for coating, and figuratively a redemption price." Translated "bribe, camphire, pitch, ransom, satisfaction, sum of money, village" (Genesis 6:14; Exodus 21:30; 30:12; Numbers 35:31-32; I Samuel 6:18; Job 33:24; 36:18; Psalm 49:7-8; Song of Solomon 1:14; Isaiah 43:3).

Thus "Atonement" means "to cover, expiate, to appease, cleanse, forgive, be merciful, pacify, pardon, purge away, put off, make reconciliation."

Note: The only place the word "Atonement" is used in the New Testament is Romans 5:11 where the Greek word is "Katallagee" and should have been translated "the reconciliation."

Under "Nature of the Atonement" we considered the word atonement while here we deal more specifically with the "Work of the Atonement." As seen previously the holiness of God coming against the sinfulness of man produces divine wrath. This wrath needs to be appeased. Sin has to be dealt with. The death of Christ was the appeasement. There the penalty of the broken law was carried out for "the wages of sin is death" (Genesis 2:17; Romans 6:23). Once the death penalty has been executed, the Law can do no more. The law is satisfied, justice is upheld.

Myer Pearlman in Knowing the Doctrines of the Bible (pp. 201-202) answers some pivotal issues concerning the Atonement, which we adapt here. Some hold that:

● Atonement is not possible for man because God's law is fixed and final. They teach that in no way can sin be remedied and the sinner brought back into a relationship with God.

● Atonement is not necessary for God is love and is too kind and gracious to demand satisfaction for His broken law, therefore forgiveness can be taken for granted. The New Testament teaches:

● Atonement is both necessary and possible. It is possible, because God is gracious as well as just; necessary, because God is just as well as gracious.

Pearlman further shows that the first two are errors concerning the very character of God. "The first over-emphasizes His justice to the exclusion of His grace; the second over-emphasizes His grace to the exclusion of His justice. The atonement does justice to both aspects of His character, for in the death of Christ God acts both justly and graciously... at Calvary, the penalty of sin was paid and the divine law honored; God was thus enabled to be gracious without being unjust, and just without being ungracious." He also states on page 202 "In the atonement, God does justice to His character as a gracious God. His righteousness called for the punishment of the sinner, but His grace provided a plan for the pardon of the sinner. At the same time He does justice to His character as a righteous God. God would not do justice to Himself if He displayed compassion to sinners in a way which made light of sin, and which ignored the tragic reality."

c. Illustration
There are a number of illustrations of the atoning work in the Old Testament but the fullest is that which took place in Israel on the national Day of Atonement. We will consider the atonement as typified in the Old Testament and fulfilled in the New Testament.

(1) The Old Testament

(a) The Daily Atonement
The regular daily sacrifices in the Tabernacle were offered as an atoning sacrifice and these were the sacrifices which brought about the expiation of sin. It was on the basis of these sacrifices that God accepted both the individual and the people corporately and could dwell among them.

(i)   Aaron and his sons were consecrated to the priesthood by means of the atoning sacrifices (Exodus 29:33-45; Leviticus 8:34).

(ii)   The altar of brass also was dedicated with atoning sacrifices (Exodus 29:36-37).

(iii)   Moses made an atonement for Israel's sin of idolatry in the making of the golden calf (Exodus 32:30).

(iv)   The Israelites were atoned for in the ordained sacrifices (Leviticus 1:4; 4:20,26,31,35; 5:6,16,18; 6:7; 7:7; 12:7,8).

(v)   Aaron made atonement for himself and the people (Leviticus 9:7).

(vi) Lepers also had to be atoned for before being brought into the camp of the Israelites (Leviticus 14:18-31,53).

(Read also Leviticus 19:22; Numbers 5:8; 6:11; 8:12,19-21; 15:25-28; 16:46-47; 25:13; 28:22,30; 31:50; II Samuel 21:3; I Chronicles 6:49; II Chronicles 29:24; Nehemiah 10:33).

(b) The Day of Atonement

Beside the regular daily atoning sacrifices and bloodshedding, there was the yearly expiation. This day was called the Day of Atonement. It was the most solemn day in national history and that which took place on this day gives us the richest illustration of the true meaning of the atonement. The details are fully covered in Leviticus 16; 23:26-32; Exodus 30:1-10 and Numbers 29:7-11. On this day the High Priest made atonement for himself, the whole nation and the sanctuary. This day was also referred to as "the cleansing of the sanctuary" (Daniel 8:13-14). On this day only, the High Priest entered within the veil, into the Holiest of All, sprinkling the blood of atonement which had been shed at the brazen altar on the mercy seat, the lid of the Ark of the Covenant.

The Shekinah glory-presence of God dwelt upon the Ark. It was God's throne on earth in the midst of His people Israel. Within the Ark were the tables of the Law. The mercy-seat acted as a lid on the Ark, thus "covering" the Law, and on the mercy seat was sacrificial blood. As the faces of the Cherubim looked towards each other and yet toward the mercy-seat, they beheld atoning blood, instead of the Law which was a ministration of death. The Law works wrath upon all who violate it. The blood on the mercy-seat was the evidence that death had taken place for death is the penalty of transgressed law. The blood now covers sin from God's sight so that it has no power to provoke His wrath.

It is this which constitutes the atonement. It is the blood on the mercy-seat which constitutes the appeasement, the cleansing, the pardon, the expiation, the propitiation, the satisfaction, the reconciliation. It is this that reveals a pardoning and merciful God. It is here that "mercy and truth have met together; righteousness and peace have kissed each other" (Psalm 85:10).

The Scriptures themselves give the best explanation of the atonement.

Leviticus 17:11 "For the life of the flesh is in the blood, and I have given it to you upon the altar to make an atonement for your souls; for it is the blood that maketh an atonement for the soul."

Exodus 12:13 "...and when I see the blood, I will pass over you and the plague shall not be upon you to destroy you..."

(c) The Result of the Atonement in Israel

(i) The sins of the nation were covered (Psalm 32:1-2; Psalm 78:38; 79:9; Leviticus 5:17-18).
Note: Animal blood in the Old Testament only "covered" sins; it did not and could not "cleanse" it. Only the blood of Jesus could do that (Hebrews 10:1-4,11).

(ii) The sinner also was covered and hid from wrath. He was accepted in the perfections of the atoning sacrifice (Leviticus 4:22-23,27-35).

(iii) Sins were blotted out (Jeremiah 18:23; Isaiah 43:25; 44:22).

(iv) Sins were removed (Isaiah 6:7).

(v) Sins were cast behind God's back and cast into the depths of the sea (Micah 7:19; Isaiah 38:17).

(vi) Sins were remitted, or sent away (Hebrews 9:22).

(vii) Sins were purged (Psalm 79:9).

(2) The New Testament
The New Testament clearly reveals that the Old Testament foreshadowed the atoning work of Christ. The writer to the Hebrews especially deals with the atoning sacrifices and emphasizes the Day of Atonement ceremony. Christ Jesus being both priest and sacrifice fulfills in Himself the Day of Atonement ceremonies.

He offered the sacrifice at Calvary's cross, the New Testament sacrificial altar. His body was broken and His blood was shed there. In His ascension He entered within the veil of the heavenly and the true sanctuary. There He presented Himself and His blood, at the throne of God, the New Testament Ark of the Covenant. He Himself is also the mercy-seat (Hebrews 6:19-20; Matthew 27:51; Hebrews 9:1-28; 10:5-22; 13:11-15,20; Revelation 11:19; 15:5). Paul says of Christ: "Whom God hath set forth to be a propitiation (Greek "Hilasteerion" or "Mercy-seat") through faith in His blood..." (Romans 3:25).

J. A. Seiss ably expressed it in the following manner: "The atonement is the actual and official presentation of the blood of Jesus Christ at the throne of God by Himself, our Great High Priest". This is the atonement, the reconciliation, and 'the finished work' (John 17:1-4; 19:30)."

What then are the results of Christ's atoning work?

(a) The sins of the believer are cleansed, not just covered (I John 1:5-7).

(b) The believer is accepted of God in Christ's righteousness (II Corinthians 5:19-21).

(c) God's wrath is appeased, He is pacified, His Law is vindicated (Romans 1:18; 2:5; 5:9).

(d) God is gracious, propitiated towards sinful man (Luke 18:13; Hebrews 9:5; I John 2:2; 4:10; Romans 3:25).

(e) Reconciliation has taken place. God and man face each other in Christ (Hebrews 2:17).

(f) The believer has a blood-sprinkled mercyseat in the throne of God by which he can approach God (Romans 3:25; Hebrews 4:16).

(g) Christ is our Great High Priest and lives in the power of an endless life (Hebrews 7:16).

(h) The blood of Jesus Christ is ever available for cleansing until the believer is brought to a state of sinless perfection (I John 1:5-7; Revelation 12:11; Hebrews 7:11).

d. Summary
Undoubtedly the greatest illustration of the Doctrine of the Atonement is that which God gave to Israel in the Tabernacle of Moses and the Temple of Solomon. In the Outer Court, at the Altar of Brass, the Israelite would see in the sacrificial victims the great truths of redemption, ransom, substitution, and propitiation. In the Holiest of All, at the Ark of the Covenant, especially on the great Day of Atonement, the great truths of reconciliation and atonement would be seen as the High Priest made the actual and official presentation of the atoning blood on the mercyseat. And then over and above the whole of the economy would be seen the revelation of God's Law and wonderful grace.

No one word is sufficient or complete in itself but the combined truths in all of these words put together constitute the atonement.

VI. THE REALIZATION OF THE ATONEMENT

A. Provision — Divine Sovereignity

We have seen how Christ Jesus made full atonement for man's sin. He paid the debt we owed. He reconciled us back to God. He has completely satisfied the demands of a holy God and His holy Law. In the cross He suffered the wrath of God that should have fallen on us and now God's amazing love and grace have been revealed. The atonement has been made. It is a finished work. Redemption is complete.

The questions now arise: Is the atonement for all, or is it a limited atonement? Are all saved, or is the atonement limited to an elect number; are the benefits of the atonement received on conditions or without conditions?

1. Provision and Extent

Theologians do not often disagree on the provision of the atonement, but they do differ concerning the extent of the atonement. The Scriptures show that the redemptive work of Christ was made in behalf of all mankind. God has excluded no-one in His merciful provision. God is not willing that any should perish, but that all should come to eternal life. No person will be cast into hell because Christ did not die for them, but because they rejected God's offer of salvation in Christ.

a. Christ died for all (II Corinthians 5:15).

b. He tasted death for every man (Hebrews 2:9).

c. God loved the world that He gave His only Son to die for the whosoever (John 3:16).

d. The Lamb of God took away the sins of the world (John 1:29; John 4:42).

e. Christ made justification available for all (Romans 5:18-20).

f. The Gospel is available and to be preached to every creature (Mark 16:15; Matthew 28:18-20; Revelation 22:17).

g. God is not willing that any should perish (I Timothy 2:4; II Peter 3:9).

h. God is no respector of persons (Romans 2:11; Acts 10:34-35).

i. Christ is the propitiation for the sins of the whole world (I John 2:2; 4:10).

j. Christ died for the elect of God who God foreknew would accept salvation on His conditions (I Timothy 4:10; Matthew 20:28; John 17:9; II Timothy 1:9; Ephesians 5:25; Revelation 13:8).

Thus the Scriptures show that provision for the salvation of all men has been made. Christ made salvation available for all, however, all will not be saved, because of their unbelief and rejection of salvation (Titus 2:11; Ezekiel 33:11; John 5:40; II Corinthians 5:18-20).

Man is a free-will agent and must respond to the convicting and soul-saving power of the Holy Spirit in order to receive the salvation provided at infinite cost. For although salvation is free, it is costly as it cost God His Son. Man is free to accept or reject the salvation which he in no way deserves nor could ever merit (Titus 3:5; Ephesians 2:5-9).

2. Provision and Application

Since Christ has rendered penal satisfaction to the Father God, He alone has the right to declare the terms upon which the benefits of His death and resurrection are to be bestowed.

Jesus Christ was not obligated to die for any man in the first place, neither is He now obligated to actually save anyone. As He was moved by grace to provide salvation, so He is moved by grace to lay down the conditions on which salvation may be experienced. The following passages point out clearly the distinction between the provision and application of the atonement.

a. Christ is the Savior of all men (provision), especially of those who believe (application) (I Timothy 4:10).

b. God so loved the world that He gave His only begotten Son (provision) that whosoever believeth in Him (application) should not perish but have everlasting life (John 3:16).

c. Christ is the author of eternal salvation (provision) to all them that obey Him (application) (Hebrews 5:9).

d. Christ was once offered to bear the sins of many (provision) and to those that look for Him (application). He will appear the second time without sin unto salvation (Hebrews 9:28).

e. There is grace and redemption in Christ Jesus (provision) and God can be just and the justifier of them that believe (application) in Jesus (Romans 3:24-26). (Read also II Peter 3:9; I Timothy 2:4,6; Matthew 1:21; Hebrews 2:3,9; I Corinthians 1:18)

Robert Clarke, in The Christ of God (pp. 111-112) says "It is universal in its scope, but limited in its application... Though God loves all, and Christ died for all and salvation is offered to all, it does not follow that all will be saved, irrespective of their response to the truth of the Gospel. Not all are saved because the application of the atoning work of Christ is limited to those who repent of sins and trust in Christ."

It is therefore important to maintain balance between the provision and application of the atonement. If divine provision is over-emphasized, then it is easy to fall into fatalism and extreme pre-destination. If human application is ever over-emphasized, then it is easy to fall into legalism and works. Divine provision is God giving. Human application is man receiving. The Scriptures contain the two streams of divine sovereignty and human responsibility, and both should be kept in proper perspective.

We now proceed to see what the Scriptures teach on the Godward side of the atonement, that is, what God has provided in Christ.

3. The Grace of God
As noted under "The Atonement Doctrinally" the provision for man's redemption stems entirely from the grace of God. It should be kept in mind that it is God who took the initiative to redeem man. When Adam sinned in the Garden of Eden, it was God who came seeking Adam, Adam was not seeking God. The atonement was God's idea, not man's (Romans 3:10-12; 5:8-10; John 6:44; 15:16).

Man could not initiate the provision of the atonement, and neither can he initiate its application. God has taken the initiative in Christ and manifested His grace to all men (Titus 2:11). All men therefore are without excuse (Romans 1:20). Grace is the ill-deserved, unmerited and unearned favor of God bestowed upon sinful man. God is not obligated to save man. Yet in providing salvation, His justice required that it be made available for all men on His terms. God is not partial, nor is He a respecter of persons.

However, although salvation has indeed been provided for all, not all will be saved. The Scriptures show that the elect will be saved, which brings us to the great doctrines of election, foreknowledge, predestination and calling.

4. The Election of God
Thiessen (page 344) defines election by saying, "By election we mean that sovereign act of God's grace whereby He chose in Christ Jesus for salvation all those whom He foreknew would accept Him. This is redemption in its elective aspect." In its simplest meaning, election refers to the intention, process and result of making a choice. It refers to an act of the will but more specifically in the Scriptures to an act of the divine will.

The Hebrew word "Bawkheer" means "to select, choose, or the person chosen (II Samuel 21:6; Psalm 89:3; 105:6; Isaiah 42:1; 43:20). The Greek word for "elect" is "Eklectos" and means "picked out, chosen by God" (I Peter 2:4,9; Revelation 17:14; Romans 8:33; Colossians 3:12; Titus 1:1). The Greek word for "election" is "Ekloge", meaning "selection, choice, the act of picking out, the person chosen" (Romans 9:11; 11:5,7,28; II Peter 1:10; Acts 9:15). Thus the word simply means "choice, chosen, selected, picked out."

a. Who are the Elect?

(1) Christ is God's elect (Luke 23:35; I Peter 2:4,6; Isaiah 42:1).

(2) The angels are God's elect; that is, those angels who did not fall with Satan (I Timothy 5:21).

(3) Israel in the Old Testament was the elect nation (Romans 9:4; Isaiah 45:4; Romans 11:28; Deuteronomy 7:6).

(4) Moses and Aaron were God's elect (Psalm 106:23).

(5) Priests were chosen as God's elect (Deuteronomy 21:5), yet many died in their sins.

(6) Kings were also elected, such as David and Saul, yet Saul died in his sins (Psalms 13:3; I Samuel 16:12; 20:30; I Chronicles 28:5).

(7) Prophets were elected, yet there were false prophets also (Jeremiah 1:5; Revelation 2:14).

(8) Apostles were chosen by the Lord (Luke 6:13; Acts 9:15; 13:17; Acts 1:2,24; 22:4; John 6:71). However, some were fallen apostles, such as Judas.

(9) The Church is now God's elect (Matthew 20:16; 22:14; 24:22,24,31; Mark 13:20,22,27; Luke 18:7; John 15:16,19; Romans 8:33; 11:5, 7; I Corinthians 1:27,28; Ephesians 1:4; Colossians 3:12; I Thessalonians 1:4; II Timothy 2:10; Titus 1:1; I Peter 1:2; 2:9; II Peter 1:10; Revelation 17:14).

Thus a consideration of the use of the word shows us that these various ones were chosen by God for specific purposes.

b. Aspects of Election
It should be noticed in the above passages of Scriptures that all who were "elected" by God were not necessarily elected to eternal life. The context of Scripture shows that there are two major aspects of election and these have to be kept distinct.

(1) The Election of Time
This is an election for temporal purpose, whether positive or negative. This refers to God's choosing of individuals or nations to fulfil His purposes in relation to time. Pharoah, Moses, Cyrus, Paul, Israel, Assyria and Babylon are examples of such choice.

(2) The Election of Eternity
That is, an election involving eternal destiny, on the basis of grace. When speaking of election in relation to the plan of salvation, we mean the sovereign act of God in grace whereby He chose in Christ Jesus for salvation all those whom He foreknew would accept Him.

Election is a **sovereign act of God,** whereby certain are chosen from among mankind for Himself (John 15:19). God is under no obligation to elect anyone, since all were lost in Adam. There was nothing of merit in any man of Adam's fallen race.

Election is wholly of **grace,** apart from human merit. Man is utterly unworthy of salvation. He deserves damnation. Grace chose to provide salvation for man.

Election is only applicable to those **"in Christ."** God could not choose man in himself because of his sinfulness and ill-deserving state; therefore God could only choose man on the merits of Christ.

5. Election and Foreknowledge

Election is solidly **based on God's foreknowledge.** God chose those whom He foreknew would accept Christ. The Greek word for "foreknow" is "Proginosko" and means "to know beforehand." The Greek word for "foreknowledge" is "Prognosis" and means "a knowing beforehand." The first is used twice of human knowledge (Acts 26:5; II Peter 3:17), but both are otherwise used of divine knowledge, referring to God's ability to perfectly know the future. Scripture states that God's works are known to Him from the beginning (Acts 15:18).

a. Christ was foreknown and foreordained to die (Acts 2:23; I Peter 1:20).

b. Israel was foreknown as God's earthly people (Romans 11:2)

c. The Church is foreknown also (Romans 8:29-30; I Peter 1:1-2).

The Scriptures definitely base God's election on His foreknowledge.

Romans 8:29 "For whom He did foreknow, them He also did predestinate..."

I Peter 1:1-2 "...to the elect...according to the foreknowledge of God the Father."

God foreknew who would respond to His offer of salvation in Christ, and who would respond to the conviction of the Holy Spirit.

Other related words are "foresee" (Acts 2:25), "foreordain" (I Peter 1:20), and "foretell." All of these words are related to God's omniscience. Because God foreknows everything, because He foresees, He can therefore foretell and foreordain. Foretelling refers to prophecy, and prophecy is not predestination, it is foreknowledge. Because God foreknew, and foresaw, He also foretold through the mouth of the prophets that which would come to pass. Thus election is founded upon foreknowledge.

6. Election and Predestination

The word "predestinate" is the Greek word Pro-orizo, and means "to previously mark out a boundary line, to pre-determine, decide beforehand." Compared with foreknowledge, predestination is used to refer to a determination made previous to its actual coming to pass and which carried with it the power to make it come to pass. Thus, it is an action of will only attributed to God Himself. We may say that foreknowledge is "to know beforehand that certain things will happen", while predestination is "to arrange or determine beforehand how they shall happen". However, foreknowledge precedes predestination. God's foreknowledge did not stem from election or predestination. Election and predestination are founded in God's foreknowledge.

a. The work of the atonement was predestined (Acts 4:28; I Corinthians 2:7).

b. The saints are predestined:

(1) To be conformed to the image of Christ (Romans 8:29-30).
(2) To become the children of God (Ephesians 1:5).
(3) To bring praise and glory to God (Ephesians 1:11-12).

Though election and predestination go hand in hand, the following distinction should be noted. Election means that God has chosen to save those He foreknew would accept His Son. Predestination means that God has fixed the destiny beforehand of those who are and who are not of His election. Thus predestination can be viewed as the bringing to pass of God's election. While election looks back to foreknowledge, predestination looks forward to destiny, yet both are based on God's foreknowledge and neither violates man's free-will choice.

7. Election and Calling

There are several words used in the Greek language relative to the calling that men receive because of God's grace.

a. Definition of Calling

(1) Kaleo meaning "to call into one's presence, invite, to call by name."
(2) Kletos meaning "called, invited."
(3) Klesis meaning "a calling to, an invitation to."
(4) Proskaleo meaning "to call to one's self, to bid to come to one's self."

These words imply a calling or an inviting and when used in relation to God being the One who calls or invites, they point to one of two major areas.

b. Distinction in Calling

(1) A call to participation in the privileges of the Gospel, that is, to salvation.
(2) A call to participation in the function of the Gospel, that is, to ministry.

c. The Calling of God

Thiessen (page 350) in relation to the atonement, defines God's call as "that act of grace by which He invites men to accept by faith the salvation provided in Christ." We may ask then who, why and by what means does God call?

(1) Who does God Call?

He calls the "whosoever"; He calls all men unto Himself (Matthew 11:28; John 3:15,16; Romans 8:30; Revelation 22:17; Isaiah 45:22; Matthew 28:19-20; Mark 16:15; I Timothy 2:4; II Peter 3:9; Matthew 22:9). God's desire is to save all and the only obstacle to any man's salvation is his own will.

(2) Why Does God Call?

He calls that men might come to a knowledge of Himself by repentance and faith in His Son. (Matthew 3:2; 4:17; Mark 1:15; Acts 2:38; 17:30; II Peter 3:9; Mark 1:15; John 6:29; Acts 16:31; 19:4; Romans 10:9-10; I John 3:23).

(3) How does God Call?

God uses various means to call men unto Himself.

(a) He uses the Word of the Gospel (Romans 10:17; II Thessalonians 2:14).

(b) He uses the ministry of the Holy Spirit to convict and convince men of righteousness, sin and judgement (John 16:7-11; Genesis 6:3; Hebrews 3:7,9).

(c) He uses the ministers of the Gospel and His saints also (II Chronicles 36:15; Jeremiah 25:4; Romans 10:14-15).

(d) He uses His providential dealings to bring man to Himself (Romans 2:4; Jeremiah 31:3; Isaiah 26:9; Psalm 107:6).

While God's election took place in eternity prior to time, based on His foreknowledge, His call to man presently resounds through out the ages of time and will continue to sound until man's "space of repentance" is ended (Revelation 2:21).

d. Summary of Calling

God in His grace, on the basis of foreknowledge, elected in eternity those He knew would respond to His calling in time, and thus predestined them to eternal happiness in heaven. Others who God knew would reject His extended grace have their destiny in everlasting punishment in hell.

B. Application — Human Responsibility

We now examine the manward side of the atonement in its application. What God has provided in Christ, man must receive and apply. Divine sovereignty and human responsibility meet together in the great redemptive plan. The foundational steps of salvation at the very beginning are (1) Repentance from dead works, and (2) Faith towards God (Hebrews 6:1-2; Acts 20:21).

1. Repentance From Dead Works

a. Importance of the Doctrine of Repentance
The first principle of the Doctrine of Christ is repentance from dead works. It is the beginning of Christ's teaching and is spoken of as the foundation (Hebrews 6:1-2). The doctrine of repentance is a most neglected, yet a most important doctrine in Christian experience. It is a word which has lost its full meaning in modern days.

A false conception of repentance comes from a false conception of sin. A false concept of sin comes from a false concept of the nature and character of a righteous, holy and loving God. Much modern-day preaching of the Gospel is a cheap and easy "only-believism" which neglects the foundation of repentance. William Booth of the Salvation Army said "The chief dangers which confront the present century are religion without the Holy Spirit, Christianity without Christ, forgiveness without repentance, salvation without regeneration, politics without God and heaven without hell."

The importance of repentance is seen in the fact that it is the first word of the Gospel.

(1) The Old Testament prophets preached repentance to the nation of Israel (Ezekiel 14:6; 18:30-32; Jeremiah 8:4-6; Matthew 12:41).

(2) John's first message and word was a call to repentance; his baptism was one unto repentance (Matthew 3:1-8; Acts 19:4).

(3) The first word Christ preached was repentance (Matthew 4:17; 9:13; 11:20-24; 12:41).

(4) The apostles called men to repentance (Mark 6:7-13).

(5) The first message of Peter at Pentecost was a call to repentance (Acts 2:37-38; Luke 24:49; Acts 3:19).

(6) Paul also preached repentance first to both Jew and Gentile (Acts 26:20-21).

(7) The very first principle of the listed doctrines of Christ is repentance (Hebrews 6:1-2).

(8) Before Christ ascended He told His disciples to preach repentance to all nations, beginning at Jerusalem (Luke 24:49).

(9) Repentance is a command to all men, without which all will perish (Acts 17:30; II Peter 3:9; Luke 13:3).

b. What Repentance is Not
Even as there are false views over so many other areas in theology, so there are false concepts of the doctrine of repentance. We will consider what repentance is not, before considering what it is.

(1) It is not conviction of sin.
Conviction precedes repentance, but not all who are convicted come to repentance (Genesis 6:3; Mark 6:16-20; Acts 24:24-25).

(2) It is not worldly sorrow.
There is a worldly sorrow and there is a godly sorrow. Worldly sorrow is a sorrow for the consequences of sin, not for the sin itself. Esau (Hebrews 12:17) and Judas (Matthew 27:3-5) exemplify this fact.

(3) It is not reformation.
Reformation is "turning over a new leaf". However, a person can reform his life without being regenerated by the Spirit of God (Isaiah 64:6).

(4) It is not being religious.
The Pharisees in Christ's day were extremely religious, but they were hypocrites. They did not come to repentance, and thus crucified Jesus their Messiah (Matthew 5:30; 3:7-12; 23:1-25).

(5) It is not 'only-believism' or mental faith.
Mental faith is merely mental assent and acceptance of a set of creeds or historical facts about Jesus without any corresponding change in the life. It is a dead faith, the faith that demons have (James 2:19-20).

c. What Repentance is
The Bible teaching on repentance shows that it involves two major areas. There is both a root and fruit of repentance when it is genuinely seen in a person's life.

(1) The Root of Repentance

(a) Hebrew
The word "repent" is used about 45 times in the Old Testament, most of the reference being used of God Himself. The Hebrew word **"Nacham"** translated "repent" means "to sigh, i.e. to breathe strongly, by implication, to be sorry, to pity, to console". It has the thought of sighing, groaning, lamenting. When it is used in reference to God, it refers to the sorrow, sighing, and lamentation that He experiences over the failures of His people, and mankind (Genesis 6:5-6; I Samuel 15:11,29; II Samuel 24:16; Malachi 3:6).

Another Hebrew word **"Shuwb"** translated "repent" means "to turn back, to retreat" and has the thought of turning and returning (I Kings 8:47; Ezekiel 14:6; 18:30). The expressions "turn" or "turn away" and "return" are used about 600 times. Thus the Hebrew thought in the word repentance involves "sighing, groaning, lamenting, turning and returning."

(b) Greek
The word "repent" is used over 60 times in the New Testament. The Greek words here define its meaning for us.

Mentanoeo meaning "to think differently or afterwards, i.e. to reconsider, feel compunction, and it is translated "repent" (Matthew 3:2; 4:17; 11:20-21; 12:41; Luke 15:7,10; Acts 2:38; 3:19; Revelation 2:5, 16,21,22; 9:20).

Metamelomai meaning "to care afterwards, to regret" and translated "repent" (Matthew 21:29,32; 27:3; II Corinthians 7:8; Hebrews 7:21).

Metanoia meaning "compunction for guilt, including reformation; by implication, reversal of another's decision; and it is translated "repentance" (Matthew 3:8,11; 9:13; Mark 1:4; 2:17; Acts 5:31; 11:18; 19:4; 20:21; 26:20; Hebrews 12:17; II Peter 3:9).

Thus repentance in the Greek involves a change of mind, thinking differently, reconsidering, caring afterwards, regret and reversal of a decision. The root meaning is a change of mind, heart and attitude and is applied particularly to sin and one's relationship with God. Repentance is a complete turnabout. It is a change of direction, from going away from God to coming towards God.

The Standard Dictionary defines repentance as: "A sincere and thorough changing of the mind and disposition in regard to sin, involving a sense of personal guilt and helplessness, apprehension of God's mercy, a strong desire to escape, or be saved from sin, and voluntary abandonment of it.''

We find that there are actually three elements involved in the nature of true repentance.

(c) The Intellectual Element
Before the fall, man's mind and heart was toward God. The fall brought about a mind in man that is in rebellion against God and His Law, a mind that desires to go its own way. These Scriptures show the state of man's mind since the fall (Colossians 1:21; Ephesians 2:3; II Corinthians 4:4; Romans 8:5-7; II Corinthians 11:3).

Repentance, brought about by the Holy Spirit, is a change of mind, a facing and turning towards God. It is a recognition of the truth of the Gospel, not just merely mental assent to a set of historical or doctrinal facts about Christ (Romans 10:17; Hebrews 11:1). It is a knowledge that one is on the wrong path, going away from God, and this knowledge is brought about by the ministry of the Spirit and the Word. It is a change of mind towards God, sin and self. The intellectual element in repentance deals with the knowledge of sin, that man is guilty before a righteous and holy God and that he is lost apart from God's saving grace. (Psalm 51:3,7,11; Job 42:5-6; Luke 15:17-19; Matthew 21:29).

(d) The Emotional Element
This element has to do with a change of feeling in that there comes a genuine sorrow for sin committed against a holy God. This element involved in repentance is that which includes lamenting, groaning, and sorrow of heart. As the soul realizes how far it has wandered from God, there comes a godly sorrow. This is sorrow for sin itself, not only for its consequences (II Corinthians 7:9-10; Hebrews 12:17; Psalm 51:1-14; Luke 10:13; Genesis 6:6; Psalm 38:18).

(e) The Volitional Element
This element involves a change of will and purpose. It is a turning from sin, an about face. It is getting off the wrong path and onto the right path and going towards God. It is a surrender of the will and life to Christ in total acceptance of His saving power. The prodigal son knew this change of will and acted accordingly (Luke 15:18-20; Acts 11:18; Jeremiah 25:5).

Thus thought, feeling and will are each involved in genuine repentance. Proper Gospel preaching which brings about true repentance enlightens the intellect, stirs the emotions and moves the will away from self and sin toward God and His righteousness. Balanced preaching of the Gospel is needed to have the Holy Spirit produce such repentance. If there is over-emphasis on the intellectual, or the emotionl, without the volitional, then the conversions are often premature births.

(2) The Fruit of Repentance
John the Baptist called for "fruit meet (answerable) for repentance" (Matthew 3:8). Paul called for "works meet for repentance" (Acts 26:29). Fruit declares the inner nature of a tree. A tree is judged by its fruit and fruit is according to root. Evidence of a genuine root of repentance is the fruit of repentance. If there is inward root, there will be outward fruit. Works speak of the outward action of the inward life. A person is judged by his works which arise out of his inward life and disposition. A genuine disposition of repentance will be evidenced by works suitable to repentance.

The fruit or works indicative of repentance are listed here:

(a) A Godly Sorrow for Sin (II Corinthians 7:10; Psalm 38:18; Matthew 27:75).

(b) A Confession of Sin (Psalm 32:5, 51:1-4; Proverbs 28:13, I John 1:9; Luke 18:9-14; 15:11; Matthew 5:23-24; James 5:16).

(c) A turning towards God through Christ (Hebrews 6:1-2; I Thessalonians 1:9; Acts 26:18).

(d) A Forsaking of Sin (Psalm 119:58-60; Isaiah 53:6; Matthew 3:8-10; Proverbs 28:13; Isaiah 55:6-7; Ezekiel 18:20-32). This is particularly pertaining to the works of the flesh (Galatians 5:19).

(e) A Turning from Dead Works (Hebrews 6:1-2; 9:14). This is especially pertaining to religious works of an unregenerate person. Any religious works done before salvation or to earn salvation, are dead works. People dead in trespasses and sins can only produce dead works, no matter how religious (Ephesians 2:1-5; Colossians 1:21; I Timothy 5:6).

(f) A Hatred of Sin (Ezekiel 6:9-19; 20:43-44; 36:31-33).

(g) A Desire for Forgiveness (Psalm 25:11; 51:1; Luke 18:13).

(h) A Restitution Where Possible (Leviticus 6:1-7; Numbers 5:5-8; Luke 19:8; 18:13; 3:1-14).

d. How Repentance is Produced

Repentance has both a divine and human side. Both work together to produce the desired end. Repentance is brought about:

(1) On the Divine Side

(a) By the conviction of the Holy Spirit (John 16:8-11).
(b) By the Word of the Gospel (Matthew 12:41; Luke 24:47; Acts 2:37-38; II Timothy 2:25).
(c) By the gift of God to the heart (Acts 5:30-31; 11:18; II Timothy 2:25).
(d) By the providential goodness of God (Romans 2:4; II Peter 3:9).
(e) By the chastisement of the Lord (Revelation 3:19; Hebrews 12:10-11; II Timothy 2:24-25).

(2) On the Human Side

(a) By acceptance of the truth of the Gospel (Romans 10:17) Touching the intellectual.
(b) By response of the soul (Psalm 38:18). Touching the emotions.
(c) By the surrender of the will (Matthew 16:24). Touching the volitional.

It should be constantly maintained that it is God who takes the initiative in repentance. It does not originate with man. No man can or will repent of himself. It is the very grace of God, who, by the Holy Spirit convicts man to bring him to a state of repentance. Man's part is simply to respond to the conviction. God commands men to repent (Acts 17:30) If He commands, He will also enable man to respond.

e. Examples of Repentance

A consideration of the following examples show the various elements of repentance, both in root and fruit.

(1) The brethren of Joseph were brought to a state of repentance by the process of Joseph's dealings with them (Genesis 42-45).

(2) The city of Ninevah manifested the ingredients of genuine repentance (Jonah 3:5-10; Matthew 12:41).

(3) The prodigal son exemplified true repentance, also, as he returned to his father and home (Luke 15:11-32).

(4) The seven churches in Asia were called upon to repent of the various things which displeased the Lord Jesus (Revelation 1-2-3). Other examples may be seen in genuine penitents such as David (Psalm 51); Daniel (Daniel 9:3-19); Manasseh (II Chronicles 33:11-13); Peter (Matthew 26:75); Saul (Acts 9:6-11); the publican (Luke 18:13), and the dying thief (Luke 23:39-43).

f. Results of Repentance

(1) The sinner is granted saving faith. Saving faith cannot be received without genuine repentance (Ephesians 2:5-8).

(2) The sinner receives pardon and forgiveness. Repentance must precede these benefits of the atonement (Isaiah 55:7; Luke 13:3; Acts 3:19).

(3) The converted sinner brings great joy to the angels in heaven (Luke 15:7,10) as well as to the messengers of the Gospel.

2. Faith Towards God

The second word of the Gospel is "believe" (Mark 1:15; Acts 20:21). The principles of the doctrine of Christ are "repentance from dead works" and then "faith toward God" (Hebrews 6:1-2). In repentance one turns from sin, while in faith one turns toward God. They are like the two sides of a coin; they belong to each other in a Biblical conversion. Just as there are false concepts of repentance so there are false concepts of "faith towards God." There is much teaching on faith which, when weighed in the balance of Scripture, is both unscriptural and even antiscriptural, as well as being out of balance. And these views have to be rooted out and pulled down before one can build and plant the truth (Jeremiah 1:10).

a. Importance of Faith Towards God

The writer to the Hebrews states for us the absolute importance of faith when he says "without faith it is impossible to please God, for he that cometh to God must believe that He is..." (Hebrews 11:6). This is faith's beginning. Faith must begin with the fact that God is, and that He rewards those that diligently seek Him. Nothing can be known or received of God unless man first believes that God is.

b. What Faith is Not

(1) Mental Assent

Though there is an intellectual element involved in both repentance and faith, Godly faith must not be mistaken for mental assent. Mental assent is simply agreement to a set of historical and doctrinal facts about Christ, God and the Bible. It is "head-faith" and not to be mistaken for "heart-faith." Mental assent alone is dead faith. It is the faith of devils (James 2:17-20). Multitudes of religious people "believe" in the Bible, God and Christ but it is merely a mental assent to facts without any real heart faith in Christ.

(2) Presumption

Presumption means to take for granted, to suppose to be true without positive proof. It means to be arrogant, insolent, over-confident, and to take liberties (Psalm 19:12-13).

Presumption is often mistaken for faith because it imitates faith. By faith the Israelites crossed the Red Sea, but the Egyptians assayed or presumed to do so and thus were drowned (Hebrews 11:29). The faith of Israel was in the received Word of God. The presumption of the Egyptians was to imitate the faith-action of Israel without having received a word from God. Presumption is to imitate the faith-actions of others without personally having the Word of God quickened to the heart.

(3) Natural Faith

Natural faith is often mistaken for spiritual faith. Natural faith trusts itself to things seen, in the realm of the natural senses and in the word of others. This is not to be mistaken for spiritual faith. Paul says "All men have not faith" (II Thessalonians 3:2). Untold numbers who exercise faith in the natural realm have no faith in the spiritual realm. Natural faith rests itself wholly on things seen, things visible and things temporal. Spiritual faith rests itself in things unseen, things invisible and things eternal (Hebrews 11:1-3,6).

(4) Faith in Oneself
The principle is "Faith towards God", not faith in oneself. Much "faith" preaching today teaches man to have faith in himself, his own abilities and latent soul powers. This kind of faith makes man his own savior and god. It is really self-saviorism and sets the latent ego up as the God one must have faith in. However, the Bible shows that true faith is in God, through Christ.

c. What Faith Is

(1) Faith Defined
The Greek word "Pistes" translated many times "faith" simply means "trust, assurance, confidence in another and another's word". Faith towards God is simply to trust God, to trust His Word and to have confidence in Him that His Word is true and that He will keep it. It is to wholly trust and rely on God and His Word.

The words "believe" and "faith" come from the same Greek word. The Greek thought of "believing" means a committal and surrender of oneself wholly over to God, to Christ and His Word, trusting Him for all, embracing and obeying His Word (Acts 16:31, Amplified).

The Bible definition of faith is found in Hebrews 11:1. We note several translations.

"Faith is the substance of things hoped for, the evidence of things not seen" (A.V.).

"Faith means that we are confident of what we hope for, convinced of what we do not see" (Moffatt's)

"Faith is the assurance (the confirmation, the title-deed) of that we hope for; being the proof of the things we do not see, and the conviction of their reality faith perceiving as real fact what is not revealed to the senses" (Amplified).

Thus faith is the foundation which upholds the believer's life. It is the assurance and confidence that we have in God's Word. It is the evidence and inner conviction of the reality of things not seen though eternal.

(2) Faith is a Spiritual Sense
Just as in the natural there are five natural senses, seeing, hearing, smelling, touching, tasting, so there are the spiritual counterparts of these senses. These spiritual senses have to be exercised. A consideration of those Scriptures show how the Bible uses these "spiritual senses" (Psalm 34:8; Matthew 5:8; Acts 17:27,28; Psalm 45:8; Revelation 2:11).

Faith is a spiritual sense. It touches and reaches things beyond the natural senses, and which the natural senses cannot lay hold of.

(3) Faith Towards God Through Christ
The Scriptures show that Bible faith is towards God through Christ (Acts 26:20-21). In "faith towards self" man is cast wholly upon man, upon what he is and what he can do. In "faith towards God" man is cast wholly upon God, upon who He is and what He has done in Christ.

d. The Source of True Faith
There is but one true and proper source of faith, the Word of God. If faith is not built upon the Word, it can never stand the storms and tests of life. The key verse to this fact is Romans 10:17 "So then faith cometh by hearing, and hearing by The Word (Greek "Rhema") of God."

To truly hear the Word is to hear the Lord Jesus Christ speaking to the heart by the Spirit. The Living Word is the Christ of God. He is the author and finisher of our faith (Hebrews 12:1-2). The source of true faith is both Christ, the living Word, and the Bible, the written Word. The written Word must become the quickened Word to create proper faith. A study of the "faith heroes" of Hebrews 11 will show that each of them received faith by a word from God, and were thus able to be and do all they were and did.

As with repentance, so there are three elements involved in faith.

(1) The Intellectual Element
It is impossible to have faith without knowledge, though it is possible to have knowledge without faith. When one hears the word of faith, it brings knowledge of God, Christ, salvation and redemption. This is to create faith, not a mental assent, as already noted (James 2:19; Hebrews 11:6; Romans 10:17; Psalm 9:10).

(2) The Emotional Element
This is the response of the heart to the truth of the Gospel. Feeling must not be mistaken for faith, but faith will involve feelings. God's order is fact, faith and feeling, never the reverse. The Christian life is not to be governed by feelings, but neither is it to be without feelings. Faith is solidly founded on the fact of the Gospel, not feelings. The feelings will follow the faith. (Psalm 106:12-13; Matthew 13:20-21).

(3) The Volitional Element
The Gospel brings enlightenment to the understanding. It creates faith and joy in the heart and moves the will to appropriation. The volitional element in faith is closely linked with that of repentance where the heart and will are surrendered to the Lord. There is the act of committal, where one commits himself to the Lord Jesus Christ for salvation.

As in repentance, so in faith, there are the divine and human aspects. Faith is a gift of God to the repentant one, and the penitent responds to God's grace (Jeremiah 31:18; Acts 3:26; Acts 3:19; 11:18; Ezekiel 33:11; Luke 22:32; Ephesians 2:5-8).

e. Aspects of Faith
The New Testament shows that there are various aspects of faith, and the believer is to proceed from "faith to faith" until he comes to the fulness of the Son of God. (Romans 1:17).

We note these five aspects of faith, with appropriate Scriptures.

(1) Saving Faith
Saving faith is God's gift to the repentant sinner that he might be saved (Ephesians 2:8). It is a looking to Christ fully for salvation. This aspect of faith is a passive faith. Here the person trusts Christ and His Word for salvation (Hebrews 11:32-35) Examples of this may be seen in Hebrews 11:4; Luke 7:50; Acts 16:31.

(2) Fruit of Faith
This aspect of faith is spoken of as a fruit of the Spirit. It is more of an active faith. It is faith with obedience. Passive faith trusts the Word when it can do nothing. Active faith obeys the Word when God has spoken it (Hebrews 11:8-10,17-19,28,30,31; Luke 5:4-6; Galatians 5:22).

(3) Gift of Faith
This aspect of faith is spoken of as a gift of the Spirit (I Corinthians 12:1-13). It is listed among the nine spiritual gifts and is a supernatural impartation of faith for the miraculous. This faith involves speaking the Word. It is given to members of the Body of Christ "as He wills". It is not to be mistaken for the other aspects of faith (Hebrews 11:29; Numbers 20:8; Joshua 10:12-14; I Kings 17:1,14; Matthew 17:20-21; Mark 11:12-14, 22-26).

(4) Doctrinal Faith
This aspect of faith is a number of times spoken of simply as "the faith". It refers more especially to the doctrinal revelation of God. It is the Word of faith, the Word of the Gospel. It refers to the sum total of the revelation of God in the whole Bible, and the whole of Biblical doctrine therein. This is "the faith" that was once delivered to the saints, which we are to contend for (Jude 3; Ephesians 4:5,11; I Timothy 6:10; II Timothy 2:18; 3:8; I Timothy 4:1; 6:10; Acts 14:22; 6:7; Colossians 1:23; 2:7).

(5) Perfect Faith
Perfect faith is spoken of as "the spirit of faith" (II Corinthians 4:3; Psalm 116:10; James 2:22). This aspect of faith will be manifested when the saints come to perfection, when every doubt and measure of unbelief will be driven from the heart. It is then that the Word will be made flesh in the believer and no unbelief will be manifested, for all will come to full faith.

This is how the believer will go from "faith to faith". Jesus was The Word made flesh, and no element of doubt or unbelief was ever found in Him. This is God's will for His people. Unbelief came by the fall, by man hearing the word of unbelief through the lips of the serpent (Genesis 3:1-6). Faith comes by redemption, by hearing the word of faith from the lips of the Lord Jesus.

f. Degrees of Faith
When the repentant man accepts Christ as his Savior, and receives saving faith, then he has to move into the life of faith. The justified are to live by faith (Habakkuk 2:4).

The Bible indicates that there are degrees or measures of faith. It is God's will that all move on in the life of faith and indeed go from faith to faith. This can only be as one maintains the life of faith in a personal relationship with Christ and His Word, the source of continuing faith. We note the measures of faith mentioned in Scripture.

(1) No faith (Deuteronomy 32:20; Mark 4:40).
(2) Little faith (Matthew 8:26; 14:31).
(3) Weak faith (Romans 14:1).
(4) Dead faith (James 2:17).
(5) Vain faith (I Corinthians 15:14).
(6) Great faith (Luke 7:9)
(7) Fulness of faith (Acts 11:24).
(8) Stedfast faith (Colossians 2:5).
(9) Rich faith (James 2:5).
(10) Unfeigned faith (I Timothy 1:5; II Timothy 1:5)
(11) Strong faith (Romans 4:19-20).
(12) Measure or proportion of faith (Romans 12:3-6; 1:17).

Faith, as repentance, is something that must be maintained through the believer's walk, as God leads and guides in the paths of righteousness. The Holy Spirit will constantly bring light. As we walk in the light there will need to be a constant maintenance of repentance and faith. Faith is not to be looked on as a work, but as a channel by which the believer receives from God all that is needed. Salvation, sanctification, victory, and spiritual life all come to the believer through the channel of faith.

Hebrews Chapter 11 is called "The Faith Chapter". It sets forth the character and exploits of faith heroes in Bible times. Jesus is the author and finisher of both their faith and ours. All saints must keep "looking unto Jesus" until the race is run (Hebrews 12:1-2).

3. Assurance of Salvation
Upon the foundation of repentance, God desires that the believer receive assurance of salvation. Many Christians never come to a full assurance of salvation because of various hindrances which will be considered in this section.

a. Definition
The dictionary defines "assurance" as "freedom from doubt, firmness of mind; confidence, to make sure or certain". It has also been defined as "a pledge or guarantee; the state of being sure or certain, security." Theologically we may say "Assurance of salvation is the inner knowledge that God has forgiven us in Christ and accepted us in His beloved Son" (Ephesians 1:6).

b. Amplification
The Scriptures teach that the believer should have assurance of salvation and acceptance before

God. Paul was able to preach the Gospel with "full assurance" (I Thessalonians 1:5). He also testified "I know in whom I have believed and am persuaded that He is able to keep that which I have committed unto Him against that day" (II Timothy 1:12). This was Paul's confidence, his security in Christ. John in his epistle, used the word "know" over 40 times, and assured the believer that he may know of his salvation and acceptance in God through Christ. The believer does not presume when he has confidence in the promises of God through Christ (I John 2:3,20,29; 3:14,19-21,24; 4:6,16-17; 5:18).

Paul teaches us concerning the three aspects of assurance in his epistles.

(1) The believer is to have full assurance of **faith** for salvation (Hebrews 10:22).
(2) The believer is to have full assurance of **understanding** (Colossians 2:2).
(3) The believer is to have full assurance of **hope** unto the end (Hebrews 6:11).

The believer experiences this assurance for ever because of peace and righteousness in the Lord Jesus Christ, (Isaiah 32:17) whom God raised from the dead (Acts 17:31).

c. Means of Assurance
There are various means by which the believer can have the inner assurance of salvation upon repentance and faith.

(1) The testimony of the **Word of God.** This is the external evidence and testimony, "It is written" (I John 5:1-2; 2:3,13,14,20,21,29; 5:15-20; John 3:36; 5:24).

(2) The testimony of the **Holy Spirit.** This is the internal evidence. He that believes has the witness in himself (I John 5:9-12; 3:19; John 16:8; Romans 8:16; Galatians 4:6; II Corinthians 1:2). The Holy Spirit bears witness with our spirit that we are born again and are the children of the living God.

(3) The testimony of a **clear conscience.** This also is an inner witness. Paul was able to speak of the fact that his conscience bore witness with the witness of the Spirit (Acts 24:16; Romans 9:1; I Peter 3:21).

(4) The testimony of the **Christian life.** The life a person lives should be in harmony with the Word of God. This is the outward evidence of the inner Christ-life. This also assures the heart before the Lord (I John 3:14; II Corinthians 13:5).

d. Hindrances to Full Assurance
We note here briefly some of the chief hindrances and things which rob believers of full assurance of salvation.
(1) Doubts and unbelief (Mark 11:22-24).
(2) Lack of a forgiving spirit (Mark 11:25-26).
(3) Spiritual lethargy and lukewarmness (Revelation 3:15-16).
(4) Grieving the Holy Spirit (Ephesians 4:30-31).
(5) Allowing the devil to rob us of assurance (John 10:10; James 4:7).
(6) Failure to do the will of God (Luke 12:47-48).
(7) Wrong companionships (Proverbs 4:14; I Corinthians 15:33).
(8) Love of the world (I John 2:15-17; James 4:4).
(9) Failure to maintain love relationship with Christ (Revelation 2:4).
(10) Wilful sin (Hebrews 10:25-29).
(11) Walking by sight, by feelings, instead of faith (II Corinthians 5:7).
(12) Disobedience to the Word of God (Hebrews 5:8-9; Acts 5:29,32).

4. Perserverance and Security
Concerning the perseverance and security of the saints, there are two major views.

a. Unconditional Security
This view holds that the Bible teaches the unconditional security of the believer. It teaches that the doctrine of perseverance is to be seen in the fact that it is God, who, by irresistible grace,

perseveres with the saints until the work of redemption is brought to its full completion. This view holds that the believer has eternal life; that once he is born into the family of God, he can never be unborn, regardless of the life he lives. In this view there is strong emphasis on the sovereignty of God. It is supported by Scriptures such as John 17:12; 10:27-30; Romans 11:29; Philippians 1:6; II Thessalonians 3:3; II Timothy 1:12; 4:18; John 3:15; Isaiah 45:17; Hebrews 5:9; 9:12 and Jude 23-24.

b. Conditional Security

This view holds that the Scriptures teach conditional security of the believer. It holds that the doctrine of perseverance is not just on God's side, but also on man's side. It teaches that God will not force people to be saved or to go to heaven against their own will (John 1:12-13). It further holds that the believer may lapse into a state or period of backsliding and unless there is return to the Lord, the believer could fall into apostasy and be eternally lost. In this view there is strong emphasis on the fact of human responsibility. This view is supported by Scriptures such as I Chronicles 28:9; I Samuel 25:1-44; Ezekiel 3:30; 33:12; Matthew 7:24-25; 25:1-46; John 15:2-6; 17:12; I Corinthians 9:27; 10:12; I Timothy 1:19; Hebrews 4:1; 6:1-6; 10:23-29; I Peter 5:8; II Peter 2:20-22 and II Thessalonians 2:1-12.

The balance between divine sovereignty and human responsibility must always be kept. If one overemphasizes grace and sovereignty, it is possible to lapse into fatalism, looseness and lawlessness. If one overemphasizes human responsibility, he can lapse into works and legalism. Both extremes need to be avoided. Paul tells the believer that he is to "work out his own salvation with fear and trembling, for it is God which worketh in you both to will and to do of His good pleasure" (Philippians 2:12-13).

The Scriptures present the two streams of truth. One stream which speaks of the believer's security in Christ; the other stream which speaks of the believer's responsibility to persevere in Christ. These streams flow together in one and it is this which brings and maintains balance. We note these two streams and consider how the Scriptures teach the perseverance of the saints and the security that is found in perseverance.

c. Perseverance of the Saints

The Scriptures abound with exhortations to the believer to persevere in the Lord and to continue in the Word. They also give many warnings against drawing back from the divine path and the dangers of apostasy from the faith. We will consider the Scriptures which encourage the perseverance of the saints as well as the warnings against backsliding and apostasy.

The word "persevere" means "to persist in any business or enterprize undertaken". In theology it means "continuance in a state of grace". The Lord Jesus exhorted His disciples to continue in His Word, to abide in Him. In John 8:31 He said "If ye continue in My Word, then are ye My disciples indeed." The word "continue" means "to stay in a given place, state, relation or expectancy". It is translated "abide, continue, dwell, remain." Hence the believer is to stay in the Word of Christ, to abide, to continue, to dwell and remain in this state of grace. The believer is exhorted to:

(1) Continue in the **faith** (Acts 14:22; Colossians 1:23).
(2) Continue in the **grace of God** (Acts 13:43).
(3) Continue in the **love of Christ** (John 15:9; Matthew 22:35-40).
(4) Continue in the **goodness of God** (Romans 11:22).
(5) Continue in **prayer** (Colossians 4:2).
(6) Continue in **faith and charity** (I Peter 1:5; I Timothy 2:15).
(7) Continue in the **Word** (John 8:31; I Timothy 4:16; II Timothy 3:14).
(8) Continue in the **Father and the Son** (I John 2:24).
(9) Continue in the **apostles' doctrine** (Acts 2:42).
(10) Continue in or abide in the **vine** (John 15:1-10).

d. Dangers of Backsliding

There are many warnings given to the believer against backsliding or drawing back from following the Lord. They are inapplicable to the unregenerate, or to the sinner. All of these warnings become meaningless to the believer if there is absolutely no possibility of falling from the state of grace. We note some of the major warnings against backsliding both in the Old and New Testaments.

(1) The Old Testament

One of the words used especially in the Old Testament speaking of those who draw back from following the Lord is the word "backslide". This word is used by Jeremiah 13 times (Jeremiah 2:19; 3:6,8,11,12,14,22; 5:6; 8:5; 14:7; 31:22; 49:4). The prophet Hosea also uses this word several times (Hosea 4:16; 11:7; 14:4). It is used once in the Book of Proverbs (Proverbs 14:14). The meaning of the word is "apostasy, heathenish, to flinch, to go back, to retreat" and it is translated "backsliding, turning away." It comes from the root word meaning "to turn back." Thus backsliding in the Hebrew has the thought of turning back, or away, being refractory, stubborn, withdrawing, sliding back, or apostasy. It should be noticed that the prophet Jeremiah and the prophet Hosea were speaking to God's chosen nation, Israel when they used this word to describe their spiritual condition. These should become warnings to all God's people today.

(2) The New Testament

The New Testament does not use the word "backslide" but it does use equivalent expressions in writing to the believer.

(a) Jesus warned that iniquity would abound and the love (Greek: "agape") of many would wax cold. It warns of the love of believers waning in such times (Matthew 24:12).

(b) Jesus also warned about "looking back" and becoming unfit for the kingdom of God (Luke 9:62; 17:32).

(c) Paul spoke of those who made "shipwreck" of the faith (I Timothy 1:18-19).

(d) Peter also spoke of those who knew the way of truth and yet returned as a sow to the mire and a dog to the vomit, their latter end being worse than the first (II Peter 2:20-22).

(e) The writer to the Hebrews warns about those who "draw back unto perdition" (Hebrews 10:38-39).

(f) Jesus spoke about believers who become like "salt without savor" (Matthew 5:13).

(g) Jesus also spoke about branches which bore no fruit and were cut out of the vine (John 15:2,6).

(h) Peter exhorts the believer to continue in the Christian virtues, saying that if he did these things he would "never fall" (II Peter 1:4-9,10).

(i) The believer is told not "to neglect so great a salvation" (Hebrews 2:3).

(j) The Lord Jesus spoke of the tree that brought forth evil fruit. He showed that the person would not be known by calling Him Lord, prophecying, casting out devils or miraculous works, but by the fruits of holy living. This passage is inapplicable to the mere professors or unregenerate (Matthew 7:15-27).

(k) Both Old and New Testaments speak of names being removed from the Book of Life. If this were not possible, then these warnings are meaningless (Exodus 32:30-33; Revelation 3:5; 20:6,14-15; 21:8; 22:18-19). Judas is an example of one who had his name blotted out of the Book of Life (Acts 1:18-22 with Psalm 69:25-28).

(l) The Apostle Paul spoke of the goodness and severity of God on Jew and Gentile in the olive tree. He spoke of God's severity on His own people who fell through unbelief and were thus broken off as branches from the life of the olive tree. He warned the Gentile believers that they would only experience the goodness of God "If thou continue in His goodness, otherwise thou shalt be cut off" (Romans 11:22,16-26). (Read also Hebrews 3:6,7,12,14)

Thus Old and New Testament alike give exhortations and warnings concerning backsliding, falling away, or turning from the Lord after having known Him. These Scriptures become meaningless if the believer is unconditionally secure.

e. Dangers of Apostasy

The distinction between backsliding and apostasy should be noted. The backslider is called to return to the Lord and may return (Hosea 4:16; 11:7; 14:4; Proverbs 14:14; Jeremiah 2:19; 3:6-12). The apostate cannot return to the Lord. Backsliding can lead to apostasy. Backsliding takes place gradually, not suddenly. It is a sliding back from God. It takes place secretly, inwardly first in the heart, and then it becomes outwardly manifested. Backsliding may be partial, not entire. The prodigal son was a "dead" and "lost" son while in the far-away country. He did come back to the Father upon repentance (Luke 15:11-32).

Apostasy, however, is the step beyond backsliding. It is at this stage that there is a deliberate and wilful renunciation and rejection of Jesus Christ. It is to "crucify afresh to themselves the Son of God, and put Him to an open shame" (Hebrews 6:6). The passages in Hebrews especially deal with apostasy, it is beyond backsliding (Hebrews 6:1-9; 10:25-31). The words "fall away" as used in Hebrews 6:6 with II Thessalonians 2:3, come from the Greek word "apostacia" from which we derive apostasy. The other word used for "fall" in the Greek language is "pipto" and has the thought of being "tripped up, or to stumble", or "to alight" (Romans 14:4; I Corinthinas 10:12; Hebrews 4:11). All believers stumble or are tripped up at times, but they get up and continue on. The apostate is one who turns deliberately and wilfully from the Lord, casting Him out of his life, and thus becomes part of "the great falling away" or "the great apostasy" of the last days.

It is apostasy which is "the sin unto death" which is not to be prayed for (I John 5:16). We note but two examples of backsliders and apostates from Old and New Testaments.

(1) Old Testament

(a) **King Saul** became an apostate from God after God's gracious dealings with him (I Samuel 10:1-10; 16:22-23; I Chronicles 10:13-14).

(b) **King David** became a backslider and was restored to the Lord upon genuine repentance (II Samuel 11-12; Psalm 51; Psalm 32).

(2) New Testament

(a) The apostle **Judas** became an apostate after being called to apostolic ministry (Matthew 10:1-4, 16-29; John 6:64-70; 13:1-30; Acts 1:15-25; Psalm 41:9; 69:25-28).

(b) The apostle **Peter** became a backslider and was restored to the Lord (Luke 22:31-34, 54-62, Mark 16:7).

f. Causes of Backsliding

The causes of backsliding, though many, may be reduced to these major areas:
(1) Lack of maintaining personal love relationship with the Lord (Revelation 2:1-7).
(2) Lack of spiritual watchfulness (Mark 13:33).
(3) Lack of spiritual fervency (Revelation 3:14-22).
(4) Lack of obedience to the Word and Spirit of God (Hebrews 5:9; Acts 5:32).
(5) Lack of prayer (Luke 22:39-46).
(6) Lack of spiritual sustenance from the Word of God (Psalm 1).
(7) Lack of fellowship with the people of God (Hebrews 10:24-25).

(8) Lack of separation from worldliness and worldly companionships (I Corinthians 15:33; I John 2:15-17; II Corinthians 6:14-18).

(9) Lack of proper humility and being lifted up in pride (Proverbs 18:12; 16:18; I Timothy 3:6).

g. Conditional Security

The Scriptures teach the perseverance of the saints. Warnings against backsliding and the dangers of apostasy show that the security of the believer is conditional upon obedience and faith in the Lord Jesus. It has been said that "Christ came to redeem man back to the obedience from which Adam fell."

The writer to the Hebrews says that Christ is "the author of eternal salvation (Greek "Soteria" safety, rescue, security, wholeness, health) unto all them that obey Him" (Hebrews 5:9).

The redemptive work of Christ does not exempt man from obedience to the Word of God. This obedience is neither a forced nor a non-volitional obedience. Obedience is the very law of security for all created beings. There can be no such thing as unconditional security. The angels are secure upon continued obedience to God's will and Word. The angels which fell disobeyed God's law. Adam and Eve were secure upon obedience to the commandment of the Lord. When they fell it was through disobedience (Romans 5:12-21). All free-will creatures are under one basic law or commandment and that is the law of loving and willing obedience. Eternal life is given to the eternally obedient. A consideration of the references listed here show that God places this responsibility upon His people saying that if they obey His voice, then He will be their God and they will be His people (Genesis 22:18; 26:5; 27:8,13; Exodus 19:5; 23:21-22; Deuteronomy 11:27-28; 30:2,8,20; Jeremiah 7:23; 11:4; Acts 5:32; Hebrews 5:9; Romans 6:17; I Peter 1:14,22; Romans 15:18).

Jesus taught that the evidences of being His sheep are "My sheep hear My voice, and I know them, and they follow Me, and I give unto them eternal life; and they never perish, neither shall any man pluck them out of My hand" (John 10:27-28). Both verses teach conditional security of the believer. Upon hearing and following the Shepherd they receive eternal life and will never perish.

It is the duty of the watchman to warn the wicked and the righteous, those without and within. The righteous are warned not to turn from their righteousness and do iniquity. If he die in his sins, all his righteousness shall not be remembered. This same principle is seen in both Old and New Testaments. The watchman is to exhort the believer to persevere in the Lord, to continue in the faith, and as he obeys the Word of the Lord, his security against backsliding and apostasy is fully guaranteed (Ezekiel 3:17-21; 18:19-32; 33:1-20; Matthew 7:15-23; II Thessalonians 3:3; Jude 24-25; I Corinthians 10:13; Philippians 1:6).

No believer need backslide or fall away from the faith, for the Lord Jesus is our advocate and intercessor. The Holy Spirit is our Comforter and indweller. The Lord gives the assurance that He "is able to keep you from falling and to present you faultless before the presence of His glory with exceeding joy..." (Jude 24-25).

5. Means of Grace

God has provided various means of grace whereby the believer may avail himself of divine strength to be and power to do. By "means of grace" we mean those divinely-appointed channels through which the Holy Spirit provides divine grace and enablements for Christian life and service.

Though there are corporate means of grace when the Church gathers together, we will refer more particularly to those means of grace which every individual believer has available to him. The two major channels of grace are the Word of God and prayer. It is by these that the Holy Spirit quickens, empowers and energizes the believer. Neglect of these means of grace results in spiritual weakness and ineffectiveness. The apostles gave themselves continually to the Word and prayer (Acts 6:4).

a. The Word of God

The inspired Word of God is an objective, external, but infallible and authoritative revelation given to man. The believer neglects the Word of God to his own peril. It is in the Word of the Lord that God reveals Himself. All that may be known of God and His creative and redemptive plan is contained in the Scriptures. This Word is the wisdom of God and the believer is exhorted to hunger and thirst after its truths. It is to be His life and spiritual sustenance (I Samuel 3:21; Proverbs 2:1-9; Job 23:12; Psalm 119:47; Jeremiah 15:16; Psalm 19:7-10; Ezekiel 3:1-3; Matthew 4:4; Revelation 10:8-10).

(1) Practical Purposes of the Scripture

The practical purposes of the Scriptures may be seen to be sixfold. The Scriptures are profitable for:

(a) Doctrine

It is the source book for all true doctrine, setting forth what we are to believe (II Timothy 3:16).

(b) Reproof

The reproofs of Scripture are the safeguards in life (II Timothy 3:16; Isaiah 8:20; I John 4:1; Jeremiah 23:31; Titus 1:9).

(c) Correction

The Scriptures correct and discipline the life style of the believer (II Timothy 3:16; Titus 2:12).

(d) Instruction

The wise believer will heed the instruction unto righteousness which the Scriptures give (II Timothy 3:16; Psalm 119:9; Micah 6:8).

(e) Comfort

Comfort and hope are contained in the inspired Scriptures (Romans 15:4; Isaiah 40:1; John 16:33; Jeremiah 15:16).

(f) Life

Man lives by the Word that is quickened in the written Word. It is the bread of life (John 20:31; Mathew 4:4).

(2) Practical Approaches to the Scripture

The believer's approach to the Scripture should be three-fold in order for him to receive their fullest benefit.

(a) Observation

The believer, in reading the Word of God, needs to ask himself: What does it say? What was it saying to the people it was written to and what was it saying to future generations?

(b) Interpretation

The believer in reading the Word also needs to ask himself: What does it mean? Scripture as a whole interprets Scripture. He may ask: What did it mean to the writers and the hearers in Bible times? What does it mean to me?

(c) Application

The believer may then ask himself: How can I apply the Word to my own life? The purpose of observation and interpretation is application. How can the timeless truths and principles of God's Word become effectual in my life? This is the goal of Scripture. If truth is not applied it remains a beautiful but lifeless theory.

(3) Practical Uses of the Scripture

How may the Scriptures be used in a practical manner? The practical uses of Scripture as an effectual means of grace may be seen in these areas. The believer should:

(a) **Hear** the Scriptures (Luke 11:28; Matthew 17:5).
(b) **Read** the Scriptures (John 5:39).
(c) **Study** the Scriptures (II Timothy 2:15).
(d) **Meditate** on the Scriptures (Joshua 1:8; Deuteronomy 6:6; Psalm 1:1-4).
(e) **Believe** the Scriptures (Mark 1:15; John 4:50).
(f) **Observe** the Scriptures (Joshua 1:8; Matthew 28:20).
(g) **Obey** the Scriptures (Romans 6:17; Joshua 2:7).
(h) **Teach** the Scriptures (Deuteronomy 6:7; Psalm 78:5).

The Word of God is a saving and sanctifying Word and is given to us as a wonderful means of grace (I Peter 1:23; Psalm 19:7; Romans 1:16; II Timothy 3:15; John 17:17).

b. The Life of Prayer
The second major means of grace is prayer. As the Word is objective and external, so the life of prayer is subjective and internal. Prayer has been spoken of as being the very breath of spiritual life. It is the believer's spiritual contact with heaven. No spiritual life can be maintained without it. Someone has defined prayer by saying: " Prayer is the soul's sincere desire, uttered or unexpressed."

(1) The Command of Prayer
Prayer in Scripture is not an option or merely a privilege, but a command (Luke 18:1; I Thessalonians 5:17; I Timothy 2:8; Colossians 4:2; I Corinthians 7:5; Ephesians 6:18). The prophet Samuel counted prayerlessness as sin (I Samuel 12:23). The disciples asked Jesus to teach them how to pray, even as John taught his disciples (Luke 11:1-4). A prayerless Christian is disobedient and powerless. The apostles gave themselves continually to prayer and then the Word (Acts 6:4; Romans 1:9; Colossians 1:9). To neglect prayer grieves the Lord (Isaiah 43:21-22; 64:6-7).

(2) The Nature of Prayer
The nature of prayer is understood by a consideration of its various elements. Certain ingredients constitute the very nature of true prayer. Prayer involves:

(a) **Adoration** — Psalm 45:1-8; Isaiah 6:1-4; Matthew 14:33; 15:25; 28:9; Revelation 4:11; Matthew 6:9.

(b) **Confession** — I Kings 8:47; Nehemiah 1:6-7; 9:33-35; Daniel 9:3-15; Ezra 9:5-15; 10:1.

(c) **Petition** — Daniel 2:17-18; 9:16-19; John 11:22; Matthew 7:7-12; Acts 4:29-30; Philippians 4:6; Psalm 42:4; 62:8.

(d) **Supplication** — Daniel 6:11; Zechariah 12:10; Luke 18:1-18; I Timothy 2:1; Ephesians 6:18; Matthew 15:22-28.

(e) **Intercession** — Acts 12:5; I Timothy 2:1; Job 42:8; Isaiah 59:16; I Samuel 12:23; Genesis 17:18; 18:23,32; Jeremiah 15:1; I Samuel 15:11,35. This involves prayer and intercession for:

(i)   The kingdom and will of God (Matthew 5:9-13).
(ii)   The rulers in authority (I Timothy 2:2).
(iii) The unsaved (Luke 23:34; Acts 7:60).
(iv)   The new believers (II Thessalonians 1:11).
(v)   The backsliders (I John 5:16).
(vi)   The saints everywhere (Ephesians 6:18; James 5:16).
(vii) The ministers of the Gospel (Ephesians 6:19-20; I Thessalonians 5:25).
(viii) The enemies of the Gospel (Matthew 5:44).
(ix)   The sick and needy (James 5:13-16).
(x)   The believer's own personal life (Jude 20; Romans 8:26-27).

(f) **Communion** — Genesis 18:33; Exodus 25:22; 31:18.

(g) **Thanksgiving** — Colossians 4:2; Philippians 4:6; Ephesians 5:20; Psalm 95:2; 100:4.

Though the Godhead is involved in the prayers of the saints, the basic redemptive approach in prayer is to pray to the Father, through the Son, and by the Spirit (Ephesians 2:18). **Prayer** to the Father, and to the Son, by the Spirit, may be seen also in these Scriptures (Nehemiah 4:9; John 16:23; Matthew 6:8; Acts 12:5; 7:59; I Corinthians 1:2; II Timothy 2:22; Jude 20; Romans 8:26-27).

(3) The Time of Prayer
The Bible shows that the saints have set times of prayer as well as special occasions of prayer. Jesus lived a life of prayer, as the Spirit of prayer was always upon Him. The believer may pray at set times or at any time. He should maintain a spirit of prayer which is the life of prayer.

(a) Saints prayed **3 times a day;** morning, noon and in the evening (Daniel 6:10; and Psalm 55:16-17).
(b) Some saints prayed at other **set times** or seasons (Acts 3:1; 2:46; 10:9,30).
(c) Sometimes Jesus prayed **all night** (Luke 6:12).
(d) Sometimes Jesus prayed **early in the morning** (Mark 1:35).
(e) Believers are exhorted to pray **always** (Luke 18:1; Ephesians 6:18; I Thessalonians 5:17).

(4) The Posture in Prayer
The posture of the body in prayer is not as important as the attitude of the heart before the Lord. The Scriptures show no set posture of the body but it does emphasize that true prayer is an attitude of the spirit.

(a) One may **stand** and pray (John 17:1; Mark 11:25; Luke 18:13).
(b) One may **kneel** and pray (Luke 22:41; I Kings 8:54; Acts 20:36; Ephesians 3:14).
(c) One may be **prostrate** and pray (Matthew 26:39).
(d) One may have his **face in his hands** and pray (I Kings 18:42).
(e) One may **lay down** and pray (Psalm 63:6).
(f) One may **sit** and pray (I Chronicles 17:16; II Samuel 17:18; Acts 2:1-4).
(g) One should always have the **spirit, heart and attitude** of prayer. This is the position of the heart before God regardless of the position of the body (Jude 20; Romans 8:26-27).

(5) The Place of Prayer
There is no place where prayer may not be made, but the Scriptures do show that all should have a place of prayer. Prayer was made in the following places:

(a) The **secret** place (Matthew 6:6; Daniel 6:10).
(b) The **desert** place (Mark 1:35).
(c) The **mountain** place (Matthew 14:23).
(d) The **assembly** place of the saints (Acts 1:14; 12:5; 20:36; Matthew 18:19-20).
(e) In **every** place (I Timothy 10:8; I Corinthians 1:2). Jerusalem was repudiated as a place of worship when Jesus said that the Father looked for true worship "in spirit and in truth" everywhere and anywhere (John 4:20-24).

(6) Hindrances to Prayer
God has laid down certain prerequisites for prayer to be made to Him. Without these prayer is of no avail; it can become an abomination, and God cannot answer it. We note a number of the major hindrances to effectual prayer.

(a) Known sin (Psalm 66:18; Isaiah 59:1-2; John 9:31).
(b) Wilful disobedience to God's Word (Proverbs 28:9; Zechariah 7:11-13).
(c) Selfish motivation (Matthew 6:5; James 4:3).
(d) Lack of genuine faith (James 1:6-7; Hebrews 11:6).

(e) Idols in the heart (Jeremiah 11:9-14; Ezekiel 8:15-18; 14:1-3).
(f) Unforgiving spirit (Matthew 5:23-24; 6:12-15; Mark 11:25-26).
(g) Hypocrisy (Proverbs 8:13; Malachi 1:6-10; Job 27:8-9; Matthew 6:5).
(h) Prideful attitudes (Job 35:12-13; Luke f8:9-14).
(i) Discord in home relationships (I Peter 3:7).
(j) Robbing God in tithes and offerings (Malachi 3:8-10).
(k) Failure to render charity to the needy (Proverbs 21:13; I John 3:17,19).
(l) Forsaking the Lord and His ways (Jeremiah 14:10-12).

(7) Helps to Prayer

The Scriptures lay out certain positive helps for the believer in using prayer as a channel of divine grace. Prayer should be made:

(a) With sincerity (Psalm 145:18; Matthew 6:5).
(b) With faith (Matthew 21:22; James 1:6; Matthew 7:7; Mark 11:24).
(c) With God's will in mind (I John 5:14; Matthew 26:39-42).
(d) With simplicity (Matthew 6:7; 26:44).
(e) With unity (Matthew 18:19-20).
(f) With earnestness (James 5:7; Acts 12:5; Luke 22:44).
(g) With definiteness (Psalm 27:4; Matthew 18:19).
(h) With persistence (Luke 18:1-8; Colossians 4:2; Romans 12:12).
(i) With fasting at times (Acts 13:2-3; 14:23).
(j) With thanksgiving (Philippians 4:6).
(k) With the Spirit (Ephesians 6:18; Jude 20; Romans 8:26-27).
(l) With the name of Jesus (John 16:23; 14:13-14).
(m) With boldness (Hebrews 4:15-16).
(n) With the promises of God's Word as our foundation and basis (Matthew 7:7-11; 9:24-29; Luke 11:13; Daniel 9:1-3; Ezekiel 36:37).
(o) With anointing and washing (Matthew 6:16-18).

(8) Examples of Prayer and Intercession

The Bible makes reference to the saints who prayed as well as many of the prayers uttered. A study of these prayers and the results show the ingredients and power of prayer in the lives of these persons, as well as in the destinies of peoples and nations. A few of the major examples of great warriors in prayer and intercession will suffice.

(a) The Lord Jesus Christ Himself is the perfect and supreme example of prayer and intercession. His whole life was a life of unbroken communion with the Father. There are many references to the prayer life of Jesus. His highest ministry now is that of prayer and intercession on behalf of His own (John 17; Hebrews 7:25; Romans 8:34). Read also the references to the prayer life of Jesus in these passages (Mark 1:35; 14:36; Hebrews 5:7; Luke 3:21-22; 5:5-16; 6:12-13; 9:18-22,28; 22:39-46; Mark 6:46; Matthew 14:23; 26:36).

(b) Abraham exemplified a man of prayer and intercession in his exercises concerning Sodom (Genesis 18-19).

(c) Moses was a great intercessor, willing to give his life for the nation of Israel (Exodus 32).

(d) Samuel the prophet counted failure to pray and intercede for the nation as sin (I Samuel 15:23).

(e) Jeremiah the prophet was an intercessor for the nation (Jeremiah 7:16; 15:1).

(f) Paul the apostle also was a man of prayer and intercession for the churnes he established (Ephesians 1:16; Galatians 4:19). The prayers of Paul in his epistles are rich in utterance.

It will be seen especially that the intercessor is one whom God calls to stand in the gap (Isaiah 59:16; Ezekiel 22:30-31). The ministry of prayer and intercession fulfills that which was symbolized in the Old Testament in the Tabernacle of Moses and Temple of Solomon in the Golden Altar of Incense. As the incense was to ascend continually before the Lord, within the veil, so the prayers and intercessions of the saints are to ascend within the veil of the true and heavenly Sanctuary. Jesus Christ, the Great High Priest, receives the prayers of the saints and offers them to the Father God (Exodus 30:1-10; Revelation 11:1-2; Luke 1:5-26; Revelation 8:1-4; Psalm 141:1-2; Revelation 5:8). Only eternity will tell the story of the results of those who prayed. The believer has been given these two great means of grace, the Word and prayer, by which he can reign victoriously in this present life. In eternity all prayer will turn to praise.

I. BENEFITS OF THE ATONEMENT

Having seen the progression and development of the Doctrine of the Atonement in its necessity, nature, origin, work, provision and application, in conclusion we proceed to consider the benefits of the atonement. These benefits are noted under various, yet related, words each having their particular facets of truth. Justification, regeneration, adoption, sanctification, salvation, glorification and perfection are the great benefits of the atonement which the believer receives.

A. The Benefit of Justification

1. Justification From Sin

a. Definition

The dictionary defines the word "justify" as "to prove or show to be just, or conformable to law, right; to vindicate as right; to declare free from guilt or blame; to absolve, to clear." Also "to pardon or clear from guilt; to treat as just; to acquit; declare righteous; pronounce sentence of acceptance." Theologically J. R. Gregory in "The Theological Student" (page 166) says: "Justification may be defined as that act of God by which He accepts as righteous the penitent sinner who believes on Christ for salvation."

(1) Hebrew

Tsaw-Dak meaning "to make right, or righteous, in a moral sense" (Genesis 44:16; Exodus 23:7; Job 9:2,20; 11:2; 13:18; 25:4; Psalm 51:4; 143:2; Isaiah 43:9,26; 45:25; I Kings 8:32; II Chronicles 6:23; Isaiah 53:11).

(2) Greek

Diakaiow meaning "to make righteous" or "to show one to be righteous, to acquit of a charge, to pronounce guiltless" (Luke 10:29; 16:15; Matthew 12:37; Acts 13:39; Romans 2:13; 3:4,20, 24,26,28,30; 4:25; 5:1,9; 6:7; 8:30,33; I Corinthians 6:11; Galatians 2:16-17; I Timothy 3:16; Titus 3:7; James 2:21,24-25; Romans 5:16, 18; 4:25).

Thus justification, according to both Hebrew and Greek thought, is to make righteous, to acquit of a charge and to absolve from guilt. It is the act of God whereby He declares righteous whoever believes on Jesus.

b. Amplification

The righteous God can only demand righteousness from His creatures. The Law demands that the righteous Judge of the earth must justify the righteous and condemn the .guilty (Deuteronomy 25:1; Exodus 23:7; Isaiah 5:23; Psalm 9:8). However, when Adam sinned, he fell from his position of right-standing before God. Now all mankind stands guilty and condemned, for "there is none righteous, no, not one" (Romans 3:10,12, 23). The death penalty for violation of God's holy law must be executed. The great problem arose as expressed by Job; "How then can a man be justified with God?" (Job 4:17; 9:1; 15:14; 25:4). How can a man become righteous before a righteous God?

There were only two alternatives by which man could seek to be justified in God's sight. He could seek to (1) justify himself by what he could do or be, which would be justification by works, or he could (2) believe God to justify him by free grace, which is justification by faith. The former was an impossibility, for no one can justify himself before God. No amount of good works could do this, for the problem is found in man himself. Man does what he does because of what he is. Man is not a sinner because he sins. He sins because he is born a sinner. He does unrighteousness because he is unrighteous.

This is one of the major purposes which God had in mind in the giving of the Law to Israel. When Israel received the Law, they said" "All that the Lord hath said we will do" (Exodus 20,24). The moment they said this, they placed themselves on the ground of works, self-effort and self justification. However, they did not know the state of their own fallen heart, that self justification was not possible before God. For 1,500 years, God allowed the chosen nation to prove to themselves and to the whole world, that none could be justified by the works of the Law, none could justify themselves. If man could justify himself, then he would have something to boast in, but not before God (Romans 4:1-4).

The great tragedy was seen in the fact that Jewry misunderstood the purpose of the Law, which was meant to be a "schoolmaster" to bring them to Christ (Romans 10:3-4). The Old Covenant was intended to bring them to Christ. However, they did not move toward Him, but rejected Him when He arrived (Galatians 3:23-25).

The righteousness of fallen man is as filthy rags before God (Isaiah 64:6) the righteousness of the Law by self-effort is also unacceptable before God (Philippians 3:9-10).

It is only by grace that a man can be justified before God. That is, God Himself must justify man by free grace. But this presents a problem, as far as sinful man and the moral attributes of God are concerned. How can God justify the guilty and Himself remain just? (Romans 3:26). This was God's problem; how to justify the sinner without justifying his sin. How can God treat a sinner as a righteous person?

Paul is given the richest revelation of God's answer to this question as well as the questions of Job and of all mankind. God's grace and love found a way in the death of Christ. In Christ's substitutionary death Christ expiated our guilt, satisfied the demands of the Law and paid sin's penalty as the righteous One (Isaiah 53:5,11; II Corinthians 5:21; Romans 4:6; 5:18-19). His death became our death, His righteousness became our righteousness. The only way man could become righteous was for God to provide him with His righteousness. This He did in Christ. Man's only hope is to accept that which is provided. He cannot pay for it. It must first be imputed, then inwrought and outworked (Romans 1:16-17; I Corinthians 1:30; Jeremiah 23:6; 33:15; Revelation 19:8; 3:4).

God's grace can now be offered because God's law has been fully met in Christ's atoning death. God can now be just and the justifier of whoever believes in Jesus. All of this is involved in the truth of justification.

The Doctrine of Justification involves three things: pardon or remission of sin's penalty, imputation of righteousness and a position of right-standing before God. This is like a "threefold cord" which should not be broken. To do so is to destroy or invalidate the truth of justification.

2. Pardon of Penalty

a. Definition
The word "pardon" means "to forgive, to absolve, to remit the penalty of, a deed conveying legal forgiveness." It has also been defined as "releasing a person from punishment; not punishing for crimes or offences; to absolve, to acquit." The word "pardon" is only translated as such in the Old Testament while the word "forgiveness" in the New Testament conveys the same truth. We note these relative words.

(1) Hebrew

(a) Nah-saw meaning "to lift (a sentence). (Exodus 23:21; I Samuel 15:25; Job 7:21; Micah 7:8).

(b) Saw-lakh meaning "to forgive". Translated "pardon" (Exodus 34:9; Numbers 14:19-20; II Kings 5:18; 24:4; Psalm 25:11; Isaiah 55:7; Jeremiah 5:1,7; 33:8; 50:20; Lamentations 3:42). "forgive" (I Kings 8:30,34,36,39,50; II Chronicles 5:21,25,27,30,39). "spare" (Deuteronomy 29:20).

(2) Greek

(a) Aphiemi meaning "to send forth", translated "forgive" (Matthew 6:12,14,15; 9:6; 18:21,35; Luke 5:21,24; 11:4; I John 1:9; James 5:15).

(b) Charizomai meaning "to grant as a favor, i.e. gratuitously, in kindness, pardon or rescue", translated "gave, frankly forgave, to be granted, deliver, freely give, forgave, forgiven" (Luke 7:21; Acts 3:14; 25:11,16; I Corinthians 2:12; Ephesians 4:32; Colossians 2:13; 3:13). Thus the word "pardon" means "to lift a sentence, to forgive, to grant as a favor, pardon, absolve, deliver, or rescue."

b. Amplification

The scene suggested by the word pardon is a court-room. The sinner has been taken to court and his case has been tried. The verdict is "Guilty" and the penalty of death has been declared (Romans 3:19). Just as the death penalty is pronounced and the prisoner taken off to jail, someone hastens to the prison with a free pardon. Someone else has taken the guilty person's penalty and died in the prisoner's stead. So Jesus took the sinner's death penalty on the cross. Now a free pardon is offered to all. However, in order for the pardon to be effective, the sinner must accept it.

In justification the one who believes in Christ receives forgiveness of sin, or remission of sin's penalty. The sinner is pardoned. Since the Lord Jesus bore man's sin, He has borne the penalty. God now remits this penalty to the one who trusts in Christ. Pardon and justification are related words. Both are legal terms. Pardon cannot be separated from justification as it is an integral part of it. It is not that God simply pardons or acquits the guilty, for this would not be just. "The soul that sinneth, it shall die" (Genesis 2:17 with Ezekiel 18:4). The death sentence for sin has already been passed. Sin must be judged. God brought in His Son who was perfect, sinless and righteous. On Calvary the sins of the world were imputed to Him. He took the guilty sinner's place and died the sinner's death (John 3:16; Romans 5:6-8). Sin's penalty has now been paid. The sentence of the Law was executed on Christ. The holiness of God has been maintained, the righteousness of the Law has been vindicated; now God can offer every offender a free pardon in Christ. Thus, sinners are not pardoned because God is gracious to excuse their sins, but because sin's penalty has been paid in the death of Christ. Sin has been cancelled out in His substitutionary sacrifice. God can only pardon that which has been judged and all has been judged in Christ.

c. Illustration

Perhaps the most suitable illustration is that seen in Barabbas. Barabbas was a guilty criminal, condemned to die, awaiting in prison for his death. At the Feast of Passover, Barabbas was released and Jesus died in his place. Barabbas was given a free pardon. The death sentence was lifted from him, for Jesus took his penalty at Calvary (Luke 23:17-26) So this illustrates what Christ has done for all sinful and guilty men. All must now accept the pardon so freely offered. Only as the pardon is accepted can it be effective in a person's life. Pardon or forgiveness is available to all through Christ.

(1) The Lord will forgive all who truly call upon Him (I Kings 8:30-39; II Chronicles 6:21-27; Psalm 25:11; Jeremiah 33:8).

(2) The Lord will abundantly pardon those who return to Him (Isaiah 55:7).

(3) Pardon or forgiveness is part of the promise in the New Covenant in the Last days (Jeremiah 31:31-34; Psalm 103:3).

(4) The Priest at the altar of sacrifice was commanded to pronounce pardon or forgiveness upon every Israelite who came to the altar in faith and obedience (Leviticus 4:20,26,31; 5:10-16; 19:22; Numbers 15:25-28).

(5) Jesus Christ is our Great High Priest, the maker of the New Covenant and because of His sacrifice and the fact that He took our penalty, pardon is available for all who will accept it (Psalm 130:4; Daniel 9:9; Mark 2:5; Luke 7:47-48; Romans 4:7; Ephesians 4:32; Colossians 2:13; James 5:15; I John 2:12; I John 1:9).

3. Imputation of Righteousness

a. Definition

The word "impute", like the word "reconciliation" is a book-keeping term. It means "to set down or to charge to one's account". Theologically it is "that act by which God charges or reckons His righteousness to our account". The great Pauline chapter on "imputation" is found in Romans 4. The theme of Romans 4 is "imputed righteousness". Righteousness being put to the account of the one who believes in Jesus.

The Greek word "Logizomai" is used about eleven times in this great chapter. It is translated "counted" (verses 3,5), "reckoned" (verses 4,9,10), and "imputed" (verses 6,8,11,22,23,24). It means "to reckon, to number or account."

b. Amplification

As noted earlier, ever since the fall of Adam, the great problem has been "How can a man be just before God?" (Job 25:4; 15:14; 4:17; 9:1). When Adam sinned all that he was and all that he did was "imputed" to the whole unborn human race. Sin left a debit on the books (Genesis 3:1-16; 2:17; Romans 5:12; 6:23). "In Adam" all sinned, and all died, spiritually and physically (I Corinthians 15:22).

When Christ died on Calvary, the sin of Adam and the whole human race was "imputed" or put to Christ's account. Because God imputed our sin to Christ, He suffered our penalty, which was death. All of our liabilities were transferred to Him, but He cancelled this debt in and by His death (John 1:29; Isaiah 53:4-6; II Corinthians 5:18-21). Christ was "reckoned (numbered, accounted) among the transgressors" (Luke 22:37).

In justification the righteousness of Christ is now imputed to those that believe. Just as our sin was imputed to Christ, so Christ's righteousness is imputed to us. The assets of Christ are transferred to us. His righteousness is credited to us, put to our account (Psalm 32:8; Romans 4:8; II Corinthians 5:21; Philippians 3:8-9). God no longer imputes sin to us but we are counted as the righteousness of God "in Christ." God does not violate His righteousness or justice in declaring us righteous. He can do this because our sins, unrighteousness, guilt and punishment were imputed to Christ on the cross. Now Christ's righteousness (the righteousness of the sinless One) is imputed to those who believe in Him. Justification pronounces the sinner legally innocent, freeing him from condemnation. The pardoned one is now declared righteous because he believes. He is declared righteous because righteousness is imputed to him. It is by this that God can be "just and the justifier of him which believeth in Jesus" (Romans 3:26). God accepts us as righteous because of the righteousness of Christ. This is pardon and imputation.

4. Change of Position

Pardon has to do with the penalty of sin being remitted, but a pardon still leaves the person unrighteous. A judge can pardon a criminal, but he is not considered a righteous man in the eyes of society. Justification, however, also declares the pardoned one to be righteous. It is having the record cleared and being put back into right-standing with God. Justification is a change of position. It is being placed in a position of right standing before God. This is to say that because the sinner is pardoned and Christ's righteousness is imputed to him by faith in Jesus, it changes his position.

From being "in Adam" and in a position of hostility and a state of condemnation, he is now "in Christ" and is given a position before the Father. He is placed in right standing. He is restored to God's favor and fellowship. When Adam sinned he lost this position before God, but now man's legal position is restored and he can stand in God's presence unashamedly because God now sees him "in Christ."

5. Summary

This may be illustrated in its integral parts by that which took place under the Mosaic economy. We view this typically, historically and doctrinally.

a. Typically

Pardon, imputation and position were seen in the sacrificial system under the Law. Even though it is recognized that the Law itself could not justify, the doctrine of justification was typically demonstrated. The offerings and sacrifices for sin presented by the Israelites had the ceremony of laying on of hands associated with them. In this act the sins of the guilty Israelite were imputed to the innocent and blemishless animal. The unrighteousness of the Israelite was put to the animal's account (Leviticus 1-7). The reverse was true also, for the innocence and perfections of the sacrifice were reckoned to the Israelites account by this act of identification. Thus the innocent died for the guilty, the sinless for the sinful. The penalty for sin fell upon the perfect and blemishless victim, and the Israelite was freed. His sins were remitted. He received a free pardon and God accepted him as righteous because of the death of another.

The laying on of hands upon the scapegoat and the Lord's goat also illustrated the doctrine of tranference of guilt to the sacrifice. (Leviticus 16). The laying on of hands was also used in Scripture for blessing, healing and ordination. It expresses the truth of imputation and identification. It is the transferral of good or evil to the person or one involved (Genesis 48:1-2; Mark 10:13; Luke 24:50; Acts 5:12; 28:8; Hebrews 6:1-2). Thus pardon, imputation and positional righteousness were set forth typically under the Mosaic economy.

b. Historically

All that took place under the Old Covenant economy set forth typically that which Christ would fulfil historically. This is recorded in the Gospels. In Christ's perfect death, He fulfilled and abolished the Old Testament sacrifices. Christ, as the righteous and sinless One became sin for us and was judged accordingly, receiving in Himself the sentence of death. The cross of Christ becomes the place of pardon, imputation and position for all who believe in Him.

c. Doctrinally

This doctrine is set forth particularly in the Pauline epistles. We consider examples of justification and its integral parts.

(1) Onesimus

Onesimus, the runaway slave, came to know pardon, imputation and a new position because of Paul's mediatorial letter to Philemon in his behalf. Paul effected a reconciliation between master and slave by assuming the debt and asking Philemon to put it to Paul's account.

So God assumed our debt and placed our sins on the account against Jesus. He has placed His righteousness to our account as we believe (Philemon 17-18).

(2) Abraham

Abraham, the father of all who believe, is set forth as the great Old Testament example of justification. He comes to know that faithrighteousness which is imputed to all who believe (Romans 4).

(3) Paul

The great example and exponent of the doctrine of justification is the apostle Paul himself. Turning from self-righteousness (Isaiah 64:6) and legal righteousness (Romans 10:3; Philippians 3:6-8; Luke 18:9), he accepted the righteousness of God in Christ which is a faith-righteousness or justification.

He came to know Jehovah Tsidkenu, "The Lord our Righteousness" in Christ Jesus (Jeremiah 23:5-6; 33:15-16; I Corinthians 1:30). Paul shows that on the cross Christ was made sin for us all, while on the throne Christ is our righteousness (II Corinthians 5:21). The epistles of Paul teach that positional righteousness must become practical righteousness. We summarize Paul's revelation of justification in the following Scriptures.

(a) Justification is not by works of self-righteousness (Philippians 3:6-9; Luke 10:28-29; 16:15).

(b) Justification is not by the works of the Law (Romans 3:19-20; Galatians 3:10; James 2:10; Galatians 2:16; Deuteronomy 25:1; Psalm 51:4; Acts 13:38-39; Proverbs 17:15).

(c) Justification is by God Himself, He is the author (Romans 3:20; 8:30,33).

(d) Justification is by grace; grace is the source (Romans 3:24; Titus 3:7).

(e) Justification is freely bestowed by God, for nothing in us merited it or moved God to do so. It was His love. This fact removes self-effort and pride (Romans 10:9-10; 3:24).

(f) Justification is by faith; faith is the channel of reception (Romans 3:26-30; 4:11; 5:1; 9:30; 10:10; Philippians 3:9; Colossians 1:23; Acts 13:28-29).

(g) Justification is through the blood of Jesus; the blood is the only foundation (Romans 3:25; 5:9).

(h) Justification is by the name of the Lord Jesus Christ (Galatians 2:16; I Corinthians 6:11).

(i) Justification is by the Spirit of God; He is the communicator to the heart and life (I Corinthians 6:11).

(j) Justification takes place at the Mercy Seat or Throne of God (Luke 18:9-14).

(k) Justification is evidenced by obedience to the Word of God (James 2:21-26).

(l) Justification is the imputed and outworked righteousness of Christ in His people (Romans 8:29-33). That is, righteousness is positional and practical, imputed, inwrought and outworked. (Revelation 19:7-8).

B. The Benefit of Regeneration

1. Definition

In regeneration a person is born into the family of God. He is born anew from above. In regeneration, man receives a new nature and a new life and is placed in the Kingdom of God.

As pardon and justification are legal terms, so regeneration and adoption are found to be family terms. In regeneration a man is born into the family of God while, as will be seen, in adoption he is placed as a son in the household. The Greek word "Palingenesia" means literally "again born". It is spiritual re-birth, spiritual renovation, new birth, renewal, re-creation, restoration of things to intended state (Matthew 19:28; Titus 3:5). The Greek word "Gennao" means "to be born, to give birth to" (John 1:13; John 3:3-8).

When Jesus talked to Nicodemus about being "born again" He meant that a person has to be literally "born from above", to be born again in a spiritual re-birth. The dictionary meaning of the word "regenerate" is "to cause to be completely reformed or improved; to form or bring into existence again; to re-establish on a new basis; to be spiritually reborn, as by a religious conversion." Thus regeneration is the change brought about by justification. It is the divine act by which God imparts to the penitent sinner the divine and spiritual life which brings him into union with God and into the family of God. It is a "re-genesis" or a new beginning, a creative act of God. The penitent is "begotten of God" (Hebrews 1:5; 5:5; I John 3:9; 4:7; 5:1, 4:18; 2:29).

2. Amplification

The New Testament uses various terms to describe regeneration. It should be recognized that these are not different experiences, but different terms used to describe one and the same experience. Regeneration is likened to:

a. A Birth

The repentant person is begotten of God, born of the Spirit and born from above. It is a creative act of God making the sinner a child of God. The natural birth symbolizes the spiritual birth (John 3:1-12; 1:12-13; I John 5:1-4,18). As the elements of seed, blood, water and breath are involved in the natural and earthly birth, so are they in the spiritual and heavenly birth (I Peter 1:23; James 1:18; I John 1:7; 5:6-8; John 3:5-6; Titus 3:5). God becomes our Father by spiritual generation (Matthew 6:9-10). God is man's creator by natural generation. Thus the penitent is born not of inherited sinful blood, nor of the will of the flesh, of self-effort, nor of man by human reformation, but by the will of God. In this birth man becomes a partaker of the divine nature (II Peter 1:4).

b. A Cleansing

Regeneration is also likened to a cleansing, a washing and a bathing from the defilements of the old life to walk now in newness of life (Titus 3:5; John 3:5-6; Acts 22:16). It is spoken of as "the washing of regeneration", or "the laver of regeneration" (Titus 3:5; Ephesians 5:26; Exodus 30:17-21; Ezekiel 36:25). Water baptism symbolizes this washing also (Acts 22:16; I Corinthians 6:11; Hebrews 10:22; John 13:1-17). The cleansing comes from the washing of water by the Word.

c. A Quickening

The word "quicken" means "to revive, to make alive, to vivify." So regeneration is the quickening of the human spirit, the making alive and the renewal by the Holy Spirit of the human spirit. New life is imparted (Titus 3:5; Colossians 3:10; Romans 12:2; Ephesians 4:23; 2:1,5,7; Psalm 51:10; Psalm 119:25, 37,40,88).

d. A Resurrection

This description is very similar to the previous but it gives a fuller picture of man's condition. When Adam fell all died in him. Man is spiritually dead in trespasses and sins and needs the miraculous power of God to be made alive. Regeneration is a spiritual resurrection by which he is raised to life. He passes from death to life (John 5:24; I John 3:14). He cannot raise himself but Jesus, the resurrection and the life, comes and performs this miracle (Ephesians 2:1-6; Colossians 2:13; 3:1; I Timothy 5:6; Romans 6:4-5; John 11:25; 5:21-27; I John 3:14; 5:12).

e. A Creation

Adam was the old creation; Christ is the fruit of the new creation (Revelation 3:14). By natural birth we belong to the old creation race, for that which is born of the flesh is flesh. By spiritual birth we become new creatures belonging to the new creation race. That which is born of the Spirit is spirit (John 3:1-5; Galatians 6:15; Ephesians 2:10; II Corinthians 5:17). Regeneration is re-genesis. It is a new beginning. Only the new creation will be able to live in the New Heavens and New Earth. The new creation has a new nature, a new character, new desires and new purposes.

f. A Conversion

The word "conversion" means "to be turned about, to revert back again to former use". This word is used a number of times in the Old Testament as also the New Testament (Psalm 19:7; 51:13; Isaiah 1:27; 6:10; 60:5; Matthew 13:15; 18:3; Mark 4:12; Luke 22:32; John 12:40; Acts 3:19; 15:3; 28:27; James 5:19-20). It is used more especially of the human response to the divine conviction of the Holy Spirit. A regenerate person is a converted person; he is "turned about" from going away from God and now is going toward God.

g. A Renewal

Regeneration is also a renewal, or a restoration. Man is renewed in his spirit back to the image of God from which he fell in Adam. Man is made new again by new birth (Colossians 3:10; Romans 12:2; Ephesians 4:23).

h. A Salvation

The word "salvation" or "saved" means "to be delivered, preserved, heal or make whole." In regeneration man is saved from the wrath of God; he is made whole, delivered from the power of Satan into the kingdom of God (Colossians 1:13; Mark 16:16; John 3:17; 10:9; Romans 10:9-13; Acts 2:21,47; 11:14; 16:30-31; Revelation 21:24).

i. A New Heart

Regeneration is the fulfilment of the Old Testament prophesies concerning the reception of a "new heart" (Ezekiel 36:26 with Jeremiah 17:9; Psalm 51:10; Jeremiah 31:31-34). The old heart is dealt with and the believer is given a new heart.

j. A Translation

Regeneration is also a change of place and position. In regeneration the sinner is taken out of his old and former position "in Adam" and now placed in a new position "in Christ". In Adam there was sickness and death and bondage. In Christ there is righteousness, health, life and liberty. It is a translation from the kingdom of darkness into the kingdom of light (Ephesians 1:3,4,6,12; II Corinthians 5:17; Galatians 6:15; Colossians 1:13-14; Acts 26:18).

k. A Relationship

Regeneration is also analogous to a spiritual relationship of the soul with Christ. Regeneration brings a person into spiritual union with the risen Lord. It is likened to a marriage where the believer is "married to Christ" (Romans 7:4; Ephesians 5:21-32; Revelation 19:7-9; I Corinthians 6:17). The figure of the vine and branches also illustrates this union (John 14:20; Romans 8:10; Galatians 2:20; John 15:5; Romans 6:5).

Sufficient reasons have been stated which show the necessity of regeneration. Man cannot act beyond the nature he is born with. Human nature can only reproduce itself. Flesh can only produce flesh. Man is by nature sinful, a child of wrath, dead in trespasses and sins. He is unable to change himself and therefore needs the regenerative work of the Holy Spirit (I John 3:10; Matthew 13:38; 23:15; Acts 13:10; Ephesians 2:1-8; John 3:1-5).

3. Illustration

Undoubtedly the greatest illustration of the truth of regeneration is that which pertains to the natural birth. The natural birth pre-figures the spiritual birth. The following analogy between the earthly and the heavenly birth show the divine agencies involved in the miracle of regeneration.

Natural Birth	Spiritual Birth
The Seed	The Seed of the Word (I Peter 1:23)
The Blood	The Blood of Jesus (I John 1:7)
The Water	The Water of Regeneration (John 3:5-7; Titus 3:5; Ezekiel 36:25-27)
The Breath	The Reception of the Holy Spirit (John 3:5-6; Titus 3:5)
The Will of Man	The Will of the Father God (John 1:13; James 1:18).

4. Manifestation

The regenerated person will have definite evidences that he has been born again.

a. Those born of God have **victory over the world,** its principles, standard and practices (I John 5:4; James 4:4).

b. Those born of God will have **victory over a life of sin** (Romans 6:14; I John 2:14). If they do sin, they do not live in sin, but seek the cleansing of the blood of Jesus (I John 1:5-7; 2:1-2).

c. Those born of God will have **love for God** and their fellowmen. Love is the very nature of God (I John 4:19; 3:14; 5:1-2; 4:21; Romans 5:5).

d. Those born of God will **live righteously** (I John 3:7; Matthew 5:44-45).

e. Those born of God will **love God's Word** and divine things (Psalm 119:97; I Peter 2:2; Colossians 3:1-2).

f. Those born of the Spirit will have the **witness of the Spirit** within themselves (Romans 8:16; Galatians 4:6).

g. Those born of the Spirit will **manifest the nature** and character of Jesus Christ (II Peter 1:4; John 1:12). Instead of manifesting the nature and character of the Devil, he will manifest the divine nature (John 8:44; I John 3:10; Psalm 51:5; Ephesians 2:1-3).

C. The Benefit of Adoption

1. Definition
Adoption is defined as that act of God whereby a born-again child is placed as a son and given the full privileges of sonship.

The Hebrew concept of adoption is similar to the English definition of the word, which denotes a changing of families.

a. Moses was adopted by Pharoah's daughter to be heir to the throne of Egypt (Exodus 2:10).

b. Abraham was inclined to adopt his servant **Eliezer** to be the heir in his house (Genesis 15:2).

c. Abraham and Sarah adopted Hagar's child, **Ishmael,** to be the heir until God forbade it (Genesis 16:1-2).

d. In Genesis 48, Jacob adopted the two sons of Joseph, **Ephraim and Manasseh,** to be his own two sons. He "placed them as sons" in the tribes of Israel. These two sons were Egypto-Israelitish boys and by Jacob's act they were thus adopted into the chosen race and entitled to inheritance among the brethren.

e. The Lord God adopted **Israel** to be His son (Exodus 4:22-23 with Jeremiah 31:9; Romans 9:4; Hosea 11:1).

f. Esther was adopted by Mordecai also to be his daughter and thus he took responsibility for her welfare (Esther 2:7). Thus she came under the protection and care of a "father" rather than paternal relationship. The Hebrew thought is the receiving into the family one who does not belong to it by birth.

The Greek word "Huiothesia" means "the placing of a son." This word is translated "adoption" 5 times in the New Testament. It seems to be more distinctly Pauline in usage (Romans 8:15,23; 9:4; Galatians 4:5; Ephesians 1:5). It should be noted that it differs from Hebrew thought and does not carry the same meaning as does the English word "adoption" whereby a child may be "adopted" from one family into another. This is not so in the Kingdom of God.

2. Amplification

a. Regeneration and Adoption
In regeneration the believer is born again, born as a child into the family of God, the household of faith (John 1:12-13; 3:3-5). This has to do with relationship rather than position. This is the impartation of a new nature and is "son-making." In adoption the regenerated believer, at the age of maturity, is placed as a son. This has to do with position and privileges rather than relationship. This is son-placing (Galatians 4:1-2). In regeneration, one receives new life. In

justification one receives new standing. In adoption one receives a new position. Adoption has to do with the legal status as a son being given full rights of inheritance.

b. Roman Custom

Bancroft in "Christian Theology" (page 240) speaks of the Roman custom of adoption. The Romans had a custom whereby at a certain time appointed of the father or the Law, the male child in the family would be formally and legally adopted. That is, he would be placed in the position of a legal son and given the privileges of a son. The legal ceremony of adoption did not bring him into the family, it only placed a child of the family as a recognized, mature son in the eyes of Roman Law. It was the taking of one's own child by birth to be a mature son, bearing the family name. This formal act, attested to by witnesses, was the act whereby the son was given position, rights, privileges and obligations of a mature son.

This illustrates what God does in Christ to His sons. The spiritual supercedes the natural custom. In the natural, the "adopted son" cannot become like the parents who adopt them as a child and heir. With God this is opposite. God makes us His sons by regeneration, thus we become partakers of the nature of our Father God. God has accepted us as His sons who were not such by natural birth, giving us the family name, family rights and the privileges of sonship (Ephesians 3:14-15; Galatians 4:1-5; Romans 8:15-19). When the repentant is born again by the Holy Spirit, the Holy Spirit comes to him as "The Spirit of Adoption" and as such brings the believer to maturity, to full sonship (Galatians 4:6). In new birth, and the baptism of the Spirit, he receives the firstfruits, earnest and seal of the Spirit. These point to the full inheritance of sonship in the Father's time. The Holy Spirit as "the Spirit of adoption gives witness to this sonship" (Ephesians 1:14; II Corinthians 1:21-22; Romans 8:23).

c. Sonship

We note some of the progressive concepts of "Sonship" as used in the Scriptures.

(1) **Angels** are called "Sons of God" (Job 2:1; I Timothy 5:21). Angels would be sons by creation, as created spirits.

(2) **Adam** is also called the Son of God. This is by creation also, but a lower order of creation than angelic beings (Luke 3:38; Psalm 8:1-4).

(3) **Israel**, as a nation, is called God's son, His firstborn. This was sonship by election, redemption and adoption (Exodus 4:22; Amos 3:2; Hosea 11:1; Romans 9:3-5).

(4) **Jesus** is the eternal and unique Son of God, not created, but begotten as to His humanity (Hebrews 1:5; John 3:16). In His humanity Jesus was placed as a Son, given His Father's name and the full inheritance of the Godhead (Acts 2:34-36; Colossians 1:19; 2:9).

(5) **Kings** of Israel were called God's sons also in their kingly position (Psalm 2:7; I Chronicles 28:6).

(6) **The believer** is God's son by regeneration and adoption. He is born as a son in new birth, a partaker of the divine nature and name, and in due time is to be placed in full sonship (I John 3:1; Romans 8:23). This distinction in the concept of sonship should be kept in view.

d. Time of Adoption

The few brief references in the New Testament concerning adoption show that there is a threefold aspect of the time of adoption.

(1) Time Past

The believer was adopted in eternity past. According to the foreknowledge of God the believer was predestined unto adoption (Ephesians 1:5).

(2) Time Present

The moment a person is born again of the Spirit of God, he receives the Holy Spirit as the

Spirit of adoption. As a born again child of God, he is to grow to full sonship. The Spirit of Adoption enables him to cry "Abba, Father" (Galatians 3:26; 4:1-5; John 1:11-12; Matthew 6:6-10; Romans 8:15-19).

(3) Time Future

The full manifestation of the believer's sonship awaits the coming of Christ. The whole creation is waiting the manifestation and unveiling of the sons of God. This adoption involves the redemption of the body, the resurrection and the translation of the saints (Romans 8:23; Ephesians 1:14; 4:30; Philippians 3:20-21; Revelation 21:7).

e. Results of Adoption

Bancroft in "Christian Theology" (page 240) outlines some of the results of adoption when he deals with the significance of this term.

(1) On the Human Side

a) As sons, we have the **family name** (Ephesians 3:14,15; I John 3:1; Revelation 2:17; 3:12).

(b) As sons, we have the **family likeness** (Colossians 3:10; Romans 8:29; II Corinthians 3:18).

(c) As sons, we have the **parents' nature** (II Peter 1:4; John 1:12,13; 3:6).

(d) As sons, we have a family affection (I John 2:9-11; 3:14-18; 4:7-8; 5:1).

(2) On the Divine Side

(a) As His children, we are the **objects of His peculiar love** (John 17:22,23; 16:27).

(b) As His children, we are the **subjects of His fatherly care** (Matthew 6:32).

(c) As His children, we are the **subjects of His paternal discipline** (Hebrews 12:6-11).

(d) As His children, we are the **subjects of His paternal comfort** (II Corinthians 1:4).

(e) As His children, we are made **heirs to an inheritance** (I Peter 1:3-5; Romans 8:17). To which may be added the following:

(f) **Deliverance** from the bondage of the Law (Romans 8:15; Galatians 4:4-5).

(g) **Indwelling** and reception of the Holy Spirit, as the Spirit of Adoption (Ephesians 1:11-14; Galatians 4:5).

(h) **Reception** of the earnest of our inheritance (Romans 8:23; Ephesians 1:11-14; II Corinthians 1:22; 5:5).

(i) **Life** in the Spirit, which is the Son of God re-living His life in His sons (Romans 8:14; Galatians 2:20; 5:18; Colossians 1:27).

(j) Father and son **relationship**, and sonship privileges as the heirs of God (Galatians 4:6; Romans 8:15).

(k) **Conformity** to the image of Christ, the firstborn among a vast family of brothers in the household of God (Romans 8:29; Ephesians 2:19; Hebrews 12:5-11).

(l) **Total redemption** of the body at the unveiling of the sons of God at Christ's coming (Romans 8:19-23).

(m) **Partakers** of the divine nature with a new heart and a new spirit (II Peter 1:4; Romans 6:4; Ezekiel 36:26; 11:19; Ephesians 4:24).

(n) **Restoration** of total inheritance, as joint heirs with Christ, which we lost in Adam (Ephesians 1:13-14; Romans 8:23; Revelation 21:7; Galatians 3:26).

3. Illustration

The development of the child to adulthood is used to illustrate the truth of sonship. The practical application of the doctrine of the believer's adoption into sonship should create the desire to come to full maturity by being conformed to the image of the pattern Son, Jesus Christ. The New Testament writers imply various stages of spiritual development and use such to encourage the believer to grow up into maturity (I John 2:12-14). We note the various stages of spiritual development in a believer's life.

a. The Infant

Several Greek words are used to set forth the infant stage of the new-born believer.

(1) **Brephos** meaning "an unborn child, a new-born child, infant, or babe." (Luke 1:41; 2:12; II Timothy 3:15; I Peter 2:2). The believer, as a new-born babe, is to desire the sincere milk of the Word.

(2) **Nepios** meaning "an infant, little child, a minor, not able to speak, untaught, unskilled, childish immature Christian" (Matthew 11:25; 21:16; I Corinthians 3:1; 13:11; Galatians 4:1,3; Ephesians 4:14; Hebrews 5:13). Paul wrote to the Corinthians and the Hebrew believers reminding them that they were babes as yet, unable to handle the meat of the Word.

(3) **Paidion** meaning "a young child, infant, a little one" (Matthew 2:8,9, 11,13,14,21; 18:2-5; 19:13,14; I Corinthians 14:20; Hebrews 2:13,14; I John 2:13,18)

b. The Child - The Growing Stage

Several Greek words are used which denote the child, or the growing stage in the believer's life.

(1) **Teknon** meaning "offspring, children, child". It is not necessarily speaking of age, but generation (John 1:12; Romans 8:16,17,21; Philippians 2:15; I John 3:1,2,10). The born-again believer is a child of God.

(2) **Pais** meaning "a child, a boy or girl" also an infant at times (Matthew 21:15; Luke 2:43; John 4:51; Acts 4:27,30).

(3) **Paidarion** meaning "a child, a boy or girl, a child up through its first school years, one who needs nurture, instruction and chastening" (Matthew 11:16; John 6:9).

c. The Teenager - Maturing Stage

Neaniskos meaning "a young man, youth, one in the prime and vigor of life, teenager, juvenile" (Acts 2:17; 5:10; 7:58; 20:9; I John 2:13,14; Matthew 19:20,22; Mark 14:22; Luke 7:14).

d. The Full Son - Mature Stage

Huios meaning "a son, mature, full-grown, having both character and privilege."

The Lord Jesus was revealed as the Son of God, a mature Son, at Jordan's baptism (Matthew 3:17). The world is waiting for the manifestation or unveiling of the mature sons of God (Romans 8:14,19, 29). (Romans 1:4; II Corinthians 6:18; Galatians 1:16; 4:6,22,30; Ephesians 4:13; Hebrews 2:10; Revelation 2:7) God's ultimate promise is that the overcomer will be His Son, restored to the image from which Adam fell.

A true son of God will hate sin, live righteously, love the brethren and walk as Christ walked in this world (I John 2:6; 4:17). Christ the son will re-live His life in His sons. The Son of God became the Son of Man that the sons of men might become the sons of God.

Regeneration	Adoption
Born of the Spirit	Matured by the Spirit
As a child	As a son
Immature	Matured
Earnest of inheritance	Full inheritance
First fruits of the Spirit	Fulness of the Spirit
Witness of the Spirit	Possessed of the Spirit
Spirit of Adoption	Adoption realized
Subject to sin and death	Redemption of the body
As a servant	As a Son perfect and mature
Discipline and obedience	Character and privileges
Made heirs	Receives the inheritance

D. The Benefit of Sanctification

1. Definition
Sanctification is the setting apart of something or someone to a particular use or service. Theologically it speaks of God setting apart the believer for Himself, from all evil use, to be wholly used for Himself and His service.

a. Hebrew
The Hebrew word "Qadesh" means "to be clean, to make, pronounce or observe as clean, ceremonially or morally". It is translated under these words: consecrate, dedicate, hallow, holy, purify, sanctify (Genesis 2:3; Exodus 29:43; Leviticus 8:10, 15,30; 10:3; Numbers 8:17; II Chronicles 7:16,20; Isaiah 13:3; Ezekiel 48:11).

b. Greek
The Greek word "Hagiasmos" and related Greek words, means "to make holy, purify, or consecrate". It is translated by these words: sanctify, sanctification, hallow, be holy, and holiness (Romans 6:19,22; I Corinthians 1:30; I Thessalonians 4:3,4,7; II Thessalonians 2:13; I Timothy 2:15; Hebrews 12:14; I Peter 1:2; Romans 1:4; II Corinthians 7:1; I Thessalonians 3:13).

Sanctification therefore means "to be separate, or to be set apart" especially for holy use.

2. Amplification
The importance of sanctification in the life of the believer is expressed in Hebrews 12:14 "...without holiness (sanctification) no man can see the Lord." Sanctification is the will of God for every believer (I Thessalonians 5:23-24; Titus 2:14). We note here the various things or persons which were sanctified by God.

a. **Days and seasons** were sanctified (Genesis 2:3; Deuteronomy 5:12; Nehemiah 13:19-22; Joel 1:14; 2:15).

b. **Places,** such as houses or fields were sanctified (Leviticus 27:14; Leviticus 27:16-22; Exodus 19:12,23; Hebrews 12:20).

c. **The Tabernacle** and its furniture were sanctified (Exodus 29:27,33,36; 30:25-29; 40:10; Leviticus 8:10; Numbers 7:1).

d. **The priests** were sanctified before their service (Exodus 29:4-9; 40:12-13; Leviticus 8:6,12).

e. The firstborn of man and beast were sanctified (Exodus 13:2; Numbers 8:17).

f. The nation of Israel was sanctified (Exodus 19:5,6,10).

g. Christ Jesus Himself was sanctified (John 17:17).

h. Believers in Christ are also sanctified (I Thessalonians 5:23).

3. Illustration
Just as pardon and justification, and regeneration and adoption are related words, so justification and sanctification are related words. Pardon and justification are legal terms, while regeneration and adoption are family terms, but sanctification is a temple term. It more especially involves priestly function and ministry. The consecration and separation of Aaron and his sons as the Tribe of Levi to priestly ministry, illustrates the vital elements of the nature of sanctification.

a. Sanctification is Separation
The priests were separated from other Israelites and from other responsibilities to the service of the Lord and His sanctuary. The Levitical tribe knew that they were a separated, sanctified tribe. The Nazarite also separated himself from various things which defile during the days of his vow unto the Lord. He was not to defile this separation (Numbers 1:47-52; 3:5-10; 18:1-7; Hebrews 5:1-5; Numbers 6:1-12).

b. Sanctification is Dedication
Sanctification has both negative and positive aspects. On the negative side it is separation from something and on the positive side it is separation unto the Lord. The believer is separated from the world to serve the Lord in His Church. He is separated unto all that is holy, clean and pure (Numbers 6:2-3; Romans 1:1-2; Hebrews 5:1; II Chronicles 29:5,15-18; Leviticus 27:14,16; Numbers 8:17; II Corinthians 6:17; II Corinthians 7:1; 6:14-18; John 10:36).

c. Sanctification is Purification
The priests in their separation to the Lord and the service of the sanctuary also experienced the ceremony of purification (Exodus 28-29; Leviticus 8-9). It involved the sprinkling of blood, washing with water and anointing with oil. By these means the priests were purified and cleansed to do the work of the Lord. The New Testament confirms the fact that the believer is also purified by the blood of Jesus, the washing of water by the Word, and the anointing of the Holy Spirit (I John 5:5-9; I Peter 2:5; Titus 3:5; Ephesians 5:26-27). Paul reminds the Corinthians that they were "washed, sanctified, justified" (I Corinthians 6:11). The sanctified believer will be purified (I John 3:3). He will be separated from all moral evil and from all that is ungodly (Hebrews 9:13; Psalm 51:7; Titus 2:14; II Corinthians 7:1; Ezekiel 36:25).

d. Sanctification is Consecration
In the sanctification of the priests was also involved the thought of consecration (Exodus 29:9). The word "consecration" here means "to fill the hand." The hands of the priests were filled with the specified parts of the ram of consecration and presented to the Lord. It was significant of the fact that the priest in his function was consecrated to the Lord. He would not appear before the Lord empty-handed. The New Testament sanctified believer also fills his hands with that which is to be presented to the Lord. He is a consecrated one and presents spiritual sacrifices, through Christ, to God (Romans 12:1-2; I Peter 2:5-9; Hebrews 13:13-15).

e. Sanctification is Service
The priests were also separated to the service of the Lord, to do His will (Leviticus 8-9; Exodus 28-29 chapters). They were no longer to do their own will but the will of God. Theirs was the service of the altar, the sanctuary, the people, and the Lord. Service was an integral part of their sanctification. So the believer is to present himself in priestly service to do the good and acceptable and perfect will of God (Romans 12:1-2; Acts 27:23; I Peter 2:5-9).

4. False Views of Sanctification
Several false views are considered as to the experience of sanctification, each of which are man's effort to be all that God intends him to be.

a. Eradication

Several groups teach that sanctification is eradication of inbred sin, the Adamic nature. They teach that the believer, by a definite work of grace, has the law of sin eradicated and can no longer sin. However, if this were practically so, then all believers would be physically free from all sickness, disease and death. For, where there is no sin, there can be no death (Romans 8:1-3; I Corinthians 15:56). This view fails to recognize the two natures in the believer, and the sin principle which is in the human nature and yet to be eradicated.

b. Legalism

This view holds that by being bound by various laws and regulations, the believer can live the sanctified life (Colossians 2:21-23). This is what the Galatian church endeavored to do (Galatians 3:1-3). However, the law and all other man-made regulations produce a legalistic spirit and approach. Legalism may be defined as the doctrine of salvation or sanctification by good works rather than that which arises out of the free grace of God. The Pharisees were legalists, following the externals of the law, believing they were sanctified and yet being corrupt within.

c. Asceticism

This view teaches that one is able to reach the experience of sanctification or a higher spiritual state by rigorous self-denial and self-discipline. This actually is a form of self-crucifixion or penance which is a voluntary suffering or self-inflicted punishment. All this is done to subdue or punish the flesh (Colossians 2:23). The theory holds that flesh or matter is evil, and the body of sins must be cut off and destroyed by ascetic practices (Matthew 5:27-30).

5. Biblical View of Sanctification

a. The Time of Sanctification

The Scripture teaches that sanctification is both instantaneous and progressive; that it is positional and practical; that it includes both standing and state; that it is judicial and experiential; an act and a process.

(1) Positional or Judicial

The moment a person is born again, they are sanctified. That is, they are separated from sin unto the Lord. This sanctification takes place at regeneration and is instantaneous. In God's sight his position is that of a separated one. He is sanctified in Christ (I Corinthians 1:2; 6:11; Hebrews 2:11; 10:10,14; Ephesians 1:4). The believer was set apart to the Lord in Christ before the foundation of the world and God reckons to him the holiness of Jesus and counts him sanctified. This is why the believer is called a saint, a sanctified one (I Corinthians 1:2; Romans 1:7; Colossians 1:2; Hebrews 10:10; II Corinthians 7:1; II Thessalonians 2:13). This is initial sanctification.

(2) Practical or Experiential

It is evident Biblically and experientially that believers, though sanctified in Christ at the time of conversion, still need a continuous or progressive work to be done in them. The Corinthian believers are but one example of this fact (I Corinthians 3:1; 5:1-8). All the New Testament epistles have their exhortations to believers to grow in Christ and to live the sanctified and separated life (Hebrews 10:14; 12:14; I Thessalonians 5:23; II Corinthians 7:1). In contrast to justification (which is instantaneous not progressive) sanctification is both an instantaneous and progressive work II Peter 3:18; II Corinthians 3:18; 7:1). This is the process of sanctification.

(3) Complete or Final

Every saint realizes that, no matter how much progress has been made in the Lord and in the life of holiness, he is still imperfect. Longings after complete holiness will never cease until the believer is brought by the power of God to a state of sinless perfection. It is at the time of Christ's coming that the believer will know full and complete sanctification. It is then that the root of sin will be eradicated and the believer's body will be immortalized and glorified (Matthew 5:48; Hebrews 6:1-2; I Thessalonians 5:23-24; I Thessalonians 3:13; Philippians 2:12-14). Thus the work of sanctification in its on-going stages may be viewed as initial, progressive and final; past, present and future; instantaneous, progressive and complete. Often a believer's "crisis experience" in the Lord has been misconstrued as a "second work of grace" or "second blessing." The total work of sanctification will show the believer that he has been delivered from the guilt and penalty of sin, he is being delivered from the power of sin, and he will ultimately be delivered from the presence of sin. This is sanctification past, present and future.

b. The Means of Sanctification
The Biblical view of sanctification indicates that there must be both the divine means and the believer's response to make sanctification both a positional and practical reality.

(1) Work of the Godhead
The Father, Son and Holy Spirit are involved in the work of sanctification.

The Father (I Thessalonians 5:23-24; Hebrews 10:11; 13:21; I Corinthians 1:30; I Thessalonians 4:3). It is the will of God the Father that all believers be sanctified.

The Son (Hebrews 10:10; 2:11; Ephesians 5:25-27; I Corinthians 1:30; Hebrews 13:12; I Corinthians 1:2; Titus 2:14). One of the great redemptive names of Jehovah is "Jehovah Mekaddishkem" or "The Lord who Sanctifies" (Exodus 31:13; Leviticus 20:7-8; 31:8,15,23; Hebrews 2:10; I Corinthians 1:30; I Thessalonians 5:23-24). Sanctification is not merely the knowledge of a doctrine but relationship with the person and work of Christ, the One who sanctifies us (Jeremiah 23:6; Titus 2:11-14).

The Holy Spirit (I Peter 1:2; II Thessalonians 2:13; Romans 8:2,13; Galatians 5:17-22). It is the Holy Spirit who applies the sanctifying power of God to the believer's life.

(2) Means of Sanctification
There are three means God has provided for the believer's sanctification. These three work together as one; each being inter-dependent upon the other for their practical outworking (I John 5:5-7).

(a) The Blood of Christ
We are sanctified by the blood of Jesus Christ. This is absolute, positional and eternal (John 19:33-34; Hebrews 13:12; 10:10, 14; I John 1:7; Hebrews 2:11).

(b) The Word of God
We are sanctified by the Word of God. This is practical obedience (Ephesians 5:26; John 15:3; Titus 3:5; I Peter 1:23; Psalm 119:9; James 1:23-25).

(c) The Holy Spirit
We are sanctified by the power of the Holy Spirit (I Corinthians 6:11; Romans 1:4; II Thessalonians 2:13; Romans 15:16; I Peter 1:1-2). The Holy Spirit comes to make us holy. He applies the power of the cleansing blood as we walk in obedience to the Word (I Peter 1:2). The Holy Spirit does the work internally. He is called "The Spirit of Holiness."

(3) Human Response
God has provided the means for sanctification. What then is the believer's response?

(a) Scriptural Knowledge
The believer must receive knowledge and understanding from the Scriptures concerning the sanctified life. He must receive from the Scriptures:

(i)   The knowledge of its necessity; the realization of his own personal need (I Peter 1:14-16; I Thessalonians 4:7).

(ii)   The knowledge that it is God's will for him to be sanctified (I Thessalonians 4:3).

    (iii)   The knowledge of its possibility here and now (I Thessalonians 5:23-24).

    (iv)   The knowledge of the divine application. That it is not by eradication, legalism or asceticism but by the divine means as seen above (Philippians 2:12-13).

    (v)   Paul emphasizes the believer's "knowing" concerning positional and experiental truth in Romans (Romans 6:3,6,9,16).

(b) Appropriating Faith

True knowledge and understanding of the Word of God creates faith (Romans 10:17). Sanctification is by faith in the Lord Jesus (Acts 26:18; Hebrews 12:10-11,14). Appropriating faith agrees with what God says about the believer. In Roman culture, a prisoner would sometimes have a dead body strapped to his back. It would be kept there, putrifying, and slowly killing the living person. It was a living death from which he could not deliver himself. Someone else had to release from him "the body of this death" (Romans 7:24). The believer is to reckon himself dead to sin, that he is freed from the body of death (Romans 6:6-23). The "old man" was crucified with Christ that the body of sin might be disannulled, so that the believer no longer serves sin. Faith reckons the Word of God to be true. It trusts that God will back up His Word in the life of the believer.

(c) Practical Obedience

The believer, as the elect of God, is sanctified by the blood and the Spirit unto obedience to the Word of God (I Peter 1:2; II Thessalonians 2:13; Philippians 2:12-13). It is as the believer walks in obedience to the Word, that the Holy Spirit continually applies the cleansing blood and the believer is living the sanctified life (John 14:16; Acts 5:32).

(4) The Two Natures in the Believer

Relative to the doctrine of sanctification and the believer's practical experience of the truth, it is important that the believer recognize that he has two natures since his regeneration. Otherwise doubts, confusion and despair will overcome him. As stated under "The Doctrine of Christ", the believer has a human nature by natural birth, and by spiritual birth is a partaker of the divine nature. The human nature has the sin principle still in it. The divine nature is to develop to full maturity and bring about that full victory over the sin principle in the human nature. This constitutes the overcoming and victorious Christian.

It should be remembered that original human nature as it came from the hand of God was not sinful. When Adam fell, the sin principle entered the human nature and corrupted it. God's ultimate intention was to fill the human nature with divine nature, with Himself. In the new birth the believer becomes a partaker of the divine nature. The divine nature is within the human nature and is to be fully expressed through it. It is the sin-principle within human nature that is the corrupting power. This has to be overcome and eventually God will eradicate it. It is then that the divine nature and the human nature will find their full expression, even as in the Lord Jesus Christ. In Him is the union of both natures in the one person, sin excepted. So shall it be in the believer.

There are a number of designations used in Scripture which show the distinction and the warfare that exists between these two natures because of the sin-principle in man. We note these with appropriate Scripture references in the following two columns.

Human Nature	**Divine Nature**
(a) Fleshly birth	Spirit birth (John 3:1-5)
(b) Natural father	Heavenly Father (Matthew 6:5-9)
(c) Natural man	Spiritual man (I Corinthians 2:14; 3:1-3)
(d) Put off the old man	Put on the new man (Ephesians 4:22,24; Romans 13:12-14; Colossians 3:9-10).

(e) First man - earthly	Second man heavenly (I Corinthians 15:47-49)
(f) No good thing in me	That good thing in thee (Romans 7:18; Philemon 6)
(g) Works of the flesh	Fruit of the Spirit (Galatians 5:16-25)
(h) Living soul	Quickened spirit (I Corinthians 15:45)
(i) The old heart	The new heart (Ezekiel 36:25-27; Psalm 51:10; Jeremiah 17:9; Mark 7:21-22)
(j) New (renewed) spirit	My spirit with your spirit (Ephesians 4:23; Ezekiel 36:25-27)
(k) You in Christ	Christ in you (Colossians 1:27; II Corinthians 5:17)
(l) Dead in sin	Dead to sin, alive to God (Ephesians 2:1-7)
(m) If any man sin	He cannot sin, seed remains in him when born of God (I John 2:1; 3:9;I Peter 1:23; James 1:18)
(n) By nature child of wrath	Partakers of divine nature (Ephesians 2:3; II Peter 1:4)
(o) The old creation	The new creation (II Corinthians 5:17)
(p) Walk after the flesh	Walk after the Spirit (Romans 8:1-13)

As the believer recognizes that he has two natures, it is his responsibility to avail himself of the divine means for living the sanctified life. He may either walk after the flesh or after the Spirit. He cannot do both at the same time. It is by the power of the cross and the Holy Spirit that the desires of the old nature are crucified. These things must be mortified by the Spirit to allow the divine nature to rule (Colossians 3:5; Romans 8:13). He must work out that which God works in (Philippians 2:12-13). As he does this, then he is living unto Christ, the sanctified life, until he comes to the perfection that is God's ultimate intention.

It is in the sanctified life that the believer recognizes the work of the cross being applied by the power of faith and the power of the indwelling Holy Spirit.

(5) The Cross and Sanctification
As with all other benefits of the atonement, the provision for our sanctification was made at the cross. There both sin and the self-life were dealt with. The three persons on the three crosses on Calvary's hill may be used to illustrate God's dealings with sin in relation to the believer's sanctification (Matthew 27:38,44; Mark 15:27-28).

(a) The Unrepentant Thief
This person had sin in and upon him. He died in sin, thus coming under rejection and condemnation before God (Luke 23:32-33,39). He became representative of all the unbelieving and unrepentant of mankind who reject Christ and the work of the cross and thus go into everlasting destruction.

(b) The Son of God
The Lord Jesus Christ had no sin in Him but He did have sin placed upon Him, as the sinoffering (II Corinthians 5:21; Isaiah 53:6,9; Galatians 3:13; I John 3:5; I Peter 2:24). Christ died for sin and thus substitution, justification and sanctification were legally provided for us. Justification deals with our deeds, what we have done while sanctification deals with our character, what we are.

(c) The Repentant Thief
This thief represents all the repentant and believing who accept Christ and the work of the cross and enter the Kingdom of God (Luke 23:32-33,39-43). He died to sin and this symbolizes reconciliation, justification, identification and sanctification.

The sinner being dead in sin speaks of our **condemnation** (Ephesians 2:1; Colossians 2:13). Christ being dead for sin speaks of our **justification** (II Corinthians 5:14; Galatians 2:17). The believer being dead to sin speaks of our **sanctification** (Romans 6:11; 8:13). Judicial truth must become experiential truth. Sanctification is the application of the cross to the self-life in spirit, soul and body (I Thessalonians 5:23). It is the Holy Spirit doing in us experientially what Christ has done for us legally.

In summary we may note the distinction between justification and sanctification. In justification we are declared righteous while in sanctification we become righteous. Justification is what God has done for us, while sanctification is what God does in us. Justification places us in right relationship with God, while sanctification is the fruit or evidence of that relationship. It is a life of separation from the sinful world and of consecration unto God. Justification declares us righteous, legally. Sanctification makes us righteous, experientially.

E. The Benefit of Perfection

1. Definition
The word "perfect" means "to be complete, whole, upright, plain, just, without fault or defect."

a. Hebrew

(1) **Shalem,** meaning "finished, whole, perfect, plain, just" (Deuteronomy 25:15; 27:6; I Kings 11:4; 15:3; II Chronicles 8:16).

(2) **Tamin,** meaning "complete, whole, perfect, upright, to end or to finish off, as a house". It is also translated "without blemish" over forty times. The sacrifices had to be "perfect" to be presented to God (Leviticus 22:21; Genesis 6:9; 17:1; Exodus 12:5; Deuteronomy 18:13; Psalm 15:2; 37:37; Proverbs 2:21; Ezekiel 46:4).

b. Greek

(1) **Telios,** meaning "complete, ended, perfect, consummation" (Matthew 5:48; 19:21; Romans 12:2; I Corinthians 2:6; 13:10; Hebrews 5:14; I John 5:18).

(2) **Katartizo,** meaning "to fit thoroughly, adjust, complete" and signifies "right ordering or arrangement". It is translated as "mended" (Matthew 4:21; Mark 1:19), "perfectly joined" (I Corinthians 1:10), "restore" (Galatians 6:1), "perfect" (II Thessalonians 3:10), "prepared" (Hebrews 10:5), "framed" (Hebrews 11:3), "fitted" (Romans 9:22).

Thus perfection has to do with completeness, wholeness, uprightness, to fit thoroughly, adjustment and being without blemish.

2. Amplification
Because God Himself is perfect, He can demand no less than perfection from His creatures. Even in fallen man there is the innate longing and striving after perfection. This itself is a testimony that man fell from this state. God Himself is the standard by which everything in the universe is measured. God desires that His redeemed be like Him. Thus God commanded perfection before Law (Genesis 17:1), under Law (Deuteronomy 18:13), and under grace (Matthew 5:48).

We consider the three kinds of perfection that the Scripture reveals.

a. Perfection as pertaining to God
This perfection, as pertaining to God, is absolute and underived, sinless perfection. It is impossible for God to sin (Hebrews 6:18; I John 3:9). God is perfect in His own nature and being. All He does, all He is and all His ways are perfect (Deuteronomy 32:4; Matthew 5:48; Job 36:4; Psalm 18:30; 19:7; 50:2; Job 11:7).

b. Perfection as pertaining to Creatures
This perfection, as pertaining to created beings, is a derived perfection. However, it was not a sinless perfection. It was an untested perfection and untried perfection. This is seen in the created beings of God, such as angels and original man.

(1) **Lucifer** was "perfect" in all his ways from the day he was created, yet it was not a sinless perfection as God had, or else he and the other angels would not have fallen (Ezekiel 28:12-18; Isaiah 14: 12-15; Jude 6; II Peter 2:4).

(2) **Adam** was "perfect" but it was an untried and untested perfection. When tempted in his state of innocency, he fell from the state of perfection he had. Adam's perfection was not a sinless perfection. No creature could have perfection in or of himself. It must be of God.

c. Perfection as pertaining to Saints
The Scriptures teach two phases of perfection as pertaining to the redeemed.

(1) Present Perfection
The Bible speaks of a perfection which is possible and attainable in this life. It is spoken of as a relative perfection and it is God who speaks of those saints who have this kind of relationship with Himself right here in this life.

   (a) Noah was perfect in his generation (Genesis 6:9).

   (b) Job was perfect before God (Job 1:1-8; 2:3).

   (c) Hezekiah had a perfect heart before God II Kings 20:2-5; Isaiah 38:3).

   (d) Abraham was called to walk perfect before God (Genesis 17:1).

It will be evident that none of these saints had "sinless perfection" for each have their faults recorded. What then was this "perfection" that God said these saints had before Him? It was a "perfect heart". That is, a heart that is surrendered and totally submitted to Him, a heart that is sold out to do the will of God; a heart that is sincere and completely after God's heart. A perfect heart is a whole-hearted desire and determination to do God's will. It is this kind of perfection that is possible before God and attainable in this present life (I Kings 11:4; 15.3; II Chronicles 25:2; 16:9; Psalm 37:37; 101:2,6; Deuteronomy 18:13).

(2) Future Perfection
The Scriptures speak of a perfection that the believer will know at the coming of Christ. This perfection will be sinless perfection, even as God has. However, it will be derived from God. Man can never realize this by himself or by His own efforts no matter how he strives after it. It is God's ultimate intention to bring the redeemed to a perfection from which it is impossible to fall (Psalm 138:8; I Peter 5:10; John 17:23; Psalm 18:32: Ephesians 4:13; I Thessalonians 3:10; Hebrews 13:20-21).

The Book of Hebrews uses the word "perfect" about 17 times. It shows how the Law was a perfect standard but could not make the Israelites perfect. Hence God brought in His Son to be the sacrifice of the New Covenant which will bring the believer to perfection. In the Old Testament, the great Day of Atonement shadowed forth the total cleansing from sin and the perfection that blood atonement would bring forth (Leviticus 16). The book of Hebrews is built around the revelation and fulfilment of the Day of Atonement (read Hebrews 9 with Zechariah 3:10). The Book of Proverbs speaks of "the Light that shines more and more unto the perfect day" (Proverbs 4:18). The New Testament speaks of it as "the day of redemption" (Ephesians 1:13-14, 4:30).

3. The Perfect Man
The Lord Jesus, as the Last Adam, was the only man who ever walked perfectly before the Father here on earth. His perfection was not only a sinless perfection, but it was also a tested perfection. As noted earlier, the First Adam had but one nature, human nature, and when tempted, fell. Jesus had the divine nature in union with His human nature and thus, when tempted, carried the human nature through victoriously. Jesus walked in human flesh in sinless perfection. Thus God had a Man here on earth who perfectly fulfilled His purpose and will. Thus it is Jesus, our Kinsman Redeemer, who makes possible the perfection for the redeemed. This is the ultimate purpose of redemption. This is the completion of the atonement.

4. Means of Perfection
Because of man's inability to bring himself to perfection, God in His grace has provided the means for it. We list a number of these divine means.

a. The Lord Jesus is the author and perfector of our faith (Hebrews 12:2; 10:14). By the body and blood of the New Covenant He will perfect us (Hebrews 13:20-21; 7:11).

b. The Word of God will perfect the saints (Hebrews 11:3; II Timothy 3:16-17).

c. Faith and obedience perfect us (I John 4:17-18; James 2:21).

d. The glory of the Lord will bring the saints to perfection (John 17:23).

e. The ministries set in the Body of Christ are given to bring the saints to perfection and maturity (Ephesians 4:11-12; Colossians 1:26-28).

f. Saints who **die in faith** are perfected in spirit (Hebrews 12:24).

g. The Church will be presented to Christ perfect, without spot or blemish and holy as His Bride by the **washing of water by the Word** (Ephesians 5:23-32).

Thus the believer is exhorted to press on unto perfection and to maintain a perfect heart until he is brought by the redeeming power of God to that state of sinless perfection from which it will be impossible to fall (Colossians 1:27-29; II Corinthians 7:1; I Peter 5:10; Philippians 2:12-13). The believer can confidently speak with the Psalmist: "The Lord will perfect that which concerneth me" (Psalm 138:8). The believer is "perfect in Christ", but that is positional truth. That which is positional truth will become experiential truth in God's appointed time as the believer presses on in God (Hebrews 6:1-2).

F. The Benefit of Glorification

1. Definition
The words "glory" or "glorified" have the meaning of "to render or esteem glorious, honorable, or to magnify." When the words "glorify" or "glory" are used relative to Christ and His saints, they have a wide variety of applications. "The Glory" speaks of the majesty, brightness and outshining of the beauty, light and honor of the Lord.

Glorification is the final work of redemption and it arises out of the perfection of the saints. The perfection and glorification of the saints are inseparable. One is an integral part of the other. When Adam fell from his state of perfection, he fell "short of the glory of God" (Romans 3:23; 8:30). The work of redemption brings the believer up to the perfection of Jesus and with perfection comes glorification. It restores man to the glory of God from which he fell in Adam. God has always desired to manifest His glory both in creation and in His creatures. Scripture references show how God's glory is revealed in created things, but the ultimate is God's glory seen upon His saints. When the redeemed are conformed to the image of Christ and have the full character of God in them, the glory of God will be fully revealed in man. The perfections of God's moral attributes and character constitute the glory of God and the glorification of the saints.

a. The Glory of God in Created Things

(1) God's glory was seen in the **burning bush** (Exodus 3).
(2) God's glory was seen in the **cloudy pillar of fire** (Exodus 16:7-10).
(3) God's glory was also seen in the **plagues of judgement** on the Egyptians (Exodus 4-12).
(4) The glory of the Lord was seen on **Mt. Sinai** (Exodus 24:16-17).
(5) The glory of God filled the **Tabernacle of Moses** (Exodus 29:43; 40:34-35; Leviticus 9:6,23).
(6) The **Temple of Solomon** was filled with God's glory (I Kings 8:11; II Chronicles 5:14; 7:1-3).

(7) Israel was the only nation that had a visible manifestation of the glory of God. The Hebrews spoke of it as "The Shekinah" (Romans 9:4).

(8) The **sun, moon and stars** and the heavens declare the glory of God (Psalm 19:1-6; I Corinthians 15:40-43).

This aspect of the glory of God speaks of the radiance, brightness and outshining of God's light and presence, and was seen in visible manifestation in the above created things.

b. The Glory of God in Christ

On the Mount of Transfiguration, Jesus manifested the glory of God in His humanity. This glory shone through His body and raiment, white as light (Luke 9:26-32; II Peter 1:17-18; Mark 9:1; Matthew 17:1-8). This is also spoken of as the glory of the kingdom. In His ascension He was revealed in the glory of the sun-light (Revelation 1:16; 10:1; Isaiah 22:24; I Corinthians 2:8). Christ Jesus experienced first the sufferings and then the glory that should follow. He is the pattern for all who follow in His steps (Romans 8:17-18; I Peter 1:11).

Various saints in beholding the glory and brightness of God in Christ were changed by that glory.

(1) Moses beheld the glory of the Lord and that glory was upon his face (Exodus 33:18-22; II Corinthians 3).

(2) Abraham saw the glory of God also (Acts 7:2).

(3) Isaiah saw the glory of God in Christ (Isaiah 6:1-6; John 12:41).

(4) Moses saw the glory of God in the burning bush (Exodus 3).

(5) Ezekiel the prophet saw the glory of God in the Cherubim (Ezekiel 1:28; 3:23; 8:4; 9:3; 10:4,18-19.

(6) Stephen saw the glory of God and Jesus standing to receive him (Acts 7:55).

(7) Paul beheld the glory of God in the face of Jesus Christ (Acts 22:11). All these saints beheld the brightness and outshining of God's light and thus were changed by this brightness.

c. The Glory of God in the Saints

It is when the saints are perfected that they are glorified. The full glory of God is manifested in them. Of what then does this glorification consist?

(1) The brightness of **God's light** upon His people, even as exemplified on the face of Moses (Exodus 33:12-23; 34:29-35; II Corinthians 3), and Stephen (Acts 7:54-60).

(2) The **resurrection body** is also involved in glorification. The glory of the heavenly bodies symbolizes the varying degrees of glory in the resurrected and immortalized saints. The saints will rise with the glory of the sun, the glory of the moon, the varying glory of the stars. They will shine eternally with these glories (I Corinthians 15:40-43; Philippians 3:20-21; Revelation 12:1; Judges 5:31; Matthew 13:43).

(3) The saints being fully conformed to the **image of Christ,** made holy in nature and character is also part of the glorification (Romans 8:17-18,30). It is the perfection of God's moral attributes now revealed in the redeemed that brings man back to the glory of God from which he fell.

(4) The **redeemed being** brought back to all that Adam fell from in the purpose of God in the creation of man under the Edenic Covenant. Redemption now makes possible the fulfillment of the purpose of creation (John 17:22-24; I Corinthians 2:7; II Corinthians 4:6,17; Colossians 3:4; Isaiah 60: 1-3; Psalm 45:13; Romans 5:2; II Peter 1:3; II Thessalonians 2:14).

The believer rejoices in hope of this coming glorification as he is being continually changed "from glory to glory" by the Spirit of the Lord (II Corinthians 3:18).

G. The Benefit of Salvation

1. Definition
"Salvation" means "to be made whole, to be delivered, made safe, preserved from destruction." The Greek word "Soteria" from which our English word "salvation" comes, is translated "salvation" (Luke 1:69), "that we should be saved" (Luke 1:71), "deliver" (Acts 7:25), and "health" (Acts 27:34).

2. Amplification
This word is used of both natural and spiritual deliverance, as the following instances show.

a. Physical and temporal deliverance from danger and fear.

(1) National deliverance (Luke 1:69,71; Acts 7:25)
(2) Personal deliverance (Acts 27:43; Hebrews 11:7)

b. Spiritual and eternal deliverance for all who accept the conditions of repentance and faith laid down by the Lord. It is deliverance and salvation in Christ by:

(1) His saving **name** (Acts 4:12).
(2) His saving **Gospel** (Romans 1:16; Ephesians 1:13).
(3) His saving **grace** (Ephesians 2:5,8).
(4) His saving **word** (James 1:21).
(5) A saving **confession** (Romans 10:9-10).

Jesus Christ is the Savior, and salvation is personalized in Him (Matthew 1:21; Luke 1:47; 2:11; Acts 5:31; Philippians 3:20; Hebrews 2:10; Isaiah 12:2; Exodus 15:2; John 4:22). In Him we are the "heirs of salvation" (Hebrews 1:14).

3. Complete Salvation
Salvation is a word which involves time past, present and future. The believer has been saved, he is being saved, and he will yet be saved. "Who delivered us (past tense) from so great a death, and doth deliver (present tense); in whom we trust that He will yet deliver us (future tense)" (II Corinthians 1:10). The word "deliver" is a synonym of salvation and this verse is illustrative of the believer's salvation in time unto eternity.

a. Time Past
We were saved (Mark 16:15-16; Romans 10:9-10; Mark 15:31; Acts 16:31; Luke 7:50; Ephesians 1:13; II Timothy 1:9). Christ died for our sins, to save us. This is our justification.

b. Time Present
We are being saved (Romans 8:24; I Corinthians 15:2; II Corinthians 2:15; 6:1-2). Christ now subdues our sins (Micah 7:19). This is our sanctification.

c. Time Future
We shall yet be saved (Romans 13:11; Daniel 9:24; I Thessalonians 5:8-9; II Thessalonians 2:13; Hebrews 5:9; 9:28; I Peter 1:4-5,9-10).

Christ will eradicate all sin. This is redemption, perfection and glorification. The writer to the Hebrews speaks of this "so great a salvation" (Hebrews 2:3). Paul tells us that it is the grace of God that brings salvation to us (Titus 2:11).

The Greek word "Sozo" translated "save" or "saved" means "to save, to make whole, to preserve, or make safe" (Matthew 1:21; 10:22; John 3:17; Acts 2:40; 16:30-31). Thus the word "saved" or "salvation" is an all-comprehensive word and it includes in itself all the benefits of the cross, the operations of the grace of God in a believer's life. Salvation includes in its scope, grace, election, predestination, calling, foreknowledge, pardon, justification, regeneration, adoption, sanctification, preservation and finally perfection, glorification and eternal life (Romans 8:27-30).

In summary of the benefits of the atonement, we say:

In Pardon, God is seen as the sovereign King who forgives the offender of His holy Law.

In Justification, God the righteous Judge, declares the pardoned sinner righteous.

In Regeneration, God the Creator imparts a new and divine life and nature to the believer, thus bringing him into the family of God.

In Adoption, God the Father places the believer as a privileged and responsible son in His family.

In Sanctification, God the Holy One, sets the believer apart from all evil unto Himself and to His holy service as a priest.

In Perfection, God the sinless One, brings the believer into complete adjustment with Himself and His will, eradicating the sin-principle of self-will.

In Glorification, God, the God of all glory, restores man to his original glory and purpose, which includes in itself creation and redemption.

Chapter 12

THE ETERNAL STATES

The Scriptures teach that man is on probation during his time on earth. Those who respond to God's grace and obey Him will be eternally rewarded in heaven, God's dwelling place. Those who willfully resist the grace of God, do their own will and serve Satan will be eternally punished in hell, Satan's dwelling place. Eternal destinies are settled here in time.

CHAPTER OUTLINE

I. TIME AND ETERNITY

    A. Time — The Probation of Man
    B. Eternity — The Rewarding of Man

II. THE DISPENSATIONS OF TIME — JUDGEMENTS AND REWARDS

    A. Innocence — Edenic Covenant
    B. Conscience — Adamic Covenant
    C. Human Government — Noahic Covenant
    D. Patriarchal — Abrahamic Covenant
    E. Law — Mosaic Covenant
    F. Grace — New Covenant
    G. Kingdom — Everlasting Covenant

III. THE RESURRECTIONS AND THE JUDGEMENTS

    A. Resurrection
    B. Judgement

IV. ETERNITY — JUDGEMENTS AND REWARDS

    A. Judgement and Rewards of Believers
    B. Judgement and Rewards of Unbelievers

V. THE ETERNAL STATES

    A. Heaven — Dwelling Place of the Redeemed
    B. Hell — Dwelling Place of the Unredeemed

I. TIME AND ETERNITY

The revelation of God in Scripture shows that God is the eternal, not limited by time. Moses said, "From everlasting to everlasting thou art God... For a thousand years in thy sight are but as yesterday when it is past, and as a watch in the night (Psalm 90:2,4). God speaks of Himself as the "I AM THAT I AM", that is, the Eternal (Exodus 3:14-15). He is the first and the last, the beginning and the ending, the Alpha and the Omega (Revelation 1:8; Isaiah 41:4). Man, however, is subject to time. He is finite and limited by time and space. Though man is a creature of time, he is made for eternity. He has a beginning but exists eternally. Man will be rewarded by God according to his works during his life whether they be good or evil.

A. Time — The Probation of Man

It is evident that when God created Adam and Eve, He placed them on a period of probation in the Garden of Eden, the earthly Paradise. They were placed under the one commandment of God and this was a test of their freewill, as to whether they would obey God or not (Genesis 2:17; 3:1-6). They failed in this probationary period. God extended grace to them and gave them space to repent and be restored to His fellowship by the atoning sacrifice. God pronounced the death penalty on man's sin of disobedience. However, there was a period of probation given to Adam as well as the entire human race. As far as man is concerned, this period is called time.

Between the birth and death of every son of Adam, there is a life-span. It is during this period of time, known only to God, that man is on probation. It is this which is "the space to repent" given to every one born of Adam's race (Revelation 2:21). No man knows how long this "space" is and it is the grace of God which comes to man during this time seeking to lead him to repentance (II Peter 3:8-9). Once this period of time is over, mortal man dies and his period of probation is forever ended. His eternal state and destiny are settled, unchanged and unchangeable. It is in this period of probation called time that man settles his destiny for eternity. For this very reason God calls all men to turn from their sin and accept His redeeming grace in Christ.

B. Eternity — The Rewarding of Man

As will be seen in due time, the ushering in of eternity as far as man is concerned is a time of reward. All men will be rewarded according to their works, whether good or evil. All will be judged according to the deeds done in the body (II Corinthians 5:10; Romans 14:10). Again, as a person's eternal destiny is settled here in time, according to character, so a person's eternal rewards are settled here in time according to works. Character, what a person is, determines their eternal state and destiny. Works, what a person does, determines their eternal rewards. Character and works cannot be separated. What a person is determines what a person does and both settle his eternal state.

II. THE DISPENSATIONS OF TIME — JUDGEMENTS AND REWARDS

God has exemplified in time that which He will do in eternity. God metes out certain judgements and rewards in time to both the righteous and unrighteous. He follows the same principle in eternity. Each of God's dispensations closed with judgement on the wicked and rewards or promises of reward to the righteous. As it was in time, so will it be in eternity (Ecclesiastes 11:9; 12:12-14; Matthew 12:36). It should be noted that the word "dispensation" as used here and in Scripture has no direct allusion to the ages of time but rather an arrangement or administrative dealing of God relative to mankind. The word "dispensation" as used by Paul in his writings distinctly means "administration of a household or estate, or stewardship" (I Corinthians 9:17; Ephesians 1:10; 3:2; Colossians 1:25; Luke 16:1-4). In God's dealings with man throughout time there is but one plan which is progressive in its unfolding. His purpose is one but His methods vary. God has but one plan of salvation but He has various ways of dealing with man in regards to this plan.

The various dispensations or arrangements cannot be separated from the divine covenants. Each covenant was a particular arrangement between God and man, having its own distinctive emphasis. Therefore the word "dispensations" as used here refers to the dealings of God with man under their respective covenants. Each closed with judgements on the wicked and the rewarding of the righteous, and each find their consummation in the judgements and rewards of eternity.

A. The Dispensation of Innocence — The Edenic Covenant

The first man Adam was placed in a perfect environment. Man was in covenant relationship with God. This dispensation was characterized by innocence (Genesis 1:26-2:25). Man was subjected to a simple test of obedience under a period of probation. He was forbidden to partake of the tree of the knowledge

of good and evil, lest he come under the death penalty. However, man exercised his free-will and chose
to partake of the forbidden fruit. He brought himself and his unborn race under the power of sin, Satan
and death.

Thus the first arrangement ended in the failure of man and God's judgement upon man in his exclusion
from Eden's Paradise. It is only by obedience to God's commandment that man will ever be rewarded
with the forfeited tree of eternal life. This is the promise of God to the one who overcomes (Genesis 2:17
with Revelation 2:7; 22:2,14).

B. The Dispensation of Conscience — The Adamic Covenant
The moment man sinned, conscience came into operation. By the conscience man was able to
distinguish between good and evil. Thus man came under the arrangement of conscience and God's
dealings with man were according to his conscience (Romans 2:14-15). Though the conscience defines
good and evil, it leaves man powerless to overcome evil and do the good. In itself it was an inadequate
arrangement. It was on the basis of the violated law of conscience that God judged the whole world of
mankind with the flood. Conscience is still part of God's dealings with man and accuses or excuses
man according to his deeds.

This arrangement brought in judgement on the ungodly world by the flood and the reward of the
righteous remnant who knew the preservation in the Ark of Noah (Genesis 6-7 with I Peter 3:20; II Peter
2:5).

C. The Dispensation of Human Government — The Noahic Covenant
Under this dispensation and the Noahic Covenant, God entrusted man with governmental authority.
The details of this arrangement are dealt with in Genesis 8-9. It was after the flood that God placed the
legal authority in the hands of man to execute murderers. This was the institution of human government and holds implicitly all other forms of punishment for violation of human rights. However, this
arrangement of human government proved to be inadequate and God brought in judgement upon
mankind at the tower of Babel (Genesis 10-11). Here the sons of Noah were divided and scattered to
their respective inheritances. God promised a reward of a city to Abraham that He Himself would build.
Abraham responded and came out of Babel, Ur of the Chaldees (Hebrews 11:10-16).

D. The Dispensation of Promise — The Abrahamic Covenant
After the tower of Babel, God chose Abraham, then Isaac, and then Jacob to be the fathers of a new
nation. The promises given involve the great Abrahamic Covenant. The promises included seed, land,
and blessings, both national or natural and spiritual. The details of this arrangement of the promises
are covered in Genesis 12-50. It was in Egypt that Israel became a nation and an enslaved people. This
arrangement was closed by the divine judgements on Egypt and the deliverance of God's people from
slavery, in fulfilment of the promises made to the fathers (Exodus 3-12).

E. The Dispensation of the Law — The Mosaic Covenant
This arrangement of God was particularly made with the chosen nation of Israel at Mt. Sinai after their
exodus from Egypt. The Mosaic Covenant involved the Tabernacle, Priesthood, Sacrifices, Feasts and
the Law. This arrangement continued from the time of Moses through to the first coming of Christ and
the ministry of the early Church. It closed off as far as a method of God's dealings, with the judgements
of God on the city of Jerusalem and the Temple in 70 A.D. The reward for the believing at this time was
escape from the terrible judgements and destruction which came upon Jewry as a nation (Matthew
23:38-24:1-2; Luke 19:41-44). Jewry has been desolate ever since.

F. The Dispensation of Grace — The New Covenant
The New Covenant was introduced by Jesus Himself as "the New Testament" or, literally "the new
arrangement" (Matthew 26:26-28). It cancelled out the Mosaic Covenant and brought in the dispensation of grace, God's dealings with man in this present period. "The Law was given by Moses, but grace
and truth came by Jesus Christ" (John 1:17; Titus 2:11; Ephesians 3:1-5). It is the grace of God which
accomplishes the eternal purposes of God in relation to man for all who receive and believe. However,
all men will not receive of the free grace of God and this dispensation will consummate with the
judgements of God upon the ungodly. When grace is spurned, there is no alternative but to judge man
(II Thessalonians 1:7-10). The second coming of Christ will usher in both judgements on the wicked
and rewards for the righteous.

G. The Dispensation of the Kingdom — The Everlasting Covenant

At the coming of Christ, the arrangement between God and man will be charaterized by man's place of dominion in the Kingdom of God. There has never been a time when the Kingdom of God has not been in existence, for the Psalmist says: "Thy Kingdom is an everlasting Kingdom" (Psalm 145:13). The King Himself is "eternal, immortal, invisible" (I Timothy 1:17).

The Kingdom of God in relation to earth has been expressed in different forms, each a part of the progressive expression of the eternal Kingdom. It is this aspect of the Kingdom which fulfils and consummates all other arrangements under their respective covenants. It brings man back to the original purpose of God through the redemption in Christ. It also ushers in the eternal order.

It is relative to this period of time that the final judgements and rewards are to be meted out. This constitutes "eternal judgment" and "eternal rewards" (Hebrews 6:1-2). It deals with all creatures whether angelic or human. All things are to be dealt with at the Judgement Seat of Christ or the Great White Throne of God (II Corinthians 5:10; Revelation 20:11-15; I Corinthians 15:24-28).

Thus we have noted briefly the various arrangements of God's dealings with man through time. They each have a point of commencement, without being abolished when another arrangement was ushered in. These arrangements have spiritual and eternal elements in them. It will have been noticed that each arrangement was ushered in by some particular judgement on the wicked and rewards for the righteous, either promised or given. All this pointed to the final and eternal arrangement, and the eternal judgements and eternal rewards.

II. THE RESURRECTIONS AND THE JUDGEMENTS

It is impossible to deal with the final judgements of God without involving the resurrections. The resurrections and the judgements of God are vitally linked. They cannot be separated. Resurrection precedes judgement and judgement necessitates resurrection. Thus the principles of the Doctrine of Christ involve "the resurrection of the dead, and eternal judgement" (Hebrews 6:1-2). (Read also Acts 17:30-31; Hebrews 9:27) Revelation 20:1-15 deals with the Doctrine of the Resurrection and then the Great White Throne judgement. Thus resurrection and judgement are inseparable.

A. The Resurrections

The resurrection is a doctrine taught and illustrated in both Old and New Testaments.

1. In the Old Testament

a. **In Testimony** (Job 19:25-27; Psalm 16:9; 17:15) The testimony of Job and the prophet David speak of the resurrection.

b. **In Type** (Genesis 22:5; Hebrews 11:19) Abraham's son, Isaac, was raised from the dead in a type. Jonah's resurrection from the fish also typified the resurrection of Christ (Jonah 1-2 with Matthew 12:38-40).

c. **In Prophecy** (Isaiah 26:19; Daniel 12:1-3; Hosea 13:14). The prophets spoke of the resurrection of the body also.

d. **In Actuality** (I Kings 17:17-24; II Kings 4:18-37; 8:5; 13:20-21; Jude 9). Elijah and Elisha knew the power of resurrection in the persons they raised from the dead.

2. In the New Testament

a. **In Teaching** (John 5:28-29; 6:39-54; Luke 16:19-31; 20:35-36). Jesus taught the resurrection of the physical body as well as a spiritual resurrection (John 5:21-25, 26-29; I John 3:14). Paul also wrote of the bodily resurrection (Acts 24:15; I Corinthians 15; I Thessalonians 4:14-18; Philippians 3:11,21). John also spoke of the resurrections (Revelation 20:4-6).

b. In Actuality (Matthew 9:18-26; Luke 7:11-23; John II:43-44; Acts 9:36-42; 20:7-12; Matthew 10:18; 27:50-53). There were actual physical resurrections in the New Testament also under the ministries of Jesus, Peter and Paul. The student is referred back to the resurrection of Christ also, for His resurrection is the sure proof of the resurrection of all men (Acts 17:30-31).

3. Two Resurrections
The Old and New Testament speak of two resurrections when it comes to the whole race of mankind. We note the Scriptures which speak of such, and the designations of each.

a. Resurrection of the Righteous.

(1) The First Resurrection (Revelation 20:4-6).
(2) The Resurrection of the Just (Acts 24:15; Luke 14:14).
(3) The Resurrection of Life (John 5:29).
(4) The Awakening to Everlasting Life (Daniel 12:2).
(5) The Better Resurrection (Hebrews 11:35).

b. Resurrection of the Unrighteous.

(1) The Second Resurrection (Revelation 20:4-6).
(2) The Resurrection of the Unjust (Acts 24:15).
(3) The Resurrection of Damnation (John 5:29).
(4) The Awakening to Shame and Everlasting Contempt (Daniel 12:2).

John tells us that these resurrections are a thousand years apart. He states "Blessed and holy are they who have part in the first resurrection." They are judged and receive eternal life and reward according to their character and works in Christ. The people of the second resurrection are cursed and unholy. They also are judged and sentenced to eternal damnation according to their character and works in this life.

4. The Nature of the Resurrection Body

a. For the Redeemed
The nature of the resurrection body is described for us in Scripture. It is to be like Christ's glorious body.

(1) A real body of flesh and bones (Luke 24:39; John 5:28; I Corinthians 15:22; Revelation 20:12; II Corinthians 5:10).
(2) A spiritual body (I Corinthians 15:44).
(3) A redeemed body (Romans 8:11-23; II Corinthians 5:4).

(4) A glorious body (Philippians 3:21; Luke 24:39).
(5) An incorruptible body (I Corinthians 15:42).
(6) A heavenly body (I Corinthians 15:47-49; II Corinthians 5:1-6).

b. For the Unredeemed
No description is given of the resurrection body of the wicked. However, they temporarily do receive one for the Lord Jesus said: "...fear Him who is able to destroy both body and soul in hell (Gehenna)" (Matthew 10:28 with Daniel 7:11). It is this which will constitute the "second death" (Revelation 2:11; 21:8). What a terrible judgement that will be to be a disembodied or naked spirit for all eternity, suffering the torments of hell.

B. The Judgements
As previously mentioned, resurrection precedes judgement and judgement necessitates resurrection.

1. Judgement Necessary:

a. Conscience of man demands it. The Law of Conscience, when violated, may be silenced, but it comes alive and active in the judgement before God's throne, and will accuse the guilty (Romans 2:14-15).

b. History demands it. The injustices of the human race through history, and the perversions of God's righteous laws demand that man be judged before the righteous and holy God.

c. Justice demands it. The justice, righteousness and holiness of God's law and being demand that He judge all sin. This He does at His throne of judgement.

2. Three Aspects of Judgement

a. Judgement Past
At Calvary, judgement was legally and judicially executed upon Satan and his hosts (Colossians 2:14-15; John 12:31; 14:30; 16:11). At Calvary the sins of the world were judged by Christ's death and all who believe in Jesus know that they have passed from death to life. Christ was judged for them (John 5:24; II Corinthians 5:21; Galatians 3:13; I Peter 2:24).

b. Judgement Present
There is a present judgement going on in the earth. In relation to the ungodly, God often steps in and judges the sins of men. Though sin contains its own judgement, the final judgement is yet to come. The believer is to judge himself so that he will not come into judgement with the world. God also divinely disciplines and chastens His people (I Corinthians 11:31-32; 5:5; I Timothy 1:20; Hebrews 12:1-10).

c. Judgement Future
Many Scriptures speak of a future judgement. All nations and cultures have this built into their understanding and conscience. All will be judged in absolute justice (I Corinthians 3:8-16; II Corinthians 5:10; I Corinthians 4:5; Hebrews 10:27; Acts 24:25).

3. The Day of Judgement
The Day of Judgement is the great reckoning day when God will bring all men before His throne to give an account of their lives as lived here on earth (Acts 17:31; Romans 2:16; II Peter 3:7; Psalm 96:13). We note in outline form some of the most important facts about the coming day of judgement.

a. There will be an **appointed day of judgement** for the believer, and for the unbeliever (II Corinthians 5:10; Romans 14:10; Acts 24:25; Revelation 20:11-15).

b. There will be the **appointed Judge,** Jesus Christ (John 5:22-27; Matthew 25:31-32; II Timothy 4:1; Acts 10:42).

c. There will be an **appointed purpose** in this judgement.

  (1) To reveal the true character of each person (Matthew 10:26; I Corinthians 4:5).
  (2) To determine the value of all the works of men (I Corinthians 3:13).
  (3) To render public reward or punishment, as men are not always punished or rewarded in this life (Matthew 16:27; Romans 2:6-9; Revelation 22:12).
  (4) To vindicate the righteousness of God in His dealings with men. His justice will be acknowledged (Revelation 19:1-2).

d. There will be **appointed principles and standards** of judgement.

  (1) Men will be judged with righteous judgement (Acts 17:31; Psalm 96:13).
  (2) Men will be judged according to God's holy standards (Romans 2:6,10,11; Revelation 22:12).
  (3) Men will be judged according to their attitudes to Christ (John 12:48; Luke 12:8-9).
  (4) Men will be judged according to the measure of light and opportunity given them (Matthew 11:21-24; Luke 12:48).

(5) Men will be judged by the infallible and omniscient Judge, Jesus Christ. There will be no chance of mistaken judgement, for He has all the hidden facts, deeds, motives and thoughts of men before Him (Ecclesiastes 12:14).

(6) Men will be rewarded or punished in different degrees (Luke 19:16-19; 12:47-48).

(7) Men will be convinced of the righteousness of God's judgement upon them. All will acknowledge that it is absolute justice meted upon their thoughts, words, deeds and motives (Jude 14-15; Matthew 12:37; Romans 2:15-16; Luke 19:22).

Thus all men, both good and bad, will be judged. They will be eternally separated into two classes. These classes are "the sheep" and "the goats" (Matthew 25:33) "the just" and "the wicked" (Matthew 13:49); "the saints" and "those that obey not the Gospel" (II Thessalonians 1:8-10). All will be eternally "blessed" or "cursed" (Matthew 25:34,41). The two destinies will be either heaven or hell.

IV. ETERNITY — JUDGEMENTS AND REWARDS

A. Judgements and Rewards of Believers

That the righteous are to be judged and rewarded is clearly stated in the Word of God. God has made many promises of reward to His people. It is not that the believer works for the reward from any wrong motives, nor does God use the promise of rewards as a bribe. The rewards are promises out of God's benevolence and as a trophy of a race well run, or a work well done. Every earthly father likes to reward his children for good work or good deeds; how much more shall our heavenly Father.

Note the following references which speak of the believer's judgement and rewards. Also, the student is referred back to "The Work of Christ" and the section "His Final Judgements."

1. Judgement of Believers

All believers must appear at the judgement seat of Christ and be judged for their works (I Corinthians 3:11-15; II Corinthians 5:10-11). All believers will stand before this seat of Christ and give an account of themselves. Responsibility necessitates accountability (Romans 14:10-12). The Lord desires that we have boldness in the day of judgement and not be ashamed before Him at His coming (I John 4:17; II Timothy 4:1,8; Revelation 11:18). This judgement actually takes place at the second coming of Christ. It is not a judgement concerning the believer's salvation, for that was settled at Calvary; it is a judgement of his works and service for the Lord. This is illustrated in the custom of the Grecian games. After the games were over, the winners were assembled before the "Judgement Seat" of the Judge and received the victor's crown. Some of the contestants had no winner's crown. In this sense there was judgement and reward.

2. Rewards of the Believers

The word "reward" is used over one hundred times in the New Testament. God speaks of rewards for both the righteous and the wicked. We list the major rewards for the believer which are given according to their faithfulness and service for the Lord. The Lord does not promise them as a bribe, but as an incentive and reward to His children (Ephesians 6:2).

  (a) The reward of faithfulness (Matthew 25:21-23).
  (b) The reward of the crown of life (James 1:12; Revelation 2:10).
  (c) The reward of the crown of glory (I Peter 5:2-4; Hebrews 2:9).
  (d) The reward of the crown of rejoicing (I Thessalonians 2:19-20).
  (e) The reward of the crown of righteousness (II Timothy 4:8).
  (f) The reward of the incorruptible crown (I Corinthians 9:25-27; I John 2:28).
  (g) The reward of the prophet and the righteous man (Matthew 10:41-42).
  (h) The reward to God's saints and servants (Revelation 11:18).
  (i) The crowns of gold (Revelation 4:4; 3:11). The Lord Jesus spoke parables which teach that believers will be rewarded (Matthew 25:20-23; Luke 19:12-19). He also said that when He comes His reward will be with Him (Revelation 22:12; Luke 6:23).

B. Judgements and Rewards of Unbelievers

That the unbelievers are to come up for judgement is necessitated by the very nature of the history of man, for many things have escaped judgement in this life. If God did not bring man up for judgement, then His own justice is violated, His righteous and holy law insulted. The character and deeds of the ungodly, which so often escape judgement in time, demand that God bring every work to judgement, and this He will at the Great White Throne judgement.

1. Judgement of Unbelievers
Although the wicked are sometimes judged in this life, the final and eternal judgement of the ungodly takes place at the Great White throne at the close of the 1,000 years of the kingdom period (Revelation 20:11-15). All are judged out of the books according to their works (Daniel 7:10, 22-26; Acts 24:28; Jude 14-15; Hebrews 9:27; Romans 2:5,16; I Timothy 2:24; Acts 17:31). The cities of the nations will be judged also, such as Sodom and Gomorrah, Tyre and Sidon, Capernaum, as well as all modern cities (Matthew 10:15; 11:20-24; 12:38-42; Ecclesiastes 11:9; 12:14).

2. Rewards of the Unbelievers
The Lord also said that He would reward the wicked according to their works. Balaam received the "reward and wages of unrighteousness" (II Peter 2:13-15). Judas also received "the reward of iniquity" (Acts 1:18). So will all the godless and wicked receive their "reward" according to their evil deeds.

V. THE ETERNAL STATES
The ultimate and eternal state, the punishment of the wicked and the rewarding of the righteous is seen in the places which Scripture call heaven and hell. Heaven is the eternal dwelling place of the righteous. Hell is the eternal dwelling place of the wicked. Whatever other rewards the believer or unbeliever receive, the eternal reward of heaven or hell will be the ultimate reward.

We consider here in outline form what the Scriptures have to teach us about these two places, for the character of the inhabitants is according to these places. Many want to believe in a heaven without a hell, but it is inconsistent to have one without the other, as will be seen.

A. Heaven - Dwelling Place of the Redeemed
Heaven is the dwelling place of God and the elect angels. It is the everlasting home of the redeemed of all mankind. The Hebrew word "Shamayin" means "heavens, or the heaved up things". The Greek word "Ouranoi" is translated "the heavens, the skies."

1. Heaven is an **actual place** (Genesis 2:1,4; Deuteronomy 10:14).

2. Heaven is spoken of as **God's dwelling place** (II Chronicles 6:25,33,35,39; Hebrews 1:10; 4:14; Daniel 4:26; Zechariah 12:1).

3. The heavens were **created by the Lord** God (I Chronicles 16:26,31; Job 9:8).

4. The Scriptures teach that there are **three heavens** and that these three heavens are the reality of the shadow cast on earth in the three places in the Tabernacle of Moses and the Temple of Solomon. The earthly sanctuary was the shadow of the heavenly sanctuary, as the book of Hebrews and Revelation set forth (Hebrews 8:1-5; 9:1-28; Psalm 19:1-6; Amos 9:6; Revelation 11:19; 15:1-5). Jesus Christ is the minister in the heavenly temple as our Great High Priest.

a. The Third Heaven
The third heaven, or the immediate presence of God, is called Paradise. It is heaven's holiest of all, or Most Holy Place. It is the very throne-room of the eternal Godhead, and the place of the brightness of God's glory. It is the original or the archotype of all that has ever been shadowed forth on earth, in the Tabernacle of Moses and the Temple of Solomon. It is called:

(1) The third heaven (II Corinthians 12:1-4)
(2) Paradise (Luke 23:43; Revelation 2:7; II Corinthians 12:1-4)

(3) Heaven itself, the Presence of God (Hebrews 9:24)
(4) Heaven, God's dwelling place (II Chronicles 6:30-35)
(5) The Heaven of Heavens (II Chronicles 6:18; 2:6)
(6) Heaven, the Throne of God (Matthew 5:34; Revelation 4:1; Acts 7:47-50; Isaiah 66:1-4).

It is this heaven which is the very center of the universe, the universe of worlds, and all revolve in orbit according to God's will, according to the power of this eternal throne (Hebrews 1:1-3; 4:14; 9:23; Job 15:15; Hebrews 8:1-2; Revelation 12:12). It is this heaven which the saints and prophets looked into when they had "open heavens" (Matthew 3:16; Acts 7:56; Ezekiel 1:1; Revelation 4:1; John 1:51; Psalm 11:4; Matthew 6:9; II Corinthians 12:1-4).

b. The Second Heaven
The second heaven, the central one, is the planetary heaven. It corresponds with the Holy Place of the earthly sanctuary of Moses. It is that heaven which has in it untold billions of planets, galaxies, star-worlds and suns, blazing and moving according to their God-willed orbits in their various glories. It is these heavenly bodies that the prophets speak of being darkened in the Last Days in judgement prior to and at the coming of the Lord Jesus Christ (Joel 2:10,30; Haggai 2:6; Isaiah 50:3; 51:6; Isaiah 13:13; 34:4). This heaven is to be shaken.

c. The First Heaven
The first heaven, from man's point of view, is the atmospheric heaven. It is the heaven immediately above and surrounding the planet earth. It is this atmospheric heaven that man depends on for breath, sustenance and earth productions, by wind, sun, rain. It corresponds to the Outer Court of the Tabernacle of Moses. This heaven is to be followed by a new heaven and new earth in due time. It is to be rolled up as a scroll and melt with fervent heat (Genesis 1:8; II Peter 3:5-16; Revelation 21:1-2). It is this heaven that is "shut up" and witholds the rain from man when he sins against God (read II Chronicles 6:26; I Kings 17:1; Deuteronomy 28:23; Leviticus 26:19; Job 1:16; Revelation 6:13-15; 20:11; 21:1; Job 15:15; Revelation 12:7-12). It is this heaven that is also polluted by the presence of Satan and his angels until they are cast out. Then will the heavens be completely cleansed.

5. The New Heaven, New Earth and New Jerusalem
The Bible shows that in time there will be a new heaven and earth. This will then be the eternal dwelling place of the redeemed. From here shall all eternal activity proceed. The new Jerusalem will be the new capitol of the universe and the place where the redeemed gather for worship and service (Revelation 21-22; Isaiah 65:17; 66:22; II Peter 3:13). The Scriptures give some indication of the character of this new heaven, new earth and new Jerusalem, for it is this which gives us the best description of our future heavenly dwelling place.

a. It will be a **new heaven and new earth,** for the former are to pass away (Genesis 1:1 with Revelation 21:1).

b. There will be **no more sea,** which speaks of separation and division of land (Revelation 21:1).

c. There will be a **new Jerusalem,** a holy city, in contrast to the old Jerusalem, which became a filthy city. This is the city which Abraham looked for, whose builder and maker is God (Hebrews 11:10-16; 13:14; Galatians 4:26; Revelation 3:12; 21:2).

d. This city will be the **Tabernacle of God,** God's dwelling place with His redeemed people. He will be their God and they will be His people, thus fulfilling the New Covenant promises as given in the Old and New Testaments (Exodus 19:4-6; Jeremiah 31:31-34; Revelation 21:3).

e. There will be **no tears,** sorrow, crying or pain there (Revelation 21:4).

f. There will be **no more death,** the wages of sin, for these things belong to the earth and the unredeemed man (Revelation 21:4).

g. The city is filled with **God's glory** and presence, even as the Tabernacle of Moses and Temple of Solomon was filled with this glory-presence as His dwelling place (Revelation 21:10-21).

h. Everything will be transparent; that is, **no shadows** or darkness or uncertainty (**Revelation** 21:21).

i. The **worship** will center around God and the Lamb eternally instead of any **earthly temple and** sacrifice (Revelation 21:22).

j. All will be **eternal light** in the New Heavens and New Earth; the New Jerusalem **has no darkness** or night there (Revelation 21:23-26; 22:5).

k. No unrighteous or unholy person shall ever be in this city. It is a righteous and holy city for the redeemed only (Revelation 21:27; 22:15).

l. The **river of life** will be there proceeding out of the Throne of God and the Lamb (**Revelation** 22:1,7).

m. The **Tree of Eternal Life** will be restored to man in this heavenly Paradise. Man lost it through failure to obey God's commandment. Now it is restored to all who obey (Revelation 22:2,14; 2:7; Genesis 2:17).

n. All the redeemed shall **see His face** and His name shall be in their foreheads. Man was driven out from the face of God because of sin. Sin is no more there (Genesis 3:22-24; Revelation 22:4; Genesis 4:14-16; Matthew 5:8; II Corinthians 3:10-18; Exodus 33:20-33).

o. The redeemed shall worship and serve God and the Lamb eternally as **king-priests** after the Order of Melchisedek (Revelation 1:6; 5:9-10; 22:5).

6. Descriptions of Heaven

God uses figurative and material glories to describe spiritual realities. Following are some of the names which are to describe the place called heaven.

a. Glory (Psalm 73:24).
b. Thy Presence and Right Hand (Psalm 16:11).
c. My Father's House (John 14:2).
d. A Place Prepared (John 14:2-3).
e. The Presence of His Glory (Jude 24).
f. With Christ (Philippians 1:23).
g. Heaven (Matthew 6:19-20).
h. Eternal Life (I John 5:11-12).
i. Paradise (II Corinthians 12:2-4).
j. The Third Heaven (II Corinthians 12:2-4).
k. The City of God (Hebrews 11:10-16; 13:14; Revelation 21:1-2).
l. The Heavenly Country (Hebrews 11:10-16).
m. The New Heavens and New Earth with the New City Jerusalem (II Peter 3:13; Isaiah 65:17; Revelation 21:1-2).

Here the believer is promised "the tree of life" (Revelation 2:7); not to be hurt of the **second death** (Revelation 2:11); a stone with a new name in it (Revelation 2:17); authority with Christ (Revelation 2:26-27); a white garment and his name in the Book of Life (Revelation 3:4-5); security in the City of God (Revelation 3:12); and ruling and reigning in the Throne of God and the Lamb (Revelation 3:21). This could only be a description of heaven, the dwelling place eternally for the redeemed of all ages. Jesus said He was going "to prepare a place" for His own, and that He would come again and receive His own to Himself, that where He was, they would be also (John 14:3). Wherever Jesus is, that is heaven. Heaven will be a place of light, love, holiness, righteousness, worship, service, joy, peace and life eternally because Jesus the Redeemer will be there. There will be no darkness, hate, sin, unrighteousness, sorrow, discord or death there. Without these things, it will be heaven indeed. What a wonderful and worthy reward of the God who redeemed us!

B. Hell — Dwelling Place of the Unredeemed

Hell is the place or state of final punishment of the wicked; of all who die in their sins and unregenerate state (Revelation 20:12-15).

1. Hell is an **actual place,** as surely as heaven is (Matthew 5:22,29,30; 10:28; 18:9; 23:15). Many like to accept that heaven is a place while rejecting hell as a place. One cannot exist without the other. Just as God has a place of happiness for the redeemed who serve Him, so God has a place of punishment for the rebellious who serve the Devil. Jesus the perfect compassionate One, spoke more of hell than all other Bible writers, and no wonder He did, for He came to save men from it.

2. Hell was not made for mankind but actually **prepared for the Devil and his angels.** However, if men choose to serve the Devil in this life, then they will dwell eternally with the Devil in hell (Matthew 25:41).

3. The Scriptures speak of **three divisions** of the underworld and each find their divisions swallowed up in Gehenna, which is the final hell.

a. Sheol or Hades

Sheol or Hades is generally recognized as being "the place of departed spirits" or "the unseen state." Sometimes it is spoken of as referring to the grave.

(1) Hebrew

The Hebrew word "Sheol" is translated as "Hell" 3 times; "Grave" 31 times and "Pit" 3 times (Deuteronomy 32:22; II Samuel 22:6; Psalm 18:5; Job 11:8; 26:6; Psalm 9:17; 16:10; 55:15; 86:13; Proverbs 23:14; 15:11; 27:20; Amos 9:2; Jonah 2:2; Isaiah 14:9,15).

A consideration of these references show that Sheol is "down", "in the depths", "beneath" and it is a place of pains and sorrows, while the righteous in the Old Testament are promised deliverance from such.

(2) Greek

The Greek word "Hades" is translated "Hell" 10 times "Grave" 1 time (Matthew 11:23; Luke 10:15; Matthew 16:18; Luke 16:23; Acts 2:27,31; Revelation 1:18; 6:8; 20:13,14; I Corinthians 15:55).

In these Scriptures Hades is seen to be "down", having gates, is a place for the spirits of the departed dead, and is to lose its victory over the righteous, and then is eventually to be cast into the Lake of Fire, the final Hell.

Thus Old Testament and New Testament confirm each other in the information concerning Sheol or Hades, which is the place of departed spirits, especially the departed spirits of human beings in the Old Testament.

b. Tartarus

The Greek word "Tartarus" is used but once in the New Testament in II Peter 2:4 and it is translated "Hell." A consideration of this verse along with Jude 6 shows that Tartarus is a prison, or jail, specifically for sinning angelic spirit beings. It is "down" and it is a place of darkness where these fallen angels are reserved and held until the time when angels are to be judged at the Great White Throne (compare I Corinthians 6:3; Revelation 20:11-15; II Peter 2:4; Jude 6).

c. Abyss

The third division in the lower down departments of the earth (Psalm 63:9; 139:15; Isaiah 44:23; Ezekiel 26:20; Psalm 88:6,13; Ephesians 4:9) is called the Abyss, the Deep, or the Bottomless Pit. It is translated various ways in the Old and New Testaments.

(1) Hebrew
The Hebrew word "Abaddon" is translated "Destruction" in the Old Testament and "Abaddon" in the New Testament (Job 26:6; 28:22; 31:12; Psalm 88:11; Proverbs 27:20; 15:11; Revelation 9:11).

(2) Greek

(a) Apollyon is the Greek word and it is translated "Destruction" and "Apollyon" in the New Testament (Matthew 7:13; Romans 9:22; Philippians 3:19; II Peter 2:1; 3:16; Revelation 9:11).

(b) The Deep, as in Revelation 9:1-3; Romans 10:7; Luke 8:31 is also the Abyss.

(c) The Bottomless Pit (Revelation 9:1-3; 20:1-3,7) is also the Abyss.

Thus we see by reading these particular references that Sheol and the Abyss are connected. It is also specifically called "a prison." The Bottomless Pit is seen to be a dungeon, a jail, and it is the abode of demon spirits, a deeper pit than Sheol or Hades. The Abyss is Destruction, Abaddon, Apollyon, The Deep, The Bottomless Pit.

Meditation on these references will show us that each place or department of "Hell", the underworld or spirit world, is a prison or jail for different created beings, who have sold themselves out to evil. The place of Sheol or Hades is a place for departed human spirits, especially for the unsaved, since the resurrection of Christ, as well as Old Testament unregenerate persons. The place of Tartarus is a place for fallen angelic spirits. The place of the Abyss or Bottomless Pit is a place for demon spirits. Just as men place accused criminals and offenders in different cells according to their crime, each awaiting their sentence and final judgement of their case, so God has various jails in which He locks up prisoners until the Great White Throne judgement, when all will be tried and sentenced eternally to the final Hell, Gehenna.

d. Gehenna
The final and eternal Hell is seen in the Greek word "Gehenna". "Gehenna" means "The Valley of Hinnom." It is translated "Hell" 12 times in the following Scriptures (Matthew 5:22,29,30; 10:28; 18:9; 23:15,33; Mark 9:43,45, 47; Luke 12:5; James 3:6). It is called "The Lake of Fire" 5 times (Revelation 19:20; 20:10,14,15; 21:8).

It should be remembered that it was the Lord Jesus Himself who spoke more of this final hell than all other Bible writers. We consider why Jesus used this terrible place with its two major features to symbolize the final state of the wicked in the final hell which God prepared for the Devil and his angels.

(1) Old Testament
The Old Testament equivalent is found in the Hebrew word "Tophet" or "Topheth" which means "Altar." The Greek word "Gehenna" is founded upon this Hebrew concept of "Hell." Tophet or Gehenna shadowed forth all that hell will be to the wicked. When Israel fell into idolatry, and began to worship Baal, they used a certain part of the valley on the east side of Jerusalem to burn their children alive, and to burn the refuse of the city with fire and brimstone. This part of the valley was called "Tophet" or "Valley of the Dead Bodies". Here wicked kings made their children pass through the fire unto the gods of Baal and Molech, the "Sun" and "Fire" gods (Leviticus 18:21; Deuteronomy 18:10; Ezekiel 23:27,39; II Chronicles 28:3-4; 33:6; Jeremiah 7:31; 19:1-12). These thousands of children were placed upon the red hot metal hands of the great idol, and, as they were being roasted alive, their agonizing screams were drowned by cymbals and the shouts of frenzied worshippers. They also beat drums to drown out the cries of the children. Thus it was called:

(a) The Valley of Hinnom (Joshua 15:8; Nehemiah 11:30; Joshua 18:16).
(b) The Valley of the Children of Hinnom (II Kings 23:10).
(c) The Valley of the Son of Hinnom (II Chronicles 28:3; Jeremiah 32:35).
(d) The Valley of Dead Bodies (Jeremiah 31:40).
(e) The Valley of the Groans of the Children (II Chronicles 28:3-4; 33:6).

The second thing about this place was that it became the place of all the refuse of the city of Jerusalem. The godly King Josiah defiled this place so that the abominations would not be carried on and from this time on it became a place for the filth and refuse of the city. Fires were kept continually burning here to consume the filth and impurity of the place. This fire was kindled by brimstone. Brimstone is a terrible substance in its action on human flesh and it becomes tortuous when thrown in with fire. Worms fed on the garbage out of reach of the fires, and vultures gloated over the scene continually. From this valley there arose stenchful and horrid smoke continually (II Kings 23:10; Isaiah 30:33).

Thus Gehenna of the New Testament is equivalent to the Tophet of the Old Testament. The Lord Jesus uses the two major features of this horrible place as a fitting symbol of the final hell, the Lake of Fire. Hell is a place where the wicked are cast, and the smoke of their torment ascends up for ever and ever. That "Gehenna" was outside the earthly city of Jerusalem. The eternal "Gehenna" is outside of the Heavenly City of Jerusalem, the Holy City of God. If it is argued that such things are only symbols, then it should be remembered that the reality is always worse than the symbol used to symbolize it. If the symbols of hell are so terrible, then the reality will be far more terrible. Thus the Lord Jesus, the One of infinite love and compassion, spoke more of Hell because He is the one who came to save mankind from this terrible place. We note then in outline form what this final Hell will be like and its inhabitants.

(2) The New Testament

(a) Hell will be the valley of the dead bodies and souls of the unregenerate (Matthew 5:22 30;18:9; Luke 12:5).

(b) Hell will be the valley of the groans, weeping and wailing of the lost of Adam's race (Matthew 13:42,50).

(c) Hell will be a place for the hypocrites, serpents and vipers in character (Matthew 23:14,15,33).

(d) Hell will be a place of fire and brimstone (Revelation 19:20; 20:10,14-15; 21:8).

(e) Hell will be a place of horrible torment (Revelation 14:9-11 with Luke 16:19).

(f) Hell will be a place of continually ascending smoke (Revelation 14:10-11).

(g) Hell will be a fire that is never quenched (Mark 9:43-49).

(h) Hell is a place where "the worm" of conscience never dies (Isaiah 66:24; Psalm 21:9; Job 24:20 with Acts 12:20-23; Mark 9:43-48). It will be terrible torment to have lusts which cannot be satisfied and a conscience that torments of past guilt and rejected grace.

(i) Hell will last eternally. The same Greek word "Aion", translated "Ages" about 20 times in the New Testament is used 16 times pertaining to God, and one time of the eternal bliss of the saints, and three times of the eternal punishment of Satan and the inhabitants of Hell. Eternal punishment is as long as eternal life (Matthew 25:46; Daniel 12:2 Romans 6:23; Jude 7; Revelation 14:11).

(j) Hell is the place where the wicked and unregenerate are "salted" as sacrifices on an altar (Mark 9:48-49). Rejecting God's sacrifice on Calvary's altar, they become sacrifices on this altar. The Hebrew word "Tophet" meaning "Altar."

(k) Hell will be some place or planet in the universe as an eternal jail for the wicked of mankind and criminal angels. God will not cause the righteous to remember such things (Isaiah 66:22-24; Revelation 14:9-11; Isaiah 65:17).

(l) Hell was prepared for the Devil and his angels. Thus the unredeemed there will find it a place of vile company (Isaiah 30:33; II Peter 2:4; Jude 6; Matthew 25:41,46; Revelation 21:8).

(m) Hell is for all whose names are not found written in the Book of Life (Revelation 2:11; 20:14; 21:8; 20:11-15).

(n) Hell is called the second death (Revelation 2:11; 20:11-15; 21:8).

(o) Hell will be outside the New and Heavenly Jerusalem (Revelation 21:8; 22:14-15).

(p) Hell will be a place of everlasting shame and contempt (Daniel 12:2; Romans 2:16).

(q) Hell will be the furnace of fire (Matthew 13:42, 50; 25:41,46).

At the present, Hell is unoccupied. The fallen angels and the wicked dead and demonic spirits are in their various prison houses awaiting the Day of the Great White Throne judgement. After this all will be cast into the Lake of Fire, including their respective prisons or cells.

(r) Hell is described by various names, thus giving us an indication of what it is like.

(i)	Destruction (Matthew 7:13; Philippians 3:19).
(ii)	Perdition (Hebrews 10:39; II Peter 3:7).
(iii)	Lost (John 17:12).
(vi)	Perish (John 3:16).
(v)	Second Death (Revelation 21:8; 2:11).
(vi)	Wrath of God (Romans 2:6-9; Ephesians 5:6; John 3:36; Romans 1:18).
(vii)	Eternal punishment (Matthew 25:46).
(viii)	Outer darkness (Matthew 8:12; 24:51; 25:30).
(ix)	Unquenchable fire (Mark 9:43).
(x)	Everlasting or eternal fire (Mark 9:43; Matthew 25:41; Jude 7; Hebrews 6:8).
(xi)	Wailing and gnashing of teeth (Matthew 13:42,50; 8:12; 22:13; 24:51; 25:30; Luke 13:28).
(xii)	Fruitless and cursed trees; burned trees (Matthew 7:19).
(xiii)	Chaff in the fire (Matthew 3:12).
(xiv)	The furnace of fire (Matthew 13:41-42).
(xv)	Tares and fish cast away and separated from others (Matthew 13:30,48).
(xvi)	Everlasting destruction (II Thessalonians 1:9).
(xvii)	Everlasting punishment (II Thessalonians 1:9).
(xviii)	Blackness of darkness (Jude 13; II Peter 2:4).
(xix)	Smoke of their torment (Revelation 14:11).
(xx)	The worm that never dies (Mark 9:44,46,48).
(xxi)	Eternal damnation (Mark 3:29; 16:16).
(xxii)	Resurrection of damnation (John 5:29).
(xxiii)	Cursed (Matthew 25:34,41; Deuteronomy 27:26; Galatians 3:10).
(xxiv)	Die in sins (John 8:21,24; Romans 6:23).
(xxv)	Lake of Fire and Brimstone (Revelation 21:8).
(xxvi)	Gehenna or Hell (Matthew 5:22; Mark 9:43-48; James 3:6).

Hell will be a terrible place separate from the presence of God, the rejected Lamb, the holy angels and the redeemed. No light, life, peace, joy, righteousness, nor salvation, but only darkness and torment of conscience will be there for those who rejected and despised the grace of God. This is the hell that Jesus Christ died to save us from.

Hell is neither annihilation nor a place of temporary punishment. It is not a place of probation or a state of non-existence. An honest consideration of the Scriptures presented will show that hell is a place of eternal punishment. Hell is a self-chosen and self-inflicted curse, the inevitable outcome of sin.

Rejecting God, rejecting Christ and resisting the Holy Spirit, the inhabitants of hell have chosen to live a life of sin here on earth. God leaves them to the choice they have made to live eternally in the sins they have chosen. God will not force any to be saved or go to heaven against their will. Yet God is not willing that any should perish (I Timothy 2:4; John 5:40; Matthew 23:37; Jeremiah 8:5,6).

God's banishment of the wicked to a place where sin and iniquity can no longer defile others, is just. Hell is therefore God's eternal jail for the criminals of the universe, never to be let loose to wreck God's new heaven and new earth, to defile the new Jerusalem or to corrupt the angels and saints.

(s) Hell has various inhabitants.

(i)   The Antichrist and the False Prophet are the first two persons to be cast into the Lake of Fire (Revelation 20:1-10).

(ii)   The Devil himself is cast into the Lake of Fire at the close of the 1,000 year period (Revelation 20:1-15).

(iii)   The fallen angels are also to be cast into hell (II Peter 2:4; Jude 6).

(iv)   The fallen demonic spirits also will be cast into hell (Luke 8:26-31).

(v)   Then the unredeemed and unregenerate of all mankind will be cast into hell, the Lake of Fire, after the Great White Throne judgement. All whose names are not written in the Book of Eternal Life are cast there (Revelation 14:9-11; 20:11-15).

(vi)   Then finally death and Hades/Sheol, Tartarus and the Bottomless Pit are all cast into this final hell, the Lake of Fire and Brimstone (Revelation 20:14; Hosea 13:14; Isaiah 25:6-8,9; I Corinthians 15:26, 54,55).

(t) The Location of Hell is somewhat uncertain.

Two major views are held as to where this final hell as a place might be. One view holds that it is some special place somewhere in the universe where God will confine the damned criminals of heaven and earth. The other view is that this present earth will become the final hell at the close of the Kingdom period and God's plan relative to earth. This view seems to be the most consistent, as a consideration of II Peter 3:3-9 with Revelation 20:11-15; 21:1 seems to indicate.

Satan has always desired to have this planet earth. Men have lived and died here, and sold themselves to Satan here on this earth. Jesus came from heaven to this earth to take the redeemed to a new heaven and new earth wherein dwelleth righteousness. Thus it seems fitting that this planet earth will be the jail of the universe of worlds that witnesses to all creatures that sin does not pay.

Wherever hell might be, it is a place to shun and warn men to escape from, turning them to the grace of God manifest in the Lord Jesus Christ (Isaiah 65:17; 66:22-24).

Undoubtedly God has a vast plan in eternity for His redeemed and it is summed up in Paul's statement in Ephesians "that in the ages to come He might show the exceeding riches of His grace in His kindness toward us through Jesus Christ." (Ephesians 2:7)

BENEDICTION

"Unto Him be glory in the Church by Christ Jesus throughout all ages, world without end. Amen" (Ephesians 3:21).

Bibliography

1. Bancroft, Emery H., **Christian Theology,** Grand Rapids, Michigan., Zondervan Publishing House, 1971.
2. Booth, William., **Handbook of Doctrine,** The Salvation Army, 1940.
3. Clarke, Robert., **The Christ of God,** London, Victory Press, 1949.
4. Evans, William., **The Great Doctrines of the Bible,** Chicago, Illinois., The Moody Press, 1912.
5. Gregory, J.R., **The Theological Student,** London, Charles H. Kelly, 1910.
6. Hammond, T.C., **In Understanding Be Men,** London, Inter-Varsity Press, 1971.
7. Hanke, Howard A., **The Virgin Birth of Christ,** Grand Rapids, Michigan, Wm. B. Eerdmans Publishing House, 1953.
8. Hodge, Archibald A., **The Atonement,** Grand Rapids, Michigan, Baker Book House, 1974.
9. Koehler, Edward W. A., **A Summary of Christian Doctrine,** Concordia Publishing House, St. Louis, Missouri, U.S.A. 1875-1951
10. Lee, Robert., **Doctrinal Outlines,** London, Pickering & Inglis.,
11. Lockyer, Herbert., **All the Doctrines of the Bible,** Zondervan Publishing House, Grand Rapids, Michigan, 1973.
12. McCrossan. T.J.. **The Bible: Its Hell and Its Ages,** 4138 Brooklyn Avenue. Seattle. Washington. U.S.A. 1941.
13. McDowell, Josh., **Evidence that Demands a Verdict,** San Bernardino, Arrowhead Springs, Campus Crusade for Christ International, 1972.
14. Offiler, W.H., **God and His Bible,** Seattle, Washington, Bethel Temple, Inc. 1946.
15. Pearlman, Myer., **Knowing the Doctrines of the Bible,** Springfield, Missouri, The Gospel Publishing House, 1937.
16. Ratz, Charles A., **The Person of Christ,** Ontario, Canada, The College Press, 1962.
17. Strong. Augustus Hopkins., **Systematic Theology,** The Judson Press, Philadelphia 1907.
18. Strong, James., **Strong's Exhaustive Concordance,** Grand Rapids, Michigan, Guardian Press.
19. Thiessen, Henry Clarence., **Introductory Lectures in Systematic Theology,** Grand Rapids, Michigan, Wm. B. Eerdmans Publishing Company, 1949.
20. Torrey, R.A., **What the Bible Teaches,** London, Nisbet & Company., Ltd.
21. Williams, Ernest S., **Systematic Theology** Vol I, II, III., Springfield, Missouri., Gospel Publishing House, 1953.

Other Resources Available by Kevin J. Conner

Kevin J. Conner

The Kingdom Cult of Self

Interpreting the Symbol & Types

The Church in the New Testament

The Name Of God

Interpreting the Book of Revelation

The Feasts of Israel

Mystery Parables of the Kingdom

Table Talks

The Tabernacle of Moses

The Tabernacle of David

The Temple of Solomon

Tithes & Offerings

Today's Prophets

Kevin J. Conner & Ken Malmin

Old Testament Survey

New Testament Survey

Interpreting the Scriptures

The Covenants